A literary History of India

A literary History of India

by

R. W. Frazer, LL.B.

Lecturer in Telugu and Tamil at University College, and the Imperial Institute; Member of Council, Royal Asiatic Society; Secretary and Principal Librarian, London Institution.

Author of
"Silent Gods and Sun-Steeped Lands"
and
"British India" ("Story of the Nations" Series)

SECOND IMPRESSION

GYAN

Published by

Gyan Publishing House
5, Ansari Road
Daryaganj, New Delhi-110002
Phone: 011-47034999, 9811692060
E-mail: books@gyanbooks.com

Distribution Network
gyanbooks.com
India, USA, Canada, UK, Australia, France

ISBN : 978-81-212-2311-9 (PB)
First Published, 1907

2nd Impression 2021

Printed at: Gyan Press, Delhi.

A literary History of India
Author: R. W. Frazer

A Literary History of India

By

R. W. Frazer, LL.B.

Lecturer in Telugu and Tamil at University College, and the Imperial Institute; Member of Council, Royal Asiatic Society; Secretary and Principal Librarian, London Institution.

Author of
"Silent Gods and Sun-Steeped Lands"
and
"British India" ("Story of the Nations" Series)

SECOND IMPRESSION

London
T. Fisher Unwin
Adelphi Terrace
1907

Literary History of India.

PREFACE

In essaying to set forth a connected history of India from such evidences as I have selected from its literature, I have been obliged to evade, and not to emphasise, difficulties everywhere patent to the scholar or specialist. In most cases, however, I have accepted the conclusions of those who are recognised authorities. In those cases where scholars still disagree I have indicated in footnotes the evidences on which I had to form conclusions of my own.

On many points, especially those relating to the significance of the early, sacrificial systems, to the origin and purport of the Epics, and to the Græco-Roman influence on the form of the Indian Drama, it was manifestly impossible, in a work such as this, to enter on any prolonged discussion.

The main outlines of the history are never likely to be materially affected by future decisions on these debatable points.

The early incursion of fair-skinned Aryan tribes, amid the darker aboriginal inhabitants, forms the starting-point. Of these Aryans, the only literary record we possess is that preserved in the Vedic Hymns, for it does not seem probable that an unaided Science of Philology will ever throw much light on their past history or religious beliefs. The early course of these invading tribes can be traced as they forced their way among the aborigines, and made their settlements in the most favoured river tracts north of the Vindhya range of mountains. The vast area over which the tribes, whose members can never have been very numerous, spread themselves prevented them from forming a united and compact nationality of their own among the ruder aboriginal races. The tribal deities lost their importance and failed to coalesce into the ideal of one national God.

As the early sacrificial cult drifted from its primitive significance the idea was evolved of a Brahman, or self-existent Cause or Force, underlying the Universe. The nature of this Brahman was ultimately declared to be Unknowable to reason, but to have been revealed in the sacred Vedic literature to the Brāhmans, or descendants of the early poet-priests who composed the hymns, prayers, or incantations to their tribal deities.

The first hope that Aryans and aborigines might become infused with a common ideal and faith dawned with the personality and teachings of the Buddha at a time when the full strength of Aryan intellectual vigour was about to culminate in phases of thought which gave rise to the schools of formulated philosophic reasoning. I have endeavoured to trace the political effects of these forces, and to indicate the causes which prevented the great civilising power of early Aryanism in India from saving the people from divisions and dissensions, which left them an easy prey to foreign invaders. The divisions of the people were stereotyped by a system of caste originally based on racial and intellectual differences. The intrusion of Scythian, Persian, Arab, Afghan, and Mughal hordes but increased the diversity of the factors into which the community was divided. The primary forces which prevented even an Akbar from implanting vital principles of union among the people were religious fanaticism, class distinctions, and race hatred. While these forces still exist, the introduction of printing into India, and the higher education of the natives through the medium of English, are implanting new modes of thought and new principles ot action among the class which claims to represent public opinion. The orthodox Brāhmans, and the high-caste natives of the old conservative school, however, remain hostile to all innovations, determined to maintain the fundamental doctrines of their religion, and preserve the best of their ancient social customs. On the other hand, the more advanced natives of the new school, whose trend of thought is, for the most part, towards agnosticism and freedom from all caste and social restraints, strive more and more to assume the position of leaders of the people and exponents of their views. The position is one produced by the deliberate and consistent policy of education in India. The stage is a stage of transition and unrest but happily for India it seems to be fraught with fewer elements of danger than the stage through which the nations of the West seem destined to pass.

Throughout the work the transliteration of native words has been of great difficulty. Cerebrals and nasals are unmarked, as the omission will not confuse any one acquainted with Eastern languages, and my experience, after many years teaching of Sanskrit, Tamil, and Telugu, is that it is impossible for any one unfamiliar with the sound of the languages as spoken in India to acquire even an approximate pronunciation of these letters.

I regret that it is impossible for me fully to acknowledge my indebtedness to the many works I have consulted. To the delegates of the Clarendon Press I am especially indebted for permission to quote from the Series of the "Sacred Books of the East"—a monumental undertaking full of evidence of the scholarship, untiring industry and wide sympathies in all matters connected with the East of Professor The Right Honourable F. Max Müller.

To the Rev. Dr Pope, the Oxford Professor of Tamil,

my sincere thanks are due for having placed valuable original translations at my disposal, and I trust that I have not too freely availed myself of his permission to quote from them. To the Editor of the Series in which this history appears I owe much for valuable suggestions and literary criticism, all of which I have most gladly accepted. To Miss C. M. Duff I am grateful for having kindly allowed me to peruse the proof sheets of her forthcoming "Chronology of India." Had I seen her work earlier I should have been spared several months of uncongenial labour in preparing a chronological framework for the present history.

R. W. FRAZER.

LONDON INSTITUTION,
5th November 1897.

CONTENTS

Frontispiece.—From "Manners in Bengal," by Mrs Belnos.

LITERARY HISTORY OF INDIA

CHAPTER I.

THE ARYANS.

NO invasion of India is feasible in the present day save by a maritime nation holding the supremacy of the seas, or by a force advancing from Central Asia with strength sufficient to break its way through the defences on the west and north-west frontiers. From Chitral in the extreme north, where the Ikshkamun and Baroghil Passes show the way across the Hindu Kush to the lonely heights of the Pamirs, southwards to where the Khaibar Pass gives access to Kābul, the Gūmal and Tochi Passes lead to Ghazni, and the Bolān still further south to Quetta and Chamān, on to the seaport town of Karāchi in Sind, a distance of 1200 miles, the whole north-west and west frontiers are held by British troops, backed by defensive entrenchments and batteries, prepared to meet the first advancing armies that venture to tread the historic paths of old that so often led the nomad hosts of Central Asia to the conquest of India. From time immemorial, bands of warlike invaders have swarmed down from beyond these barrier passes to conquer the effete inhabitants of the fertile river-valleys of the plains of India, only themselves in turn to fall subdued by the enervating influence of the climate, and be swept away by succeeding bands of hardier invading races.

When the history of India first dawns in literature, it is through these same bleak mountain passes that tribes of warrior heroes, bred in cold and northern climes, are seen slowly advancing to seek new homes beneath the warm and southern sun. Proud in their conquering might, these tribes called themselves Ārya, or "Noble," a term denoting the contempt they felt for the dark-skinned races they found in possession of the land. Full four thousand years ago, these first historic invaders of India must have stood gazing, in wonder and amazement, from the lofty heights of some one of these northern passes, on the rich valleys lying smiling at their feet. To their gods they sang their songs of thanksgiving that at length their weary journey from colder realms was at an end, and that victory had been given them over their foes, who lurked amid the mountain forests, and opposed their progress with fierce cries and rude weapons. These invading tribes were a fair-skinned race[1] with whom all Brāhmans and twice-born higher castes of India now claim kindred,[2] holding themselves aloof from the darker-skinned descendants of the aboriginal inhabitants. The birthright of the Brāhmans of India is to keep preserved in their memories the early hymns sung by their Aryan forefathers. These hymns—every stress and accent marked as in days long past, every syllable and word intoned according to ancient usage,

[1] "A tall fair-complexioned dolichocephalic and presumedly lepterhine race."—Risley, "Study of Ethnology in India," p. 249; *Journal Anthropological Institute* (February 1891).

[2] It must be borne in mind that in using the term, "Āryan," with reference to modern India, it merely refers to those people who speak Aryan languages, no suggestion being made that these people are necessarily of Aryan descent. As clearly stated by Max Müller, in a letter to Mr Risley ("Biographies of Words," p. 245): "Aryas are those who speak Aryan language, whatever their colour, whatever their language. In calling them Aryas, we predict nothing of them except that the grammar of their language is Aryan."

remain the sacred treasure of their hereditary custodians, so that the utterances of the early Aryan invaders of India live to-day as clear and distinct as when first sung by the Vedic poets. These treasured verses, as collected together in the 1028 hymns, known as the "Hymns of the Rig Veda," are all that are left to enable us of to-day to pierce the mists of the long past history of India. To all orthodox Hindus, they are held as having been breathed forth as a divine revelation from before all time. The reducing of them to writing, and even the hearing of their recitation by foreigners, or by any but the twice-born castes, is still looked upon as sacrilege and profanation by those who claim the sole right to hear their sacred sound.

The first of a long line of priestly legislators who strove to reduce all the laws and customs of the people of India to ideals founded on priestly ordinances declared[1] that a Sūdra, or one of non-Aryan blood, who dared to listen to the recitation of the Vedic Hymns, should have his ears filled with molten tin or lac; should the Sūdra repeat the words he had heard, his tongue should be cut out; should he remember the sound, his body should be split in twain.

These Hymns, though they are still held as revelations from the Creator of the universe, tell nothing of the long, dark night that preceded the advent of these Aryan tribes, who loom so indistinct on the horizon of the literary history of India.

To the Vedic bards, standing as they did on the threshold of a new world, the story of their nation's past faded into insignificance before the brightness of its present. Enthroned in the pride of race, the poet sang of the might of his people, of his own power to win, by the magic of his words and cunning of his spells, the favour of the gods, so that they might lead the Aryan tribes to victory. For him the hand of time passed by unnoticed. To have told of the

[1] "Gautama," chap xii. 4-6, S.B.E. vol. ii.

past in the intoxicated fervour of his imagination, as he alone could have done it, would have dimmed the glory of the present. The time had not come when his mind, grown full of halting fears, would brood in misgivings over the future. Yet, strange to say, the very words over which the poets lingered in syllables of soft cadence, or which came rushing from their lips with the sound of the heavy roll of war chariots, held the secret, not only of their own, but of many other people's past.

The torch of learning, set aglow by the first Aryan invaders of India, was kept for long alight by an hereditary line of Brāhman priests, poets, and philosophers, who ministered, sang, and reasoned far and wide—from the holy land of Aryāvarta, to the distant seminaries in the South; from the Buddhist monasteries in the West, to the renowned schools of logic in the East. Fresh conquerors appeared in the land, but still the Brāhmans kept on their even way. At length the advancing wave of a Western civilisation, founded on new ideals, crept up the banks of the sacred rivers of India, and spread all over the land. In the eager race for wealth that ensued on the entry of these new invaders, the whole foundations on which the fantastic structure of the religious and social life of India was based remained unnoticed, as though Vedic song had never been sung in the land, and Brāhman had never existed.

The first to take note of the ancient learning of the land was the English Governor-General Warren Hastings, who summoned eleven Brāhmans to Calcutta, there to compile for their new rulers a code of Hindu religions and customs.[1] The reasons set forth by the Governor-General for thus desiring to ascertain somewhat of the laws of the Brāhmans

[1] The first published translation from Sanskrit into any European language was "Bhartrihari's Śatakas," by Abraham Roger, first Dutch chaplain at Pulicat (1631-1641), Grierson, "Satsaiya of Bihari," p. 2.

was, that "the Hindus had for long fallen under the Muhammadan rule, so that terror and confusion had found a way to all the People, and Justice was not impartially administered."[1] The work compiled by these eleven Brāhmans reached England in the year 1776, but still the Sanskrit on which it had been founded held its secret safe. Nine years later (1785) a young merchant, J. Wilkins, sent forth his translation of the Indian Song of Songs, the "Bhagavadgīta," and two years later (1787), the collection of Hindu stories, known as the "Hitopadesa," the original source of the famed fables of Bidpai. Yet the West woke not up to the fact that India possessed aught of more value than bales of calico, rich spices, and gems. Two years later, a drama of Kālidāsa, the Shakespeare of India, was given to the West by Sir William Jones. This drama, the now well-known "Sakuntalā," showed that India possessed a literature. To Kālidāsa Alexander von Humboldt allotted "a lofty place among the poets of all ages," and of the drama itself Goethe sang in raptures in his well-known lines:—

> "Willst du die Blüthe des frühen, die Früchte des späteren Jahres,
> Willst du was reizt und entzückt, willst du was sättigt und nährt,
> Willst du den Himmel die Erde, mit einem Namen begreifen ;
> Nenn' ich Sakuntalá dich und so ist alles gesagt."

The attention, not only of men of taste but also of scholars,[2] was naturally attracted to these works, and efforts were made in Europe to study and master the Sanskrit in which they were composed. So far an interest—an interest of curiosity—was aroused in the literature of India, but no expectations were entertained that the West had anything further to learn from the lore of the East.

[1] Halhed's Introduction to "The Code of Gentoo Laws" (London, 1776).

[2] F. Schlegel (1808), "Upon the Language and Wisdom of the Hindus," where he derives the Indo-Germanic family from India.

Soon, however, it came to light[1] that India not only possessed a sacred literature, that of the Vedic Hymns, but that the Sanskrit of these hymns was of a primitive and archaic type, preserving in structure and grammatical forms affinities with the Aryan languages of Europe. At once the belief arose that this Vedic Sanskrit was the primitive language of humanity,[2] and the old belief that the East was the cradle of the human race gained new strength. It was fondly hoped that the Brāhmans of India had preserved the parent speech, out from which had grown the Greek, Latin, Iranian, Celtic, Lettic, Teutonic, and Slavonic languages. Soon these hopes were doomed to disappointment. Sanskrit was found to be but one branch of the great Indo-European family of languages, and not even as such to have preserved a structure which can be considered more primitive than that of the other known branches.[3]

The plea for India as the lost home of primitive man died away, and in its place the belief[4] that the nations of Europe had migrated in early days from the Bactrian plains of Central Asia, was held as a fundamental axiom in all enquiries into the origin of the Indo-European races. Even the routes by which these early people spread from their Asiatic home towards Europe were clearly traced out,[5] and acknowledged as correct. The ablest scholars[6] accepted this Asiatic

[1] F. Rosen (1838), "Rig Veda, Sanhita Sanskritè et Latinè."

[2] Weber, "Modern Investigations on Ancient India" (1857).

[3] "Although no historic conclusions may be drawn from the primitiveness of Sanskrit, that primitiveness itself remains the same as ever."—Max Müller, "Biographies of Words," p. 99.

"Of all the existing tongues of the whole great family, the Lithuanian or the Baltic retains by far the most antique aspect."—Whitney, "Language, and the Study of Language," p. 203.

[4] Grimm, "Geschichte der Deutschen Sprache," pp. 113-122.

[5] Pictet, "Origines Européennes," 1859.

[6] Max Müller, "Lectures on the Science of Language."

theory, while Sayce[1] agreed that "it is in the highlands of Middle Asia, between the sources of the Oxus and Jaxartes," that the first traces of the Aryan languages appear in history.

The most pathetic instance of the unrelenting vindictiveness meted out by orthodoxy to originality, is to be seen in the ridicule showered on Dr Latham, when he ventured[2] upon the enunciation of a new suggestion, that the original home of the Aryans might be sought in Europe rather than in Asia.[3] Various theories followed in rapid succession. It was not long before grounds were found for locating the primitive Aryans somewhere to the north[4] of the Black Sea, from the Danube to the Caspian, while again on further investigation, the home was shifted to Central and West Germany.[5] The habitat was then removed to the whole of North Europe,[6] from the shores of the Atlantic to the confines of the Ural range of mountains, until at length the theory was propounded that the Aryan people have always occupied the same relative position they now hold, and that linguistic varieties arose *in situ*.[7]

In 1878, Poesche,[8] met by the difficulty arising from connoting unity of race, with unity of language, called in

[1] "Principles of Comparative Philology" (1874), p. 101.

[2] First in "Native Races of the Russian Empire," 1854. *See* Rendall, "Cradle of the Aryans," p. 8. *See* Schrader, "Prehistoric Antiquities," p. 85.

[3] Max Müller still declares himself "more inclined to the Asiatic hypothesis" (*Athenæum*, April 4, 1896).

[4] Benfey's Introduction to Fichte's "Wörterbuch der Indo-Germanischen-Grundsprache" (1868), p. ix. and "Geschichte der Sprachwissenschaft," 1869.

[5] Geiger, "Zur Entwicklungsgeschichte der Menschheit" (1871). *See* Schrader, p. 87.

[6] Cuno, "Forschungen in Gebiete der alten Völker-kunde" (1871). *See* Schrader, p. 89.

[7] *See* Taylor, "Origin of the Aryans," p. 36.

[8] "Die Arier, Ein Beitrag zur historischen Anthropologie" (1878). In the marshes of Pinsk, "the phenomenon of depigmentation or ablinism is of extremely common occurrence, and is clearly marked in men, animals, and plants," and accounts for the blonde colour of Indo-Europeans. *See* Schrader, p. 100.

the aid of anthropology and archæology, and propounded his theory that there was but one true Aryan race, a race tall, blue-eyed, fair-skinned, with a dolichocephalic skull, whose ancestral home he assigned to a clime where plants, animals, and men soon became bleached, to the Rokitno swamps of Russia.[1]

More plausible and fascinating was the theory[2] that Scandinavia was the original home of the typical Aryans, who are now only to be found in North Germany and Scandinavia, language alone being left in other parts of Europe and in India as a sign of an Aryan conquest, the Aryan race itself having succumbed in Southern climes to climatic influences. That there did exist a people, living united somewhere, probably in Europe,[3] known to us as Aryans, who spoke a language from which the modern languages of Europe have diversified, as well as the languages spoken by the Zend-speaking Iranians of Persia, and the Sanskrit-speaking peoples of Vedic times in India, admits of but little doubt. That these Aryan-speaking people separated the one from the other in some ancient period, the ancestors of the Indo-Iranians travelling East to seek new pasture-lands and homes, the Europeans holding together until they reached a halting ground, probably bordered on[4] the South

[1] Taylor, "Origin of the Aryans," p. 43.

[2] Penka, "Origines Ariacæ" (1883); "Die Herkunft der Arier" (1886). "The Ice Age drove the majority of the human race from central Europe. The Aryans remained, and it is "the climate of the Ice Age, and the struggle with their environment that they have to thank for their blonde hair, blue eyes, gigantic limbs, and dolichocephalous skulls."—Schrader, p. 102.

[3] Huxley, *Nineteenth Century*, 1890, pp. 750-777:—"As to the 'home' of the Aryan race, it was in Europe, and lay chiefly east of the central highlands and west of the Ural." Van den Gheyn has in "L'Origine Européenne des Aryas" (1885), analysed all these theories.

R. von Ihering in "The Evolution of the Aryan" (*tr.* A. Drucker, 1897), has adopted "the prevailing opinion that the original home of the Aryans was in Ancient Bactria (Central Asia)," and holds that "the ancient Aryans lived in a hot zone" (*see* pp. 1, 2).

[4] Schrader, "Prehistoric Antiquities," chap. xiv. p. 434.

by the Danube, and on the West by the Carpathians, where they evolved the elements of their future civilisation, seems now the most reliable conjecture. From the Celts who followed their ever-waning fortunes towards the Main and Rhine; from the Teutons who stolidly marched along the Vistula and Oder; from the Greeks who found a resting-place at the foot of Mount Olympus, thence to send South tribes of Ionians, Æolians, Achæans and Dorians; from the Latin, Slav and Lithuanian races, the Indo-Iranians parted for ever, to carry to the East the intellectual vigour and physical energy they inherited, in common with all races bred and nurtured amid the harsh necessities of a northern clime. Of the long pilgrimage of these eastward-travelling tribes, along the pasture-lands of the Oxus and Jaxartes—the only natural route—neither archæology nor philology can throw any light. On this long march the eastern-going tribes first became known as Aryans.

Speaking some language, older in its primitive form than Zend or Sanskrit, the Indo-Iranians held long together, until at length a feud, probably religious, arose and divided them for ever. All that is certainly known is, that one division of the tribes, the Iraṇian, sought a home in Persia, the other, the Indo-Aryans, passed onwards towards the Indus, to seek new homes in the sunlit plains of India.

CHAPTER II.

THE GREY DAWN MISTS.

FOR long it was hoped that the Science of Comparative Philology might weave out a history of the period before the Aryan people separated to build up their own distinctive languages and civilisations. In spite of the brilliant results at first obtained,[1] it is now recognised that only here and there a few faint clues can be found as to the mode of life of these Aryans before the time when their literary records rise from out the dim mists of the prehistoric days.

The Science of Language, in the words of Dr Schrader, "can only give us a skeleton, and to cover the dry bones with flesh and blood is the prerogative of the Comparative History of Culture. That the Indo-Europeans did possess the notion of a house the philologists show us, for the Sans. *damá*, Lat. *domus*, Greek δόμος, Slav. *domŭ*, correspond; but how these houses were constituted the historian of primitive culture alone can ascertain."[2]

For the construction of such a skeleton, the strict rules of philological research demand, in order that a word may be

[1] The earliest list of common Aryan words was by Colebrooke (1803). *See* Max Müller's "Biographies of Words," p. 128; Schrader, "Prehistoric Antiquities," p. 149.

[2] Schrader, p. 149.

taken as a fossil of prehistoric life, that it should not only be represented in at least one section of the European and one of the Asiatic groups, but that it should also agree in suffix as well as root.[1] Care must also be taken to eliminate from consideration such concepts as may possibly have been borrowed by one language from another.[2]

Allowing for all these and similar restrictions, which hold the imagination ruthlessly bound to the dry accuracy of scientifically-proved fact, some flickering gleam of light can still be shed on the dim past of the Indo-Aryans—before history dawns in the Vedic Hymns—as they emerge on the North-West passes, thence to descend down the river-valleys of the Ganges and Jumna, take up their abodes in the fertile plains, send their warriors and missionaries across the Vindhya range of mountains, only to see their vaunted pride droop before the eternal decrees of Fate, which ever bid the Aryan succumb, as he drifts further from the cold realms wherein his warlike manhood was first nurtured.

Philology, however, affords but vague and uncertain evidence respecting the thoughts, beliefs, and ideals of the primitive Aryans before they left their cold northern homes. It may be assumed that, as human beings, they had their own aspirations towards the ideal, and longings for a knowledge of the Divine. It may be held for certain that they had not sunk their heritage as reasoning creatures to the level of the brute instincts of the flocks they pastured.

The chilling hand of science, however, lies heavy on those who fain would paint a brilliant sunlit background to light up the simple picture of the life and homes of our earliest historic forefathers.

[1] Schrader, p. 30; Rendall, "Cradle of the Aryans," p. 9.

[2] *See* also Max Müller, "Contributions to the Science of Mythology," vol. i. p. xi.

It has even been held[1] that the early Aryans were devoid of all religious ideas. Again they are declared merely to have "believed in a multitude of ghosts and goblins, making offerings to the dead and seeing in the bright sky a potent deity."[2]

Professor Max Müller, however, still contends[3] that not only had the Aryans, before their arrival in India, gods who were the personified representations of the phenomena of Nature, but that they, in common with the undivided branches of the Aryan family, had an abiding faith in deities known as "asuras," or "devas."[4] These were the gods of whom the myths were told, chief of them all being the supreme deity of the sky; for, as the same authority says: "Even the most stubborn opponents of all attempts at tracing Greek and Indian gods back to a common source seem to have yielded an unwilling assent[5] to the relationship between the Greek Ζεύς-πατήρ, the Vedic *Dyaush-pitar*, the Latin *Jupiter*, and the Teutonic *Týr.*"[6]

Yet in India in the first utterances of the Vedic Hymns, Dyāus appears merely as a designation of the visible sky, his personality as a supreme god having faded before the purely Vedic "devās," or bright ones.[7] According to Dr

[1] Otto Gruppe, "Die Griechischen Kulte und Mythen." *See* Schrader, p. 410.

[2] Sayce, p. 890, British Association (1887).

[3] Max Müller, "Contributions to Science of Mythology," vol. i. p. 74.

[4] *Ibid.*, vol. ii. p. 448, arguing from Lat. *crēdo*, etc., "the idea of faith also must have been realised," etc. *See*, however, Schrader, p. 415.

[5] "Many equations of names once made in the first enthusiasm of discovery and generally accepted, have since been rejected, and very few of those that remain, rest on a firm foundation. *Dyaúś*—Ζευς, is the only one which can be said to be beyond the range of doubt."—A. A. Macdonell, "Vedic Mythology" (Grundriss), p. 8.

[6] Max Müller, "Contributions to Science of Comp. Mythology," vol. ii. p. 498.

[7] Sans. *dēvás*, Lat. *deus*, O. N. *tivár* and *dív.* Lat. *flāmen*, Sans. *brāhman*—worshipping. Schrader, "Prehistoric Antiquities," p. 416.

Schrader,[1] "the personification of the sky cannot have gone very far in that prehistoric period, else it would be difficult to see why the meaning of 'sky' should have got the upper hand again in later times." The Aryans, in fact, present in their Vedic Hymns the first literary landmarks in the history of India, and beyond those same Vedic Hymns, little can be definitely asserted as to their mythology or their beliefs in God or the after life.

Philology can, however, tell that the Aryans came from a land where the climate was, for the most part, cold, although a summer was known.[2] Time was there measured by the moon; the year was lunar, unadjusted to a solar year, and time itself was computed by the night, a reminiscence of which computation still lives in the English fortnight and sennight.[3]

That they had made some advance towards civilisation is clear. Copper was probably known, but it is doubtful if iron, gold, or silver were in use.[4]

The people were grouped together in clans; each member within the separate clans bearing, as a distinctive appellation, the name of some common ancestor or father, under whose patriarchal authority the "sib," or clan would have remained if he were living.[5] The clans united together for warfare, defence, or corporate management, formed the tribe. Strangers were held as enemies, so that with them no trade or commerce was possible. Inside the tribe, exchange

[1] Schrader, "Prehistoric Antiquities," p. 417.

[2] "That the Aryans did not come from a very southern clime has long been known, since they possessed common names for winter, such as Sanskrit, *himâ*, Greek, *χειμών*, Latin, *hiems*, Old Slav. *zima*, Irish, *gam*."—Max Müller, "Biographies of Words," p. 103.

[3] *See* Schrader, "Prehistoric Antiquities," p. 311; Tacitus, "Germ." XI.: *Nec dierum numerum sed noctium computant.* *See* Schrader, chap. vi; Sayce, British Association (1887), p. 889.

[4] Max Müller, "Biographies of Words," p. 180; Rendall, "Cradle of the Aryans," p. 12.

[5] Schrader, "Prehistoric Antiquities," pp. 398-9.

was carried on by barter, the standard of value being the cow. Marriage was as a rule monogamous, the bride being purchased from a neighbouring tribe, or captured by force from a hostile tribe. On entering her new home, the wife fell absolutely under the dominion of the patriarchal head of the household. The term "daughter" may be derived from a common root, which, according to one view, would pleasantly depict her as filling up the outlines of an idyllic picture, as the milkmaid of the household,[1] or, according to the more probable, though more prosaic, rendering, would view her as nothing more than a mere nourisher of offspring.[2] However this may be, the husband's power over his wife was absolute. He had the right to decide if her offspring should be allowed to live, or, in consequence of infirmity or sex, be exposed to die. In the words of Dr Schrader, "the wife belongs to the man, body and soul, and what she produced is his property, as much as the calf of his cow and crop of his fields."[3] Philology affords no evidence of any matriarchate system under which the children and property would belong to the mother, the father being a subsidiary element in the family life.[4]

The word "father" itself may be traced back through a series of equations which would represent him as the protector of the family, and the word "mother"[5] through a parallel series, representing her as a mere maker or fashioner of children, or, according to Sir John Lubbock and others, those very terms "Pa" and "Ma," which denote protection and fostering, may have been evolved from the earliest spon-

[1] Grimm, "Geschichte der Deutschen Sprache," p. 694; Max Müller, "Selected Essays," I., p. 124.

[2] Rendall, p. 11: "The derivation from *duh*, 'suck,' has rather better phonetic warrant."

[3] Schrader, p. 388.

[4] Max Müller, "Biographies of Words," p. xvii.

[5] Schrader, p. 371; Max Müller, "Biographies of Words," p. xvi.

taneous utterances of a child by mere labial or dental suppression of its breath.[1]

In their original habitat the early Aryans were, for the most part, pastoral, though agriculture[2] was practised to some extent. The ploughs, however, were primitive and simple, being made of bent wood shod with stone. Seeds were sown, the cereal rye at least was grown, the reaping-hook and mill-stone were used, as was the yoke for oxen. Cows were milked; oxen drew such rude waggons as were fashioned. Horses were kept in droves for milk or food, but not until Vedic and Homeric times were they ridden.

The tribes, for the most part pastoral nomads, drove their flocks from grazing-ground to grazing-ground, ever ready to migrate and seek more favoured pasture-lands. Their houses were domed, of basket-work, daubed with mud, or else the family lived underground. Scraped skins sewn together by bone-needles, or wool close pressed together and made with glutinous fat into felt,[3] formed their clothing, while a mead made from honey was an intoxicating beverage to which they seem to have been addicted.

Such is the main outline of the meagre skeleton which philology builds up of the life lived in common by the primitive ancestors of the European peoples, and by those of the first Aryan invaders of India. It shows them tied down to a neolithic primitiveness, preparing for an advance to an Age of Bronze.

At what period these Aryans entered India is unknown.

[1] Lubbock, "Origin of Civilisation," p. 427; Westermarck, "History of Human Marriage," p. 88.

[2] "When we say that the Aryas before their separation were agricultural, we mean no more than that they did not depend for their food on mere chance, but cultivated the soil and grew some kind of corn."—Max Müller, "Biographies of Words," p. 134.

[3] "All the other arts which we ascribe to the Ancient Aryans, such as plaiting, sewing, spinning, weaving, must all be conceived as most simple and primitive."—Max Müller, "Biographies of Words," p. 135.

Pride of race, and pride of birthright still hold the imagination of the pious and orthodox Brāhman of to-day to the fond belief that the Vedic Hymns were a revelation from before all time. Even though this be considered no longer worthy of credence, yet the Brāhman views, with impassive face, the efforts of historic enquiry to pierce through the mists of an antiquity he still feels to be beyond the ken of man. To the unbiassed enquirer the period of civilisation, which witnessed the composition of the Vedic Hymns, seems to fade further into distant time, instead of, as might be hoped, drawing nearer to such historic dates as fall within the limits even of Homeric time. From 1200 to 1500 years [1] before the Christian era was for long held the earliest period to which, with safety, the composition of the Vedic Hymns could be assigned.[2] Should the latest theories, based on astronomical data, fail to win adherents to the conclusion that the period of Vedic civilisation extended back as far as 4500 years B.C., and the Hymns themselves to 2500 B.C., it seems daily to grow more probable that the whole period of early Sanskrit literature must be placed at a much earlier date than that to which it has until lately been allotted.[3]

Be the date what it may, it is in these Hymns that must be sought the evidences as to what were the hopes and ideals of the times, for in them is contained all that the tribe, sib, or family of the poets who composed them deemed worthy of being preserved as a record of the best the age knew, as a record of the literature of their race.

[1] Max Müller, "India: What Can It Teach Us," p. 202 (1500 B.C.); Kaegi, "Rig Veda," p. 11 (2000 to 1500 B.C.); Haug, "Introd. to Ait Brāh.," i. 47 (2400-1400 B.C.).

[2] Max Müller, "Biographies of Words," p. 153:—"Within sight of the Indus and its tributaries, the undivided South-Eastern Aryas spoke a language more primitive than Sanskrit or Zend, about 2000 B.C."

[3] *See* Barth, "Ind. Ant.," September 1894.

CHAPTER III.

THE EARLY BARDS.

ON the first dawn of Vedic history, the Aryans appear amid the bleak mountain ranges in the north-west of India, where the Swāt, Kābul, Kumār, and Kuram rivers find their way through unfrequent fertile valleys to the lowland plains and land of the Five Rivers of the Panjāb. These rivers the Aryans had to cross before they could set aside their conquering arms, and, beyond the sacred Sarasvatī, seek rest in the holy land of Brahmāvarta,[1] thence to spread their civilising mission down the rich river-valleys of the Ganges and Jumna, and claim all India north of the Vindhya as the abode of their race—as the renowned Aryāvarta.[2] For weary centuries the tribes had journeyed on towards the rising sun, their hopes buoyed up by stories told of the warm, sunlit plains. These once gained, no longer would the sacred and first duty of each head of a family be to nourish and cherish, as the chief great friend of their race, the heaven-sent "Agni," the God of Fire.

[1] "Manu," II, 17:—"Between the two divine rivers, Sarasvatī and Drishadvatī, lies the tract of land, which the sages have named "Brahmāvarta," because it was frequented by gods."—G. C. Haughton.

[2] *Ibid.*, II, 22:—"As far as the eastern, and as far as the western oceans, between the two mountains, Himālaya and Vindhya, lies the tract which the wise have named Aryāvartā, or "abode of the learned."

Then there would be time for peace, and rest, and sleep, and thought; for once the dark aborigines were conquered or propitiated, to them could be allotted all manual labour. No wonder that the imagination of the Vedic poet was stirred to its deepest depths as he stood amid the moving times. From the shadowed recesses of the silent forests bordering the mountain ranges, murmuring echoes answered back the poet's exulting song of joy and the tribesmen's fiercer notes of warlike might. From the far-off plains the rain-clouds rolled on towards the mountain passes, in black and heaving billows, while from out them dashed the vivid gleam of an Indian lightning as the thunder sent its peals from mountain peak to peak. It was down in the arid, lowland plains that Indra, the God of Rain, became the Aryan tribesmen's champion—the god who won their battles, broke open the heavenly fortresses, and let the waters forth to cool the parched fields. It was Nature[1] that held spell-bound the imagination of the new-come Aryans, and it was to glorify her, and seek the aid of her powers—vaguely personified as "devas," "deities," or "bright ones,"—that the Vedic poets composed their songs of praise. Of history, pure and simple, the hymns tell but little. The comings and goings of the people, the trivial life of mankind, appeared but as a breath when compared to the mystery of the unchanging vault of Heaven, the depths of the clear, starlit nights ever soothing to rest, the sad rise and wane of the moon, the glad, red blush of the dawn as it awoke all Nature to life, the unchanging passings of the sun in its three steps across the sky, until, in the silence of eventide, it descends towards the land of the fathers, there to abide until it again rises towards morn over the land of the living.

[1] *See* Regnaud, p. 64, for the theory that the adoration of Nature in Vedic times was only an illusion produced by the phraseology, or rather by the rhetoric of the hymns.

To those whose ears are not attuned to the sound of the music that throbs through every stanza of the Vedic Hymns, the whole secret of the power they held over the hearts of the people will be lost. Held as sacred treasures of the race, they have been handed down from generation to generation, as all that has been deemed worthy of preservation, as the best the age brought forth. In verses full of the sound of the rush of moving waters, the poet tells, with swelling pride, the glories of the new-found land his race had come to claim and make its own, as far as from the Sindhu or Indus in the West, away to the distant Ganges in the then unknown East:—

"Let[1] now the poet, here waiting in the place of sacrifice, tell, O rivers, your chief glories. The Rivers have come forth by seven and seven from three quarters, the Sindhu surpassing all in her glory. From the mountains onward towards the sea, the Sindhu hasteneth in her strength, rushing in the path that Varuna had smoothed out; eager for the prize, she surpasses in the race all that run. Above the earth, even in the heavens, is heard the sound of her rolling waters; the gleam of bright light lengthens out her unending course. From the mountain-side the Sindhu comes roaring like a bull, as from the clouds the waters rush amid the roll of thunder. The other rivers run to pour their waters into thee.

"From both sides thou drawest on the flowing streams like to a conquering king rushing to the front, leading his following hosts. O Ganges, Jumna, Sarasvatī, Sutlej, and Ravi, and you also, O Asiknī, Marudvridhā, hearken O Vitastā and Ārjīkīyā with the Sushomā, listen now to this my praise. Flashing, sparkling, gleaming, in her majesty the unconquerable, the most abundant of streams, beautiful as a handsome, spotted mare, the Sindhu rolls her waters over the lands.

"Mistress of a chariot, with noble horses richly dressed, golden, adorned, yielding nutriment, abounding in wool, youthful, gracious, she traverses a land full of sweetness. May she grant us vigour in this struggle; for greatly celebrated is the glory of that unconquered, illustrious, and much-lauded Sindhu.[2]

[1] Re-translated with the aid of Muir's "Sanskrit Texts," vol. v. p. 343; *cf.* R.V., x. 75, and Max Müller, "India: What Can It Teach Us?" pp. 164-5 (1892); Griffith, R.V., p. 251.

[2] Muir, vol. v. p. 344.

It was in the extreme north-west of India that the Aryans first made their homes. Thence tribes spread South as far as the junction of the Indus, with the rivers of the Panjāb;[1] Yet all those who remained there, as well as all those who formed alliances, matrimonial or political, with the aboriginal inhabitants, were held by the orthodox Aryan of later times as impure. They were considered as having fallen from the ranks of those Aryans who left the plain-land of the Five Rivers behind them, and passed onwards to the Sarasvatī, Ganges and Jumna, there to rest and collect the treasured hymns of their forefathers into what is now known as the Sanhita of Vedic Hymns. Centuries, not years, represent the period of the composition of these verses, but 1017 or 1028[2] in number, which contain 153,826 words, and now hold all that will ever be known of the past of the Aryan forefathers of the great priestly families of India.

Of the aboriginal inhabitants whom the Aryans found in possession of the land history has preserved no record. The Vedic Hymns merely mention their existence in order to revile them as Dasyus[3] *(foes)*, as slaves. To the fair-skinned Aryans these dark aborigines were no-nosed and fierce, eaters of raw flesh, and godless. Yet of their forts and castles there is mention, and of their wealth there are clear indications,[4] while there is ample evidence that with many of them the Aryans made matrimonial connections, and that the offspring formed a new class, considered as of more or less pure blood and social position. The Aryans, however,

[1] In the North, probably in Kashmīr, tribes known as the Kuru-Krivis (in later times renowned as the Panchālas), are held to have taken up their abode; to the further West, in the valleys of the Kābul and Kuram, the tribes known as the Gandhāra found a home; while even as far South as Sind, tradition tells of the tribe known as the Yādavas (*see* Baden-Powell, "Ind. Vill. Com.," p. 97; and Zimmer, "Alt. Ind. Leben.," pp. 122-124).

[2] Max Müller, "Hibbert Lectures," p. 153.

[3] *See* Muir, O.S.T., vol. i. p. 174 (ed. 1890); Zimmer, "Alt. Ind. Leben.," pp. 115-118.

[4] R.V., 3, 34, 9.

for the most part lived as joint families, united in their ancient sibs, or clans, into settlements[1] under a common chief.[2] When the clans or settlements joined together for war or defence, they formed the tribe.[3] The king, or "rājā," was elected from among the chieftains,[4] as their chosen representative, though the office soon became practically hereditary.

By the king's side stood his priestly counterpart, the "purohita,"[5] who, by his solemn invocations and charms of noted potency, held his position secure. On the election of a chieftain to be king, the chosen poet of the people poured forth his benediction in flowing verse, such as has been so aptly translated by Mr Griffith:[6]—

"Be with us; I have chosen thee; stand steadfast and immovable.
Let all the people wish for thee: let not thy kingdom fall away.
Be even here; fall not away: be like a mountain unremoved.
Stand steadfast here like Indra's self, and hold the kingship in thy grasp.

. . . .

Firm is the sky, and firm the earth, and steadfast also are these hills.
Steadfast is all this living world, and steadfast is this king of men.

. . . .

On constant Soma let us think with constant sacrificial gift.
And then may Indra make the clans bring tribute unto thee alone."

Other verses tell of the power and influence of the king's "purohita," or domestic chaplain:—

"May this prayer of mine be successful; may the vigour and strength

[1] "Viś," Schrader, pp. 399, 403.

[2] "Viś pati," Zimmer, "Alt. Ind. Leben.," p. 172.

[3] Baden-Powell, "Ind. Vill. Com.," p. 204 (*cf.* R.V., 2, 26, 3), in which the tribe, clan, or minor clan, or connected single families held together by some tie of descent. Robertson Smith, "Religion of the Semites," p. 34.

[4] Jevons, "Introduction to History of Religion," for separation of Kingly and Priestly Functions, originally united, p. 275.

[5] Probably, as a rule, an Atharva priest (*cf.* "Yājnavalkya," i. 312), Bloomfield, S.B.E., vol. 42, p. xlvi, also lviii.

[6] R.V., x. 173.

be complete, may the power be perfect, undecaying, and victorious of those of whom I am the priest (*purohita*). . . . May all those who fight against our wise and prosperous (prince) sink downward, and be prostrated. With my prayer I destroy his enemies, and raise up his friends. May those of whom I am the priest be sharper than an axe, sharper than fire, sharper than Indra's thunderbolt. I strengthen their weapons; I prosper their kingdom rich in heroes. . . . Ye with the sharp arrows smite those whose bows are powerless; ye whose weapons and arms are terrible (smite) the feeble. When discharged, fly forth, O arrow, sped by prayer. Vanquish the foes, assail, slay all the choicest of them; let not one escape."[1]

To their kings the people rendered obedience. The offerings or tribute to the chosen chief were held to be voluntary, though there are verses[2] that liken a king unto a fire that burns up the forest, in the way he sweeps up the goods of the rich. There are also hymns,[3] which tell how the king sat, decked with gold and jewels, in what is described as a palace, with a thousand pillars and a thousand doors. Headed by their chosen king or chieftain, the tribes advanced to battle, and, as they marched, the proud song of the king's elected "purohita," or poet-priest, rang in their ears. Not by the king's valour nor by his well-known heroic might, not by the impetuous rush of the conquering tribes was the victory to be gained. It was the incantations of the haughty purohita who summoned the gods to hover near and win the day, that cheered on the clansmen and made them sure of victory. The knowledge that the gods fought on their side, added to the war-chant of the chosen poet-laureate, inspired the god-intoxicated enthusiasm of all ranks alike, and held the Aryans united against their darker foe. The weird influence of the magic of the priestly spell, the sound of the blast of the tempest, and the

[1] Muir, O.S.T., pp. 283-4; "Atharva-veda," III, 19, 1.
[2] R.V., 1, 65, 4.
[3] Zimmer, "Alt. Ind. Leben.," p. 167; R.V., 8, 5, 38; 1, 85, 8; 10, 78, 1.

howl of battle-rage subtly mingled in the inspiring chant of the purohita, who proudly sings the song of war:[1]—

> "Increased is now this prayer (*brahma*), the might, the power. Increased the warrior sway of which I am the conquering Purohita. I lengthen out the lordly rule with heaven ascending smoke-incense, I hew asunder the foemen's arms. Let those who rage against our mighty king sink low, with this my prayer (*brahma*) I vanquish all who are not friends and raise up those near. Advance and conquer, heroes! Let now your arms be fierce. Strike down with pointed arrows the weak bowmen, strike with fierce weapons the powerless foe."

No translation could give the full force of these lines, changing as they do in the original from sound to sound to suit the sense. In the last verse, calling on the tribes to advance and conquer, the fierce passion of battle strife seems to shake the utterances of the inspired poet, as he repeats again and again the harsh sounds which thrill through the last two sounding lines,[2] calling on the Aryans to strike down the foe.

Though there were kings and purohitas and sacrificial priests (*brahmans*); though there were warriors and the great body of the people, cultivators, artisans, or dealers in articles of food, in grain or merchandise, there is no evidence that anywhere were the people tied down to the rigidity of a caste[3] system where a fixed hereditary occupation was allotted to the members.

The composers of the Vedic Hymns, or *Brahmans*, as they were called, belonged to no one class or order. He on whom the gift of song had fallen became the poet-priest. One poet[4] tells how that, although he is a maker

[1] "Atharva-veda," III, 19.

[2] "Pretâ jayantâ nara ugrâ vâh santu bâhavah.
Tiksńesavo abala dhanvano hata ugrâ ayudhâ abalān ugrabâhavah."

[3] "Caste is a European word, but it has become so completely naturalised in India that the vagueness of its meaning seems to have reacted on the native mind. The Sanskrit word for caste is *varna*, literally 'colour' or *jâti*, literally 'breed,' or 'kith.'"—Max Müller, "Biographies of Words," p. 247.

[4] "Rig Veda," ix. 112, 3.

of the hymn he sings, yet his father was a physician, while his mother ground grain between millstones. Every one, he says, has a different occupation and varied opinions—the carpenter seeks something to mend, the physician some one in distress, the priest one who has an offering to make. All in the world stand waiting for wealth, even as the cowherd stands watching his cattle. The horse longs for a cart that runs smoothly; those who love talking long for those who talk; frogs long for water, and desire roameth wild after that which it desireth. In one well-known hymn,[1] of which the language and tenor is modern, compared with the rest of the collection, the people are described as divided into four distinctive classes.

The hymn tells of the creation of all things from the sacrifice of a fabulous monster-man, or "Purusha," his severed limbs giving birth to the world. As is pointed out by Mr Andrew Lang,[2] the same primitive mode of accounting for creation is found in the Norse legend, where the earth, the seas, water, mountains, clouds, and firmament, are formed by dividing up the body of the Giant Ymir. So also in the Chaldæan story a monster woman is divided in twain by Bel, to form the heavens and earth. The same story runs through the myths of the Iroquois in North America, as well as through those of Egypt and Greece. In the Vedic legend the monster Purusha has a thousand heads, a thousand eyes, and a thousand feet. So great was this primeval being, that he spread over the earth and yet ten fingers' breadth beyond. By the gods he was offered up in sacrifice. From him sprang forth all the creatures of the air and all animals, wild or tame, also the three Vedas—the "Rig," "Sāman," and "Yajur"—horses, and all creatures having two rows of teeth, goats, and sheep.

So far the story runs close to those of other folk. The

[1] R.V., x. 90.
[2] "Myth. Ritual and Religion," vol. i. p. 243.

conception points back to a very early phase of thought, almost to the childhood of mankind. The Vedic account, however, goes on to add that from Purusha also sprang four castes or classes of the people. There is no escape from the conclusion that this is an attempt to force an antiquity for a modern social system by connecting it with an undeniably ancient legend. The four castes are held to have existed from before all time. The Brāhmans, as a distinct class of priests who recited the *brahman*, or "prayer," are said to have been created from the mouth of Purusha; the "Rājanya," or warriors, to have sprung from his arms; the "Vaiśya," or main body of the Aryan people, agriculturists or tradesmen, were born from his thighs, while last and lowest born were the Sūdras, the servile conquered foes, created from the feet of Purusha. The Brāhman priesthood were thus held to have been divinely created, according to the revealed evidence of the Vedic text, as supreme above kings, warriors, or servile workers. All alike were made to feel the power thus placed in the hands of the Brāhmans.

In the "Atharva-veda," where much more of the life-throb of the people is felt than in the more dignified and stately "Rig Veda," clear evidence is given of the unrelenting vengeance of the Brāhman priests towards those who intrigued against them or sought to take their wealth:—

> "He who thinks the Brāhman mild," declares one hymn,[1] "and slays him, he who reviles the gods, lusts after wealth without thought, in his heart Indra kindles a fire; him both heaven and earth hate while he lives."

More fierce than this is the invective poured forth

[1] "Atharva-veda," v. 18, 5 (Bloomfield); S.B.E., vol. xlii; Muir, O.S.T., vol. i. p. 285.

against those unbelieving oppressors of the priest who holds the magic spell :—

"The Brāhman's tongue turns into a bow-string, his voice into the neck of an arrow; his windpipe, his teeth are bedaubed with holy fire; with these the Brāhman strikes those who revile the gods, by means of bows that have the strength to hurt, discharged by the gods."

"The Brāhmanas have sharp arrows, are armed with missiles, the arrow which they hurl goes not in vain, pursuing him with their holy fire and their wrath, even from afar do they pierce him."[1]

The earlier Vedic Hymns show the Aryans free from all caste restraint, priestly aggression or kingly oppression. The poet or maker of the Vedic Hymns merely calls upon the king and people to be liberal in gifts,[2] for those who are liberal sink not into sin nor sorrow; they abide for ever glorious, living long lives and reaping rich rewards hereafter. One poet praises the liberality of a chieftain who dwelt on the bank of the Sindhu, or Indus, from whom one hundred horses, sixty thousand kine, eight cows, all good milkers, and one hundred necklaces had been received.

Between the two famed poet-priests, Vasishta and Visvamitra, of whom every Hindu household in India to-day holds legends, the rivalry was great to secure the favour of the renowned king Sudās, who led the white-robed Tritsu tribe to battle against ten other kings who had raised the standard of revolt.[3]

Visvamitra at length was obliged to retire before his rival Vasishta, who remained to sing the praise of his patron, the conquering Sudās. It was Vasishta who, by his mystic prayers, brought the aid of Indra to the king, and hurled

[1] S.B.E., vol. xlii. p. 170; Muir, O.S.T. (1890), p. 258, for use of word brăhmăn, first as "a sage, a poet," next as an officiating priest, and later as a special description of priest, or even as "a priest by profession," and Brāhmana as the son of a brăhmăn, denoting the hereditary transmission of the function.

[2] R.V., x. 107, 2; 7, 33, 6; 3, 53, 12.

[3] Zimmer, "Alt. Ind. Leben.," p. 170; R.V., vii. 18, 23.

back Visvamitra and his warlike friends the Bhāratas. To Vasishta wealth and honour were poured forth; two chariots with mares were given him, along with four horses decked with pearls, so that the seven rivers of the Panjāb might spread abroad the liberality of Sudās. No greater glory could the devout Aryan win than to bestow his wealth on the tribal laureate.[1] Those who gave rich garments lived long; those who gave gold enjoyed undyingness:[2] liberality was held the best armour for a wise man to wear. The coming of the rich man is awaited with joy by maidens gleaming in fine garments; the abode of the liberal man is a lake of enjoyment spread with lotus leaves. The *brăhmăn*, or maker of the prayer, became, as time rolled on and the sacrifices to the gods more frequent, complicated, and relied on, of greater importance. The "purohita," or domestic chaplain, swayed the policy of the tribe and ruled the king's thoughts. The purohita was elected from among the ranks of the poet-priests[3] or Brāhmans, who knew or had composed hymns honoured as of special merit or potency. In course of time, as the ritual developed, other sacrificing priests were appointed to chant the hymns, perform the sacrifice, or assist in various subsidiary duties.

The Brāhmanas or Brāhmans, sons or descendants of the early poet-priests, were trained to hold in their family the general supervision over the entire sacrificial system.

Changes such as these came not until the Aryans had advanced far into India, and found time, leisure, and opportunity to develop the primitive system of worship of their deities by mystic prayers.

In the early hymns of the "Rig Veda" the Aryans are,

[1] R.V., 10, 107, 2.

[2] *Amritatwam.*

[3] For the plea raised by the Atharvan priest that from amongst them the Brâhman should be chosen, *see* S.B.E., vol. xlii. p. lxv.

for the most part, pastoral tribes. These tribes are often referred to as five in number,[1] references that, however, can hardly be taken to denote any special division of the people, since the word "five"[2] is often used to express any indefinite number. Although the pastoral habits of the tribes are often described—horses, kine, sheep and ewes[3] being frequently mentioned—yet agriculture was common. Wheat and barley were sown and reaped, though, strange to say, there is no reference to rice. Watercourses are mentioned, and it seems as though they had been specially constructed for the purpose of irrigation. In course of time the Aryans allowed all direct agricultural operations to lapse, for the greater part, into the hands of the aboriginal darker race, becoming themselves landlords[4] and co-sharers of the lands where they found a home, the darker races being then, as the Dravidians are to-day, skilled builders of irrigation reservoirs or "tanks," and apt in terracing sloping land for cultivation. In the Veda the plough and ploughshare are addressed as objects of Divine worship. One hymn[5] is addressed to a deity, vaguely personified as the lord who presides over the fields, he being prayed to direct the plough straight in the furrow, or "*sītā*," to keep the land sweet, so that the husbandman may cheerfully drive the oxen with his goad.

Trade was carried on by barter, and although the medium of exchange was the cow, gold pieces are referred to, as are also usurers, yet there was no recognised system of coinage.

[1] Muir, Original Sanskrit Texts (3rd ed.), vol. i. p. 177.

[2] *Ibid.*, p. 179.

[3] R.V., x. 91, 14:—"Horses, bulls, oxen and barren cows offered for sacrifice," also (x. 89, 14), "a place of slaughter mentioned" (Muir, vol. v. p. 463).

[4] Baden-Powell, "Ind. Vill. Com.," p. 89:—"Whatever customs regarding land are of Aryan origin, they are the customs of a conquering race, or at least of a race which took the superior position in everything. The tenures that arose from their State arrangements, and their locations of Chiefs, were all essentially overlord, or at least landlord tenures."

[5] R.V., iv. 57.

Weaving and working in leather were well-known, garments being made from the wool of sheep.[1] Women are described as well adorned, as wearing jewels, having their hair braided, and well-oiled. The white-robed tribe of the Tritsus adorn their hair in special coils, as do also the deities, Rudra and Pūshan.

The raging storm-deities[2] are described as having gold breastplates and anklets, and as wearing gold crowns, while their white horses[3] are depicted as caparisoned with gold chains and trappings.

Like unto a barber shaving a beard,[4] so fire is said to clear the stubble from the earth, while the pious pray that they may be sharpened even as a razor, or pair of scissors is sharpened by a barber.

It is doubtful if the early Aryans ever knew of the ocean. The seas of water they mention may have referred to the wide-stretching Indus. Ships, however, are frequently referred to, and one oft-quoted incident records how Tugra abandoned in the midst of the waters his son Bhujyu, who was rescued by the Aśvins in a ship with a hundred oars.[5]

From the earliest Vedic Hymns, making all allowances for poetic exaggeration, a picture of social life is seen, far removed from primitive simplicity. The Aryans, in fact, emerge on the horizon of Indian history as entering through the North-west Passes, in well-organised tribes, holding their popular assemblies, led by renowned chieftains or kings, honouring their bards and priests, free from social distinction, and possessing many of the arts and refinements of civilisation. Even physicians[6] are mentioned, who collect herbs for the curing of diseases, magic spells being recited when the herbs were applied to the patient.[7]

[1] *See* Muir, O.S.T., pp. 462 *ff.*

[2] R.V., v. 54, 11.

[3] *Ibid.*, v. 54, 11; iv. 2, 8; iv. 37, 4.

[4] *Ibid.*, viii. 4, 16; x. 142, 4.

[5] Muir, vol. v. 245, 465.

[6] R.V., x. 97, 6.

[7] *Ibid.*, x. 97, 19.

To the Aśvins laud is given, for that when, in the time of battle, a leg was severed like a wild bird's pinion,

> "Straight ye gave Vispalā a leg of iron that she might move what time the conflict opened."[1]

Stranger still, the Aśvins restore the eyesight of one blinded for his evil deeds.

Other traits, however, both social and religious, are to be found, recalling faint reminiscences from a distant past. The aged[2] were left forlorn and deserted, and their property divided, a custom not far removed from that of the ancient Germans, where the useless father, when over sixty, was either killed or turned to menial work by his son, who took possession of his property; or from that of the Romans who threw the aged into the Tiber.[3] The position of woman had in many respects improved from that of the Indo-Germanic period, when she was treated as a chattel, the absolute property of her lord and master. Possibly the many hardships encountered during the long march of the Aryans towards India, the losses and opposition met with from opposing tribes, may have given woman time and opportunity to work out her own individuality, whilst her lessened numbers must have gained for her a consideration she would not otherwise have received. The further fact that the conquered were made slaves,[4] must have given the women of the Aryan tribes a dominant position, independent of household drudgery, the full benefit of which they naturally would not be slow to avail themselves.

[1] R.V., i. 116, 15.

[2] *Ibid.*, viii. 51, 2; Zimmer, "Alt. Ind. Leben.," 327; R.V., i. 70, 5: "Parting as 'twere an aged father's wealth."

[3] Kaegi (*note* 50), p. 112; Zimmer, "Alt. Ind. Leben.," pp. 326-328.

[4] For women being made slaves, viii. 46, 33; ix. 67, 10, 11. For whole subject of slavery in India, *see* Article by W. Lee Warner, "Jour. Soc. Arts," February 1897.

Polygamy was, no doubt, common in Vedic times, yet the general custom seems to have favoured monogamy, either from necessity or from the growth of a refined sentiment.

The woman who was handsome is recorded to have been allowed to choose her own friend or lover ;[1] and the hymn which records the custom, states, with dry humour, that no one would object to a man carrying off the blind daughter of another.

There is no evidence to show that women were in these early times curtailed of their freedom or confined to the solitude of their own homes, as is the custom now in India among the respectable Hindu families, a custom primarily due to the fear of insult from foreign conquerors. In one Vedic hymn[2] the story is told of the wrath of the wife of Indra, whose path was obstructed by an offending demon. The goddess rails that, great as were her swelling charms, great as her joy in Indra's love, the demon had checked her course, although she urges that it was the custom for women to go openly to the festival, and to the place of sacrifice.

Again the Dawn is depicted as coming forth, as women throng to a festal meeting, while in many cases it was the custom for husband and wife to perform the necessary sacrifices together. Not only was this so, but one hymn to Agni[3] is ascribed to a poetess Viśvavārā, in which she prays the deity to maintain the well-knit bonds of wife and husband.

More suggestive of the true position held by woman in this early period are the verses[4] recited at the wedding of Soma and Sūrya, the Moon and Sun, an idealised type of all earthly ones. For the bride and bridegroom fortune, prosperity, and sons are besought; for the bride it is

[1] R.V., x. 27, 12.
[2] *Ibid.* v. 28.
[3] *Ibid.*, x. 86.
[4] *Ibid.*, x. 85.

prayed that she may rule over her household and bear affection to her husband. The assembled people are prayed to bid the bride good fortune, and as the bridegroom takes her by the hand, he declares that the gods have appointed her head of his household, to share his joys, to twine her arms around him, and love him fitly, so that they both may reach old age together. At the threshold of her new home the bride is bidden to enter, and bring down a blessing on all who dwell there, so that the home may grow full of happiness, full of joy and mirth, full of sons and grandsons.

In some respects the life in these archaic times seems to have been not far different from that to be seen in many parts of India to-day. One hymn[1] tells of the vintner's house, and of the wine-skins kept within. The Aryans then ate flesh and drank deep.[2] The intoxicating juice of the Soma plant was poured out at the sacrifice until it came to be worshipped as a loved deity. The Indo-Aryans, wandering in search of new homes and gods, may well have cried out in the words of the Persian poet:[3]—

> "Yesterday this Day's madness did prepare
> To-morrow's Silence, Triumph, or Despair,
> Drink! for you know not whence you come, nor why,
> Drink! for you know not why you go, nor where."

Drinking, fighting, and living free, despising the darker skinned aborigines, the Vedic Aryans, except for their belief in their gods and sacrifices, stand out as a race in many points akin to the Greeks of Homeric days. No gloomy speculations are to be found over the mystery of the soul and terrors of an hereafter. To the Aryan,

[1] R.V., i. 191, 10.

[2] *Ibid.*, viii. 58, 11, refers to all the gods as being intoxicated. "Ait. Brāh.," v. 11, states that at the mid-day libation the gods are totally drunk.

[3] Omar Khayyam.

Nature was instinct with joy, while love was bold and untamed.

Gambling in ancient, as in modern, India, was a favourite vice. One despairing gambler pours forth his lament in terms which, in spite of their archaic setting, might well find an echo in many a modern Rājput household. He bemoans[1] how, though his wife had never shamed him, had never blamed him, had never turned away from him or from his friends, but had been ever gentle, yet for one throw of the dice he had for ever turned his face from her. He then continues:[2] "My mother-in-law detests me, my wife rejects me, I cannot discover what is the enjoyment of the gambler. Others pay court to the wife of the man whose wealth is coveted by the impetuous dice. Yet as soon as the brown dice when they are thrown make a sound, I hasten to their rendezvous like a woman to her paramour. Hooking, piercing, deceitful, vexatious, delighting to torment, the dice dispense transient gifts, and again ruin the winners. They appear to the gambler covered with honey. They roll downward, they bound upward, having no hands, they overcome him who has. The destitute wife of the gambler is distressed, and so, too, is the mother of a son who goes she knows not whither. It vexes the gambler to see his own wife, and then to observe the wives and happy homes of others. In the morning he yokes the brown horses (the dice); by the time when the fire goes out he has sunk into a degraded wretch. Never play with dice, practise husbandry; rejoice in thy property, esteeming it sufficient."

There is no doubt evidence,[3] for those who care to pursue the subject, that women's vows were as frail in ancient

[1] R.V., x. 34.
[2] Muir, v. 426-7.
[3] Pischel and Geldner, "Vedische Studien." (1889-92), for evidence of existence of *hetairai*.

Vedic times as they are to-day, and that monogamy, the ideal bond of earthly union, carried in its wake some far from submissive swains. Charms against rival wives, charms to hold the flickering love of man or woman, are given in the hymns of the "Atharva-veda," which evidently goes back in its underlying basis as far as do the hymns of the more stately "Rig Veda." Bloomfield, in his recent translation of the Atharvan Hymns, has given a number of these spells, some of which are said in the spells themselves to have travelled from distant places. One of these spells[1] is as follows:—"From folk belonging to all kinds of people, from the Sindhu thou hast been fetched, the very remedy for jealousy. As if a fire is burning him, as if the forest fire burns in various directions, this jealousy of him do thou quench, as a fire is quenched by water."

More pleasing is the love-charm for a bride and bridegroom, as translated by Griffith:[2]—

"Sweet are the glances of our eyes, our faces are as smooth as balm,
Within thy bosom harbour me, one spirit dwell in both of us."

Another potent charm tells how to bind the love of a reluctant maiden:[3]—

"My tongue hath honey at the tip, and sweetest honey at the root,
Thou yieldest to my wish and will, and shalt be mine and only mine.
My coming in is honey sweet, and honey sweet my going forth;
My voice and words are sweet: I fain would be like honey in my look.

Around thee have I girt a zone of sugar-cane to banish hate.
That thou may'st be in love with me, my darling, never to depart."

There are verses of the "Rig Veda"[4] which allude to the

[1] A.V., vii. 45; S.B.E., vol. xlii. p. 107.
[2] *Ibid.*, vii. 36.
[3] *Ibid.*, i. 34.
[4] R.V., iv. 19, 9; iv. 30, 16; 11, 29, 1.

sons of unwedded women, sometimes to the birth of children in secret shame.[1] The union of a widow in "levirate" marriage[2] with her brother-in-law, for the purpose of raising up offspring to the deceased husband, gives evidence in itself of, at least, the non-universality of the ancient Aryan custom of the widow being put to death on the decease of her husband. On death the body of the deceased was burned,[3] though burial was also in vogue. In one hymn[4] it is prayed that both those who are burned and those who are not burned may hereafter gain the perfect path,[5] and a body such as they desire. One hymn gives the entire funeral surroundings when the tribe brings forth its deceased kinsman to restore him to mother earth. Round the burial-place the friends and relatives of the deceased assemble and commence their wail to death.

From amid the throng the cry of the bard goes forth to Death :—

"Go thou now far away, I speak to thee who seest not, and hearest not, injure thou not our children nor our fighting men. These all standing here are now divided from the dead. We look to dance and song, we long to lengthen out our days. Let all here live a hundred years. Between those living and him now dead we heap up stones ; let none advance beyond them ; by this stone we now set up, let death be kept away. Let first the women not yet widowed, those with noble husbands go hence, weeping not, strong, adorned with jewels, let them go first towards the house.[6] Now let the wife of the dead man arise. Let her go to the world of the living. Your husband's life is fled, you are now the widow of him who grasps your hand and leads you forth.[7] Take now the bow from the hand of him who lies dead. Enter, O

[1] Zimmer, "Alt. Ind. Leben.," p. 324.

[2] Deuteronomy, ii. 5, 5 ; R.V., x. 40, 2.

[3] Oldenberg, "Rel. des Vedas," p. 570.

[4] R.V., x. 15, 14.

[5] *Asunîti.*

[6] "Ārohantu janayo yonim agre."

[7] "Du bist die gattin dessen geworden, derjetzt deine Hand ergreift und dich aufstehen macht."—Oldenberg, "Rel. des Vedas," 575 (*note*).

lifeless one, the mother earth, the widespread earth, soft as a maiden; in her arms rest free from sin. Let now the earth gently close around you, even as a mother gently wraps her infant child in soft robes. Let now the fathers keep safe thy resting-place, and let Yama, the first mortal who passed the portals of death, prepare for thee a new abiding-place."

It would be rash to affirm from this hymn that widow-burning was totally unknown in Vedic times. The custom was an old one, and survived in India down to very recent days. In the "Atharva-veda,"[1] it is referred to as an ancient custom, so that it will be safer[2] to accept the conclusion that the custom was not one belonging to the family or tribe of the poet who composed the Vedic Hymn. The fact, too, that the bow was taken from the hand of the deceased and gold substituted, shows an advance on the older custom, where the belongings of the dead man were burned with him,[3] and may tend to support the suggestion that the widow was similarly rescued by a special rite.

The one great perplexing question for all mankind—the question as to what becomes of man after death—still remained to perplex the Indo-Aryan mind, if haply it might find some solution, and then hand on the weary quest as a heritage to occupy the subtle thought and untiring efforts of succeeding generations. Death, so far as can be learned from the Vedic literature, was held to be the going-forth from the living of his breath,[4] or of the thinking part, the mind, which was held to reside in the heart. Yama was the first mortal to find the after world.

Those who had done good in this world; those who had

[1] A.V., xviii. 3, 1.

[2] "Dharma purāna 'als uralte sitte.'"—Zimmer, "Alt. Ind. Leben.," pp. 329-31.

[3] "Nicht anders steht es mit der Wittwe—sie besteigt den Scheiter haufen, und es bedarf eines eignen rituellen Āctes um sie von dort zur Welt der Lebenden zurückzuführen."—Oldenberg, "Rel. des Vedas," p. 587.

[4] For this, the *asu*, or physical breath, *see* Oldenberg, p. 525 (*note* 2). For the *manas*, the subtle body of the Sanhhya, R.V., x. 15, 1. *See* Barth for the *ajobhagas*, x. 16, 4.

performed sacrifices, been liberal, warriors or ascetic saints, gained the happy heaven where dwell Yama, the fathers[1] and the gods who have passed to the land similar to that described in the Odyssey:[2]

> "To the plain Elysian, where light-haired Rhadamanthus doth dwell.
> Where restful is life and ever with men it goeth full well."

There they met with Yama, who was guarded by two four-eyed brindled dogs, with broad nostrils, Death's messengers among men, though again the Dove[3] is mentioned as Death's envoy. They dwell with Yama as the Fathers who have again gained spirit or breath,[4] knowing right, and returning to earth to eat the funeral oblations, to which they are periodically summoned. These Fathers are prayed[5] not to injure the living. It is they,[6] who, with Soma, have stretched out the heavens and the earth, set the stars in the firmament, and given the great light.

In this happy after-life the body of the deceased, though not in the form it bore during life, takes part, and pines for raiment and nourishment,[7] provided for it by devout sons at the funeral oblation. So when the deceased is cremated the deity of the Fire is besought[8] not to consume him entirely, not to scatter his body or skin, but to give to the fathers, endowed with breath and clothed with a new body, any portion that may have been injured by bird, ant, serpent or beast of prey, fully restored.

[1] "Ancestor worship and the cult of the dead have no place in the Homeric world, and can have none."—Schrader, p. 424.

[2] Avia, "Odyssey," x. 561.

[3] R.V., x. 165, 4.

[4] *Ibid.*, x. 15, 1: "Asum ye Iyuh" (Muir, v. 295).

[5] *Ibid.*, iii. 55, 2.

[6] *Ibid.*, viii. 48, 13.

[7] Oldenberg, "Rel. des Vedas," v. p. 529. For a later idea, *see* "Śat. Brāh.," x. 4, 4, 4, where the deceased has human passions in Heaven. "Śat. Brāh.," xi. 2, 7, 33, good and evil deeds are weighed, and recompense given accordingly ("Śat. Brāh.," vi. 2, 2, 27; x. 5, 4, 15).

[8] R.V. x. 16, 1.

The home of the dead is said to lie at the back of the sky:[1] it is, again, a place where there is uncreated light,[2] a world wherein the sun is placed; it is within the sky's deepest depths. Again, it is in the third firmament,[3] in the third sky, where there is joy and delight, attainment of all wishes, where one dwells immortal, and the fathers wander as they will. Another verse[4] tells how those, who have given rich offerings to the priests during life, go to the highest heaven; those who have given gifts of horses dwell by the sun. Yet again the deceased is addressed in a hymn[5] which tells the good deeds done by those who have won the happy shores, where a mead made from honey, or Soma, awaits those who, by their penance,[6] have become invincible and gained the light. There dwell warriors who in the fight have given up their bodies, and those who have on earth upheld the right.

Heaven, a happy hereafter, was all that was looked forward to by these Vedic Aryans. Throughout the hymns there is no weariness of life, no pessimism. The day's work had to be done, a new home won with sword in hand, and there were friendly gods to cheer on the warriors. The time had yet to come, as come it does to all, when the sword is laid aside, and man shudders at the thought that in the fight for advance and progress he must take his weaker brother's life, and blast all the ideals which set peace and goodwill to all men as the prototype of heavenly mercy.

As to the future of the evil-doer and the sinful, there is

[1] R.V., i. 125, 5.

[2] *Ibid.*, x. 14, 7.

[3] R.V., ix. 113, 9: "In the third sphere of inmost heaven, where lucid worlds are full of light" (Griffith).

[4] *Ibid.*, x. 107, 2.

[5] *Ibid.*, xv. 4.

[6] Tapasâ, "durch askese" (Oldenberg, 534). "Through religious abstraction" (Muir, O.S.T., vol. v. p. 310). "By fervour" (Griffith).

but faint allusion. In one verse[1] Indra and Soma are prayed to cast the wicked into the depths,[2] into a darkness profound, from which they emerge not. Again, in another verse, it is said that a deep place[3] has been made for those maidens without brothers who wander about doing evil; for women who deceive their husbands, who are sinful, unrighteous, and untruthful.

[1] R.V., vii. 104, 3.
[2] "Abyss" (Muir, p. 312); "In den Kerker" (Oldenberg, p. 538).
[3] R.V., iv. 5, 5.

CHAPTER IV.

THE TWILIGHT OF THE OLDER AND THE DAWN OF NEWER DEITIES.

As the Aryan tribes wandered on through mountain passes, gloomy forests, and scantily cultivated river-valleys towards the lowland plains of India, the sacred duty of each householder was to preserve bright within his homestead the once-kindled spark of fire. In Greece, Hestia, the goddess of the domestic hearth, had the sacred fire ever kept lighted in the Delphic Temple. Vesta had her temple at Lavinium, and there the sacred fire brought first from Troy by Æneas was kept burning with pious care. To-day, in India, when the sedate Hindu awakes to feel the cold, grey dawn creep slowly through the early morning mists, he rises, and from amid the ashes, carefully heaped together the night before on the household hearth, unfolds the glowing spark, and with his palm-leaf fan kindles again the friendly fire. No defiling breath from his impure mouth is ever wafted on the sacred friend of man. No Hindu, however low or fallen, would dare to extinguish a burning light by profanely blowing on it as do the foreigners.

Should once the life go from the gleaming spark, and it lie cold as man lies cold in death, then the kindling sticks of Arunī wood are brought forth, one twirling piece is placed in the bored-out hollow of the other, and twirled round so that the skilled hand of a native soon brings again to life the sacred flame. Here to the primitive mind, untrained in scientific terminology, is an exact type of all birth and re-creation. To-day everywhere may be seen, in households and by the roadside, emblems outwardly phallic in their form, yet symbolic of the wooden implements whereby a new birth takes place, whereby something is produced which is endowed with a vital life. The new-born fire has a will, a potency of its own, as much as has man. It is animated by a soul, it breathes, it goes free, rejoicing, laughing, crackling ; it is a friend in the household, a friend as it rushes through the undergrowth, drives the foe from his hiding-places, and burns down his strongholds. It is a god resembling, more or less, in the thoughts of the perplexed observer, something which must be human, endowed with human powers and attributes, the assistance of which must be courted, the great power of which must be won as an aid to the conquering Aryans. So all the phenomena of Nature become more or less vaguely personified in one form or another, and prayers, charms, and incantations are composed and sung to sway these deities, to make them more propitious and extend their aid to their worshippers.

In times of danger from increasing foes, in times of victory or public rejoicing, in times of drought, in times when the storms burst forth, the thunder rolls, and the terror-striking lightning gleams along the clouds, bursts through the heavens, and sends its thunderbolts to tear with heavy crash the sobbing earth asunder, then the people turn to their gods, and the tribal sacrifice is made. Those of the tribe on whom the gift of music and of song have fallen are then called forth to carry out the sacrifice, so that the gods may be drawn near.

In Vedic sacrificial times, an open space, or large thatched hall was first prepared. There the sacrificial altar was set up, and the posts, to which the sacrificial victims were bound, adorned. Priests[1] move busy to and fro amid the scene. Seven officiating priests[2] are named. The duty of the Brāhman, who in later ritual becomes the chief over-seeing priest of the entire sacrifice, is referred to as that of kindling[3] the fire, and the recital of the hymns to Indra.[4] Three fires were the number to be prepared within the sacrificial hall. The first represented the household fire, always lighted from fire obtained by drilling one piece of hard Aruni wood into another. It was the fire before which, in the private sacrifices, each householder recited such Vedic Hymns as were held in his family to have special potency to summon the deities, to whom chiefly the intoxicating Soma juice was offered, so that it might please and exhilarate them as it did man. The second, known as the "Southern Fire," stood to the eastward; it was kindled from the household fire. From the South were held to come unclean spirits, malignant influences, and the spirits of the departed; these the "Southern Fire" was supposed to ward off from the sacrifice held sacred to the gods alone. The third fire stood yet further to the East. It was the chief fire of the ceremony.

First used and kept ready to destroy all of the offering not consumed by the gods, it came to be the place whence amid the flames and incense, nourishment was wafted towards the heavens and eager deities. Near at hand were placed seats of sacred grass, on which the gods were prayed to be seated, and partake of the offering. One strange relic of bygone days was the offering of human blood.

[1] R.V. i. 162, 5 (Griffith), for sixteen priests.

[2] The "Hotár," "Potár," "Neshtar," "Agnídh," "Praśāstar," "Adhvaryu," and "Brahman" (*see* x. 91, 10; Haug, p. 12; "Ait. Brāh.").

[3] R.V., x. 52, 2.

[4] Oldenberg, p. 396, holds him to be the Brāhmanācchamsin. Wise sons of Brāhmans are mentioned in eight hymns.

Only this year the natives fled from Bombay in thousands, not for fear of the plague, but because the whisper had gone forth[1] that their foreign rulers had prepared a holocaust of human victims, to appease the divinity of the Queen-Empress, whose statue in Bombay had been insulted. Among the Khonds of the wild hill-tracts of Ganjam, human victims, purchased from the lowland traders, were until lately sacrificed, and their blood and flesh given to the earth to ensure its fertility, and increase the redness of the turmeric by its magical and physical influence.[2]

In the Vedic Hymn the story is told of how the youth Sunashepa was bound as a victim to the sacrificial post, and by his supplications to the gods released from his fate. In another hymn[3] the order of procession, when a horse is led forward to be sacrificed, is detailed. The horse itself goes first, then follows a cart, then a human being (*martyo*) succeeded by cows and troops of maidens.

In the more refined Vedic Hymns there are few traces to be found of human sacrifice, the commonest form of all savage rites. In later days, when the details of the fully developed sacrificial system were set forth in the prolix and wearisome prose manuals,[4] it is declared that in the beginning the sacrifice most acceptable to the gods was man. The text then goes on to tell how, for the man a horse was substituted, then an ox, then a sheep, then a goat, until at length it was found that the gods were most pleased with offerings of rice and barley. Here in the

[1] The evidence for this is founded on indisputable authority, and was referred to by Lord Reay in the course of remarks on Surgeon-Captain Burton Brown's Paper at the Royal Asiatic Society, on the "Ruins of Dimāpur" (March 1897).

[2] *See* Frazer, J.G., "Golden Bough," vol. i. pp. 384-390.

[3] R.V., i. 163, 8; Macdonell, J.R.A.S. (1895), p. 960. *See* Oldenberg, "Rel. des Vedas," p. 365:—"Was sonst für die Existenz vedischer Menschenopfer angeführt wird, scheint mir nicht jeden Zweifel auszuschliessen." Barth, "Rel. of India," p. 35, for the offerings of melted butter, curdled milk, rice, soups, and cakes, and Soma mixed with water or milk.

[4] "Śat. Brāh.," xii. 3, 5.

ancient manual, is clearly set forth the gradual passing of mankind through the early stages of primitive culture.

First, they start as wild and savage hunters, then turn to pasturage, tending horses to be used for food and milk, then to taming the wilder animals, and at last settle down to agriculture, from which laborious mode of life—the most laborious of all save mining—they gained those habits of perseverance and patient industry which led them onwards to the invention of mechanical appliances.

One other great offering to the deities was the intoxicating Soma juice, squeezed from the succulent stems of a plant now unknown in India. This offering of the Soma juice became in time the type of all true sacrifices.[1]

From the Vedic Hymns may be imagined the hall or open space strewn with grass; the sacrificial stakes well decorated; the trembling animals led near; the altars built and prepared; the three fires flaming upwards. The Soma plants are standing ready in a cart, to which are harnessed two goats; the officiating attendants prepare the straining presses and goat-hair strainer, through which the juice drops down like glistening rain; the sacrificing priest waits ecstatic, he is already in communion with the gods, he is indeed a god himself. The Vedic Hymns are being murmured or chanted, every accent, stress, and intonation carefully marked, for the least mistake would vitiate the whole ceremony, and bring danger to all present.

The gods are invited to take their places, eat of the viands or drink the Soma juice, yet nowhere can the forms of gods be seen. There are no idols present, the time was yet to come when the sacrificial post, well-carved and ornamented, would be brought within a temple as the idol or form of the god, to be honoured, fed with offerings and worshipped. Who then are the gods invoked by these early Aryans at the domestic altar, or before the triple

[1] Stevenson's "Preface to the 'Sama Veda,'" p. vii.

fires? Each god has his defined rank, each has his allotted ritual. In the mind of the Vedic priest there was no haziness as to the god he adored.[1] Yet the gods all move to and fro, so far as the hymns depict them, in nebulous anthropomorphic forms. The singer, as he recites the praise of each god in turn, lauds and exaggerates the attributes of the deity he carries for the moment before him in his imagination. The deity at its highest is some personified phenomenon of Nature. It is addressed as if it were man-like, endowed with human will and potency, yet in the mystic utterances of the poet, it never assumes the objective reality, with which it would have been endowed by a Semitic or Greek dramatic genius.

So indistinct is the delineation of the gods, as fashioned by the Vedic poet, that Professor Max Müller,[2] with all his vivid imagination, has but been able to trace the shadowy forms of various gods, each rising in turn to be supreme and highest god.

First of all the gods is Fire, or "Agni." He is the great loved god of the Aryans, to whom the opening hymn of the Vedas is addressed as the deity praised by new poets as well as by old. Yet though Agni is father of all the gods, he is but a younger deity,[3] for originally Fire merely consumed the offerings left from the repast of the other gods; so he is son[4] to all the other gods, and had no part in the drinking of the Soma juice. Thrice born was Agni. From the heavens he fell to earth as lightning, on earth he is produced by the rubbing of the firesticks, in the water[5] also he finds his birth as lightning in the clouds, or as sprung from the wood which holds water as its essence.[6]

[1] Oldenberg, "Rel. des Vedas," p. 101 (*note* 1).
[2] Max Müller, "India: What Can it Teach Us," p. 147.
[3] Oldenberg, p. 104.
[4] Muir, vol. v. p. 221; Oldenberg, p. 44; R.V., vii. 1; iii. 13, 4.
[5] Oldenberg, p. 108.
[6] *Ibid.*, p. 114.

He finds his place in the three sacrificial fires,[1] and at the domestic hearth he is worshipped three times a day by all Hindus. Strong when born[2] he never ages, he never sleeps,[3] he is ever beautiful, he has ruddy limbs, yet he is not to be touched[4] for his locks are flames.[5] He is the guest in every dwelling;[6] he is the bearer of messages; his ears are ever listening, he carries the sacrificial food to the gods. He is the charioteer of the worshipper. As he goes on his way, rich in splendour, and adorned with gold and glittering ornaments, he carries his banner of smoke and his flames of war, "like the roaring waves of the Sindhu."[7] His black trail is to be seen in the brushwood; he is never tired and ever greedy; when the butter is poured over him his back shines like that of an anointed youth who runs a race.[8] His jaws are fiery, his strength is as that of a bull, he breaks down the stronghold of the Dāsa foe.[9] To win his aid "wise men fashion forth spells,"[10] for "he upholds the sky by his efficacious spells." To him "three hundred gods, and three thousand and thirty more did honour."[11] As the poet composes his best song he prays: "May this well-composed prayer, O Agni, be more welcome than a badly composed one."[12] It is Agni who protects the man who speaks the right and the truth.[13] To Agni the sinner prays:—

> "Whatever sin, O youngest god, we have committed against thee in thoughtlessness, men as we are make thou us sinless before Aditi; release us from guilt on all sides, O Agni."[14]

[1] R.V., v. 3, 1. [2] *Ibid.*, iv. 7, 10. [3] *Ibid.*, i. 143, 3.

[4] R.V., ii. 10, 5. [5] *Ibid.*, i. 141, 8.

[6] *Ibid.*, v. 4, 5. "As dear house friend, guest welcome in the dwelling" (Griffith).

[7] *Ibid.*, v. 44, 12 (*tr.* Oldenberg, p. 38).

[8] *See* Pischel, "Vedische Studien.," vol. i. p. 151.

[9] R.V., iii. 12, 6.

[10] *Ibid.*, i. 67, 4.

[11] *Ibid.*, iii. 9, 9; x. 52, 6.

[12] Oldenberg, S.B.E., vol. xlvi. p. 142.

[13] "Rita," S.B.E., vol. xlvi. p. 316; R.V., iv. 2.

[14] R.V., iv. 12, 4 (*tr.* Oldenberg, S.B.E., vol. xlvi.).

Agni is four-eyed; he watches his worshippers on all sides;[1] he accepts the praise of the poor; to him the prayer goes up:—

> "Have mercy upon us; thou art great."[2]

And again—

> "Forgive, O Agni, this our fault, look graciously on the way which we have wandered from afar."[3]

He is prayed to carry the sacrifice to the gods, "for whenever we sacrifice constantly to this or to that god, to thee alone the sacrificial food is offered."[4] He flames forth against all those who are wicked, and against all sorcerers.[5] He drives away sickness, and ever stays near his worshippers as a father stays near to a son; and he is chief of all the clans.

He is the god, indistinct, and clothed in all the subjective mysticism of his worshippers, who is prayed to come to the sacrifice, and take his place on the sacred grass among the gods as Hotar, Priest and Purohit, and giver of treasure.

Such are the Vedic gods of whom it may be said, in the chastened language of Andrew Lang:[6] "The lights of ritualistic dogma, and of pantheistic and mystic and poetic emotion, fall in turn like the changeful hues of sunset, on figures as melting and shifting as the clouds of sunset."

In such forms the gods everywhere crowd through the three regions and hover round the altars. Some, abstract conceptions,[7] such as Wrath, Faith, Speed, and Abundance; others, the personifications of active agencies,

[1] R.V., i. 31, 13.
[2] Oldenberg, i. 36, 12; S.B.E., vol. xlv. 1.
[3] R.V., i. 31, 16; S.B.E., vol. xlvi.
[4] Oldenberg, i. 26, 6; S.B.E., vol. xlvi.
[5] R.V., i. 12, 5; S.B.E., vol. xlvi.
[6] "Myth. Ritual and Religion," vol. i. p. 161.
[7] Macdonell, J.R.A.S. (1895), p. 948.

as Tvashtar, the lord[1] who forms all things, who fashions the sun in the heavens and the child in the mother; Pūshan, the Guide, who shows the path of death to the sacrificer; and Savitar,[2] the Quickener or Inspirer, who with his raised arms holds forth his blessing and giveth hope to all. Brihaspati or Brahmanaspati, the lord of the *Brăhmăn*, or "prayer," takes shape and form as does Prajāpati, the lord of all creatures, for "the image of the Creator floats hazily among others in the great, grey, shapeless mist which surrounds the world of creation."[3]

As the imagination strives to pierce through the mists, and form out one by one the Vedic gods, a figure glides gently out from amid the rest, rising, clothed in garments of purest light, as the loved maiden-goddess, the gleaming bride, the Dawn. As she draws near, the youth with ruddy limbs and locks of flame, grows pale and fades away, while the dark Night rises to make place for her loved sister, the glowing ever-welcome light, the first-born daughter of the Sky. Seated on her car she cometh; ruddy horses speed her over the land of her worshippers. At her coming the birds fly up from their nests, and man rises from sleep to gaze in solemn wonder at the fair goddess who steals forth as a dancer, never resting, her breasts bared, her garments adorned, for he remembereth how—

> "All those who watched for thee of old
> Are gone, and now 'tis we who gaze
> On thy approach; in future days
> Shall other men thy beams behold."

With the Dawn rise two horsemen, the Aśvins, her twin brothers or husbands,[4] sons of Dyaus. They are ever inseparable, like to the Dioscurī, sons of Zeus, who in

[1] Wallis, "Cosmology of the Veda," p. 9.
[2] Macdonell, J.R.A.S. (1895), p. 951; R.V., i. 95, 7.
[3] Oldenberg, "Buddha," p. 22.
[4] Hopkins, "Rel. of India," p. 80.

Attica freed their sister Helena from Theseus. They yet dwell ever apart; they are wonder-workers,[1] of "golden brilliancy." Swift as young falcons, wearing lotus garlands, their chariot is triple-wheeled and threefold in its parts, with golden reins and drawn by swift-flying birds.[2] The Aśvins are the physicians of the gods, bringing health to all: they are the friends of all lovers.[3] Yet so indistinctly do they loom in their forms and attributes, that they have been held to be the morning and evening star,[4] and yet again the blending light and darkness of morning dawn, or else the Heaven and Earth, the Sun and Moon, or Day and Night.[5]

Before Sūrya, the Sun-god, who supports the sky even as truth supports or upholds the earth, who springs from Aurora, his mother,[6] and speeds forth on his chariot, drawn by seven swift steeds, the Dawn fades away:—

> "But closely by the amorous Sun,
> Pursued and vanquished in the race,
> Thou soon art locked in his embrace,
> And with him blendest into one."[7]

It is as Savitar, the Quickener, the Inspirer,[8] that the Sun "stands forth as the golden deity, yellow-haired, surrounded by a golden lustre,[9] and with upraised arms holds forth blessings and hope to his worshippers." As he arises the chant bursts forth:—

[1] R.V., viii. 5.

[2] Muir, vol. v. p. 241.

[3] *Ibid.*

[4] Oldenberg, "Rel. des Vedas," p. 213.

[5] Macdonell, J.R.A.S. (1895), p. 953, *et seq.*; Muir, vol. v. p. 234.

[6] R.V., iii. 61, 4; vii. 63, 3; Hopkins, "Rel. of India," p. 42.

[7] Muir, vol. v. p. 196.

[8] Macdonell, J.R.A.S. (1895), p. 951.

[9] Muir, vol. v. pp. 162, 163.

D

"Uprisen is Savitar, this god to quicken, Priest who neglects not this most constant duty.
To the gods, verily, he gives rich treasure, and blesses him who calls them to the banquet.
Having gone up on high, the God, broad-handed, spreads his arms widely forth that all may mark him.
Even the waters bend them to his service; even this wind rests in the circling regions."[1]

In later mythology the solar deity emerges from the brotherhood of all the Vedic gods as Vishnu, the preserving god of the world, who moves in three steps over the universe,[2] bearing in his hand as symbol of his origin the solar disc, and having by his side the heavenly bird, Garuda.

So Rudra, the bearer of the thunderbolt and father of the "Maruts" or Storm-gods, arising clear from the seething flux of changing thought, lives to-day in Indian worship as the dread god, Śiva, the "Auspicious,"[3] the potential Destroyer of the Universe. In Vedic times he was the demon bred in forests and in mountains, bearer of his dreaded message of fever and disease.[4]

From around the altars of the Vedic Aryans older deities pass away and are forgotten; for them hymns are no more fashioned. Newer deities inspire the poets' praise as fulfilling new functions in the course of the people's changing life. Dyaus, the Sky, the Father of the Silent Heavens, and Mother Earth herself early vanish from the scene. So also Trita sinks to rest, while the great encompassing Sky,

[1] Griffith, R.V., ii. 38; i. 2.

[2] Macdonell, J.R.A.S. (1895), pp. 170, *et seq.* Oldenberg ("Rel. des Vedas," p. 228) holds Vishnu to be the vast wideness of space, and names him the "Wanderer." Macdonell (J.R.A.S., 1895) holds his three steps to be in air and earth, and the last leading to his dwelling-place in Heaven.

[3] *Ibid.*, p. 957.

[4] Oldenberg, "Rel. des Vedas," p. 223:—"Auf Berge und Wälder sowie seine schädliche krankheitbringende Macht begründet zu sein."

the ancient Varuna,[1] the Avestan Ahura Mazda, gives place as a popular deity to Indra, as the Sun-god Mitra, the Avestan Mithra, does to Savitar. Even the hymns to the Dawn pale before those to Agni and Soma when fire became the symbol of sacerdotal power, and Soma the personified deity of the intoxicating beverage from whence the seers derived their inspiration.

Yet Varuna was the deity who rose nearest to the heights of monotheistic greatness as sole ruler of the universe. It was he who by his magic measured out the earth with the sun, and he was the god who saw into the hearts of all, knowing the guilty as they came trembling before him to confess their guilt:—

> "If we have sinned against the man who loves us, have ever wronged a brother, friend or comrade, the neighbour ever with us, or a stranger
> O Varuna, remove from us the trespass. If we as gamesters cheat at play, have cheated, done wrong unwittingly or sinned of purpose
> Cast all these sins away like loosened fetters, and Varuna, let us be thine own beloved."[2]

The poet prays to Varuna to forgive man for the laws broken day by day. He seeks to bind the deity with a new song, as he wails sadly in soft, pleading tones, the full sense of which lies only in the sound of the Sanskrit:—

> "Parā hi me vimanyavah patanti vasya ishtaye.
> Vayo no vasantir upa."

No translation can give the full throb which beats throughout the lines. Like all the rest of the Vedic Hymns

[1] Hopkins, "Rel. of India," pp. 71, 72. The equation Varuna (Οὐρανος) is not accepted by Oldenberg; but *see* Macdonell, J.R.A.S. (1894), p. 528; also Grundriss, d. I.-A. Philologie u. Altertumskunde, "Vedic Mythology," A. A. Macdonell (1897):—"The equation, though presenting phonetic difficulties, seems possible;" also Barth, "Rel. of India," p. 17.

[2] Griffith, R.V., v. 85, 7, 8.

the meaning alone can be given :—"Yet my wearied mind turns only to thoughts of gaining wealth, even as a bird flies to its resting-place." But the beauty and spirit of the Vedic Hymns can only be known or judged when heard recited in the land of their birth. The poet having in the above lines attuned the sound of his verses to the lament of his soul over its own impotent strivings to reach the ideals he had ever set before him, again bursts forth in a triumphant peal of ringing melody, skilfully designed to echo forth the glory of the god on whom all efforts of man depend :—

"Kadā Kshatra sriyam narramā Varunam Karāmahe,
Mṛilīkaya urucakshasam."

("When shall we turn him the Lord of Strength, the Hero,
the Beholder of All, the god Varuna.")

Or as the same idea is expressed later on in the translations, so often here chosen for the fidelity with which they express the sense of the original :—

"Thou, O wise god, art Lord of all, thou art the king of earth and heaven :
Hear, as thou goest on thy way." [1]

The great heroic deity of the conquering Aryans was not the passive Varuna, the judge of good and evil, the god who, with his gentler attributes toned down by philosophic refinements, escaped the vulgar gaze; it was Indra, the god of battle and of storm, the Soma-drinking boon-companion of rough-and-ready warriors. Indra rose to power when the Dasyu foes had to be driven from their stronghold, when the Aryans settled in the lowland plain, and prayed for the Thunderer to sound throughout the heavens, and bring the rain-clouds near. When the lands were parched, and the

[1] Griffith, R.V., i. 25, 20.

cattle driven to the forest-clad mountains there to graze—as they are to-day in India in all villages during the long, hot weather, or when famine rages—the people longed to see the coming of the rain, and watch with glad joy the herdsmen drive back again their well-fed herds. Indra was the great deity who slew the dreaded Drought Sushmā, which held back the light and waters. In heaven and on earth,[1] the combat raged. The Pānis were the robber chieftains, who held the clouds, or cows, deep hidden in the cave, where Vala,[2] the Demon of the Cave, had concealed them, and Śaramā was the messenger sent by Indra to demand their release. As the combat rages, and the sacrificing priests call on Indra to take his seat before the altar and quaff the invigorating Soma juice, there grows to life no clear figure of this great deity. If Indra be sought amid the assembled throng of Vedic deities, the first clue to his identity is his great thirst. How much more is typical of Indra, as distinguished from the other gods, so that he might be painted as a dramatic figure of life-like interest, would be hard to say. So when Śaramā gives her message to the Pānis, with doubting laughter they reply :—

> "Who is he? What does he look like, this Indra,
> Whose herald you have hastened such a distance,
> Let him come here, we'll strike a friendship with him,
> He can become the herdsman of our cattle."[3]

In his hand Indra carries the flaming lightning; he is seated upon a golden chariot, and by his side the Storm-gods, or "Maruts," ride through the heavens, with all the rush and fury of tempests. As he advances to slay Sushmā the Drought, and Ahi the Snake, and Vritra the Demon,

[1] Oldenberg, "Rel. des Vedas," p. 151.

[2] For connection of Paris with the Pānis, etc., *see* Oscar Meyer, "Quæstiones Homericæ" (1867), p. 10, *et seq.;* also Kaegi, "Veda," p. 137.

[3] Kaegi, p. 42 *tr.* of x. 108, 3.

he shines with all the beauty of the dawn, with all the glory of the sun; he "speaks in thunder;"[1] he "gleams like the lightning":—

"Yet not one form alone he bears,
But various shapes of glory wears,
His aspect changing at his will,
Transmuted, yet resplendent still."[2]

By the side of Indra hasten the Maruts, with phantom, anthropomorphic shapes as created in the lyric effusions of the Vedic Soma-inspired bards.

The cracking of their whips is heard as they advance to the hall of sacrifice. The earth trembles as the roll of their chariot wheels is heard; they drive spotted deer, with a red one for leader. They are slayers of demons, tall and manly like unto giants.[3] They are seven, thrice seven, and again thrice sixty in number.[4] They are born from the clouds, and Rudra was their father. They are like wild elephants who eat up the forests, yet they are handsome like gazelles, and the golden tyres of their chariot gleam as they glide down to take their seats before the sacrificial altar and drink the Soma juice. They have golden helmets on their heads, golden daggers in their hands, golden chains on their breasts, quivers on their shoulders and glittering garments. To few is their birth known; it is a secret, possessed, perhaps, only by the wise.[5] They are prayed to grant strong sons to their worshippers, and to lead the way across the waters towards new lands, to be won by their conquering aid. The Soma juice they drink was the loved drink of all the deities and of men. As its drops fall to the ground, pressed forth from the straining pans by the gold-

[1] Hopkins, "Rel. of India," p. 92.
[2] Muir, "Metrical Sketch of Indra," vol. v. p. 129.
[3] R.V., i. 64, 2.
[4] Hopkins, "Rel. of India," p. 98.
[5] R.V., vii. 56, 2, 4:—"Verily no one knoweth whence they sprang: they and they only, know each other's birth" (Griffith).

adorned hands of the sacrificial priests, it fell to earth like the glistening rain, and so was held to induce the clouds to shed their moisture by the sympathetic magic of its charm, just as in our later days the frame of man is supposed to fade when his waxen image was placed before a fire and melted away. The mystery of the Soma plant may never be disclosed. No one knows whence it came;[1] no one knows truly how the intoxicating juice was fermented and prepared, although the great Soma sacrifices are asserted to be still occasionally performed in India, as are other great fortnightly and four-monthly offerings before the three sacred fires.[2] As on earth the Soma juice was poured forth, so was it in the heavens, where the gods themselves were supposed to sacrifice. The yellow moon, the reservoir of the dew, was held to be the source of the heavenly Soma juice, and as such to represent the earthly Soma.[3] Yet in the Vedic Hymns this is a secret known only to the wise, so the identification of the Soma with the moon, alluded to in the later hymns,[4] can hardly be taken to signify that the moon, and not the earthly Soma plant, personified as a deity, was the centre of the Vedic worship.[5]

Each poet as he sang the praises of his favoured deity strove in his song to magnify its attributes. To him the main conception of each deity was determined and defined, yet its glory was enhanced by ascribing to it universal powers, and giving to it praises, couched in sounding words and sentences, applied equally to it and all the other deities. The entire worship is pervaded by a common and early

[1] Max Müller, "Biographies of Words," p. 234, for a suggestion that "hops and soma" were one and the same thing (*Academy*, 1885).

[2] *See* Bhandarkar, "Ind. Ant." (1874), p. 132.

[3] Hillebrandt, "Vedische Mythologie," vol. i.

[4] R.V., x. 85, 3.

[5] Oldenberg, "Rel. des Vedas," pp. 599-612.

pantheistic phase of thought. Nature in all its phenomena was held to be endowed with soul life.

With patient strife and long pondering the poets strove to pierce the secret of the Universe, tear from the moaning tempests the message they bore, catch the whispered voices that stole, as the evening fell, through the deepening stillness of the forest :—

> " Goddess of wild and forest who seemest to vanish from the sight,
> How is it thou seekest not the village? Art thou afraid?
>
> . . . .
>
> Here one is calling to the cows, another there has felled a tree.
> At eve the dweller in the wood fancies that somebody hath screamed."[1]

This is Nature worship; the expression of the vague unaided intuitions of the soul as it seeks for some solution of that which lies beneath the reality of things. It is expressed throughout the stately Vedic Hymns, the earliest recorded answer of man, in rhythmic lines, which wail to us still, with all their echoing charm of solemn and majestic resonance.

To these poet-priests Nature had indeed manifested herself in all her solemnity, in all her glory and beauty, so that their voices burst forth in poetic raptures over their new deities, and such of their old as had come to dwell in the new-found homes, with renewed brightness and vigour.

Old deities fade away amid the moving times; the forms of others become more clear, while the faint outlines of gods, such as Rudra and Vishnu, loom but barely recognisable as the prototypes of those personifications of Destruction and Preservation, now worshipped everywhere in Hindu India. At times, as the fervour of some singer bursts forth in the vague raptures of his Soma-inspired song, it seems as if the many gods were about to blend into

[1] Griffith, R.V., x. 146, 1-4.

the conception of one supreme god who for a time stands forth as sole deity.

Thus one hymn tells how

> "They call him Indra, Mitra, Varuna, Agni, and he is the heavenly winged Garutmân.
> To what is one, the Sages give many a title, they call it Agni, Yama Matarisvan."[1]

And again when the question is asked

> "What pathway leadeth to the gods? Who knoweth this of a truth, and who will now declare it?"[2]

The answer quickly comes back:[3]—

> "One All is Lord of what is fixed, and moving, that walk, that flies, this multiform creation."

Yet soon the soul's triumph dies away in the moan of despair, as the Hymns declare that all the gods are unreal, that the Universe must have existed before the gods, or any of the gods arose from out the mundane darkness, that still the weary search remains to find "kasmai devāya havishā vidhema" ("to what god shall we now offer our sacrifices?").[4]

So in vague and mysterious fancies[5] the thought of the poet wandered. Hymns there are which peal with the sound of fiercest battle-strife; others which tell in softer strains of the daily life of the people; others which echo with the triumphant note of some new-born prophet who, in his lofty pride, declares the will of the gods and the secret of this and the after-life.

[1] Griffith, R.V., i. 164, 46.
[2] *Ibid.*, iii. 54, 5 (Griffith's translation).
[3] Wallis, "Cosmology of the Veda," p. 51.
[4] Muir, R.V., x. 121, 1; vol. iv. pp. 15, 16.
[5] Barth, "Rel. of India," p. 28.

From the Vedic Hymns of these Indo-Aryans, proud in their intellectual power and subduing strength over alien foes, glorying in their conquests, standing on the threshold of creating a philosophy which, in its metaphysical subtleties, has seen as deep, though perhaps not so clear, as any Western philosophies, there arises the sad wail, set to sadder music, of the soul's lament over the defeat of human hopes to pierce the secret of the Omniscient and Omnipotent Cause, which existed from before all time:—

"Then there was not Being, and Non-Being there was not; there was not Air, nor yet beyond that Sky.
What covered all? What held all safe?
Where was the deep abyss of waters?
There was not Death, and Non-Death there was not, and change neither of Day nor Night.
One alone then breathed, calm and self-contained, naught else beyond nor other.
Darkness first was hid in darkness, all this was one Universe unseen.
What lay void and wrapt in darkness, that by fervour grew.
Desire then in the beginning arose, the first germ of the mind.
The bond 'twixt Non-Being and Being, as knowledge wise men find hid in their hearts.
The Bond that knit all things, was it below or up above?
First source of life sprang forth, and all was heaving unrest.
Who knows this? Who can here tell whence all this issued forth?
The gods themselves came afterwards,
Who then knows whence it all became?
Who knows it all, if it was made or not?
He who rules it all in the highest realms, He indeed knows, or perchance He knows it not."

The gods were but created in mobile anthropomorphic form out of the lyric raptures of the poet's heart. None springs to birth instinct with the same dramatic reality with which the genius of a Hebrew prophet, a Homer, an Æschylus or Sophocles would have endowed their fancies.

It was the mystic ecstatic song, often poured forth under the influence of the intoxicating Soma juice, just as the Delphic oracles were declared by the priestess "maddened by mephitic vapours,"[1] that, for weal or woe, held sway over the imagination of the people, who deemed that the cry went forth with power to influence even the gods themselves. The poet-priest was held to be in actual communion with the deity invoked. The Hymns were considered as prayers, which not only swayed the deities and held them bound, but compelled them, when strengthened and invigorated by the sacrificial food, to hearken to the people's call, and do their bidding. Without the prayer the sacrifice was in vain.[2] The prayer, the *brahman* (neuter) had to be intoned with exact precision by the brāhman (masc.), or offerer of the prayer; one word wrongly pronounced or misplaced would vitiate its whole magic influence. The prayer could be offered by any who knew, or who composed the spell, for though sons and descendants (brāhmanas) of brahmans are mentioned, it is not until later times that the Brāhmans became a hereditary and professional class of overseeing priests. So words, when poured forth, either in the rhapsodies of a Delphic oracle; in the wild broken accents of a savage chieftain, who sacrifices all to emotion, that he may raise his tribesmen's untamed instincts; in the mystic effusions of a Vedic seer; or in the chastened utterances of an absolute poet, where the forms assimilate more and more to the "concrete and artistic expression of the human mind in emotional and rhythmical language,"[3] will ever ensure to him who holds the divine gift of poetry and eloquence, a certain power over the emotions and thoughts of man.

[1] G. L. Dickenson, "The Greek View of Life," p. 29.

[2] Muir, vol. i. (1878), p. 241; vol. iii. pp. 128-144; R.V., x. 105, 8.

[3] "Encyclopædia Britannica" (*Poetry*).

In the Vedic Hymns themselves, Speech became personified as the goddess Vāc, who declares of herself:[1]—

"I am the greatest of all deities.[2] I am the Queen, the first of all those worthy of worship. I am she to whom the gods have given many places, set in many homes, and sent for abroad. He who hears and breathes, who listens to the spoken word, eats food. They know me not, and yet live near. Let the wise man hear. I tell that which is to be believed.

I sing myself the truth dear to gods and men,
Whom I love I make mighty, I make him a Brāhman, Seer and Wise.
I for Rudra bend the bow, so that the arrow may pierce the hater of the hymn.
I make the people join together, I have entered both Heaven and Earth.
I have revealed the heavens to its inmost depths, I dwell in waters and in sea,
Over all I stand, reaching by my mystic power to the height beyond.
I also breathe out like the wind, I first of all living things.
Beyond the heavens and this earth here, I have come to this great power."

One more hymn to Vāc, or "Speech," declares that when she was first sent forth, all that was hidden, all that was best and highest, became disclosed through love. Through sacrifice Speech was sought out and found, yet though some looked, they saw her not, and though some listened, they heard her not; her beauty she keeps closed, as the loving wife shows hers but to her lord alone. He wanders about in vain delusion who knows not the flower and fruit of Speech.

With the conscious pride and haughty tone of a nation which has won its way to victory, these vague guesses

[1] R.V., x. 125.

[2] In the "Śat. Brâh.," *Vāc* becomes "the mother of the Vedas" (iii. 8, 8, 5).

swell in solemn resonance through the stately periods of the Vedic Hymns: yet, under-lying all is no uncertain sound of the sad wail that ever and again murmurs from the seer's soul, declaring that man's proud answers but mock at its yearning cry to know the invisible, the unbound. The true end of the struggle is found in the one verse handed down from Vedic times, and murmured by all orthodox Hindus of to-day, as they wake to find the reality of the world rise up around them, and still know that beyond the reality is that which they still yearn to know. Like all the best of Vedic Hymns, this hymn, known as the "Gāyatrī," has its form in its sound, and therefore remains untranslatable in words, even as does music which rouses, soothes, and satisfies in its passing moods. It still holds its sway over the millions who daily repeat it, as it also held entranced the religious fervour of countless millions in the past. The birthright of the twice-born was to hear whispered in their ear by their spiritual preceptors this sacred prayer of India:—

> "Om.[1] Tat Savitur vareṇyam bhargo devasya dhīmahi
> dhiyo yo naḥ pracodayāt."[2]

Once heard in the land of its own birth, once learned from the lips of those whose proudest boast is that they can trace back their descent from the poets who first caught the music which it holds in every syllable, it rings for ever after as India's noblest tribute to the Divine, as an acknowledgment of submissive resignation to the decrees which bid man keep his soul in patience until the day dawns when all things shall be revealed.

[1] The syllable is a syllable of permission, for whenever we permit anything we say, *om*, "yes." "Taitt. Bráh.," ii. p. 1.

[2] Let us meditate on the to-be-longed-for light of the Inspirer; may it incite all our efforts.

As the life of the nation is traced in its literature, it will be found that, down to the present day, the ceaseless cry, first heard in Vedic times, has ever since sent its echo down through the ages, so that now it sounds as clear as it did when first moaned sadly forth—

"To what god shall we now offer up our sacrifice?"[1]

[1] R.V., x. 12, 1; Muir, vol. iv. pp. 11, 16.

CHAPTER V.

BRĀHMANISM.

FROM the arid mountains and the intervening fertile valleys lying to the north-west of India, the Aryans slowly made their way down to the plains of India. Along the rivers and close to the mountains they formed their settlements, even as far South as Sind on the lower Indus Valley, sometimes engaging in conflict, sometimes forming alliances with the ruder races. In the Vedic Hymns those who opposed the new-comers are described as demons and goblins. It was the god, Indra, who conquered those slaves, as they are also called, and who gave their land to the Aryan tribes. To the Aryans, these dark, flat-nosed aborigines were without sacrificial rites or gods; they were revilers and despisers of Indra, haters of *brahman*, or "prayer"; they were fierce foes and cannibals.[1] The colour, or "varna" of the aborigines, their "black skins"[2] became the sign of servitude, and Indra was prayed to drive it far away from the sight of the fair-skinned invaders. There are no valid grounds for holding that the dark-complexioned and broad-nosed people,[3] whom the Aryans

[1] R.V., x. 87, 2 *ff.*

[2] Muir, ii. p. 391; R.V., ix. 41, 1; i. 130, 8.

[3] Risley, "Tribes and Castes of Bengal," vol. i. (Preface), p. 32.

found in possession of the river-valleys, and cultivating the cleared lands on the forest sides, differed in essential characteristics or in the fundamental framework of their social relationships, from the present Dravidian races of India.

At the present day the process whereby the rude aborigines who inhabit the highlands of Central India, the forest tracks above the eastern and western ghāts, and the slopes of the more important mountain ranges, gradually receive the impress of civilisation from settlers who immigrate from the lowland tracts[1] can be clearly traced, and it cannot be far different from that of Vedic times. All traces of social intercourse with the darker races have in the Vedic Hymns been eliminated perhaps by the vanity of the early Aryan immigrants.

In the later literature evidence is everywhere forthcoming to show how a compromise was made between the more advanced religious notions of the Aryans and the more primitive cults of the earlier inhabitants.[2] To discriminate now in how far the religious practices of modern Hinduism have been derived from the elements introduced by the Aryan invaders, and how much is an accretion from the savage rites of the more primitive aborigines, would be a task leading to but slight profitable results, except, perhaps, to the augmentation of the reputation of the enquirer for ingenuity. Even in the simple question as to the social position assumed by the Aryans among the earlier inhabitants, the evidence is equally evasive and delusive.

In North India of the present day, where the Aryan influence is more strongly marked than in the South, those

[1] Hewitt, "Ruling Races of Prehistoric Times," p. 46.

[2] For phallic worship, the "śiśna deva" of R.V., x. 27, 19; x. 99, 3; vii. 21, 5, *see* Hewitt, p. 207, and Zimmer, "Alt. Ind. Leben.," p. 116; also Muir, vol. ii. p. 391.

races who approach most to the typical Aryan type are found to be in landlord[1] possession of the villages, or to hold the land in joint-partnership, or under a late developed system of joint-family ownership,[2] the actual cultivation of the soil being relegated to the dark-skinned folk. In the South of India, where the Aryan infusion is of a relatively late date, the land remains, for the greater part, in the hands of the Dravidian people, who themselves own it and cultivate it, acknowledging no over-right except that of the ruling power, to exact its share of the produce in exchange for its protecting rule.

There are evidences that even in the Vedic times the aborigines had attained to a considerable degree of material civilisation.

The Śambara, a race living amid the mountains, against whom the Aryan chieftain, Divodāsa, father of the renowned Tritsu king, Sudās, waged many a war, are said to have possessed castles of stone, one hundred in number.[3] Against the cities and castles of these Śambara the Aryans advanced again and again, until Indra came to the aid of his chosen people, and broke in pieces the iron strongholds of the aboriginal foes with his thunderbolts.[4] The Hymns tell how it was to gain the land and cows[5] of these foes that the Aryans advanced with their horses and chariots, and more striking evidence still of the wealth of the aborigines

[1] The whole subject has been treated by Hewitt in Essay II, pp. 106-131, "Ruling Races of Prehistoric Times," where he brings a store of erudition to evolve his theory that "village communities originated in India, and that this communal system, together with the matriarchate form of government instituted by their founders, was brought by the Indian cultivating races and their allies into Europe." The main outline of this movement is stated as follows:—"It was immigrants from the South, who, during the Neolithic Age, introduced into Europe the agriculture they had learned in these Southern villages, while North-Western Europe was made uninhabitable to tillers of the soil by the rigorous climate of the Palæolithic period" (Preface, pp. vi., vii.).

[2] Baden-Powell, "Ind. Vill. Com.," p. 241:—"The joint-village is, in fact, coterminous with the range of Aryan and later conquests."

[3] R.V., iv. 30, 20. [4] *Ibid.*, ii. 20, 8. [5] Muir, vol. ii. p. 384.

is an account given of how they possessed treasures of gold,[1] and of rich jewels.

Across the Five Rivers of the Panjāb the Aryans pressed until they reached the land to the East, renowned ever afterwards as Brahmāvarta, and described as a land "created by the gods, lying between the two divine rivers, the Sarasvatī and Drishadvatī."[2] There the Vedic Hymns were collected together, and the entire sacrificial system elaborated. The land of the Five Rivers was then no longer looked to as a fit abiding-place for the Aryan race. The later literature of the Epic period declared that "in the region where the Five Rivers flow . . . let no Aryan dwell there even for two days. . . . There they have no Vedic ceremony nor any sacrifice."[3]

The Panjāb evidently saw no extensive settlement of the Aryan tribes; it was in the land further to the East, in Brahmāvarta and Kurukshetra, that the rise of the Brāhmans to power, and the glorification of their priestly office can be traced. The land left behind became accursed, the abiding-place of impure tribes, such as the Bāhīkas, "who are outcasts from righteousness, who are shut out from the Himavat, the Gangā, the Sarasvatī, the Yamunā, and Kurukshetra, and who dwell between the Five Rivers."[4] "The women who dwell there are addicted to incestuous practices, and are without shame;"[5] they are "drunk and undressed, wearing garlands, and perfumed with unguents, sing and dance in public places, and on the ramparts of the town."[6]

As the Aryans advanced further into the plain-country the time was forgotten when they were designated, as in the Vedic Hymns, "the five" people,[7] or people of the five tribes.

[1] R.V., iii. 34, 9; Baden-Powell, "Ind. Vill. Com.," 84.
[2] "Manu," ii. 17, 19. [3] "Mahābhārata," v. 20, 63.
[4] "Mahābhārata," viii. 202, 9 *ff.* [5] Muir, vol. ii. p. 483.
[6] *Ibid.*, v. 20, 35; *Ibid.*, vol. ii. p. 482.
[7] *Pancajanāh.*

When they passed beyond the sacred abode lying between the Sarasvatī and Drishadvatī, and reached the fertile land along the Jumna, praised[1] as the country where wealth in kine and wealth in steed was to be gained, and thence made their way onward to the high banks[2] of the Ganges, they no longer preserved their ancient tribal names. The Tritsus, loved of Vasishtā, and the Bhāratas to whom Visvāmitra turned in his wrath, had united as friends, and with the third great Vedic tribe, the Purus—whose king, Kutsa, had led the Bhāratas and allied ten tribes[3] in Vedic war against Sudās, king of the Tritsus—fused together to form the great alliance of the Kurus,[4] who dwelt in the plains of Kurukshetra, and who afterwards built their renowned capital at Hastinapura on the Ganges, sixty-five miles north-east of Delhi.

South-east of the land claimed by the Kurus,[5] a second Aryan tribe, who early in Vedic times dwelt in the valleys of Kashmīr, and was there known as the Krivi, took up its abode, and became renowned as the Panchālas, with its capital at Kampilya on the Ganges. Kurukshetra[6] became the great place of sacrifice for the Aryans, the place where the sacred literature was compiled and elaborated, the place where the Brāhmans consolidated their power, established their schools of learning, and thence spread abroad their civilising influence.

From the Brāhmanic families of the Kuru Panchālas trained scholars went abroad to the outlying tracts where adventurous Aryans had made their settlements, until gradually the whole of India fell subdued to the sacerdotal

[1] R.V., v. 52, 17. [2] *Ibid.*, vi. 45, 31.

[3] *See* Oldenberg, "Buddha," pp. 404-5, for original identity of Tritsus and Bhāratas, and Ludwig, "Mantra Literatur," p. 175.

[4] For identification of these, *see* Hewitt, p. 115. For the allies of the Tritsus, *see* Zimmer, "Alt. Ind. Leben.," p. 434; Hewitt, p. 114.

[5] Zimmer, p. 102; Oldenberg, "Buddha," p. 401; "Śat. Brāh.," xiii. 5, 47; Eggeling, p. xli.

[6] Oldenberg, "Buddha," p. 395.

ordinances of their priestly guides. The succeeding history of India, as preserved in its literature, is one unending struggle of the Brāhmanic power to assert its supremacy, and to promulgate far and wide the ordinances it laid claim to formulate under Divine sanction. Never, since the Kuru Panchālas first settled on the upper reaches of the Ganges and Jumna, has the struggle ceased, and never has the Brāhman failed to take from the hands of his opposing foes the weapons they used, and add them to his already skilfully-arranged armoury. Against the priestly ordinances free thought and philosophy revolted; against the long array of Vedic texts, on which the existence of a soul to man and a Divine Ruler to the Universe was postulated, the agnosticism of Buddhism strove in vain in its efforts to win the allegiance of man, born to live in wonder and die in hope.

The power of the Brāhmans, temporal and spiritual, remained supreme, so that Manu [1] was able to declare that, from a Brāhman born in the plain of Kurukshetra, "immediately after Brahmāvarta," where dwell the Kurus, the Panchālas, the Matsyas, and the Surasenas, all men on earth should learn their duties, for it was the ever-famed abode of the Brahmarshis or Brāhmanical sages.

From the collection of hymns known as the "Rig Veda," such hymns as were chanted by the Udgatar priest at the sacrifices, where the clarified juice of the Soma plant was offered to the deities, were collected together into a "Sanhita," or metrical text, known as the "Sāma Veda," the verses of which were set to a tune or melody in "Gāna," or Song-books. The entire sacrificial system, with varied explanations of the significance of each act, were set forth in a third Veda, named the "Black Yajur Veda," a text-book compiled for the instruction of the Adhvaryu priests, whose duties were connected with the

[1] "Manu," ii. 17, 19, 20, 21.

performance of the practical details of the great Horse and Soma sacrifices. The "Black Yajur Veda" was later simplified and systematised in a clearer arrangement, called the "White Yajur Veda."

All this extensive literature was not considered sufficient for the exposition of the religious history of the Aryans, and the elucidation of the mysteries of the sacrificial system. To each of the Vedas were attached, by succeeding generations of priests, long, wearisome discourses, often in prose, describing in minute detail the entire Brāhmanic ritual, so far as its origin could be traced, or its significance understood, by the sacrificers themselves, whose minds were intent more on its practical import at the time than on its historical purpose or development.

These treatises are known as the "Brāhmanas." The centre of the period during which they were composed may be placed at somewhere not far removed from the tenth century before our era.[1]

In these "Brāhmanas" it is found that not only had the Aryans spread across the Sarasvatī, and reached the banks of the Ganges and Jumna, but that adventuring bands had penetrated as far to the East as Oudh, Benares, and North Behar. The Kāsis had gone as an advance guard, and made the land around Benares their own, and the Magadhas had gone even further East. The Kośālas settled in Oudh, and the Videhas established themselves in North Behar, where they were destined to take a prominent position in the history of India, though in the early period, when the Brāhmanic system was being developed in the homes of the Kuru Panchālas to the West, they had no part in the Vedic culture or sacrificial rites.[2]

During the Brāhmanic period the centre of Vedic culture

[1] Oldenberg, "Buddha," p. 18:—"Somewhere between the ninth and seventh centuries before the Christian era."

[2] *Ibid.*, p. 391.

lay from the divine Sarasvatī beyond Kurukshetra to the Jumna in the East. It was there that the Kuru Panchālas and allied tribes had their homes; it was there that Vāc, or the divine "Speech," was held to be purer than elsewhere; it was the place where the great Vaidik or Śrauta sacrifices were performed before the three sacred fires. The full number of these sacrifices reached to upwards of a thousand, and some of the more important extended to long sessions of from ten to one hundred years in length.[1]

According to the classification of the "Śrauta Sūtras," the shorter rules formed for the preservation of the Brāhmanic teaching, the chief sacrifices fall within three chief groups, each of seven typical sacrifices. The first seven were the great Soma sacrifices,[2] performed with three fires, at one of which, the Vājapeya, chariot races and games[3] took place, and the intoxicating "sūra" was drunk. The next seven sacrifices consisted of oblations of butter, milk, rice, and meat. These were known as the Havir sacrifices. The first was performed on the setting up of the sacred fires in the home of a new householder. This rite lasted for two days, and required the presence of the four priests, the Brāhman, Hotar, Adhvaryu and Agnīdh. The other six Havir sacrifices were those of daily oblation; those on days of full and new moon; those in times of harvest; four monthly sacrifices; animal sacrifice; and lastly, a special expiation for over-indulgence in drinking the Soma.

These fourteen were the types of Vaidik ceremony. The third group of seven sacrifices consisted of rites performed before the domestic hearth with oblation of cooked food. These seven were called the Pāka[4] sacrifices,

[1] "The legendary history of India knows of such sessions, which are said to have lasted for one hundred and even for a thousand years."—Haug, "Ait. Brāh." (Introd.), 6.

[2] The great type was the Agnishtoma sacrifice, which lasted five days.

[3] Weber, "Ueber den Vājapeya" Sitz. ber. Berlin Acad., 1892.

[4] "Sānkhāyana Grihya Sūtra," i. 1, 15; "Gautama," viii. 15.

performed in winter, on new and full moon days, at times of the Śraddhā, or funeral sacrifices, and four falling due in specified months—Śrāvana, Āgrahāyanī, Chaitra, and Aśvina.

For all sacrifices there had first to be a sacrificer, and by him were selected the priests to whom gifts and presents were given. The place of sacrifice was usually a room within a Brāhman's house. For important sacrifices, such as the Soma sacrifices, a large shed was erected in an open place, the floor in all cases being covered with the sacred Kuśa grass, the favourite food of the black antelope. The East, or Āhavanīya fire-place was square; the South, or Dakshināgni, was spherico-triangular,[1] the West, or Gārhapatya, was round. The altar itself was a low wall running in a serpentine curve from fire-place to fire-place. One direction[2] for the construction of an altar for a Havir sacrifice stated: "Let the Altar measure a fathom across on the west side; they say that namely is the size of a man, and the Altar should be of the man's size . . . let him make it as long as he thinks fit in his own mind."

A significant description is given as to the shape of the altar in the same text:[3] "The altar should be broad on the west side, contracted in the middle, and broad again on the east side; for thus shaped they praise a woman, broad about the hips, somewhat narrow about the shoulders, and contracted in the middle (or about the waist). Thereby he makes it (the altar) pleasing to the gods."

A further essential feature of the altar follows immediately after the above direction. "It should be sloping towards east, for the east is the quarter of the gods; and also sloping towards north, for the north is the quarter of men. To the south side he sweeps the rubbish (loose soil), for that is the quarter of the deceased ancestors. If it (the

[1] Stevenson, "Sama Veda" (Introd.), viii.

[2] "Śat. Brāh.," i. 2, 5, 14.

[3] *Ibid.*, i. 2, 5, 16.

altar) were sloping towards south, the sacrificer would speedily go to yonder world."

In the case of the sacrifice of animals, besides the three fires and altar, a sacrificial pillar, for the tying of the animal, has to be hewn and erected, for it is directed:[1] "There are both an animal and a sacrificial stake, for never do they immolate an animal without a stake. And as to why this is so—well, animals did not at first submit thereto that they should become food, as they are now become food; for just as man here walks two-footed and erect, so did they walk two-footed and erect."

The pillar was hewn with an axe, care being taken to utter the incantation: "O axe, hurt it not."[2]

As a further precaution, a blade of "darbha" grass was placed between the axe and the tree, so that it might receive the first blow. When the tree, out of which the sacrificial part had to be hewn, was cut down, offerings were made upon the stump, "lest evil spirits should arise therefrom."[3] The sacrificial stake was then carved eight-sided, ornamented with a top ring, anointed and dedicated to Vishnu.[4] The Adhvaryu priest then girds (the stake with a rope of Kuśa grass). Now it is to cover its nakedness that he girds it, wherefore he girds it in this place (viz. on a level with the sacrificial navel) for it is thus that this (nether) garment is (slung round). He thereby puts food into him, for it is there that the food settles; therefore he girds it at that place."[5] One of the chips hewn off the post was then placed beneath the rope. In the description of the ceremonies, as given in the "Aitareya Brāhmana,"[6] the Hotar priests recited the Vedic Hymn, and adored the sacrificial post as a youth[7] well robed, fastened by the sacrifice to the

[1] "Śat. Brāh.," iii. 7, 3, 1. [2] *Ibid.*, iii. 6, 4, 10. [3] *Ibid.*, iii. 6, 4, 15.
[4] *Ibid.*, iii. 7, 1, 19. [5] *Ibid.*, iii. 7, 19.
[6] Haug, "Ait. Brāh.," p. 77.
[7] R.V., iii., 8, 4-6; *see* Oldenberg (*tr.*), S.B.E., vol. xlvi. pp. 252, 253.

earth, fashioned by the axe, as divine, as standing before the worshippers to grant them treasures and offspring.

To the ancient Brāhmanic expounders of the sacrificial system the whole primitive significance of the sacrifice had been lost. The protracted ceremonies are minutely described, and laboured explanations of them are given, but nowhere is there any clue given as to the true history of their primitive origin. The altar itself was clearly but a developed table, or hearth, arising out of the primitive altar, which, as "among the northern Semites as well as among the Arabs, was a great stone or cairn at which the blood of the victim was shed"[1]

The importance of these details of the early sacrificial system in the history of India is self-evident. The tendency would have been for an advance from the worship of the Vedic deities to a grand conception of monotheism, if the Aryan tribes had remained combined into united and compact bodies, with a commonly accepted ideal of one tribal God. The actual result was a lapse into idolatry and unrestrained polytheism after the political forces widened and weakened themselves by compromises with worshippers of strange idols and fetishes. Of peculiar significance are the words in which Jehovah directed Moses to deliver unto the children of Israel His ordinances as to the setting forth of the altar:—

> "An altar of earth thou shalt make unto me, and shall sacrifice thereon thy burnt-offerings, and thy peace-offerings, thy sheep and thy oxen. . . . And if thou wilt make me an altar of stone, thou shalt not build it of hewn stone: for if thou lift up thy tool upon it, thou hast polluted it."[2]

In the Canaanite and Hebrew sanctuaries was the altar, and also near at hand the pillar of stone, such as Jacob set up and anointed, so that it "shall be God's house." The altar was the place on which the sacrificial blood was

[1] Robertson Smith, "History of the Semites," p. 185.
[2] Exodus xx. 24, 25.

drained, so that its sanctity should not pass into the earth, and the pillar on which the blood was sprinkled "was a visible symbol or embodiment of the presence of the deity"[1] which, in process of time, came to be fashioned and carved in various ways, until, ultimately, it became "a statue or anthropomorphic idol of stone, just as the sacred tree or post was ultimately developed into an image of wood."[2] It can be traced[3] how the pillar or post became gradually more artistically developed, was placed in a house, or temple, and became the idol.

According to the Brāhmanic theory, the sacrifice on earth took place merely as a counterpart of a divine sacrifice held periodically by the gods. Prajāpati, the Lord of all Creatures, was held[4] to have been the first sacrificer, the reason given for the motive which impelled him to sacrifice being, that he "having created living beings, felt himself, as it were, exhausted." Eleven were the sacrifices he offered, so that "the creatures might then return to me; the creatures might abide with me, for my food and joy."[5]

In imitation of the sacrifice by Prajāpati, all sacrificers were directed to offer eleven victims. The first victim was sacrificed to Agni, chief of all the gods, the father of the gods, and by that sacrifice the offerer becomes reunited with Agni. By a second sacrifice to Sarasvatī, the goddess Vāc, or Speech, the sacrificer "becomes strong by speech, and speech turns unto him, and he makes speech subject unto himself."[6] By a third sacrifice to Soma, food becomes subject; by a fourth to Pūshan cattle become subject; by a fifth to Brihaspati, the priesthood becomes subject; by a sixth to the Viśve Devās, or all gods, the sacrificer becomes

[1] Jevons, Introd. to "History of Religion," pp. 13, 178.
[2] Robertson Smith, "History of the Semites," p. 187.
[3] Jevons, p. 135. [4] "Śat. Brāh.," iii. 9, 1, 1.
[5] *Ibid.*, iii. 9, 1, 2. In "Śat. Brāh.," xi. 7, 1, 3, flesh is called the highest food. Raj. Mitra, "Indo-Aryans," vol. i. pp. 361-374.
[6] *Ibid.*, iii. 9, 1, 7.

"strong by everything; everything turns to him, and he makes everything subject to himself." By a seventh sacrifice to Indra, the God of Warrior Might, the sacrificer gained valour and power. By the eighth sacrifice, that to the Maruts,[1] who are said to personify the clan and abundance, abundance was made subject; by a ninth to Indra and Agni the double energies of these gods were made subject; by a tenth to Savitri, the Impeller of the gods, all wishes were made subject to the sacrificer, while by the eleventh and last sacrifice, that to Varuna, the sacrificer freed himself "from every noose of Varuna, from every guilt against Varuna."

So far, it can be seen that the sacrifice of an animal was supposed to be efficacious in endowing the sacrificer with both natural and supernatural powers, similar to those he sacrificed to obtain. There was but a slight advance on the primitive idea, generally found at some stage in the history of humanity, of the sacrifice of an animal, and the actual drinking of its blood and partaking of its flesh in order that the sacrificer might become endowed with the supernatural powers of the animal he thus sought to become kin with. The phase of thought on which these ideas are based has risen naturally from the primitive construction of society.

Everywhere primitive man is found to hold together in sibs, or clans, where the bond of blood relationship is the sole security from attack or treachery. Should a stranger seek to join the brotherhood, the blood of the adopted kindred must be made to flow in his veins by actual inoculation.[2] This is the blood covenant, and outside its limits there is neither friendship nor kindred. Not only with his brother man does primitive humanity in the early struggle for existence find himself at variance, but he is

[1] Jevons, p. 242, for Mars as a vegetable deity; and Haug, p. 92, for the Maruts being the "Vaiśyas," or subjects of the gods.

[2] *Ibid.*, p. 97.

confronted with the whole supernatural powers of Nature, with which he would willingly be in alliance. Man finds himself surrounded by strange manifestations of an unknown power, over which his mind knows not how to reason. The very animals have strange cunning, and in all savage folk-tales they speak naturally as human beings. For defence or attack animals unite together; their kinship within their own species is as that of man within the brotherhood. Should an animal be slain, the enmity of its species is aroused against the slayer; it can be equally a friend or a foe, though different from man, its powers are outside the reach of primitive intelligence.

So the savage seeks to be on good terms with, and win the friendship of, such animals as he is most brought into contact with, or regards with special fear and reverence. To do this, there is but one way, and that is to follow the analogy of the human race and claim a blood relationship. The savage, therefore, wears the skin of some animal loved or feared of his sib; he decorates his head with its horns, and, similarly to its body, he mutilates or paints his own, so that he may become endowed with its virtues or supernatural powers. There is but one step further, and that is to cement a blood covenant with the clan [1] or species to which the animal belongs. The animal or object whose alliance is thus sought, then becomes the "Totem" [2] of the common brotherhood. A social bond has been made with the species. The animal and the human clan are regarded as having sprung from a common ancestor, the animal, and as being of one kindred. More important is the aspect of the religious bond which binds the human clan in affection to

[1] Frazer, J. G., "Golden Bough," p. 26.

[2] *Ibid.*, "Totemism," p. 1:—"A Totem is a class of natural objects which a savage regards with superstitious respect, believing that there exists between him and any member of the class an intimate and altogether special relation." *See*, however, Frazer, J. G., "Golden Bough," vol. ii. p. 38:—"It is not yet certain that the Aryans ever had Totemism."

the animal supposed to be supernaturally endowed. There can be no more fitting way to cement these bonds than for the human clan periodically to assimilate to themselves all the qualities of the animal, by actually partaking of its flesh and blood.

The animal is of necessity slain for this purpose, yet the act of killing is one arising from affection,[1] not from lust or desire for food. The act itself is sacrilegious. The blood as it falls is "taboo"; it is received on the altar, no part must touch the ground. Everywhere throughout the Brāhmanic sacrifice, traces are to be found of the repugnance to shed the blood of the victim, and scrupulous care is taken to remove all traces of it, the pillar being left as a sign that the ground is to be avoided. One peculiar result is recorded in the "Brāhmanas":—"Now those who made offerings in former times touched the altar and the oblations while they were sacrificing. They became more sinful, and those who sacrifice not become righteous, they said."[2]

It was the sacrificer who struck the first blow and who partook of the flesh and blood that became endowed with the supernatural qualities of the animal slain. He became reborn with the powers of the animal slain. He emerged from the sacrifice as the god himself, possessed of all the powers which the alliance of the animal had brought. The sacrifice in its primitive signification in no way indicated a gift or payment by the worshippers to their deities. It was a bond, an act of communion[3] between the worshippers and the animals, or any natural object they held possessed of supernatural powers, whose aid they sought to win for themselves.

[1] The cow, though sacred, was slain for sacrifice.

[2] "Śat. Brāh.," 1, 2, 5, 24.

[3] Robertson Smith, "History of the Semites," pp. 365, 442:—"The sacrifice was in no sense a payment to the god, but simply an act of communion of the worshippers with one another and their god."

The sacrifice had its foundation laid securely in the mental structure of all mankind. It was the highest expression of religious instincts which at all times and in all places impelled the individual to seek close union with the ineffable mystery of the Divine, in which no powers of reason will ever persuade him he has no part. With the forces which he sees underlying all Nature—animals, trees, and plants—he hopes at first to form a bond of friendship. As the animals become domesticated, and agriculture is introduced, the sacrifice assumes the form of a gift of an animal, or harvest offerings to the god whose aid it was sought to secure, the primitive idea of the necessity of incorporating it as kin to the clan fading away.[1]

In India, even down to the time of Manu, it was held that the land "where the black antelope naturally roams, one must know to be fit for the performance of sacrifices; the tract different from that is the country of the "Mlecchas" (barbarians).[2] It would be hazardous[3] at present to assert that the Aryans in India held the black antelope for a Totem, or that it ever was a Totem for them, inasmuch as they had for long passed beyond the early stage of civilisation out of which the primitive ideas of sacrifice arise. Nevertheless, the place taken by the black antelope during the Brāhmanic ceremony shows that it had assumed, metaphorically at least, the position which would have been devoted to a tribal Totem. The great sacrifices were, in these Brāhmanic times, performed for the benefit and at the

[1] *See* Jevons, Introd. to the "History of Religion," p. 331, *et seq.*, for the introduction into Greece in the sixth century B.C. of the North Semitic tendency to abandon, under stress of national calamity, the gift idea of sacrifice, and to revert to the primitive conception of the sacrificial meal being an actual participation of the essence of the god by the worshippers.

[2] "Manu," ii. 2, 3.

[3] Hewitt, "Ruling Races of Prehistoric Times," p. 367; Max Müller, "Mythology," vol. i. pp. 8, 200:—"Sanskrit scholars would certainly hesitate before seeing in Indra a Totem, because he is called . . . . . . bull." *See* Oldenberg, "Rel. des Vedas," pp. 85, 415.

cost of some pious householder, who had first to prepare himself by a ceremony of initiation,[1] through which he became re-born into a condition in which he was supposed to enter into actual communion with the deity worshipped. The ceremony as described in the "Brāhmanas" is conclusive on the subject. The sacrificer is first sprinkled with water, "for water is seed."[2] He is then anointed with butter, for by such anointing, "they make him thrive." His eyes are then darkened with collryrium by which lustre is imparted, and he becomes a "Dīkshitā." They then "rub him clean with twenty-one handfuls of darbha grass," they thus make him pure. He then enters a place prepared for him, which represents a place of birth; he is thus supposed to become an embryo. "In this place, he sits as in a secure abode, and thence he departs. Therefore the embryos are placed in the womb as a secure place, and thence they are brought forth (as fruit). Therefore the sun should neither rise nor set over him, finding him in any other place than the spot assigned to the Dīkshitā; nor should they speak to him." The succeeding portion of the ceremony is so clear as to the underlying significance of the rite, and points out so unmistakably the origin of the triple thread still worn by all people of India to-day, who call themselves twice-born, that it is quoted in full from Dr Haug's valuable translation, which unfortunately is now out of print. The sacrificer remains in the place chosen for the new birth, while the priests "cover him with a cloth. For this cloth is the cowl of the Dīkshitā (with which he is to be born like a child).

[1] Max Müller, in his "Comp. Mythology," p. 227, contending against Oldenberg's views that this Dīkshâ, or initiatory ceremony, was "to excite an ecstatic state which helps forward an intercourse with gods or spirits," concluded by stating his opinion "that this initiatory ceremony was meant as an act of propitiation and sanctification; or, like the Upanâyana, as a symbolical representation of that new birth which distinguishes the three upper classes as fit for sacrifice."

[2] Haug, "Ait. Brâh.," p. 8.

Outside (this cloth) there is (put by them) the skin of a black antelope. For outside the cowl there is the placenta. Then they cover him (symbolically by the skin of the antelope) with the placenta. He closes his hands. For with closed hands the child is born. As he closes his hands, he thus holds the sacrifice and all its deities in his two hands closed."[1]

The ceremony ends by the sacrificer removing the skin of the black antelope, and then, still wearing the cloth, purifying himself by bathing.

A similar account of the initiatory ceremony is given in the well-known "Śatapatha Brāhmana,"[2] attached to the "White Yajur Veda."

Here the place of sacrifice is where the ground is higher than any surrounding ground, "for it was thence that the gods ascended to heaven, and he who is consecrated indeed ascends to the gods."

An enclosed shed is erected, with its beams running West and East, for the gods come from the East, and the sacrifice is to be performed facing East. The sacrificer must be one of the Aryan race, a Brāhman, Kshatriya, or Vaiśya, for the gods have no commerce with Sūdras.

The sacrificer's hair and beard is shaved,[3] the hair being first touched with the sacred grass, both the hair and grass being laid in water; his nails are cut, and he then bathes, so as to become pure. He then clothes himself in a new linen garment, and is anointed five times, for the five

[1] The original is—"jajnam ca eva tat sarvās ca devatā mushtyo kurute."

[2] "Śat. Brāh.," iii. 1, 1.

[3] The explanation, according to the Brāhmana, of the shaven head is as follows:—"Then as to the Sacrificer shaving his head all round. Now yonder sun, indeed, faces every quarter; it drinks up whatever moisture it dries up here; hence this Sacrificer thereby faces every quarter, and becomes a consumer of food."—"Śat. Brāh.," ii. 6, 3, 14. An objector to this theory remarks:—"What in the world has it to do with his face, even if he were to shave off all the hair off his head? . . . let him therefore not trouble himself about shaving his head."—"Śat. Brāh.," ii. 6, 3, 17.

seasons, from head to foot with fresh butter; his eyes being touched with a reed stalk. When further purified by being stroked with one, seven, or twenty-one stalks of sacred grass, he then enters the hall of sacrifice, and walks about at the back of the Āhavanīya fire, which faces the east door, and in front of the Gārhapatya fire, which faces the west door, the altar lying between these two fires. "The reason why this is his passage until the Soma pressing is this: the fire is the womb of the sacrifice, and the consecrated is the embryo; and the embryo moves about in the womb."[1]

Two black antelope skins are then spread on the ground, on which the sacrificer sits down with his hands folded, like unto an embryo. He then places round himself a triple hempen cord, in which is twined a reed; he covers his head, ties a black deer's horn to his garment, and lays hold of a staff of Udambara wood (*Ficus glomerata*)[2] and so remains silent. "Thereupon someone calls out, 'Consecrated is this Brāhman, consecrated is this Brāhman,' him being thus announced, he thereby announces to the gods: 'Of great vigour is this one who has obtained the sacrifice; he has become one of yours, protect him.'"[3]

The sacrificer remains silent until sunset, when he becomes reborn, a god himself, and is fed with milk and barley to which vegetables are sometimes added. The reason why the food must be cooked is because "he who is consecrated draws nigh to the gods and becomes one of the deities. But the sacrificial food of the gods must be cooked, and not uncooked: hence they cook it, and he partakes of that fast-milk and does not offer it in the fire."[4]

It must be borne in mind that the speculations of the

[1] "Śat. Brāh.," iii. 1, 3, 28; S.B.E., vol. xxvi. (Eggeling's translation).

[2] For the *Ficus glomerata* as the parent tree of the trading races who introduced the Soma sacrifice, *see* Hewitt, "Ruling Races of Pre-historic Times," p. 367.

[3] "Śat. Brāh.," iii. 2, 1, 39. [4] *Ibid.*, iii. 2, 2, 10.

priestly compilers of the "Brāhmanas" were earnest and sincere efforts to explain the hidden meaning of the complicated ritual that had in process of time grown up around the sacrifice. Not only are the rules which bear on the ceremony set forth, but every effort is made to give rational explanations of every step of the ritual.

Philosophic disquisitions abound as to the intention of the early sacrificers, and philological reasons are given for special uses of Vedic texts. Stories of ancient sacrificers and legends of former sacrifices are introduced, with an evident intention of expounding, so far as it was understood, the necessity for the due performance of the religious ceremonies in the new-found homes of the Aryans. In the course of ages the true meaning of much of the ritual had been lost to the priesthood, much remained obscure, and on many points in the ceremony there were held varied opinions and practices.

At times the sacrifice is declared to be man; it is the representation of the sacrificer himself;[1] therefore the altar extends as far as a man's outstretched arms on the West side, and it is in human shape. Again the sacrifice is prayer, or speech,[2] for it is handed down from priest to priest by speech. It was first taught by the gods to man, who handed it on from father to son.[3] By the sacrifice the gods gained their place in Heaven, and then fearing that man by the same means might conquer their celestial home, they concealed it until man found it again for himself.[4]

The most striking and most important account of the ancient sacrifice is that given in connection with the legend of the Flood, as preserved in the "Śatapatha Brāhmana." The account differs in so many respects from

[1] "Śat. Brāh.," i. 3, 2, 1; Eggeling, S.B.E., vol. xii.

[2] *Ibid.*, i. 5, 2, 7.

[3] *Ibid.*, i. 6, 2, 4.

[4] *Ibid.*, iii. 4, 1, 17; iii. 9, 4, 22.

the Biblical record of the deluge, that at present there is no evidence to connect the Indian with the Semitic tradition.

In the Brāhmanic story, Manu[1] takes the part of Noah in the Old Testament, though with striking dissimilarities. The story commences with a description of how when Manu was one day washing his hands he found that he had seized a small fish. To his surprise the fish spoke, and prayed to be saved from destruction, promising in return that he would in time to come preserve Manu from a great danger. The danger that was to come was foretold by the fish to be a flood, that would sweep away all creatures. So Manu kept the fish and placed it in a jar. When the fish grew large it told Manu the year in which the flood would come. It then counselled Manu to build a great ship, and enter into it when the waters rose, saying, "I will save thee from the flood." Manu accordingly built the ship, and as the fish had grown too big to remain in the jar, he placed it in the sea. As the fish had foretold, the flood came. When Manu entered into his ship the fish swam towards him, and Manu tied the ship to a horn on the fish's head, and was towed to the Northern Mountain where he tied the ship to a tree. Then the waters receded and Manu was left alone. The narrative is simple, natural according to primitive ideas, and, as annual floods are common in all tropical lands, there is at present no necessity for holding that it contains more than the record of a wide-spread catastrophe. The real interest of the story is not in the suggested connection of the words Manu, ship, flood, with Noah, ark, deluge, but in the side light which is thrown on the primitive history of the sacrificial cult. This is to be seen in the steps taken by Manu to acquire supernatural power and reproduce creation.

At first Manu, "being desirous of offspring, engaged

[1] "Śat. Brāh.," i. 8, 1, 1.

in worshipping and austerities; during this time he also performed a '*pāka*' sacrifice: he offered up in the waters clarified butter, sour milk, whey, and curds. Thence a woman was produced in a year." The woman then announced to Manu that she was his daughter, that she had been produced through his offerings, declaring to him: "I am the blessing: make use of me[1] at the sacrifice; thou wilt become rich in offering, and cattle." With the woman "Manu went on worshipping and performing austerities. Through her[2] he generated this race, which is the race of Manu; and whatever blessing he invoked through her, all that was granted to him."[3] A further important reference to the position of the woman[4] in the sacrificial ritual is the injunction given that after the rice had been poured from the winnowing basket into a mortar[5] preparatory to its being ground between the two mill-stones[6] as an offering, the sacrificer should be summoned forward, an injunction followed by the important remark, so full of significance in the history of the development of the ritual, that, "now in former times it was no other than the wife of the sacrificer who rose at this call."

The ancient custom of the participation of women[7] in harvest offerings, as well as harvest festivals—a custom to be traced in much of the folk-lore of India to-day—is in

[1] "Śat. Brāh.," i. 1, 4, 16-17, for the actual sacrifice of Manu's wife:—"When she had been sacrificed the voice went out of her, and entered into the sacrifice." Also *Ibid.*, i. 8, 1, 9.

[2] "Idā. Śat. Brāh.," i. 8, 1, 11.

[3] "Śat. Brāh.," i. 8, 1, 10.

[4] "As a rule, the wife of the sacrificer was present, with hands joined to her husband" ("Taitt. Brāh.," iii. 3, 10). "The wife has to confess at the sacrifice" ("Śat. Brāh.," ii. 5, 2, 20).

[5] "Śat. Brāh.," i. 1, 4, 8.

[6] *Ibid.*, i. 1, 4, 13.

[7] "Gobhila Grihya Sūtrās," i. 3, 15:—"If they like, his wife may offer the morning and evening oblations over the domestic fire. For his wife is (as it were) his house, and that fire is the domestic fire." *See* also Hillebrandt, "Rituel Litteratur," p. 70.

the above texts clearly referred to as being remembered at the time of the Brāhmanic sacrifice, although for priestly reasons it was overlooked, or but obscurely hinted at.

The explanation of this appearance of women on the scene arises from the fact[1] that in primitive times the duties of agriculture lay, for the most part, in the hands of women.

The historical development of this portion of the sacrifice is tersely summed up in the words of Mr Jevons: "It is therefore an easy guess that the cultivation of plants was one of women's contributions to the development of civilisation; and it is in harmony with this conjecture that the cereal deities are usually, both in the Old World and in the New, female."

Agriculture, however, when its benefits became thoroughly understood, was not allowed amongst civilised races to continue to be the exclusive prerogative of woman, and the Corn Goddess, maiden or mother, had to admit to the circle of her worshippers the men as well as the wives of the tribe. The gradual transition from the early sacrifice of human beings, to the stage in which horses, kept in droves and tended by man during the pastoral stage, were sacrificed, thence on to the substitution of various animals as they became domesticated, ending with the offering of the fruits of the earth when agriculture became known, is set forth as a recognised fact in the "Aitareya Brāhmana." The account given is that man was the primitive form of sacrifice, but that in time the sacrificial essence went out of man and passed into the horse.[2] From the horse the sacrificial essence went to the ox, which was sacrificed; in the same manner for the ox, sheep were substituted, for sheep, goats, which remained the best suited for sacrifice. From the goat the sacrificial essence passed into the earth, and so

[1] Jevons, Introd. to "The History of Religion," pp. 240-1.

[2] For the great Horse Sacrifice, *see* "Taitt. Brāh.," iii. 8. For the year the horse was allowed to roam, sacrifices being performed by day.

finally the sacrificial part turned into rice.[1] It is also laid down as an injunction that no one of these animals, out of which the sacrificial essence had gone, should be eaten. This special prohibition evidently indicated that the eating of flesh was a custom in ancient India. In the "Śatapatha Brāhmana" there is a direction that the flesh of cows or oxen should not be eaten, although Yājnavalkya declared: "I for one eat it, provided that it be tender."

When the animal was killed for the sacrifice, every limb was preserved, the offal being buried in the earth. According to the later custom, the animal was killed by beating it to death.[2] The priest during the slaying averted his eyes;[3] any blood that fell was received on the sacred grass, and considered an offering to the Rākshasas, or demons. To the officiating priest, and to the sacrificer, allotted parts of the cooked food were presented. In the "Aitareya Brāhmana"[4] the animal had to be divided into thirty-six portions, for the priests, the sacrificer, and his wife.

To those who thus divided the offering into thirty-six parts, the animal "becomes the guide to Heaven. But those who make the division otherwise, are like scoundrels and miscreants, who kill an animal merely for gratifying the lust after flesh."

The origin of human sacrifice may be traced back to early Aryan times,[5] when a chieftain's wives and attendants were slain, in order that they might accompany him to the after-world. Its introduction into the Brāhmanic ritual as an atonement for the guilt of some

[1] Haug, "Ait. Brāh.," p. 91. [2] *Ibid.*, p. 85.

[3] "Śat. Brāh.," iii. 8, 1, 15: "Then they step back to the altar and sit down—lest they should be eye-witnesses to its being strangled."

[4] Haug, "Ait. Brāh.," p. 443.

[5] Tylor, "Primitive Culture," vol. i. p. 464; Jevons, Introd. to "The History of Religion," p. 161.

member of the community[1] is indicated in the well-known story of Śunahśepa, as narrated in the "Aitareya Brāhmana."

The story is one always to be recited with an accompaniment of one hundred Vedic verses before a king, so that his blood-guiltiness as a warrior may be removed. The Hotar who recites it must be rewarded with a gift of a thousand cows and a silver ornamented carriage drawn by mules. To the Adhvaryu priest who, during the recital makes the fitting responses, a hundred must be given, and upon Adhvaryu and Hotar, as an additional reward, a gold-embroidered carpet must be bestowed. To all who hear the story, the gods will allot long days and offspring. The story is as follows:—

Hariśchandra of the Ikshvāku race, mighty king though he was, had no son. To his household priests he poured forth his sorrow, asking them why it was that every one had so great a desire for male offspring. The answer, ancient though it may be, is one that would be given by all pious Hindus of modern India. "A son is ever to be desired, for a son hands down his father's life; the wife who bears a son re-creates the father: a son shines as a light in Heaven. He is the greatest of all earthly possessions; he gains immortality for the father. *A daughter is but an object of compassion.*" The holy advisers of the king told him that the desire was unconquerable, that all wondered at such Brāhmans as turn from a family life, and go forth as wanderers over the earth to live as hermits in the forest, or as religious mendicants.

So the king prayed to Varuna, the god who fulfils all wishes, and swore that were he but permitted to see the face of a son, he would sacrifice the child when born to

[1] "This was probably the origin of the sacrifice of human beings to the gods amongst the Mediterranean peoples. Amongst the Americans it was . . . due to the lack of domesticated animals."—Jevons, p. 161.

Varuna. The god granted the king's desire, and a child, Rohita, was born. The king put off from day to day the fulfilment of his vow, until Rohita grew to manhood, and became a warrior. When his father's vow was made known to Rohita, he fled into the wilderness, and there hid himself, whereupon Varuna caused a grievous illness to fall upon the king. Rohita remained concealed for the space of six years, at the end of which time he met a Brāhman sage, who had three sons, the second of whom was named Śunahśepa. For a gift of one hundred cows, the Brāhman gave his son Sunahśepa as a ransom sacrifice to Varuna. The good god Varuna on hearing of this, bowed his head and accepted Śunahśepa as a sacrifice in place of the king's son, for he knew that the offspring of a Brāhman was of more value than the son of a king.

At this time the great priest Visvamitra was the Hotar to King Hariśchandra, and the renowned Vasishta was the "purohita," yet no one could be found to bind Śunahśepa to the sacrificial post. Then the father of Śunahśepa, on receiving a further gift of one hundred cows, consented to bind his own son to the sacrificial post. The sacrificial fire was prepared, the Vedic texts ordained for such a sacrifice were duly recited, yet no one could be found to slay Śunahśepa. For a fourth gift of one hundred cows, the father of Śunahśepa agreed to slay his own son.

When the sharpened knife was raised, Śunahśepa prayed to Prajāpati, to Agni, to Savitri, to Varuna, to the All Gods, to Indra, to the Aśvins, and to the Dawn, and as he prayed, the fetters which bound him fell off one by one, and King Hariśchandra was restored to health.

The evidence for the actual existence of human sacrifice[1]

[1] The "Taitt. Brāh." gives a list of various men and women fit for sacrifice to one hundred and seventy-nine gods."—Barth, "Rel. of India," pp. 57, 58. "Der Purushamedha ist eben der Uberrest eines barbarischen Zeitalters des wir fur Indiens so evenig wie für andere Länder zu leugnen haben."—Hillebrandt, "Rituel Litteratur," p. 153.

during the Brāhmanic period, rests on accounts such as that of Śunahśepa, where, however, as in the Biblical accounts of Abraham and Isaac, the victim is released, showing that the rite was one then no longer in use. In the "Śatapatha Brāhmana"[1] it is stated that the animals used for sacrifice are "a man, a horse, a bull, a ram and a he-goat."

With regard to these the direction to the sacrificer is:[2] "Let him slaughter those very five victims as far as he may be able to do so; for it was those Prajāpati was the first to slaughter, and Syāparna Sāyakāyana the last, and in the interval also, people used to slaughter them. But nowadays only these two are slaughtered, the one for Prajāpati, and the one for Vāyu." The two animals here referred to are he-goats.[3] The fact that the compiler of the texts records the name of the last sacrificer who performed a human sacrifice, shows that the practice had died out in the home or family of the compiler.

It would be futile to seek for clear matter-of-fact statements or commonplace explanations of the sacrificial system in the early Brāhmanic literature.

The entire ritual was a cult falling more and more into the hands of a hereditary class of priests, determined to hold the power they thus obtained free from outside criticism or attack. The commanding position the priesthood obtained in the community by their exclusive knowledge of the complicated details of the sacrificial system, which so closely hemmed in the whole life of every Aryan householder, would naturally incline them to attach to their office and to all its duties not only an esoteric significance, but further in every way to heighten and exaggerate the supernatural basis on which they were primitively founded. Over the whole ceremony the superintending Brāhman priest hovered, as a man possessed of divine knowledge and divine power.

[1] "Śat. Brāh.," vi. 2; 1, 15. [2] *Ibid.*, vi. 2; 1, 39. [3] *Ibid.*, vi. 2, 2, 1.

He was the central figure, looming mysterious in his carefully preserved silence, yet held to possess powers potent enough in their overshadowing might never to call for their actual manifestation. For days or for years the rites might drag on their mysterious ways; it was the Brāhman alone who held the knowledge and power to set in motion the whole performance; his nod or word could break the thread of the ceremony, and bring the direst results to all engaged.[1] At the morning libation he gave permission that the Vedic Hymns might be chanted by uttering the words, "Bhūr! ye may sing!"[2] So at the mid-day libation he muttered, "Bhuvah! ye may sing!" and at the evening libation he says, "Svar! ye may sing!" He stood overseeing all as a very god. "Verily there are two kinds of gods, for indeed the gods are the gods, and the Brāhmans who have studied and teach sacred lore are the human gods. The sacrifice of these is divided into two kinds; oblations constitute the sacrifice to the gods; and gifts to the priests that to human gods."

The Brāhman wisely left all the outward signs of power in the hands of his serving priests. At the bidding of the Brāhman, the reciting priest, the Hotar, a class from which the Brāhmans were chiefly recruited,[3] commenced the recitation of such Vedic Hymns as were ordained for use. As the stately music of the words, intoned by the Udgātar priest, rose and fell, it cast around its spell of magic power, moving amid the people as though it subtly bound their souls to the gods who thronged around them. Should the Hotar desire to deprive a sacrificer of life, or sense, limb, strength, or speech, he had but to omit a Vedic verse in his

[1] A special remark made by the renowned Ārunī, who composed many of the sacrificial formulæ, is as follows: "Why should he sacrifice who would think himself the worse for a miscarriage of the sacrifice? I for one am the better for a miscarriage of the sacrifice."—"Śat. Brāh.," iv. 5, 7, 9.

[2] Haug, "Ait. Brāh.," pp. 377, 378.

[3] S.B.E., vol. xii.; Eggeling (Introd.), xx.

recitation, or pronounce it confusedly, it was held that by his so doing the union of the sacrificer with the gods would at once be broken, and the whole sacrifice rendered futile,[1] the wish of the Hotar alone resulting. To deprive a sacrificer of his wealth, or a king of his subjects, the Hotar had but to recite a hymn out of its proper order, and so great was the inherent power of the sacred word that the required result would inevitably follow. Should the priest desire to deprive a sacrificer of the whole fruit of the sacrifice, he had but to pronounce a verse in a different tone from that in which it should be pronounced, and the sacrifice would fall useless. Not only did the priestly power reign supreme over the religious life of the people, but, politically it extended side by side with that of the tribal chieftain or king.[2] No king could succeed in deeds that were not founded on priestly advice, and the gods are said to turn away from the food of a king who has no "purohita" or Brāhman guide.

It is said that a king who appoints no family priest or "purohita" is cast out from Heaven,[3] deprived of his heroism, of his dignity, kingdom, and subjects. To the king who has a "purohita," Agni Vaiśvanara gives protection; he surrounds the king[4] as the sea surrounds the earth; such a king dies not before he has lived one hundred years; he dies not again, for he is not reborn; his subjects obey him "unanimously and undivided."[5]

Imprecations almost fiendish in their malignity are called down on one who should curse the Hotar at any part of the ceremony, all being finally summed up:[6] For in "like

[1] The various means for rectifying blunders are given in the "Kauskītaki Brāhmana," vi. 11. One opinion is given: "As far as the blunder extends, so far let him say it again, whether a verse, a half verse, a foot, a word, or a letter."

[2] For union of the two offices, king and priest, as the first sacrificer, *see* J. G. Frazer, "Golden Bough," vol. i. pp. 8, 223.

[3] Eggeling, xiv.

[4] *Ibid.*, S.B.E., vol. xii. p. xii.

[5] Haug, p. 530.

[6] "Śat. Brāh.," i. 4, 3, 22; S.B.E., vol. xii.

manner, as one undergoes suffering, on approaching the fire that has been kindled by means of the kindling verses, so also does one undergo suffering for cursing a priest (brāhmana) who knows and recites the kindling verses."[1]

With the "purohita" swaying the councils of the king by his sacerdotal power, backed as it was by an assumed knowledge of sorcery and incantation; with the priesthood enclosing the whole daily life of the people with complicated religious rites, the efficacy of which depended on the supposed supernatural influence of the Brāhmans over the gods themselves, the national independence of thought and exuberant free-play of imagination, which in earlier times had produced the poetry and visions of the "Rig Veda," passed away for ever, to give place to fatalism and the quiescence of pantheism.

To their growing powers the priesthood failed not to add that of wealth. For each sacrifice the officiating priests demanded their "dakshina," or reward of gold and kine; one text[2] mentions the liberality of a worshipper who gave 85,000 white horses, 10,000 elephants, and 80,000 slave girls adorned with ornaments, to the Brāhman who performed the sacrifice.

Throughout the early history of India, tradition tells of fierce conflicts between the Brāhmans and the warrior class, out from which the Brāhmans ever emerged victorious. Prajāpati,[3] the lord of all creatures, was held to have created divine knowledge and the sacrifice for Brāhmans, not for warriors. At the inauguration of a king, when he was anointed by the sprinkling of water and admitted to

[1] The ancient mode of destroying an enemy by making an image of wax and placing it before a fire is narrated in the "Sāmavidhāna Brāhmana":—"The image of the person to be destroyed or afflicted is made of dough, and roasted, so as to cause the moisture to exude, and then cut in pieces and eaten by the sorcerer."—Burnell (Introd.) p. xxvi.

[2] Weber, "Ind. Stud.," x. p. 54. *See* also "Śat. Brāh.," ii. 6, 3, 9; iv. 5, 1, 11; iv. 3, 4, 6; "Taitt. Brāh.," iii. 12, 5, 11-12.

[3] Haug, "Ait. Brāh.," p. 471 (*tr.*).

the drinking of the Soma juice, he had for the time being to lay aside the signs of his warriorhood,[1] his horse, his chariot, his armour, his bow and arrow, and take up the signs of the sacerdotal power, the sacrificial implements, and become a Brāhman so long as the inauguration lasted. With the natural tendency of a class rising to almost supreme power, the priesthood sought in every way to consolidate its position and enforce its rules and ordinances on those whom it could force to submit.

The king and his "purohita," originally holders of a joint office,[2] stood apart and separate in their functions, both a type of the class or caste division into nobles and priests, of those who held power over the labouring community.[3]

The agricultural or trading members of the Aryan clans held themselves proudly aloof from the despised black-skinned and broad-nosed aborigines, with whom for the most part they abstained from intermarriage or social intercourse.

The road was gradually being prepared for the division of the people into distinctive classes, a system ultimately to develop into a modern theory of caste, founded on differences of colour, descent, occupation, or livelihood.

The Aryans by the close of the Brāhmanic period had spread far to the East, where those tribes or clans, who were furthest removed from the homes of the Kuru Panchālas and the sacrifice, were to rise in opposition to the whole theory on which Brāhmanic supremacy was founded, and inaugurate a revolt which culminated in the formulated doctrines of Buddhism.

[1] Haug, "Ait. Brāh," p. 472 (*tr.*).
[2] Frazer, "Golden Bough," vol. i. p. 224.
[3] Senart, "Castes dans l'Inde," p. 149.

CHAPTER VI.

FROM BRĀHMANISM TO BUDDHISM.

THE "Brāhmanas" tell how, from the plains of Kurukshetra, from the abodes of the Kuru Panchālas, Brāhman priests went to carry to the homesteads of those adventuring warriors, who had gone further east to seek new fortunes, the knowledge of the sacrificial mysteries, the power they held to sway the gods, and to claim in return some share of the wealth that had fallen to the Aryan race. To the East, as far as to the banks of the Sadānīra, or Modern Gandak, which flows into the Ganges near Patna, the Kośālas had made their homes, while the Videhas had ventured to cross the cold water of the same stream, and take up their abode in the rich land beyond.

The ancient literature of India still tells how once the land to the east of the Sadānīra, "she who is always filled with water," was for long "very uncultivated and very marshy,"[1] and how no Brāhmans dwelt there. By the advancing Aryans the sacred fire was at length carried across the deep stream, and by it the undergrowth burned away and the forest trees cleared. The story as told in the "Brāhmana of One Hundred Paths," is one of the few facts regarding the people and their movements that the times thought it worth while recording.

[1] "Śat. Brāh.," i. 4, 1, 15.

"Nowadays," narrates[1] the chronicler of the advance of the Aryans eastward to Videha, "the land is very cultivated, for the Brāhmans have caused Agni to taste it through sacrifices. Even in winter that river, as it were, rages along: so cold is it, not having been burned over by Agni Vaisvānara."

"Mādhava, the Videgha, then said to Agni, 'Where am I to abide?' 'To the east of this river be thy abode,' said he. Even now this river forms the boundary of the Kośālas and Videhas; for these are the Māthavas or descendants of Mādhava."

The wandering course of tribes other than the Kośālas and Videhas can also be traced in early Vedic literature.

Tribes known as the Kāsis found an abiding-place round the modern city of Benares, the sin-destroying Kāsi, within sight of whose myriad temples all who die are said to pass straight to the heavens of the Hindu gods. Beyond the Kāsis lived the Magadhas and Angas, tribes who wandered far beyond the pale of Aryan civilisation[2] to venture their fortunes amid the fever-smitten tracts,[3] where they might live free from the strict rules of sacerdotal orthodoxy.

In the history of the times there is no evidence that over any of these tribes—far as they may have gone to the East, or long as they may have settled in the fertile valleys of the Ganges and Jumna—the enervating influence of climate, sloth, or luxury, had cast its fatal spell. The wild untrammelled play of fancy that had inspired the lyric outburst of early Vedic song gave place, it is true, to the reasoned and more ordered train of thought, seen in the prose, diffuse and artificial though it be, of the "Brāhmanas,"

[1] S.B.E., vol. xii.; "Śat. Brāh.," i. 4, 1, 16-17.

[2] *See* Oldenberg, "Buddha," p. 400.

[3] S.B.E., vol. xlii.; "Atharva-veda," p. 2:—"Destroy the fever that returns on each third day, the one that intermits each third day, the one that continues without intermission, and the autumnal one. To the Gandhāris, the Mūjavantas, the Angas, and the Magadhas, we deliver over the fever, like a servant, like a treasure."

"Āranyakas," and "Upanishads." Full as the "Brāhmanas" are of evidences how the Kuru Panchāla Brāhmans sought, for the purpose of their own aggrandisement, to gain a temporal and spiritual dominion over the superstitious mass of the people, yet in Magadha, in the far East, the almost sublime figure of Buddha stands forth, not only as a personification of stately self-restraint, but also of heroic protest against the usurpation by men of power over the eternal destinies of their fellow-creatures. In the leading principles of the "Upanishads," which contain the free and earnest speculations of a rising class of philosophers—priests, kings, and warriors alike—who thronged to the courts of the chieftains of Kośāla and Videha, there is to be found the bursting forth of an advanced order of thought, and though this may be peculiarly, and exclusively Indian in the deeply religious and intensely subtle mode of its expression, yet as a phase of thought, it was a natural growth from the preceding religious history of the people, and as such shows nothing unworthy of taking a foremost place in the intellectual history of the world at the period in which it arose. That the Aryans advanced into India in numbers sufficient to oust the aboriginal tribes, and themselves to colonise the vast area over which their influence can be traced, has never been held as probable, or even possible. The previous inhabitants were numerous, and more or less civilised. At the present day, the only evidence India affords of an invasion of Aryan people in Vedic times, outside the literary record and existence of the great group of northern Aryan languages, derived from Sanskrit, is the presence of an upper stratum of fair-skinned and refined families in the great mass of the dark-skinned, and more illiterate agricultural population.[1] The very

[1] The case of South India, where the Aryan influence spread later, is typical. "It has often been asserted, and is now the general belief of ethnologists, that the Brāhmans of the South are not pure Aryans, but are of mixed Aryan and Dravidian race."—H. A. Stuart, "Madras Census Report" (1891). Mr Edgar

denunciations in the early Sanskrit literature against matrimonial relationship between members of the Aryan community and those of the aboriginal tribes, as well as the relegation of any offspring to despised or inferior classes of mixed descent, show plainly that the intermingling of the newcomers with the earlier inhabitants was far from uncommon. Even though this may have been so, to a greater extent than at present it would be safe to assert, it is certain that the Aryans, in the course of their migrations from the Sarasvatī to the limits of Western Bengal, left the impress of their language and culture over the whole of this extensive area, assuming, as must be done for the present, that Buddhism, in its primary significance, was a legitimate outcome of Aryan thought. These Aryans, as they spread far and wide, remained, for the most part, united into clans and tribes, each under its own local chieftain. As in the earliest Vedic times so down to the time of Buddha in the sixth century B.C., and even later, these scattered tribes show no inability to push their way amid opposing foes, or even, if opportunity afforded, to take possession of the territories of those of their own race than whom they found themselves more powerful. The

Thurston, who has taken a series of anthropological measurements ("Madras Government Museum Bulletin," No. 418, 1896), states that the Brāhmans of the South "are separated from all the classes or tribes of Southern India which I have as yet investigated, with the exception of the Kongas of Coimbatore, by the relation of the maximum transverse diameter to the maximum antero-posterior diameter of the head (cephalic index). Though the cephalic index of the Kongas is slightly greater, the mean length and breadth of their heads are considerably less than these of the Brāhmans, being 17·8 cm. and 13·7 cm. against 18·6 and 14·2." Again: "The length of the head of Brāhmans, Kammalans, Pallis, and Pariahs show that the average length is the same in all except the Kammalans, in whom it is slightly (·2 cm.) shorter." Also: "In all except the Paniyans the average width of the nose is the same, but the length is slightly greatest in the Brāhmans." "I came across many dark-skinned Brāhmans with high nasal index." Finally, he sums up his results: "The Brāhmans are characterised by the greatest weight, greatest breadth of head, greatest distance from the middle finger to the patella, and the largest hands" (p. 229).

more the once-united and compact body of Aryans diffused themselves over the vast extent of Northern India, separating into groups under chieftains, each desirous of extending his possessions and influence by conquest over, or by alliances with, other rich and powerful chieftains, aboriginal or Aryan, the more their life-history becomes disseminated into devious courses, never again to re-unite into one combined nationality.

Popular religious movements, such as those of Buddhism and Jainism, which appealed to the understanding and sympathies of the mass, had undoubtedly an influence in infusing the community with a common purpose and enthusiasm.

These movements had their results in ancient India, as similar popular religious movements have had, and undoubtedly will have in the future, in modern India, and were taken advantage of by chieftains anxious to seize the opportunity of extending their local influence. Yet from their very nature they proved powerless to unite for long the diverse elements which went to make up the community into a combined body, powerful and coherent enough to resist the disintegrating effects of a rude shock from foreign invasions. These movements left their own peculiar literary record, though the history of the phase of thought out of which they arose, preserved as it is in the earlier "Brāhmanas" and "Upanishads," is one of the most obscure in the whole range of Indian literature.

While the Aryan people were bereft of all hope of ever seeing a great national leader arise among them to combine the scattered elements, into which the people were drifting, into one political unity, it would be as vain to seek, in the history of the times, for the growth of any tendency to evolve a clearly-defined conception of a monotheism, as it would be to seek for any great literary outburst in which could be read the national expression of the desire of the race for expansion. At the most, it must be expected that the literary history of the period is one in which all that was left of the past was fostered and elaborated or developed along its own inherent lines by the peculiar genius of a gifted race, able to preserve its intellecual power amid the crumbling ruins of its political career. In the literature we find not the record of an intellectual movement, sinking deeper into despondency and despair from climatic or priestly influences,[1] but rather the free discussion among the outlying portions of the community of the whole religious tradition and new-founded claims of the priesthood, the enunciation of doctrines in many cases subversive of such claims, and, unhappily, in many cases showing evidences of the incorporation of beliefs, superstitions, and debasing cults of alien races, with whom the more orthodox Aryans had entered into social and political relations.

The evidences for the changing order of things are to be sought in the philosophic disquisitions of the earlier "Upanishads."[2]

At the court of the renowned Janaka, the patron of all wise men and chieftain of Videha, there stands forth the figure of a celebrated Brāhman priest, Yājnavalkya,[3] who was deeply versed in all the ritual of the sacrificial cult as practised in the holy land of the Kuru Panchālas. The fame Yājnavalkya brought to the land of the Videhas[4]

[1] Garbe, "Monist," p. 50 (1892):—"India was governed by priests, and the weal of the nation was sacrificed with reckless indifference." The same learned writer also remarks that "it is no exaggeration to say that priest-rule was the ruin of India." It should not, however, be forgotten that the drifting of the destinies of a nation, or even of a movement, into corrupt or incompetent hends, is but one of the symptoms of decay, not the cause.

[2] P. Regnaud, "Matériaux pour servir à l'Histoire de Philosophie dans l'Inde," p. 30.

[3] For his instructor, Āruni, *see* Oldenberg, "Buddha," p. 396 (*note*); "Śat. Brāh.," iii. 3, 4, 19.

[4] Where he compiled the "White Yajur Veda" and its "Śatapatha Brāhmana."

even aroused the anger and jealousy of Ajātasatru, the chieftain of the distant Kāśis.

Janaka, proud of the fame he had won, held a great sacrifice,[1] and offered a reward of one thousand cows, bearing each ten pieces of gold fastened to their horns, to the wisest of all the assembled Brāhmans, who had gathered together at his court from the western lands of the Kuru Panchālas. Then Yājnavalkya directed his pupil to drive away the cows, for he held himself to be the wisest of all wise men. Challenged as to his knowledge, he silenced all enquirers by repeating the whole sacrificial cult. Yet there was one question put to him he would not answer before the assembled warriors, or in the hearing of those who placed their salvation in the hands of the priesthood and in the efficacy of the duly performed sacrifice. So Yājnavalkya turned to his enquirer with the remark: "Take my hand, O friend, we two alone shall know of this; let this question of ours not be discussed in public."[2] The question Yājnavalkya would not answer before the assembled crowd was for him a perplexing one, an answer to which it was the mission of Buddha to proclaim openly before all men. It was the question as to what became of man after he departed from this world, and in the heavens had received the reward of all his labours.

In the hands of the Brāhmans the rites of the sacrifice lay. It was solely on the efficacy of the sacrifice that the welfare, here and hereafter, of all depended. The practical result of the disquisition was that the two friends arrived at the conclusion that, from all good deeds, sacrifice included, only good results would flow, and from bad deeds, non-sacrifice included, only bad results would flow. The words of the "Upanishad" state:—"Then these two went out

[1] "Śat. Brāh.," i. 4, 1, 10; Oldenberg, p. 398; S.B.E., vol. xii. p. xliii.; "Brih.-Aran. Up.," iii. 1, 2, 1:—"Many presents were offered to the priests of the Aśvamedha."

[2] "Brih.-Aran. Up.," iii. 2, 13.

and argued, and what they said was *Karman* ("work"); what they praised was Karman; viz. that a man becomes good by good work, and bad by bad work."

The soul might pass after death into different habitations according to its acts; but the question referred to the position of those who had gained a knowledge that was to lead to the overthrow of the whole sacrificial system. It opened up the whole question of the knowledge which man possesses of the true nature of the world as it is presented by the senses, including, as it necessarily does, the relationship of man to the changing scene of birth and re-birth, of ever-ceaseless becoming and never-abiding being, in which he finds himself move as a factor in the great scheme of creation.

The weary cry raised by the Vedic poets that their gods were many, and that, amid them all, they still wondered to what god they should offer their sacrifice, had died away in echoing murmurs that though all the gods are of equal might and majesty, yet no man knew where stood the tree, nor where grew the wood out from which the heavens and earth were fashioned.[1] At the close of the early Vedic times, when all the sacerdotal learning of the priestly caste of Kurukshetra had been brought to the Eastern lands, where dwelt the Videhas, Kośālas, Kāsis, and Magadhas, there to be sifted by the ruthless logic of more independent minds, the triumphal answer came that "Brahman" was the tree, that "Brahman" was the wood out from which the world was hewn.[2]

When Yājnavalkya was again questioned at the court of Videha by a proud woman, Gārgī Vāchakanavī: "In what are the worlds of Brāhman woven, like warp and woof?" he answered: "O Gārgī, do not ask too much lest thy head

[1] R.V., x. 81, 4:—"Ye thoughtful men enquire within your spirit whereon He stood when He established all things" (Griffith).

[2] "Taitt. Brāh.," ii. 8, 9, 6; *see* Deussen, "Das System des Vedānta," p. 51.

should fall off. Thou askest too much about a deity about which we are not to ask too much."[1] When the woman cried out against the learned priest:—" O Yājnavalkya, as the son of a warrior from the Kāsis and Videhas might string his loosened bow, take the pointed foe-piercing arrows in his hand, and rise to battle, I have risen to fight thee."[2] He was forced to reply to the question she put to him: "That of which they say that it is above the heavens, beneath the earth, embracing Heaven and earth, past, present, and future, tell me in what it is woven, like warp and woof?" The answer given forms the basis of the whole philosophic thought of the time. The sacrificial system was once for all placed in a subsidiary position in relation to a new doctrine of salvation which looked upon the performance of religious practices, and the doing of good deeds, merely as a basis whereon should be founded the true aim of mankind: the attainment of a true knowledge of the relationship of the Self to the Self of the Universe.

Yājnavalkya declared to Gārgī, of him who did not possess this true knowledge, that "though he offer oblations in this world, sacrifices, and performs penances for a thousand years, his works will have an end." He "departs this world; he is miserable, like a slave."

There remained but two simple concepts for the future of India to brood over with all the fervour and subtlety of its unrivalled powers of insight into the true nature of things. First, the whole reality of the world, as perceived by the senses, had to be pierced through, and that which underlay it, that which gave it being, ascertained and defined. So when Gārgī questioned Yājnavalkya as to what underlay all objective reality, what permeated all, what wove all together, like warp and woof, there came the answer that there remained only "Brahman," that which

[1] "Brih.-Aran. Up.," iii. 6, 1. [2] *Ibid.*, iii. 8.

"is unseen but seeing; unheard but hearing; unperceived but perceiving; unknown but knowing. There is nothing that sees but it; nothing that hears but it; nothing that perceives but it; nothing that knows but it."[1]

So far there remained, as the result of the earliest phase of philosophic thought in India, nothing but the Unconscious Brahman, yet, as the Indian sage himself asserts, he knew, too, that he himself also exists, for no man says, "I am not."

It was not given to the East to undertake an analysis of the human thinking faculties, and see how far the external appearances of things were thereby conditioned. It therefore became necessary to explain in what relationship that which man postulates the existence of—his own Self, his own Soul—stood in regard to the Imperishable, the Brahman. The Indian mind had to seek for knowledge that was of more value than sacrifice or good deeds, the knowledge not only of Brahman, but of that which told all men that even if their perceptions of the objective reality of the world be founded on nescience, there yet remained, calling for some explanation, the subjective evidence man possesses of his own Self, of his own existence.

Whilst the Indian mind was thus searching for the Cause from which issued the objective form of the world, it was, at the same time, seeking out from the subjective reality the underlying Self or Soul by which man knows he exists. The answer respecting the Cause was clear.

From "Brahman" proceeded the creation of the world, the form of whose arrangement no mind can grasp, where all becoming has its own time, and place, and cause.[2] The word Brahman itself is formed from a root, *brih*, signifying bursting forth, expanding, spreading, growing.[3] From *brih*

[1] "Brih.-Aran. Up.," iii. 8, 11; S.B.E., vol. xv.

[2] "Brahma Sūtras," i. 1, 2.

[3] "*Ibid.*, i. 1, 1:—"Root *brih*=to be great"; *see* Gough, "Philosophy of the Upanishads," p. 38; Max Müller, "Vedānta," pp. 21, 148.

the word Brahman was first formed; it was the prayer sent forth by the Vedic seer to invoke the near presence of the deities. Brihaspati was the lord of prayer,[1] the lord of speech.[2] From the prayer, from the creative fervour of the poet's imagination and aspiration, all the gods had sprung to birth, the triple "Vedas," on which all truth is founded, had sprung to life. "Brahman" was that from which all the universe, extended in name and form, was issued forth. It was the tree and the wood from which the heavens and earth were hewn; it was that in which all things are woven, like warp and woof. In its full definition, as later given,[3] "Brahman" was held to be that Omniscient and Omnipotent Cause from which came the birth, the stay, and the decay of this Creation, as seen spread out by name and form, wherein abide many actors and enjoyers, wherein arises the fruit of good and evil deeds, all having their own time, and place, and cause; a Creation, the planning of whose form no mind can grasp. The answer respecting the Soul or Self had further to be formulated.

From earliest times the wondering powers of the primitive mind were set to fathom sleep and death, and their surrounding mysteries. In sleep are seen visions of well-known faces; scenes are fancied forth; joys and fears come and go; yet, as man moves not, the first solution is that something—the breath, the spirit, or the soul—has gone forth to wander free. From death there is no awakening; the shade,[4] the breath, soul, or spirit has gone forth and

[1] R.V., ii. 23, 1:—"Als Priestlicher Schachtgott"; Oldenberg, "Rel. des Vedas," p. 67, as "sacerdotal side of Agni's nature"; Macdonell, J.R.A.S. (1895), p. 948.

[2] R.V., x. 98, 2, 3; x. 71, 1. Vachaspati, *see* Max Müller, "Vedānta," p. 149. For Brāhman as Logos of Fourth Gospel, *see* Deussen, p. 51; Max Müller, "Vedānta," p. 148:—"He created first of all the Brāhman"; *cf.* S.B., vi. 1, 1, 8, which is translated:—"He created first of all the word."

[3] "Brāh. Sūtras," i. 1, 2.

[4] Huxley, "Romanes Lecture," p. 40; Rhys Davids, "Hibbert Lectures," p. 83.

returns not. The lifeless body is still loved by friends,[1] and feared by those who were foes. Efforts are made by friends to recall the soul, to guide it to the place where it once dwelt, food is placed near, offerings made, and all the means so familiar to students of folk-lore, taken to hasten it on its journey. To these spirits, Pitris, or fathers, who had gone away[2] ("preta") along the path first trodden by Yama, the Vedic Soma[3] was poured forth, and they were summoned to take their place[4] among the assembled gods, and partake of the sacrifice. In the "Taittiriya Brāhmana" the souls of the deceased are said to dwell in the heavens above as stars,[5] and again[6] in the stars are "the lights of those righteous men who go to the celestial world." In the "Śatapatha Brāhmana"[7] death is the sun whose rays attach to mortals their life breath, yet, as the "Katha Upanishad"[8] declares: "No mortal lives by the breath that goes up and the breath that goes down. We live by another in whom these two repose."

There was something which went out of man in sleep and death; something underlying the Ego, the I, the vital breath, more subtle than life.

In the "Rig Veda,"[9] the sun, though it holds the life breath of mortals, is something more. It is the Self, or the "Ātman," of all that moves and moves not, of all that fills the heavens and the earth. So of man there is also the Ātman,[10] "the Self, smaller than small, greater than great, hidden in the heart of that creature." A man who is free

[1] Jevons, "History of Religions," pp. 46, 54.

[2] Max Müller, "India: What Can It Teach Us?" p. 220.

[3] R.V., x. 15, 1:—"The fathers who deserve a share of the Soma."

[4] *Ibid.*, x. 15, 11:—"Fathers whom Agni's flames have tasted, come ye nigh: in proper order take ye each your proper place. Eat sacrificial food presented on the grass" (Griffith).

[5] "Taitt. Brāh.," v. 4, 13.

[6] "Śat. Brāh.," vi. 5, 4, 8.

[7] "Śat. Brāh.," x. 3, 3, 7, 8.

[8] "Katha Up.," ii. 5, 5; S.B.E., vol. xv.

[9] R.V., i. 115, 1.

[10] "Katha Up.," i. 2, 20.

from desires and free from grief sees the majesty of the Self by the grace of the Creator.[1]

It is this Ātman, or Self, more abstract in its conception than soul, Psyche, or "anima," that becomes also the Universal Self, the Self of the World, "bhūmiyāh ātman," of which the "Veda"[2] speaks: "When that which had no bones bore him who has bones, when that which was formless took shape and form."

The Indian sage, seeking out the primal cause of creation, had first to sweep away all that which had been produced, even the gods themselves, and to his gaze there remained but the neuter essence, Brahman, from which all things issued forth, and into which all things resolve themselves. There remained also the Self, the Soul, the Ātman of man. There was but one step further to be reached by the Indian mind, and that was taken when all duality vanished, and the Brahman became the Great Self, the "Paramātman," the Universal Self, into which was merged the Ātman, or Self, of man.

In the closing scenes of the teachings of the priest, Yājnavalkya, at the court of Videha, this doctrine of the Ātman, which was to have so great an influence on the future of India, is set forth in clear and plain language.

Maitreyī, the wife of Yājnavalkya, appeared and prayed her husband, who was preparing to go forth from his home and end his days, according to the custom of the time, as a hermit in the forest, to expound unto her the secret of death and immortality. Yājnavalkya replied to his wife: "Thou art, indeed, dear to me, therefore I will explain it to you, and mark well what I say."[3]

So he told her that to all the world was dear; that wives and sons were dear; wealth, the gods, sacrifice, and knowledge, for the simple reason that they were all held in the

[1] "Dhātu prasādāt," *see* Max Müller, "Vedānta," p. 50.
[2] R.V., i. 164, 4. [3] "Brih.-Aran. Up.," iv. 5, 5.

Self, that they were all permeated by the Self, that they were all one in the Self. "Verily, the Self is to be seen, to be heard, to be perceived, to be marked, O Maitreyī! When the Self has been seen, heard, perceived, and known, then all this is known."[1]

The futility of the efforts to inculcate these philosophic speculations among the people, so that they might become potential principles of a new religious movement, a consummation only effected by Buddha with respect to the doctrines he taught, is dramatically set forth and artistically foreshadowed by generally putting forth women such as Gārgī and Maitreyī to receive instruction. This can be seen in the answer made to Yājnavalkya by his wife. Then Maitreyī said: "Here, sir, thou hast landed me in bewilderment. Indeed, I do not understand."[2]

The remark gave Yājnavalkya the opportunity for setting forth, in the simplest language, the doctrine of the unity of the Self of Man and the Self of the Universe, the peculiar Eastern mode of expressing "the Monistic doctrine of the All in One which has had the greatest influence on the intellectual life of modern times."[3] In the answer of Yājnavalkya there is no exulting cry of one seeking, by the keenness of his intellect, to overthrow rival creeds; there is no vaunting boast that the riddle of existence had been solved; there is but the sad wail that the mind had pierced as keenly into the nature of things as it was able, and that even then there was room for wonder—room not only for wonder, but room for doubt that any reasoned thought of man would ever satisfy the eager thirst of humanity to seek out a living faith in keeping with the instincts which make its manhood. Nowhere in the history of the world's thought can there be found more earnest efforts to seek out for suffering mankind some

[1] "Brih.-Aran. Up.," iv. 5, 6. [2] *Ibid.*, iv. 5, 14.
[3] Garbe, "The Monist," p. 58 (Oct. 1894).

solution of the perplexing questions which surround his life than in those sedately and reverently-expressed speculations of the awakened thought of India. Yet, strange to say, these speculations never touched the hearts of the people. They worked no such revolution as did the crude agnosticism of Buddha.

From the sedate and learned priest, prepared as he was to leave wealth and fame, wives and sons, and end his days in subdued submission to the scheme of things which held him powerless, and was soon to claim his life, came the gentle answer to his wife Maitreyī:—

"O Maitreyī, I say nothing that is bewildering. Verily, beloved, that Self is imperishable and of an indestructible nature. For when there is, as it were, duality, the one sees the other, one smells the other, one tastes the other, one salutes the other, one hears the other, one perceives the other, one touches the other, one knows the other; but when the Self alone is all this, how should one see another, how should one smell another, how should one taste another, how should one salute another, how should one hear another, how should one touch another, how should he know another? How should he know him by whom he knows all this? That Self is to be described by no, no! He is incomprehensible for he cannot be comprehended; he is imperishable for he cannot perish; he is unattached for he does not attach himself; unfettered, he does not suffer, he does not fail. How, O beloved, should he know the knower? Thus, O Maitreyī, thou hast been instructed. Thus far goes immortality. Having said so Yājnavalkya went away into the forest."

The Indian mind had, however, long to wait before it clearly saw its course to Monism, notwithstanding the answer here given by Yājnavalkya as the last result of his long efforts to rest within the dreamy depths whence the reality of the world fades away into the Universal Self, outside of which there is no duality.

As yet this Self is but that which pervades and underlies all things; it stands apart, yet from out it springs Creation. Close to a pure idealistic conception of the

Universe and the unreality of everything, the perception of which by our senses is mere delusion, comes the well-known teaching of Uddālaka to his son Śvetaketu in the "Chandogya Upanishad"[1] where it is declared: "In the beginning, my dear, there was that only which is (τὸ ὄν) one only without a second. Others say, in the beginning there was that only which is not (τὸ μὴ ὄν), one only without a second, and from that which is not, that which is, was born."

"But how could it be thus, my dear?" the father continued. "How could that which is, be born of that which is not? No, my dear, only that which is, was in the beginning, one only without a second."

So far it might seem as if there could exist no reality nor duality from which the creation of anything outside the One Universal Self could rise. Yet the teaching goes on to declare that what in the beginning was one only without a second thought, "may I be many, may I grow forth. It sent forth fire."

It remains still that Self out of which the heavens and earth were made.[2] It is still, as the one piece of clay gives its name to the whole piece of clay,[3] that from which all creation derives its name and form. It still has thought,[4] and from its thought plurality springs forth, first fire, then water, food, and earth. It is still the Self which Death declares to Nachiketas, who had gone to the realms of Yama to redeem a vow made by his father.[5] From Yama Nachiketas claimed a boon, for Death, who had been busy among mortals, had kept him waiting, and the boon he claimed was, that Yama should declare to him what was

[1] "Ch. Up.," vi. 2 1. [2] "Taitt. Brāh.," ii. 8, 96. [3] "Ch. Up.," vi. 1, 4.

[4] *Ibid.*, vi. 2, 3:—"It thought, may I be many, may I grow forth. It sent forth fire." S.B.E., vol. i.; Oldenberg, "Buddha," p. 41:—Therefore "involving the duality of the subject and object."

[5] "Katha Up.," p. 54, for which Oldenberg claims a pre-Buddhistic origin.

the great secret beyond the grave. In vain Death prayed[1] not to be asked the question. He offered to Nachiketas fair maidens, and chariots, and song. Yet of them Nachiketas cried: "They last till to-morrow, O Death; they wear out the vigour of all the senses. Even the whole of life is short. Keep thy horses; keep dance and song to thyself." Nachiketas but desired to know the mystery of death. So Death told him all that the mind of man had been able to fathom of the unknown the portals of which had been fashioned out from fantastic dreams of evanescent fancy, still more dear to the mystic mind of the East than the stately portals of Western constructive thought, where each line is laboriously laid down to serve a purpose. So Death weaves a web through which one may seek the infinite, fine-spun and vague as the thread of thought which stretched from Vedic times towards Buddha's feet.

"Fools and blind leaders of the blind,"[2] Death says, "are they who fall into my hands. They are those who deem there is no world but theirs, who know not the truth of Self. The Self is not to be known by the 'Veda,' nor by the teaching. It is not born; it dies not; it sprang from nothing; nothing sprang from it.[3] It is hidden in the heart of every creature. The wise who knows the Self as bodiless within the bodies, as unchanging among changing things,[4] as great and omnipresent, does never grieve, but he who has not turned away from his wickedness, who is not tranquil and subdued, or whose mind is not at rest, he can never obtain the Self (even) by knowledge." Amid all these strange guesses which the enquiring mind of the Indian philosopher hazarded respecting the nature of Soul and

[1] Max Müller, "Hibbert Lectures," p. 335.

[2] S.B.E., vol. xv. pp. 10-12; Oldenberg, "Buddha," pp. 53-7; Max Müller, "Hibbert Lectures," pp. 333-7.

[3] "Katha Up.," i. 2, 18.

[4] *Ibid.*, i. 2, 23:—"He whom the Self chooses, by him the Self can be gained."

Supreme Being, and their connection, in which all of the old is held fast, for as yet the sage is not satisfied that he has pierced to the truth, there comes one belief stranger to our ears than all others, declared as follows:[1] "Self cannot be gained by the 'Veda,' nor by understanding, nor by much learning. He whom the Self chooses, by him the Self can be gained. The Self chooses him (his body as his own)."

So from thought to thought the mind wandered on in its own course, over the anxious questions never to be solved yet never silenced. "Breath to air, and to the immortal,"[2] cries the dying soul; "then this my body ends in ashes. Om! mind, remember! Remember thy deeds. Mind, remember! Remember thy deeds."

"He who knows at the same time both the cause and the destruction of the perishable body, overcomes death by destruction, and obtains immortality through knowledge of the true cause."

"When to a man who understands the Self has become all things, what sorrow, what trouble can there be to him who once beheld that unity?"[3] "And he who beholds all beings in the Self, and the Self in all beings, he never turns away from it."[4] "All who worship what is not the true cause enter into blind darkness; those who delight in the true cause enter, as it were, into greater darkness."[5]

The full doctrine of the "Brahman" and the "Ātman" is set forth in the well-known "Śāndilyavidyā,"[6] or sayings of the sage, Śāndilya, so often quoted in succeeding disquisitions :—

> "All this is *Brahman* (neuter). Let a man meditate on that (visible world) as beginning, ending, and breathing in it (the Brahman).
>
> Now man is a creature of will. According to what his will is in this

[1] "Katha Up.," i. 2, 23. "Māndukya Up.," iii. 2, 3, gives the same.
[2] "Isa. Up.," 17; S.B.E., vol. i. p. 313. [3] *Ibid.*, vol. i. p. 312.
[4] "Isa. Up."; S.B.E., vol. i. p. 312. [5] *Ibid.*, vol. i. p. 312.
[6] "Ch. Up.," iii. 14; "Vedānta Sūtras," iii. 3, 31.

world, so will he be when he has departed this life. Let him therefore have this will and belief.

The intelligent, whose body is spirit, whose form is light, whose thoughts are true, whose nature is like ether (omnipresent and invisible), from whom all works, all desires, all sweet odours and tastes proceed; he who embraces all this, who never speaks, and is never surprised; he is my Self within the heart, smaller than a corn of rice, smaller than a corn of barley, smaller than a mustard seed, smaller than a canary seed or the kernel of a canary seed. He also is my Self within the heart, greater than the earth, greater than the sky, greater than Heaven, greater than all these worlds.

He from whom all works, all desires, all sweet odours and tastes proceed, who embraces all this, who never speaks, and who is never surprised—he, my self within the heart, is that *Brahman* (neuter). When I shall have departed from hence, I shall obtain him (that Self). He who has this faith has no doubt; thus said Śāndilya, yea, thus he said."

This is the teaching which has ever had the deepest fascination for all succeeding thought in India. It was the teaching in which Ajātasatru, King of the Videhas, instructed the proud Brāhman, Gārgya Bālāki, remarking as he did so: "Verily, it is unnatural that a Brāhmana should come to a Kshatriya hoping that he should tell him the Brahman."[1]

It was the knowledge of the Self and its oneness with Brahman that inspired Brāhmans to give up all desire for sons, for wealth, and a life amid the gods, to go forth from their homes and wander as mendicants.[2] The knowledge was not one to be obtained by argument,[3] and "he who has not first turned away from his wickedness, who is not tranquil and subdued, or whose mind is not at rest, he can never obtain the Self even by knowledge."[4] The path to the Self is difficult to pass over; it is sharp as the edge of a razor.[5] The Self is seated in the body as if in a chariot; the intellect drives, the mind becomes the reins, yet the senses

[1] "Brih.-Aran. Up.," ii. 1. 15:—"Then let me come to you as a pupil."
[2] *Ibid.*, iii. 5, 1.
[3] "Katha Up.," i. 2, 9.
[4] *Ibid.*, i. 2, 24.
[5] *Ibid.*, i. 3, 14.

are as vicious horses which speed it along, over a road strewn with the objects of sense.[1]

The Agnihotra, the new moon, the full moon, the four-monthly, the harvest sacrifices[2] lead to the heaven of the gods. They lead the sacrificer, "as sun rays,[3] to where the one Lord of the Devas dwells; they lead him to where there is rejoicing[4] over his good deeds." But they are[5] "fools who praise this as the highest good; (they) are subject again and again to old age and death."

"Fools, dwelling in darkness, wise in their own conceit, and puffed up with vain knowledge, go round and round, staggering to and fro like blind men led by the blind. Considering sacrifice and good works as the best—these fools know no higher—and having enjoyed (their reward) in the height of heaven, gained by good works, they enter again this world or a lower one."

Yet, before the teaching of the "Vedas" and "Upanishads" was systematised in the "Brahma Sūtrās," and commented upon by the greatest of all commentators, Śankarāchārya, a strange belief had arisen in India, which for upwards of one thousand years set its impress on the history of the land, and gave to its literature a rich wealth of treasure, the full value of which is but now dawning on the nations of the world. The belief was that known as Buddhism, claiming for its founder the Sākya chief, Siddārtha, greater than whom there came but One other among the sons of men to preach the gospel of peace and goodwill unto all.

[1] "Katha Up.," i. 3, 4. [2] "Māndukya Up.," i. 2, 3. [3] *Ibid.*, i. 2, 5.
[4] *Ibid.*, i. 2, 6. [5] *Ibid.*, i. 2, 8, 10.

CHAPTER VII.

BUDDHISM.

THE sacrificial fires still burned in India. From the three altars still arose to the gods the incense-bearing smoke. The Brāhmans still chanted their Vedic Hymns, and preserved the ancient traditions of their race; still strove to hold their place amid the councils of the local chieftains, and gain rich lands, kine, and wealth.

The sacrificial victims were still slain, harvest-offerings made to all the gods. Priestly ordinances hemmed in the life of each Aryan householder to fixed and immovable rites, to customs all bearing a divine sanction. There were Brāhmans and laity, men and women alike, who had, however, turned their gaze from the sacred fires, and no longer saw their gods personified as in days of yore. Beyond the heavens, beyond the gods, beneath the throb of life, there lay, not one great personal God, Creator of the World, but the imperishable Brahman, "the Unconscious Self of the Universe," "never contaminated by the misery of the world."[1] Deeper than the transmigratory soul, which reaped the reward of good and evil deeds, lay the Self of man, that moved free, undivided from the Self of the

[1] "Katha Up.," ii. 5, 11.

Cosmos, when man rests in dreamless sleep,[1] when he no longer distresses himself with the thought: "Why did I do what is good? Why did I do what is bad?" By a knowledge of the true nature of Brahman, and Self, all duality vanishes;[2] the Self of man recognises itself as but temporarily separate from the Self of the Universe. "All the world is animated by the supersensible. This is true; this is Self. That art thou."[3]

The mystic charm of idealistic Monism stole over the minds of many with all the soothing rest of a mid-day *siesta* in a tropical clime, where the heavens, the waters, the earth, and all that it contains, the very air itself, seems to rest profound and calm in the unison of sleep.

From the earliest Vedic times[4] there had been ascetic sages who had cut themselves adrift[5] from all the cares of life to wander free from observance of sacrificial rites or priestly ordinances. In the laws[6] set forth by the Brāhmans for all the Aryan community, the position of these ascetic dreamers had to be considered, and their claims to sever themselves from the duties of a householder acknowledged.

So it was held[7] that the ascetic might leave his home, and discontinue the performance of all religious ceremonies,

[1] "Ch. Up.," vi. 8, 4; Huxley, "Romanes Lecture," p. 18:—"Practical annihilation involved in merging the individual existence in the unconditioned, the Ātman in Brahman."

[2] "In zahlreiche Gleichnissen suchen die Upanishads das Wesen des Brahman zu beschreiben, aber diese Betrachtungen gipfeln in dem Satze, dass das innerste Selbst des Individuums eins ist mit jener alles durch dringenden Urkraft (tat tvam asi, das bist du)."—Garbe, "Śānkhya Philosophie," p. 109.

[3] "Ch. Up.," vi. 15; Gough, "Phil. of the Upanishads," p. 90.

[4] R.V., x. 154, 2; i. 69, 2; *see* Barth, "Rel. of India," p. 34.

[5] For the existence of women ascetics, *see* Oldenberg, "Buddha," pp. 62, 154; Fichte, "Die Sociale Gliederung in N.O. India," p. 42, *et seq.;* Arrian, "Indica," xii. 8, 9.

[6] "There can be no doubt, from the laws laid down respecting them, that they had a recognised position about the eighth century B.C." (Jacobi).

[7] "Vasishta," x. 1, 4.

"but never let him discontinue the recitation of the 'Veda.' By neglecting the 'Veda' he becomes a Sūdra, therefore he shall not neglect it."

There were other rules laid down, even before the time of Buddha,[1] for these wanderers from village to village and hermit-dwellers in the forest. Those who chose to wander free from all bondage or restraint, from all Vedic observances, had first to take five great vows. The first great vow was not to injure any living thing. The other four vows were to be truthful, to abstain from the property of others, to be content and liberal. Besides these five chief vows there were five lesser for all these saddened sages who withdrew themselves from the busy ways of men, and turned their backs for ever on the blind struggle to live as others lived, preferring to go to the forest and dream out their own lives apart, or wander from land to land seeing if any knew or had heard the truth of the Brahman and the Self. Many of these wandering folk were, no doubt, corrupt and vicious, given to the practice of unholy rites, hoping to obtain insight into the unknown and gain supernatural powers by self-imposed tortures, by mesmeric trances, and by all the varied means so common in later India. For the guidance of these strict rules were necessary, so it was held that a true ascetic should take the vows to be free from all anger, to be obedient,[2] not rash, cleanly, and pure in eating.

The ground had been well prepared for the growth of new beliefs[3] and new doctrines outside the orthodox bulwarks of Brāhmanism.

[1] "He who has finished his studentship may become an ascetic immediately."—"Baudhāyana," ii. 10, 17.

[2] To his *guru*.

[3] *See* Bühler, "Ind. Ant." (1894), p. 248:—For the worship of Narāyana, as taught by the Bhagavatas or Pancaratras, had taken root, a cult afterwards to develop into the deification of the heroic Krishna. For reference to Krishna and dramatic representations of scenes in his life by Patanjali (take as second century B.C.), *see* Bhandarkar, "Ind. Ant." (1874), p. 14.

It was amid this changing flux of thought that Buddha moved, and wove out for himself the solution of the riddle of the Cosmos, which placed man's fate, for weal or woe, here and hereafter, in man's own hands, and taught him to look not beyond himself for hope or aid.

The birthplace of Buddha has lately been sought and found in the now forest-grown and fever-laden tract of country lying along the southern slopes of the Himālayas, almost 200 miles to the northward of Benares.[1] Burial topes and mounds, inscriptions carved on stones, all still lie buried beyond the dense jungle that, during the last fifteen hundred years,[2] has crept over the rich land where once the Buddha lived happily.

According to the account of the Chinese traveller, Hiouen Tsang who left his own country in 629 A.D., to learn in India the tenets of Buddhism, the country of the Sākya people, among whom Buddha was born, "is about 4000 li (sixty-four miles) in circuit. There are some ten deserted cities in this country, wholly desolate and ruined. The capital, Kapilavastu, is overthrown and in ruins. The foundation walls are still strong and high. It has been long deserted. The people and villages are few and waste. . . . The ground is rich and fertile, and is cultivated according to the regular season. The climate is uniform, the manners of the people soft and obliging."[3]

Different from the account of the Chinese traveller is that recorded in the Pāli Scriptures by a Brāhman,

[1] Bühler, *Athenæum* (March 6, 1897):—Where Niglīva is placed 13 miles from Paderia, the site of Buddha's birth, 8 miles from Kapilavastu. Barth (*Jour. des Savants*, Feb. 1897) places Niglīva "à 37 miles au nord-ouest de la station Ushka du North Bengal Railway, par 83° E. of Greenwich."

[2] "In Fa Hian's time, about A.D. 400, the country was already a wilderness, with very few inhabitants, and full of ancient mounds and ruins."—Bühler, *Athenæum* (March 6, 1897).

[3] Beal, "Budd. Rec. of West. World," vol. ii. p. 14.

Ambattha,[1] who visited Kapilavastu, and there found that the rude warrior clan had no respect for the lofty claims advanced by the haughty priest. "The Sākyan race," the young Brāhman angrily complained, "is fierce, violent, hasty, and long-tongued. Though they are naught but men of substance, yet they pay no respect, honour, or reverence to Brāhmans."

More full of interest is the Buddha's recorded reply to the Brāhman, pointing out that there was no occasion for wrath, for it was well known that the Sākyas, as Kshatriyas, held themselves aloof from the Brāhmans; that they refused to acknowledge the offspring of one of their class and a Brāhman as a true Sākyan, while the Brāhmans accepted such as pure Brāhmans. In the important article by Mr Chalmers here quoted, it is further pointed out that "the young Brāhman is forced to admit that, if a Kshatriya is expelled by his fellows, the Brāhmans will welcome him as one of themselves, and he will rank[2] as a full Brāhman; whereas, an expelled Brāhman is never received by the Kshatriyas." The position of Brāhmanism in relation to Buddhism is clearly indicated in the words of the "Sutta,"[3] where it is declared that "it is mere empty words to give it out among the people that the Brāhmans are the best caste, and every other caste is inferior; that the Brāhmans are the white caste, every other caste is black; that only the Brāhmans are pure, not the non-Brāhmans; that the Brāhmans are the legitimate sons of Brahma, born from his mouth, Brahma born, Brahma made, heirs of Brahma."

The land of the Sākyas lies within the Nepalese Terai, north of the district of Gorakhpur. To the south of it lay,

[1] Chalmers, "Madhura Sutta," J.R.A.S. (April, 1894):—Where he quotes above from the "Ambattha Sutta of the Dīgha Nikaya."

[2] *See* Rhys Davids, "Hibbert Lectures" (1881), p. 24; "In Valley of Ganges":—"No Kshatriya could any longer become a Brāhman."

[3] Chalmers, J.R.A.S. (1894), p. 360.

in the time of Buddha, the land of the Kośālas, before whose power it was soon to fall subject. The Sākyas themselves were a warrior clan, and if of Aryan descent, had, in their distant retreat, mingled their blood with non-Aryan folk, and accepted many of their habits. They refrained from intermarriage with other Aryan families, being forced from their isolation "to develop the un-Aryan and un-Indian custom of endogamy."[1] The tradition, however, still remains that they claimed descent from Ikshvāku,[2] the fabled first king of Oudh, the son of Manu, and progenitor of Purukutsa, the king of the Purus. With the Vedic sage, Gotama, they also claimed alliance, so that the great glory of their race was known not only as Buddha, "The Enlightened," and Siddārtha, "one whose aim has been accomplished," but as the ascetic Gautama, the descendant of Gotama, the reputed founder of his family.

In the land of the Sākyas, the father of Buddha owned some part of the fertile lands that now lie waste, and there he became renowned as Suddhodhana, "the possessor of pure rice." These are but dull facts. Better tradition with its imagination, its romance, and poetry, that tells how the Buddha's father was a king, and how the queen, Mayadevī, conceived miraculously. Facts seem now to support tradition so far that in the middle of the sixth century B.C. the Buddha was born to Mayadevī in the garden Lumbini. The route to this spot was marked out towards the close of the second century by a row of pillars stretching north from Patna, the capital of Asoka, the Constantine of Buddhism, who journeyed to Kapilavastu, there to see for himself the place where the Sākya prince was born.

It was to the West, with all its stern love for realism, that the honour fell of discovering the long-fabled garden

[1] Bühler, *Athenæum* (March 6, 1897).

[2] Zimmer, "Alt. Ind. Leben.," p. 130; Oldenberg, "Buddha," p. 403; "Śat. Brāh.," xiii. 5, 45.

where Mayadevī housed on her journey to her father's home, and where the Buddha was born. The news came to England in a brief telegram of the *Times* of December 28, 1896, and there it passed unnoticed and unremarked. From the time when Hiouen Tsang and Fa Hian visited the spot, the miasma of the forest had warded off all stray travellers, and left the deserted ruins a grazing-place for cattle until, in the strange vicissitudes of time, the mystery was unravelled that had so long hung round the birthplace of the sage, whose teaching held India spellbound for one thousand years, and is now accepted, in more or less perverted forms, by so large a proportion of the human race in Ceylon, Siam, Burma, Nepal, Tibet, China, and Japan.[1]

Asoka, who visited the spot in his own day, erected a pillar there, engraved with an inscription. This pillar was seen and described by Hiouen Tsang during his travels. Since then all memory of the pillar and its inscription faded away from memory until it was found by Dr Führer, and the inscription thereon interpreted by Hofrath Professor Bühler as follows: "King Piyadasi (or Asoka), beloved of the gods, having been anointed twenty years, himself came and worshipped, saying: 'Here Buddha Sakyamuni was born,' . . . and he caused a stone pillar to be erected, which declares, 'Here the worshipful one was born.'"[2]

In his father's home the future Buddha must, like all other Kshatriyas, have been trained to take his part in defence of his home and homestead. All had to join in the tribal fights against surrounding clans or encroaching principalities. Hiouen Tsang states that when he visited the ruins of Kapilavastu, "within the eastern gate of the city, on the left of the road, is a stupa (burial mound);

[1] *See* Max Müller, "Chips from a German Workshop," p. 214.

[2] Bühler, *Athenæum* (March 6, 1897)

this is where the Prince Siddārtha practised athletic sports and competitive arts."[1] The tribe, not able to hold its own, was soon subdued by another more powerful, and the tradition tells how the Kshatriyas murmured because Siddārtha neglected to train himself as a warrior and prepare himself to fight in case of war. Thus challenged, Siddārtha came forth and "contended with Sākyas in athletic sports, and pierced with his arrows the iron targets."

Round all the early life of the Buddha, tradition loves to set a halo of mystery and miracle. Hiouen Tsang states that he himself had seen a fountain, the clear waters of which had miraculous powers of healing the sick, for, as he says, "there it was, during the athletic contest, that the arrow of the prince, after penetrating the targets, fell and buried itself up to the feather in the ground, causing a clear spring of water to spring forth."[2] So succeeding ages have woven into the early life of Buddha a fantastic web of legends, which find their source in the poetic and pious imagination of those who saw in all the deeds of the ascetic sage something more than human.

From all this legend may be sifted out the fact that, at the age of sixteen, the Buddha was married to his cousin, Yasodharā, daughter of the Koliyan chief, and ten years later a child, Rahula, was born. The story has been framed in poetic fancy of how, to Buddha, the woes of life were borne home by visions of decrepitude, of old age, of palsied sickness, and of death. Buddha at length saw a means to escape these haunting terrors in the vision of an ascetic sage who had wandered forth from his home, resolved that never more should his eyes behold the unaided sufferings of those to whom he had knit his soul. So Buddha rose and in the

[1] Beal, "Hiouen Tsang," vol. ii. p. 23.
[2] *Ibid.*, vol. ii. p. 211.

night-time passed forth from his wife and child, from his home and homestead, to find if, amid the fair villages and peaceful groves of India, where sedate and learned Brāhmans, ascetic hermits, and strange recluses dwelt, there were any who knew the secret of the mystery of life and death, of sorrow and suffering.

The time was one when strange unrest and strange forebodings had everywhere been borne to the soul of man. Near at hand in Persia, Zoroaster had proclaimed, as some solution of the bitter wail of mankind, the existence of the two ever-conflicting principles of good and evil. In Palestine, Jeremiah poured forth his lament "that all his days are sorrow, and his travail grief. That which befalleth the sons of men befalleth beasts." At Ephesus, Thales had struck the first note of independent thought and unorthodox belief by declaring that water was the primal germ of all things, to be followed by Heraclitus, who saw everywhere evidences of unresting change, the mere glow and fading away, like unto fire, of all things, an eternal becoming, and a never-existing Being, as of flowing water, wherein no firm resting-place remained for man but in some negation of change,[1] some cessation of the entire scheme of Creation.

So to the soul of Buddha crept the sad murmur of the bitter wail that "the millions slept, but a hushed and weary sound told that the wheel of life still revolved."[2] There was a question Buddha had perforce to face—a question to which if there came no answer, to the soul of man all joys and pleasures fade as transient dreams. What to Buddha, what to all men, are the rewards of life, the love of wife, of parents, offspring, the fond memory of those who have passed the chilling gates of death; what the hopes and aspirations that hover round life if they are all

[1] Huxley, "Romanes Lecture," p. 39 (*note* 2).
[2] E. Garnett, "An Imaged World," p. 91.

but mockeries of man's vain efforts to raise himself above the brute beasts? All had better be relinquished than be retained at the relentless nod of a jeering destiny, than grow bright only to be severed by the decrees of an impotent Cosmos, that answers back the moan of suffering with the cold stare of nescience, wherein can be read no gleam of purpose working to an omniscient end. Better for Buddha that he should have cast from him all ties which daily grew closer round him, and made life more dear, than that they should clasp him tighter and drag him down to a darkness profound amid his unavailing cries for help, when neither from Brāhmans nor from burned-offerings could he find the aid for which his soul cried out.

For Buddha, and for all men in whom reasoned thought had risen, the religious systems of the time held forth no hope. The Vedic gods were gods for a conquering folk whose future had but dawned. They were friendly gods who led the way to victory, and so long as victory was assured, a united people sang their praise.

The Sākyan land was far removed from homes where the Aryan brotherhood held its traditions firm amid alien foes. The echoes of an Aryan past that came to its borders were vague and uncertain ere they fell on Buddha's ears. He may have heard of the doctrines of the early "Upanishads,"[1] how rest was to be sought by knowledge of the Brahman and Self. His efforts, after he had left his wife, and child, and fatherland, seem to have been to gain, by asceticism, morbid fancies, and religious austerities, some supernatural or mystic power whereby his soul might rise free from all the trammels of the desires of the body, and be no longer subject to the domain of death. If Buddha was versed in Brāhmanic lore,[2] as many have

[1] Rhys Davids, "American Lectures," p. 29.

[2] *Ibid.*, p. 102, states that Buddha, in his early probation at Rājagriha, received a teaching on the problems "discussed by such *later* schools as the Sānkhya and Vedānta." He continues: "It is certainly evident that Gotama,

sought to prove, he must have been appalled not only by the visions of a hereafter, which confronted himself and those he held dear, but by the drear future which lay before all mankind. Long before his days the weird doctrine of the transmigration of the soul through endless births and re-births had crept its way into the beliefs of the people.

In the early Vedic times there seems to have been no gloom or despair surrounding the idea of death or the hereafter.

Agni [1] was besought to bear those who died to the abode of the Fathers, where there was joy and happiness. Later [2] Agni was declared to be the bond, the bridge leading to the gods, with whom the dead dwell in friendship. The man who sacrifices goes [3] after death to abide with the gods. The more he sacrificed, the greater was his piety, the closer he became in his nature to that of the gods.[4] As the thought grew, it was with his own true body [5] that man gained immortality, and great became the care [6] in Indian life that none of the bones of the deceased were missing when his funeral rites were performed.

There were some who sacrificed, and some who neglected the sacred duty, some who gave rich rewards to the priests, some who were niggardly, against whom the sacred texts are vehement in their denunciations. So for the Aryan

either during or *before* this period, must have gone through a very systematic and continued course of study in all the deepest philosophy of the time." I agree with the learned Professor, with the exception that I do not see that any evidence is forthcoming that Buddha had any such knowledge when he left Kapilavastu; he obtained it in Magadha. Even if the Śānkhya, as a philosophy, existed before the time of Buddha, there is no evidence that it was known to, or influenced, Buddha. *See* Oldenberg, "Buddha," p. 64; Rhys Davids, "American Lectures," p. 29; and for opposite view, Garbe, "Śānkhya Philosophie"; and Huxley, "Romanes Lectures," p. 17.

[1] R.V., ix. 133, 66.

[2] "Taitt. Brāh.," iii. 10, ii. 1.

[3] "Śat. Brāh.," ii. 6, 4, 8.

[4] *Ibid.*, x, 1, 5, 4.

[5] *Ibid.*, iv. 6, 11, xi. 1, 8, 6, xii. 8, 3, 31; Weber, Z.D.M.G., ix. 237 *ff*; quoted in Muir, "Sans. Texts," vol. v. 314-15.

[6] "Śat Brāh.," xi. 6, 3, 11, xiv. 6, 9, 28.

householder there grew to be the rewards and punishments in the next world according to how he performed his duties in this world, according as he completed the full course of the stated sacrifices. The idea was that in the next world his deeds were weighed in a balance,[1] and according to the result his award was meted out, for he "is born into the world which he has made."[2]

So the thought wanders hazily along. The whole world, to the primitive mind, is animated with soul life. The trees, animals, the running brook and solitary mountain, the petrified fossil over which man wonders, the dreaded snake and abhorred reptile, are all endowed equally with souls or spirits; there is no broad line drawn between man and the rest of that into which the Divine has breathed life. So the bewildering idea is set forth—bewildering only to the learned, not to those who love to watch the flowers in the changing warmth and cold of Spring-time, who conjure up the eager contest between St George and the dragon, and who dread to see in May the "Three Great Ice Kings." "Now the Spring assuredly comes into life again out of the Winter, for out of the one the other is born again; therefore, he who knows this is, indeed, born again in this world."[3]

Not in modes of formal thought, but in the dreamy fancy of one who loves to walk in the fallacious paths of specious analogy, comes the reasoning over the soul of him who has not won by his acts release from the common course of Nature's working. "Whoever goes to yonder world not having escaped Death, him he causes to die again and again in yonder world."[4] Of all good acts that man could do, the performance of the sacrifice was highest, and of all sacrifices the Agnihotra sacrifice was best. So "verily he

[1] "Śat. Brâh.," xi. 2, 7, 33, xi. 7, 2, 23.

[2] *Ibid.*, vi. 2, 2, 27:—"Man is born into the world made by him."

[3] *Ibid.*, i. 5, 3, 14.

[4] *See* also *Ibid.*, ii. 3, 3, 1.

that knows that release from death is the Agnihotra, is freed from death again and again."[1]

The full tragedy of this phase of thought, of this destiny of mankind—a destiny to which the direst of Greek tragedies, pursuing to its relentless end the result of act or omission, presents but a pale and colourless contrast—is summed up in the appalling words of the "Chandogya Upanishad,"[2] believed not only in Buddha's time, but also in India to-day: "Those whose conduct here has been good will quickly attain some good birth—the birth of a Brāhman, or of a Kshatriya, or a Vaiśya. But those whose conduct here has been evil will quickly attain an evil birth—the birth of a dog, or a hog, or a *chandāla*."[3] Another "Upanishad," having allotted the place of the Soul to the Moon, sets forth the same idea of transmigration, in more laboured fashion: "According to his deeds he is born again here as a worm, or as an insect, or as a fish, or as a bird, or as a lion, or as a boar, or as a serpent, or as a tiger, or as a man, or as a something else in different places."

Probably no scholar has shown more dogged determination to view Buddhism from a purely historical and philosophic standpoint than Professor Rhys Davids, yet, when he approaches the realms of metempsychosis, he seems almost to shudder at the monstrous aberrations of thought which beset man in his cherished beliefs over the soul theory: "Thus is the soul tossed about from life to life, from billow to billow, in the great ocean of transmigration. And there is no escape save for the very few who, during their birth as men, obtain to a right knowledge of the Great Spirit and then enter into immortality, or as

[1] "Śat. Brāh.," ii. 3, 3, 9; *see* also ii. 3, 3, 8:—"Whoever goes to yonder world not having escaped Death, him he causes to die again and again in yonder world."

[2] "Ch. Up.," v. 10, 7; S.B.E., vol. i.

[3] Offspring of a Sūdra and a Brāhman woman.

the later philosophies taught, are absorbed into the Divine Essence."[1]

Some such doctrines the Buddha must have learned during his early probation near Rājagriha, the capital of Magadha. It was his mission to view with his own master-mind all the current phases of thought that were struggling forth among the scattered people, as the expression of what the ages had produced, and combine them into the structure known as Buddhism. This master-work of Buddha stands out colossal in awe-inspiring loneliness as a memorial that the Eastern world had, for the time, closed itself in from all hope of knowledge of the Divine. It is well typified by the dome-shaped mounds of Sanchi, Bharhut, and Amrāvati, wherein were shut all that was left for the Buddhist to reverence, the relics of the Sākya prince. These mounds remain the outward form of Buddhist thought, just as the Parthenon and the memory of Pallas Athene remain the memorials of Grecian ideals of beauty and of reasoned thought; just as Shah Jahan's Taj Mahal and Akbar's tomb shadow forth the hopes that were bursting forth in India in Mughal times, only to fade away in dreams, as soft and pleasing as those of the sister Taj Mahal and stately bridge that was designed to span the waters of the far-stretching Jumna.

So the dome-shaped mounds in India, left as memorials of the artistic conception of Buddha's mission, tell their own story—the story of how man turned his gaze from the heavens above and entombed his soul, so that never more might his aspiring hopes be roused to fancied dreams by stately minarets or soaring spires.

The new reformer had been born into the world to view, from a lonely standpoint, and weave into an artistic whole, the thoughts the age had brought forth. From the earliest

[1] Rhys Davids, "Hibbert Lectures," p. 86.

Vedic times there were those who had denied the existence of even the Vedic deities.[1]

The Vedas themselves had been denounced, reviled, and held as unworthy the consideration of wise men.[2] Atheists (*nāstikas* = *na asti*, *i.e.* non est) flourished and spread abroad their unbelief. A worldly sect known as the Lokayatas had freely declared:[3]—

"There is no heaven, no final liberation, nor any soul in another world.
Nor do the actions of the four castes, or orders, produce any real effect.
. . . .
While life remains let man live happily, let him feed on *ghee* even though he runs in debt.
When once the body becomes ashes, how can it ever return again?
If he who departs from the body goes to another world,
How is it that he comes not back again, restless for love of his kindred?
Hence it is only as a means of livelihood the Brāhmans have established here
All these ceremonies for the dead—there is no other fruit anywhere.
The three authors of the 'Vedas' were buffoons, knaves and demons."

There is yet another phase of thought which must be considered in connection with the underlying factors out of which grew Buddhism.

In the sixth century B.C., a great reforming preacher, Mahāvira, had spread abroad the doctrines of Pārśva, the founder of the Jaina sect, who had lived in the eighth century B.C.[4] He, like Buddha, was a Kshatriya. His father is said to have been named Siddārtha, a chieftain of the Kundagrama village, his mother being a sister of the chieftain of Vaisāli, the chief town of the Licchavis, and also related to Bimbisāra, King of Magadha. At the age of

[1] R.V., ii. 12, 5:—"They ask, Where is He? Or verily they say of Him, He is not" (Griffith).

[2] Monier-Williams, "Buddhism," p. 8.

[3] Cowell and Gough, "Sarva Darśana Sangraha," p. 10.

[4] "Ind. Ant.," p. 248 (Sept. 1894).

twenty-eight he set forth on his mission, and became known as the Jina, "The Conqueror," and his teaching as Jainism, just as Buddha is known as "The Enlightened," and his teaching properly as Bauddhism.

By the Jains the world is held to be eternal, and made up of atoms. Time revolves in two ever-recurring cycles of fabulous age, in the first of which goodness increases only to decrease in the next. Twenty-four Jinas appeared in the past cycle; they are now reigning as gods; twenty-four have appeared in the present cycle—a cycle in which goodness is ever decreasing—and twenty-four are yet to appear in a future cycle.

The great object of the Jain is to attain victory over all worldly desires; to free his soul and so become divine like unto the Jinas. These were known as Nirgranthas,[1] "those who have no bonds," and in the middle of the fourth century B.C. they parted into two great sects, those known as the Śvetāmbaras, "who are attired in white raiment," and those known as the Digambaras, or "sky-clad," who show how they have cast off from themselves everything of the world by wandering about unclothed. The Jains are still numerous in India,[2] the faith being followed by the wealthy Seths, the great banking families. The costly Jaina temples, where the images of the Jinas live in lonely isolation on the summit of Mount Abu, still preserve the highest ideals of pure Hindu architecture. In many points the history of Jainism closely resembles that of Buddhism, a system from which it was for long considered an offshoot. The Jains, like the Buddhists, have lay members, "Śrāvakas," who are in and of the world, and also ascetic monks, "Yatis," who live apart in monasteries. For the Jaina generally there were three "gems" by which the soul obtained liberation, or "Moksha."

[1] Jacobi, Z.D.M.G., xxxviii. 17; Hopkins, "Rel. of India," p. 284.

[2] "Census of India," (1891):—"Jains now number 409,715; Buddhists only 243,677."

These three were, right insight (*darśana*), right knowledge, and right conduct. In the observance of the last injunction the monastic Jaina monks were vowed never to tell lies; never to steal; never to be immoderate in thought, word or deed; never to desire too much; but above all, never to kill or injure any living thing. So the Jaina monk to-day upholds hospitals for the care of all animals, even for the nurture of foul insects. The water they drink they first strain in hopes of removing all life; they sweep the ground before them as they walk, so that their feet may not fall on any living thing; they even wear veils over their mouths that nothing with life may be drawn in by their breath.

Even if Buddha had not heard in his own home of any of these doctrines of the Vedāntic or Śānkhyan philosophies, of Jainism, of agnosticism, or of the Brahman and Ātman, nevertheless, the spirit of the times was moving towards them, and the practical success of his mission shows that he had, with true insight, set forth an ideal which in the East received assent from wondering myriads of men and women who lived and died in simple and devout reverence of his teaching and his Order. The force he sent forth was sufficient for a time to overshadow that on which the rising power of Brāhmanism was based.

Inasmuch as Buddhism found its truest abiding home in Scythian or Turanian lands, it might be held that it was not the true outcome of Aryan thought, yet a parallel is to be seen in the spread of Christianity among Teutonic races.

When Buddha, at the age of twenty-nine, departed from the northern home of the Sākyas, he made his way towards Rājagriha, where ruled Bimbisāra, the chieftain of the Magadhas, over a district extending over one hundred miles south of the Ganges, and one hundred miles east of the Son. To the north of the Ganges were the Licchavis, whose chieftain, Kataka, ruling at his capital, Vaisāli, was brother to Trisalā, the mother of the Jaina saint, Mahāvīra.

Still further to the east of Magadha was the land of the Angas, with their capital at Chompā, while away to the north-west lay the Kośālas, whose king, Prasenajit, ruled at Srāvasti, whither the ancient capital had been removed from Ayodhya. At Rājagriha Buddha met two Brāhmans,[1] Udraka and Alāra, and from them he learned the means whereby they sought to vanquish all that held them bound to take their part in life—a part which at its best, many of to-day would say, is not worth taking unless some firm faith or trust in its Divine purpose be the guiding light.

From the two Brāhmans Buddha could have obtained no such light. They could but point to their wasted frames, to their own sunken eyes. They could but have told him of their austerities, of their hopes that light might some day come, when the mystery which shrouded their lives would pass away, and they become as gods with insight more than human.

From the two Brāhmans Buddha parted. His quest still lay before him, for still he knew and felt

> "I am as all these men
> Who cry upon their gods and are not heard,
> Or are not heeded.—Yet there must be aid!
> For them, and me, and all, there must be help!"[2]

From Rājagriha he wandered on to the lonely forests of Uruvela, near to the present temple of Buddha Gāyā, south of Patna, where pilgrims now bring from far lands their votive gifts to lay, in lowly reverence, on the spot where the feet of their master and teacher once pressed.

For five weary years Buddha strove to seek out his own salvation. Penances, austerities, fastings and contemplation brought neither superhuman knowledge nor power. Five ascetic sages sat by and watched the lengthened struggle,

[1] Oldenberg, "Buddha," p. 106; Hopkins, "Rel. of India," pp. 303-4 Rhys Davids, "American Lectures," p. 102.

[2] Edwin Arnold, "Light of Asia."

wondering if at last one mortal might pierce the Infinite, and grasp eternal knowledge of the Divine.

From the lips, thin and bereft of colour, there came no murmur; from the eyes, sunk deep beneath the arching brows, there came no gleam to show that the soul of the sage had been quickened by a knowledge more sustaining than earthly food. The Buddha remained silent and suffering. At length in despair he turned from his asceticism, and his five companions left him.

One night—the sacred night of Buddhism—while Buddha dreamed on alone beneath the sacred Bo-tree,[1] whose shade yet falls on Buddhist pilgrims, he clearly grasped in his own mind the whole cause of the world's sorrow, and the means whereby the soul might free itself for ever from the continued course of birth and re-birth. The attainment of enlightenment by Gotama, who by it became the Buddha, "The Enlightened," has been surrounded by later tradition[2] with miraculous events and supernatural portents. When the powers of darkness struggled to hide the light from Sākya Muni, the mountains trembled, the earth shook, the storms broke loose, the sun hid itself away, and the stars moved from their spheres. The truth, however, slowly worked its way to Buddha's soul. Then Māra, "the Evil One," crept close and sought, with soothing words and visions of delight, to stay The Enlightened from proclaiming abroad the knowledge he had attained. Muchalindra, "the King of the Snakes," folded itself as a safeguard round the Buddha's body. Brahmā Sahāmpati descended from his heaven and bade the Muni go forth and free all mankind from the bondage of birth, old age, and death. While Buddha wondered to whom he should first proclaim his doctrine, he learned that his two former teachers, Alāra and Udraka, were dead, so he turned towards Benares to seek out the

[1] *Ficus religiosa.*

[2] Rhys Davids, "American Lectures," p. 104.

five ascetics who had watched his early struggles. He found them seated in the Deer Park, three miles north of Benares, then known as Varānasī. But as he approached they said one to another:[1] "Friends, yonder comes the ascetic, Gotama, who lives in self-indulgence, who has given up his quest and returned to self-indulgence. We shall show him no respect, nor rise up before him, nor take his alms-bowl and his cloak from him; but we shall give him a seat, and he can sit down if he likes." Their subsequent conduct, however, shows how it was Buddha's own personal influence, an influence founded on an absolute belief in himself and in his own mission, supported and extended by his overpowering eloquence, and the mesmeric charm a powerful and determined mind has over others, that won for him success as a teacher and propagator of his doctrines. When all this had departed, Buddhism lived in its purity only so long as those who remembered his personality exercised their influence to preserve the faith simple and uncorrupted.

He was the first to show that the races of India were capable of being infused by a firm master-mind with a common purpose, and of being held together by a common bond of union. It was through the work commenced by Buddha that Asoka,[2] the first temporal Chakravarti, or emperor, was able to unite the scattered Aryan tribes and alien races beneath his sceptre.

Once Buddha's personality faded away, his religion found its chief rallying-point in the cohesion of a mendicant order of monks, who transformed their Buddha into a god,[3] and mingled legend, miracles, idolatrous practices

[1] Oldenberg, "Buddha," p. 125 (quoted from "Mahâvagga," i. 6-10).

[2] Neither Chandragupta nor Bimbisâra were Buddhists, nor Asoka until the twentieth year of his reign.

[3] Rhys Davids, "Buddhism," pp. 200-1, for the rise of the worship of the Buddhist trinity, Maitreya Buddha, Manju Sri, and Avalokitesvara; also p. 128:—"Gautama was very early regarded as omniscient, and absolutely sinless"; p. 189:—"After his death the miracles and exaggeration increase."

and debasing beliefs with the moral teachings of the founder which they had forgotten to follow.

When Buddha approached nearer to the five ascetics, who watched his approach in the Deer Park near Benares, they could no longer abide by their resolution to show him no respect. They rose and prostrated themselves before him, and as they listened to his burning words, poured forth in the soft and pleading Pāli, each of the ascetics felt as though the Master addressed him alone. These five were his first disciples, so that, "at that time there were six Arahats (persons who had reached absolute holiness) in the world."[1]

To the five ascetics the Master first declared that he had at length found the great truth which all had sought —a truth giving freedom from bondage and from re-birth, leading to enlightenment, to *Nirvāna* in this life, and then to *Parinirvāna*, when the body falls to decay bereft of all *Karma*. He then told them how the truth could not be found in wordly pleasures nor yet in morbid asceticism. There was but one path whereby it could be reached. This was the Middle Path, journeyed through by the following of the Eightfold Precepts, whereby he had obtained emancipation of the mind which "cannot be lost; this is my last birth; hence I shall not be born again."[2] This Eightfold Path consisted of Right Views,[3] Right Aspirations,[4] Right Speech,[5] Right Conduct,[6] Right Living,[7] Right Effort,[8] Right Thought,[9] and Right Self-Concentration.[10] Such was the simple Middle Path for

[1] "Mahāvagga," i. 7, 3; S.B.E., vol. xi. (Rhys Davids' translation).

[2] S.B.E., "Mahāvagga," i. 6, 29.

[3] Free from superstition and delusion.

[4] High and worthy of the intelligent, earnest man.

[5] Kindly, open, and truthful.

[6] Peaceful, honest, pure.

[7] Bring hurt or danger to no living thing.

[8] In self-training and self-control.

[9] The active, watchful mind.

[10] In deep meditation on the realities of life.—Rhys Davids, "American Lectures," pp. 137-38.

those to follow who desired to obtain peace, enlightenment, and freedom from re-birth.

The centre point of Buddha's faith, round which all his teaching revolves, was the doctrine of Karma, one of the most important and far-reaching philosophic theories ever reached by the intuitive reasoning powers of man. It was a new and enormous contribution to the sum of human speculation. Its importance in the history of Indian social and political life cannot be over-estimated. No other theory at all similar to it was ever enunciated by any of the philosophic schools of India with the same clearness, the same breadth and depth of view regarding its bearings, and absolute certainty regarding its transcendent importance, as was this master-stroke of one who "saw deeper than the greatest of modern idealists."[1]

Two of the most important philosophic theories which the thought of India has produced—important not only in their practical influence in the past, but in being the two theories forming the whole basis on which the orthodox classes in India at present confront the advances of Christianity—are theories which rest on assumptions incapable of substantiation or proof. They have to be taken on faith, and therein consists the strength of their position. The first is the doctrine of Karma.

The ancient doctrine of transmigration of the soul had taught the Indian sage that: "Every sentient being is reaping as it has sown, if not in this life, then in one or other of the infinite series of antecedent existences of which it is the latest term."[2] It was the act, or character, of individuals "which passed from life to life and linked them in the chain of transmigrations; and they held that it is modified in each life, not merely by confluence of parentage, but by its own acts. They

[1] Huxley, "Romanes Lecture," p. 19.
[2] *Ibid.*, p. 14.

were, in fact, strong believers in the theory, so much disputed at present, of the hereditary transmission of acquired character."[1]

Inasmuch as Buddha denied the existence of a Soul, for which his scheme had no place,[2] he had, by some other theory, to account for that which was continually taking place, the ever-becoming, the never-being.

Buddha had to show a cause for the condition of sorrow into which man is born; he had to give some reason for the necessity of following his Eightfold Path, which had four stages leading from acceptance of his doctrines on to greater and greater freedom from re-birth to absolute Arahatship. If there were no soul, and all enquiry respecting the existence of God were but vain labour, as Buddhism asserted, then there must be some cause to condition the becoming, the re-birth, which Buddha admitted. This re-birth was that of a sentient being in no way connected by bonds of blood with the previous being; it had no bond with the past except through the one mystery of Karma, or act. It must, however,

[1] "That the manifestation of the tendencies of a character may be greatly facilitated or impeded by conditions of which self-discipline, or the absence of it, are among the most important, is indubitable; but that the character itself is modified in this way is by no means so certain. It is not so sure that the *transmitted character* of an evil liver is worse, or that of a righteous man better, than that which he received. Indian philosophy, however, did not admit of any doubt on this subject; the belief in the influence of conditions, notably of self-discipline, on the Karma, was not merely a necessary postulate of its theory of retribution, but it presented the only way of escape from the endless round of transmigrations."—Huxley, "Romanes Lecture," p. 15.

[2] "Granting the premises, I am not aware of any escape from Berkeley's conclusion, that the 'substance' of matter is a metaphysical, unknown quantity, of the existence of which there is no proof. What Berkeley does not seem to have so clearly perceived is that the non-existence of a substance of mind is equally arguable, and that the result of the impartial application of his reasonings is the reduction of the All to co-existences and sequences of phenomena, beneath and beyond which there is nothing cognoscible. It is a remarkable indication of the subtlety of Indian speculation that Gautama should have seen deeper than the greatest of modern idealists."—Huxley, "Romanes Lecture," p. 19.

be clearly borne in mind how this theory differs from the modern theory of evolution and the disputed theory of transmission of character from parent to offspring.

When a man died, when the elements which Buddha held to constitute man passed away—and in these elements there was no abiding soul—all that remained, according to Buddha, was his Karma—his doing, the result of his good and evil actions, of his words, and of his thoughts. This Karma had to work out its potentiality; it had to receive punishment or reward; so a new conscious existence, unconnected with the old, was produced as a habitation for its working.

The assumption was an ingenious hypothesis to account for transmigration without the necessity of assuming the existence of a soul, or of any underlying substance of matter or of mind.

It is but seldom that the weakness of the entire system of Buddhism is recognised. Professor Rhys Davids, who has so clearly recognised the historical importance of Buddhism, has pointed out[1] the factors which inspired the faith of its followers: "On one side of the keystone is the necessity of justice, on the other the law of causality." At the same time he clearly recognises how they "have failed to see that the very keystone itself, the link between one life and another, is a mere word."[2]

According to Buddha, man is made up of aggregates, or Skandas, of "*material* qualities, *sensations*, abstract *ideas*, *tendencies* of mind, and mental *powers*."[3]

Nowhere amid these Skandas, nor in their sub-divisions, is there any such thing as Soul. The Skandas exist alone, ever passing from change to change, leaving no abiding

[1] Rhys Davids, "Buddhism," p. 105. [2] *Ibid.*, p. 106.

[3] *Ibid.*, p. 90; or Oldenberg, "Buddha" p. 128 (*note*):—"Corporeal form, sensations, perceptions, conformations (or aspirations), and consciousness."

principle whatsoever. When a sage attains Nirvana, when there is no result of his Karma calling for new existence to work out its effects, the body truly remains, and "while his body shall remain, he will be seen by gods and men but after the termination of life, upon the dissolution of the body, neither gods nor men will ever see him."

The first of the "Four Noble Truths" laid down by Buddha shows that sorrow is inseparable from birth, old age, disease, and death; from union with those not loved, and separation from those loved; from non-attainment of what one desires—in fact, a clinging to all that springs from the five Skandas.

The second "Truth" was, that the thirst (*Trishnā*) for existence led to new becomings "accompanied by pleasure and lust, finding its delight here and there." [1]

The third "Truth" was, that sorrow comes only from "the destruction in which no craving remains over, of this very thirst; the laying-aside of, the getting-rid of, the being-free from, the harbouring no longer of, this thirst." [2]

The fourth "Truth" was, that if the Eightfold Path of Right Discipline be followed, suffering will be extinguished. By following the Eightfold Path, the Buddhist first frees himself from all delusion of Self, from doubt as to the teachings of Buddha, from trust in rites and ceremonies, and reaches a stage, "better than universal empire in this world, better than going to heaven, better than lordship over all worlds." [3] By further progress in the Right Path the Buddhist becomes almost freed from all bodily passion, from ill-feelings towards others, from desire to live on earth; his Karma will but act to produce one new birth. So the course goes on, until all remnant of longing for life on earth or in heaven, all pride, ill-feeling, bodily passion,

[1] S.B.E., "Mahāvagga," i. 6, 20.
[2] Rhys Davids, "American Lectures," p. 137.
[3] *Ibid.*, "Buddhism," p. 108.

self-righteousness, and ignorance vanish, the man becoming a perfect Arahat having attained Nirvana.[1]

The Nirvana gained, there ensues the one great sinless and actionless state of mind, in which the Karma is deprived of "potential." The "wheel of life"[2] stands poised, there being no longer a motive force, springing out from ignorance and leading on to despair, to speed it on its saddened round of desire, attachment, birth, death, and re-birth.

It was strength, and daring strength, that sent Buddha forth to seek out for his times some solution of the question of how the Creator

> "Would make a world and keep it miserable,
> Since, if, all powerful, he leaves it so,
> He is not good, and if not powerful,
> He is not God?"[3]

It was genius unequalled among the sons of men that inspired the Buddha's teaching. It was genius, commanding in its dictatorial strength, that held together his Order. It was genius, the first and last that India saw, that, in its lofty aims and universality, foreshadowed the possibility of uniting the people into one great nationality, if such had ever been possible.

It cast no shadow over Indian thought. It gave it in the doctrine of Karma the best and surest motive it could ever reach unaided for the deepening of a sense of individual responsibility,[4] for act, thought, deed, or speech.

[1] It is neither annihilation nor everlasting bliss, it is "but an epithet of a state of mind to be reached and enjoyed only in the present life."—J.R.A.S. (1897), p. 407.

[2] Rhys Davids, "American Lectures," pp. 120-21.

[3] Arnold, Sir E., "Light of Asia."

[4] *See* an important article (J.R.A.S. 1897, p. 410) by Mrs Rhys Davids, pointing out the danger of introducing "ill-fitting Western terminology" into questions dealing with Eastern modes of thought. It may be generally said that all the plausible similarities pointing to connection between Eastern and Western modes of thought, are either fallacious or unhistorical. Their discussion would entail a considerable space, and the result, in nearly all cases, would be so problematic that they have been unnoticed to a great extent in

In viewing Buddhism in its historical significance, in its being the culminating point to which the wave of Indian thought had reached, the wreckage of the past that still clung around it, and was carried on with it, must not be confused with the wave itself. Amid this wreckage much can be found to delight the prurient mind, much from which a system could be framed for morbid mysticism, and much to encourage those who seek for themselves a reputation for the possession of prophetic and supernatural powers, such as were undoubtedly ascribed by the common mind to Buddha, if not in his own days, at least shortly after his decease. To those who study the past of India down through the ages, and look for the future which is yet to dawn, when all her latent intellectual and spiritual forces will once again awaken to add their strength to the history of the world's progress, the chief point of interest in Buddhism is to ascertain how high the wave of thought reached in Buddha's time, not to probe how low to the earth the instincts and superstitions of the mass could creep.

Buddha, in his own life-time, could defend his teaching and maintain his Order by his own power of eloquence and by the force of his own character and personal influence. Of these the Order was deprived on his death. The stately structure that the architectonic genius of Buddha had raised to impress and fascinate the Eastern world had to be sustained by means other than those which the master-builder could alone employ. So long as he lived he claimed no Divine birth, no miraculous power, no supernatural insight.

From the literature as we now possess it—for we possess

the body of this manual. The author is not prepared to admit any classical influence on the Indian drama, and can only see very special and exceptional evidences of Greek or Roman art having affected Indian architecture. The whole of Indian thought and art is impressed indelibly with an individual stamp of its own, and for the present the evidences of this must remain more a matter of feeling than one for profitable discussion.

no work of which even the author or date is known before the middle of the third century B.C.,[1] and books in manuscript[2] are not known until long afterwards—it is almost impossible to extricate the real teachings of Buddha as he formulated them, yet the earliest burial mounds erected to his memory, and temples wherein his sayings were recited, show plainly that the whole system is free from superstition, idolatry, or the worship of Buddha as a divine being to whom miraculous or supernatural powers were ascribed.

For forty-four years Buddha wandered to and fro, enrolling Brāhmans, Kshatriyas, Vaiśyas, low-caste men, and even women within his Order. There was no distinction made on account of caste; the Buddhist monks had but to declare that they desired to take refuge in Buddha, his Law, and his Order. Once they donned the orange-coloured robes of Buddhism and assumed the Eastern form of tonsure, they abandoned their families, went forth as mendicants to live a life of seclusion, meditation, chastity, and moderation in all things. Far and wide the monks were sent, yet never in twos, to preach the fame of Buddha, and proclaim the knowledge that had dawned from out the Sākyan race. Buddha himself journeyed all through the Aryan homes inculcating everywhere his Four Great Truths, his Eightfold Path, and Four Stages leading to Nirvana. To those who sought his help and counsel he told the stories of the good deeds done in former births by good or evil livers, the Karma of which was but working out its results in the joys and sorrows the people suffered. From Magadha to Kapilavastu, from Kośāla to Videha, his fame went forth: it was soon evident

[1] "The Kathā Vatthu: or, Account of Opinion," "written by Tissa, son of Mogali, about the year 250 B.C."—Rhys Davids, "American Lectures," p. 64.

[2] Professor Bendall, whose search for Sanskrit MSS. in Nepal have yielded such valuable results, informs me that an MS. of the third century A.D., in Kharosthi character, has been found recently by a Russian Consul in Kashgaria. *See* also J.R.A.S. (April, 1897).

that a new power had arisen among the Aryan people, and that strange changes would arise from out the new awakened life. At Magadha, the chieftain, Bimbisāra, listened to the words of Buddha, and gave him a grove[1] close to his capital. At Kośāla the chieftain, Prasenajit, received him at his capital Srāvastī,[2] and there a wealthy merchant, Anāthapindika, purchased land for golden pieces sufficient to cover its extent, and gave it to Buddha, and there the monastery, Jetāvana, arose.

At Kapilavastu he enrolled his son, Rāhula, in the Order, but conceded to the request of his father, Suddodhana, that no more would sons be admitted to the Order without the consent of their parents. At first the people cried out against Buddha and his Order, for the system meant the destruction of family life. This Buddha could not help. The Buddhist had to remain celibate, for a woman was, above all things, to be avoided; she was as "a burning pit of live coals."[3] At length the Buddha gave way so far as to allow women to enter the Order, and his widowed wife, Yasodharā, was admitted in the fifth year of his travels, and in the following year, Kshemā, the wife of Bimbisāra.

In temporal affairs Buddha's influence was soon felt. In a dispute between the Sākyans and Koliyans respecting their claims to the waters of their boundary river, Kohāna, he had to adjudicate. When Ajātasatru[4] ascended the throne of Magadha—it is said by the murder of his father, Bimbisāra—he consulted Buddha as to the success of an expedition he was about to undertake against the advancing tribe of Wajjian Turanians, north of the Ganges, and Buddha's answer was that those who remained united, and held to their ancient customs, would retain their independence.

[1] Veluvana, identified in Cunningham's "Ancient Geography of India," p. 451.

[2] *Ibid.*, p. 407. [3] "Cullavagga." [4] 485 to 453 B.C.

Towards the end of his career, in the forty-fourth season of his itinerary, Buddha crossed the Ganges at the site of the modern city of Patna. There he found the ministers of Ajātasatru laying the foundations of Pātaliputra, the modern Patna, a city destined to become the capital of the rising kingdom of Magadha, and the centre of Indian life for almost one thousand years, a greatness foretold by Buddha. Thence he passed on to Vaisāli, the chief town of the Licchavis, whose proud nobles he insulted by receiving, in preference to theirs, the hospitality of the dancing-girl, Ambapālī, who refused to give up to her rivals her right to feed the Buddha: "My lords, were you to offer all Vaisāli, with its subject territory, I would not give up so honourable a feast."

From Vaisāli he journeyed on to Belugāmaka, and thence to Kusinagara, a town eighty miles east of Kapilavastu, and one hundred and twenty north-east of Benares.

To his favourite disciple, Ānanda, he poured forth his last injunctions: "I, too, Ānanda, am now grown old and full of years; my journey is drawing to its close. I have reached my sum of days; I am turning eighty years of age. Therefore, O Ānanda, be ye lamps unto yourselves. Be ye a refuge to yourselves. Betake yourselves to no external refuge. Hold fast to the truth as to a lamp. Hold fast as a refuge to the truth. Look not for refuge to any one besides yourselves."

To Ānanda he also declared: "I have preached the truth, Ānanda, without making any distinction of exoteric or esoteric doctrine; for, in respect of the truths, the Tathāgata has no such thing as the clenched fist of a teacher who keeps some things back."[1]

To his disciples Buddha left no other guide save the Law and Rules of his Order. They were to work out their

[1] Rhys Davids.

own salvation, ever following the Eightfold Path. His last words for the Mendicant Brotherhood were an exhortation that they should remember how "everything that cometh into existence is ever passing on; permanency abideth nowhere; and so strive without ceasing."[1]

The clearer the simplicity of Buddha's teaching stands out, the more sublime rises the figure of the Eastern sage with saddened face and folded hands, a man born of woman, not divine nor arrogating to himself any divinity, sending forth his plaintive wail that man is for ever shut out from piercing the mysteries of creation so long as he hopes to find the clue through his own limited intuitions of time, space, and cause.

It was not long after the death of Buddha that strange changes crept over the land as well as over the spirit of his religion. The year before Buddha's death, Ajātasatru, the King of Magadha, conquered Srāvasti, the chief town of the Kośālas and centre of Buddhism, and razed to the ground Kapilavastu.

Not much more than one hundred and fifty years from the date of the death of Buddha, Chandragupta,[2] with whom the successor of Alexander the Great in the East was forced to make a treaty, became King of Magadha, and Emperor of all North India, an empire consolidated by the greatest native ruler India has seen, the famed Asoka, the Constantine of Buddhism, whose life and deeds have, strange to say, found no place in the "Rulers of India" Series. Though Asoka adopted the Buddhist faith, many changes had taken place in it since it had lost the guiding hand of its founder.

On the death of Buddha, five hundred of his disciples gathered together in a cave, known as the Satapanni Cave, near Rājagriha, where all the teachings, the rules, and

[1] Oldenberg, "Buddha," p. 202; *see* also Rhys Davids, "Buddhism," p. 83.

[2] 315 to 291 B.C.

precepts, as remembered by those who had listened to Buddha's words, were collected together, learned, and recited by the whole Council, so that they should ever be remembered. The stricter Buddhists of Ceylon hold that in these Pāli books of the three Pitakas, they possess the full doctrines of Buddha as chanted at the first Council.

One hundred years rolled on during which time but little more is known of the Buddhists. India was on the verge of revolution. The Empire of the Magadhas had not only broken in pieces the separate power of the outlying chieftains, and brought them under its own sway, but low-caste usurpers[1] were to seize the empire for themselves, while the time was approaching when Alexander the Great was to break through the isolation which separated India from communion with the thought and beliefs of the Western world.

The second great Buddhist Council met at Vaisāli, the ancient capital of the Wajjians, in 377 B.C., and signs of coming changes were apparent. The edifice raised by Buddha was to receive the first rude shock which ultimately shattered it to pieces in India, and left its crumbling ruins to form a relic of the past in Ceylon, Burma, and Siam, and an ignoble and debasing refuge for the myriad peoples classed as Buddhists in China and Tibet. The Wajjians of Vaisāli, at the Council, strove to formulate ten indulgences, including the right of the Buddhists to receive gold and silver, and over these ten indulgences the Council divided. With the Wajjians the Buddhists of Mālwā joined, while the representatives of the more remote outlying Southern and Western countries clung to the older and more orthodox teaching of Buddha. But of the orthodox and un-orthodox parties, eighteen sects arose, all belonging to the

[1] The Sisunāga dynasty of Magadha lasted from 600 B.C. to 370 B.C., and then the Sūdra dynasty of the Nandas held possession for fifty years, till the time of Chandragupta, 32 B.C.

Little Vehicle, or Southern school,[1] and not to the Northern, or Turanian school, which followed what came to be known as the Great Vehicle, a debased form of Buddhism. The unorthodox party subsequently formed a council of their own, known as the Great Council, and by the Southern school their proceedings were denounced as heretical:—

> "They broke up the old scriptures and made a new recension.
> A discourse put in one place they put in another.
>
> . . . .
>
> These monks, who knew not what had been spoken at length,
> And what had been spoken concisely,
> What was the obvious, and what the higher meaning,
> Attached new meaning to new words as if spoken by the Buddha,
> And destroyed much of the spirit by holding to the shadow of the letter."[2]

Henceforth the history of Buddhism in India no longer touches the life-history of the thought of the people. It merges itself into the political history of the time, being used as a state religion to support the authority and position of emperors whose existence it had made possible.

In the early burial mounds, such as that of Bharhut, where the freest and most artistic indigenous work in sculpture that India has ever produced is to be found, the bas-reliefs merely depict the good deeds done by Buddha in previous births; and in the early temples, such as those of the Lomas Rishi, and those at Bhāja, and Kārli, between Bombay and Poona, there is no trace of idolatrous worship of Buddha or infusion of debasing superstition or primitive native cults. All is severe and simple, such as Buddha himself might have designed. In

[1] Rhys Davids, J.R.A.S. (1892-3); Dutt, "Ancient India," vol. ii. p. 295, where he states that the "Eastern opinions were subsequently upheld by the Buddhists of the Northern (Turanian) school."

[2] Rhys Davids, "Buddhism," p. 217 (quoting the "Dīpavamśa").

the later burial mounds, such as those at Sānchi, somewhere about 250 B.C. to the first century A.D., and Amrāvati, perhaps one hundred years later—domes adorned with all the art which India could furnish forth or bring to her aid from foreign lands—Buddha is fashioned as a god, not man, crowned with a nimbus, guarded by snakes, while near at hand are sculptured trees and snakes all equally entitled to worship. In time the old forms of spirit-worship grew again and claimed the people's superstitious awe. The Soul of man assumed its old place. Buddha became the immaculate offspring of his mother, Māyā; he was enthroned a god in the highest heaven, there to be adored in an outward form of worship, more simple in its forms, and more congenial to the monks and laity than the tedious following of his precepts. Bodhisatvas—those enlightened saints who have deemed it best not to follow Buddha's path and gain Nirvana, but allowed their Karma to work so that their good deeds might benefit humanity—were placed side by side with Buddha, and claimed the reverence once paid solely to the founder of the Buddhist doctrines. The whole future history of Buddhism in India is the history of the receding of the wave of thought that in the sixth century B.C. had reached its culminating point. The surging force that sent it onward was Brāhmanism, and that was a force with strength enough to sweep Buddhism from before its path, and drive it to its natural resting-place amid the Scythian race. The final wave of Brāhmanism covered in its course all India, and there it still rests, so that the dove may wing its way to and fro and never find a resting-place from which it can discern any sign that the flood may pass away, and leave the land and people free from its depths of brooding waters.

CHAPTER VIII.

THE POWER OF THE BRĀHMANS.

WHILE Buddha held aloft the standard of revolt against priestly hierarchy, endeavouring to establish among the people of the land through which he passed a religious order, whose rallying point was a disregard of all distinction founded on race, class, or caste, the Brāhman power was carrying on the ancient tradition of its own past.

The Brāhmans had been for long the sole custodians of the treasured wealth of Aryan lore. They had grown to power side by side with kings and chieftains. They held the sacred guardianship of the mysteries of the sacrificial cult, the necessity of which was, from an unknown past, implanted in the very mental fibre of those who gathered round the smoke-ascending incense. The power which Buddha strove to eradicate had its roots implanted in the religious, social, and racial instincts of the Aryan folk. So long as this was so, and so long as Brāhmanism allowed not its strength to be wholly sapped by the ever-increasing foreign elements with which it was surrounded, its vitality remained unimpaired.

Down to the present day Brāhmanism preserves its power through all the wreck of ages—possibly as a mere phantom shadow of its past—because those it admits within its ranks acknowledge not only the high claims of the Aryan priesthood to be the custodians of Divine ordinances, but also bow before the laws and customs of caste, which ever tend to preserve them from change in creed, thought, or mode of life.

Buddhism, viewed from its political aspect, strove to break through those mighty barriers which separated race from race and caste from caste. It was a consummation which even centuries of advanced thought have been unable to accomplish in the West, even between the neighbouring Celts and Teutons, where none but a Celt feels how deep the separation lies.

India saw the fatuity of Buddha's efforts, not in the thrusting out of his religion by the Brāhmanic power, but in the impossibility for an Asoka, a Sivajī, or Ranjīt Singh,[1] to combine the varied peoples of India into one united whole, capable of sending forth the message that, as their land holds one-fifth of the human race, they can demand a recognition of their right to stand forth as more than a subject people.

From the extreme north-west, in early days, the Aryans had spread their influence from the sacred Sarasvatī to far beyond Magadha in the east, so that the land where they settled became renowned as Aryāvarta, "the land of the Aryans," where "the rule of conduct which prevails is authoritative."[2] From the Himālayan mountains south to the Vindhya range, over the rich land where the black antelope wanders,[3] the Brāhmans established their sway,

[1] The failure of Akbar is not a case in point.

[2] "Baudhāyana," i. 1, 2, 9; "Vasishta," i. 10.

[3] *Ibid.*, i. 13; "Baudhāyana," i. 1, 2, 12. "The Oryx cervicapra selects for its home the well-cultivated rich plains of India only, and is entirely wanting in the sandy, mountainous, or forest districts, which are now, just as in ancient times, the portion of the aboriginal tribes."—Bühler, S.B.E., vol. xiv. p. 3 (*note*).

holding that where they dwelt could alone be found "spiritual pre-eminence."[1] Down the valley of the Indus other tribes, such as the Yādava, went and made their settlement in Sind; others took up their abode in the Panjāb, the Land of the Five Rivers. For long the Vindhya range shut out the south from the Aryan advance. As time went on,[2] even this geographical barrier to all incursion from the north gave way before the fair-skinned race that spread along the Narbadā and Tapti, across the Deccan, so that even before the Christian era a great kingdom—that of the Andhra[3]—was established between the Krishna and Godavari, with its capital at Amrāvati, not fifty miles from the eastern sea. As the Aryan people spread to the further east and to the south, the Brāhmans followed in the wake of the conquering chiefs, gaining reward in land and wealth for their learning, sacred knowledge, and the right they held to dictate the laws and ordinances of the people. Writing must have been known in those days,[4] but the Brāhmans preferred to hold their sacred texts preserved in their own memories, so that

[1] "Baudhāyana," i. 1, 2, 12; "Vasishta," i. 13.

[2] Even earlier than the sixth century B.C. Barth, "Ind. Ant." (1894), p. 246; *see* Burnell quoted, p. 91; Nelson, "View of Hindu Law"; Bühler, S.B.E., vol. ii. p. xxxvi.: "There can be no doubt that the South of India has been conquered by the Aryans, and has been brought within the pale of Brahmanical civilisation . . . long before the authentic history of India begins, at the end of the fourth century B.C." Baden-Powell, J.R.A.S. (1897), p. 247; "Study of the Dakhan Villages":—"At the western extremity the 'Vindhyan' barrier ceases, some way before the coast is reached, and thus the interesting country of Gujarāt is open . . . and once in Gujarāt, it would not be difficult to dominate the Narbadā valley, and to extend to the Tapti valley, to Berār, and to the Dakhan."

[3] S.B.E., vol. ii. p. xxxvi.

[4] For the Northern alphabet, known as Kharosthi, used in Asoka's inscriptions, and on the Græco-Indian coins, and derived from the Aramaic alphabet, used by the Achæmenian dynasty, ruling N.W. of India from 550 B.C. to the time of Alexander the Great, 327 B.C., as well as for the Brahmi alphabets, derived from Phœnician traders, *see* Bühler, "Indische Palæographie," p. 19, *et seq.*

as far as possible—for Aryans other than the Brāhmans claimed a right to be taught the texts—their power and influence should remain in their own hands.

Trained as the memories of the Brāhmans were—and even yet there are Brāhmans able to repeat the Vedic text of their own school by heart, and others who learn the whole grammar of Pānini, with all the "Vārtikhas," or explanation of Kātyāyana, and the interpolations of the "Mahābhāshya" of Patanjali—it would have been impossible thus to preserve, free from corruption, the long prose ramblings of the Brāhmans, and the later sacred literature. At every centre of Brāhmanism there were schools for imparting instructions in the sacred texts, and from these schools trained Brāhmans went forth to act as priests, advisers, and counsellors of kings and chieftains, or to become teachers of their particular recension of the "Veda," and subsidiary treatises founded thereon. The rules for the Vedic sacrifices, for the domestic rites, for the construction of the altars, and for the duties and customs of the Aryans, were therefore reduced to the most concise and condensed form possible, and strung together in leading aphorisms, or "Sūtras," so that they might be easily carried in the memory. These "Sūtras" were not held, like the previous literature, to be of Divine revelation. They were professedly compiled by human authors for the convenience of teaching the essential elements of the subjects they expound. So there grew to be different "Sūtras" ascribed to different authors, who followed in their teaching one or other of the recensions of the four "Vedas" preserved in their family.[1]

[1] *See* Max Müller, letter to Prof. Henry Morley, S.B.E., vol. ii. (Preface) pp. ix., x. The "Sūtras" relating to the Vedic sacrifices were known as the "Śrauta Sūtras"; those of the domestic rites, the "Grihya Sūtras"; those relating to laws, the "Dharma Sūtras"; and those relating to the building of the altars, which dealt with geometry, the "Sulva Sūtras." The whole four being known as the "Kalpa Sūtras."

It may be safe to take the whole of this Sūtra period as extending from the fifth to the first century B.C.[1]

One Brāhmanic family, known as the Mānavas, followed their own recension of the "Black Yajur Veda," and though the Sūtra Aphorisms of their laws are now lost, they are often quoted, and from them the later metrical law book, popularly known as the "Laws of Manu," was compiled. The earliest work in which an account of the laws and customs of the Aryans is to be found, is that known as the "Aphorisms of Gautama," a Brāhman law-giver, who followed the recension of the "Sama Veda" of his own school. Gautama was succeeded by Baudhāyana, whose teaching is accepted in India, south of the Vindhyan range[2] of mountains, after whom came Āpastamba in the fifth century, B.C.,[3] who, like Baudhāyana, followed the "Black Yajur Veda," and is of authority in the south.[4] The school of the fourth great law compiler, Vasishta,[5] who followed the "Rig Veda," was probably that in vogue in a school of North India.[6] From the Brāhmanic codes of law, it can be clearly seen that, wherever the Brāhmans spread over India, north of the Vindhya, and south to the Godavari, the ideal aimed at, whatever the practice may have been, was to preserve the sharp distinction between the Aryan race and the aboriginal inhabitants; to stereotype for ever the traditions that had set the priestly clans as custodians of

[1] Max Müller fixes the date of the Sūtra period between 600 and 200 B.C. Bühler places the origin of the Āpastambiya school probably "in the last five centuries before the beginning of the Christian era."—S.B.E., vol. ii. p. xviii. *See* "Jaina Sūtras," p. 30; "Encyclopædia Britannica," p. 279; "Ind. Ant." (1894), p. 247; Jolly, "Recht und Sitte," pp. 3, 6.

[2] "There are also some faint indications that the Andhra country is the particular district to which Baudhāyana belonged."—Bühler, S.B.E., vol. xiv. p. xliii.

[3] *Ibid.*, vol. ii. p. 43.

[4] *Ibid.*

[5] For connection with the Vasishta of the "Rig Veda," *see* S.B.E., vol. xiv. p. 12.

[6] *Ibid.*, vol. xiv. p. 22.

the Divine decrees and expounders of the laws and customs of the people.

The dark-skinned Sūdras,[1] the aboriginal settlers, were outside the Aryan pale. If the Sūdra "assumes a position equal to that of a twice-born man in sitting, in lying down, in conversation, or on the road, he shall undergo corporal punishment."[2]

No pride of conquering race, or pride of white-skinned birth could run higher than it did in India over two thousand years ago. Should a Sūdra dare raise his eyes to an Aryan woman, the law declared that he should be slain or mutilated. If he listened to a recitation of the Vedic texts his ears were to be filled with molten lac or tin; if he repeated the sacred words his tongue was to be cut out; if he remembered them, "his body shall be slit in twain."[3] The penalty for the slaughter of a Sūdra was the same as that for killing "a flamingo, a crow, an owl, a frog, or a dog."[4] Elsewhere a higher price was placed on the dark man's skin, the penalty for slaying a Sūdra being placed at ten cows.[5] The sole object for which the Sūdra was created was servitude; yet contact with him was so abhorred that "a Brāhman who dies with the food of a Sūdra in his stomach will become a village pig in his next birth, or be born in the family of that Sūdra."[6] Food touched by a Sūdra becomes unfit for eating.[7] Should an Aryan, when eating, even be touched by a Sūdra, he had to abandon his food.[8]

1 "Nous ne saurions discerner si la population comprise sous la dénomination de Sūdras était uniquement composée de ces éléments aborigènes qui rencontrèrent les Aryens en immigrant du nord-ouest dans l'Inde, ou si elles englobaient des éléments mélangés. La point est secondaire. D'Aryens à Sūdras il y a certainement à l'origine une opposition de race, qu'elle soit plus ou moins absolue."—Senart, "Les Castes dans l'Inde," p. 146.

2 "Gautama," xii. 7; "Āpastamba," S.B.E., vol. ii. 10, 27, 16; "Manu," viii. 281.

3 "Gautama," xii. 6.

4 "Baudhāyana," i. 10, 19, 6.

5 "Baudhāyana," i. 10, 19, 2.

6 "Vasishta," vi. 27.

7 "Āpastamba," i. 5, 16, 22.

8 *Ibid.*, i. 5, 17, 1; ii. 2, 3, 4.

Āpastamba,[1] however, also declares that a Sūdra may prepare the food of a householder if he is under the superintendence of men of the three higher castes. Gautama,[2] while laying down that the duty of a Sūdra is to serve the three higher castes, to wear their cast-off shoes and garments, to eat the remnants of their food, shows that the rules of class differences had not in his time crystallised themselves into the strict laws of the professional and trade castes of later times. His laws state that the Sūdra may live by mechanical arts. The laws of Manu, some three hundred years later, declare that a Sūdra could only support himself by handicraft when he was unable to find service under a twice-born Aryan, or when he was in danger of dying from hunger.

From intermarriage, and from all fellowship and contact with the Sūdras, the three Aryan classes of Brāhmans, and Kshatriyas, and Vaiśyas were, above all things, exhorted to abstain. The Sūdra race was a burial-ground,[3] therefore "let one not give advice to a Sūdra, nor eat what remains from his table, nor let him explain the holy law to such a man, nor order him (to perform) a penance."[4] The twice-born Aryan who "declares the law to such a man, and he who instructs him in (the mode of) expiating (sin), sinks together with that very man into the dreadful hell."

The practical tendency of such rules was to exclude the great mass of the population from entering into combination, or alliance, with the Aryan race to form a new nationality.[5]

1 "Āpastamba," x. 55-67.

2 *See* also *Ibid.*, x. 40, where a Sūdra of eighty years of age was to be honoured.

3 *Ibid.*, i. 3, 9, 9; "Vasishta," xviii. 11.

4 "Vasishta," xviii. 14, 15; "Manu," iv. 80-81.

5 "The Indian caste system is a highly developed expression of the primitive principle of *taboo*, which came into play when the Aryans first came into peaceful contact with the platyrhine race, which we may provisionally call Dravidian. This principle derived its initial force from the sense of difference of race as indicated by difference of colour, and its great subsequent development has

The division between race and race, thus stereotyped by the Brāhmanic laws, was to penetrate even further as the tendency became stronger for each separate group to formulate for itself its own peculiar laws and customs, and to engage only in such occupations as were hereditary. Intercommunication, eating or drinking with members of outside groups was surrounded with the same Divine sanction as the Brāhmans fulminated against those of the Aryan race who mingled, ate, or drank with the darker-skinned Sūdras.

The offspring of a Sūdra with a Brāhman woman became a Chandāla,[1] whom "it is sinful to touch . . . to speak to, or to look at."[2] The son of a Brāhman and a Sūdra woman is as "that of one who, though living, is as impure as a corpse."[3] By the Brāhmanic law the varied peoples and races of India sprang from the forbidden union between those of a different class. The offspring, for instance, of a Sūdra and Vaiśya became a Māgadha,[4] with whom the Yāvanas, the Ionians, or Bactrian Greeks were classed likewise as descendants of a Sūdra woman.

been due to a series of fictions by which differences of occupations, differences of religion, changes of habitat, trifling divergences from the established standard of custom, have been assumed to denote corresponding differences of blood, and have thus given rise to the formation of an endless variety of endogamous groups."—Risley, "Study of Ethnology in India" (*Anthropological Journal*, 1891, p. 260). Mr J. Kennedy, in a peculiarly instructive review of "The Tribes and Castes of the North-Western Provinces and Oudh," by W. Crooke, has summarised the results of Mr Crooke's laborious work by his conclusion:—"The cephalic index proves that the whole population has a large intermixture of Dravidian blood; the nasal index shows, with equal clearness, that the higher castes are of purer blood than the lower." The question of caste and nationality therefore reduces itself, according to Mr Kennedy, to this position:—"We know on historic and linguistic grounds that the Dravidian population which covered Northern India were invaded at various times by Aryan and Turanian tribes. These invaders were exogamous, and intermarried freely with the aborigines; they subsequently formed themselves into endogamous groups, and the whole social hierarchy now professes to be based on a superiority of descent."—J.R.A.S., July 1897.

[1] "Vasishta," xviii. 1.
[2] "Vasishta," xviii. 10.
[3] "Āpastamba," ii. 1, 2, 8.
[4] "Baudhāyana," i. 9, 7.

To Baudhāyana,[1] the inhabitants of Mālwā, Behar, Guzārat, the Deccan, Sind, and the South Panjāb were all of mixed origin and not pure Aryans. For an Aryan who visited the people of the Panjāb, those of South India, or those of Bengal, a penance had to be performed; while "he commits sin through his feet who travels to the country of the Kalingas.[2] This prohibition against visiting tribes held to be degraded, such as the Kalingas, the people dwelling south of Orissa to the mouths of the Krishna, shows clearly how the Aryan law-givers strove, with what at first sight seems an infatuation almost suicidal, to curb any tendency towards cohesion of the varied people, or intrusion of outside influence which might have infused the old with new life. The power of these Brāhmanic laws in their own sphere was no mere phantom. Down to to-day, no Brāhman can dwell among the nations of the West without risk of forfeiting his social rank, or without being obliged to perform costly and irksome penances on his return home. The history of this subject is dismal, and would be trivial were it not that it forms the turning-point for the future of India. It shows how the Aryans spread among inferior races in numbers insufficient to exterminate them, or drive them from before their path, as was done by the Aryans in America or Australia. They dared not chance the risk of intermingling with them, and depend on their own physique and constant recruitment from new arrivals to preserve their own racial characteristics predominant. As a consequence, the Brāhmans followed the only course open to them if they were to preserve their own national characteristics, and impress their language and culture, such as it was, over the lands where they spread. They had to hold themselves, as far as possible, free from any contaminating influence which might probably have undermined their very existence as a more

[1] "Baudhāyana," i. 1, 2. [2] *Ibid.*, i. 1, 2, 15.

gifted, more refined race, with higher developed mental tendencies than the dark-skinned people with whom they found themselves in contact. As the Brāhmans spread in ever-diminishing numbers to the extreme south, into Bengal and Orissa, the disaster followed which the race foresaw, and in their own wisdom sought to provide against, for in these lands it would often be impossible to discern how those dark-skinned Brāhmans, who claim Aryan ancestry, have preserved any of the typical Aryan characteristics; they have, in fact, been swamped by intermarriage with other peoples.[1]

One very important statement of Baudhāyana[2] shows how confusion had already sprung up in his time, and how carefully it had to be guarded against. He states that in the south the custom was for Brāhmans to eat in the company of one uninitiated,[3] "to eat with one's own wife, to eat stale food, or marry the daughter of a maternal uncle or of a paternal aunt." He also states that in the north, Brāhmans, as they do now in Kashmīr,[4] were wont to deal in wool. There were also those who drank spirituous liquors—an evil which is becoming all too prevalent in India—and of which Āpastamba declared, "A drinker of spirituous liquor shall drink exceedingly hot liquor so that he dies."[5]

Another custom of the northern Brāhmans was to go to

[1] Senart refers to Mr Nesfield in the following words:—"La communauté de profession est, à ses yeux, le fondement de la caste—il exclut délibérément toute influence de race, de religion. C'est pour lui illusion pure que de distinguer dans l'Inde des courants de populations diverses, aryens et aborigènes, etc."—"Les Castes dans l'Inde," p. 186.

[2] "Baudhāyana," i. 1, 2, 3.

[3] "A Rome il suffit de la présence d'un étranger une sacrifice de la gens pour offenser les dieux. La Sūdra est une étrangère elle n'appartenent pas à la race qui par l'investiture du cordon sacré, nait à la plenitude de la vie religieuse."—Senart, "Castes dans l'Inde," p. 212.

[4] Bühler, "Baudhāyana," *note* to i. 1, 2, 4.

[5] "Āpastamba," i. 9, 25, 3.

sea.[1] Another was "to follow the trade of arms," a custom which at the time of the Mutiny led to fatal results. With respect to this northern custom of Brāhmans becoming warriors, Gautama held that a Brāhman might only use arms if his life were threatened, while Āpastamba declared that a Brāhman shall not take a weapon into his hand though he be only desirous of examining it.[2] The following of any other practices in any country except where they prevail is, according to Baudhāyana,[3] a sin. The standard rule of conduct was that which obtained in Aryāvarta.[4] Gautama, on the other hand, held that the laws of countries, castes, or families, are of authority if they are not opposed to the teachings of the "Vedas," and subsidiary sacred books; while, at the same time, "cultivators, traders, herdsmen, money-lenders, and artisans have authority to lay down rules for their respective classes.[5]

From the time of Warren Hastings the Brāhmanic law books consulted—or such of them as were known to the Brāhmans—have been held to set forth the laws and customs of the people of India. As a matter of fact, the great mass of the population has never heard of the sacred law books of the Aryans.[6] These law treatises were separately compiled as the received tradition of a school or class of Brāhmanical families, who strove, by all means at their command, to inculcate their teaching among the community, and impress the importance of their observances at the courts of the kings or chieftains with whom they had gained influence. As for the mass of the people, the dark-skinned aborigines, they could

[1] "Āpastamba," ii. 1, 2, 1. A custom which he afterwards declares entails loss of caste.

[2] *Ibid.*, i. 10, 29, 6.

[3] "Baudhāyana," i. 1, 2, 5.

[4] "Baudhāyana," i. 1, 2, 11, 12.

[5] "Gautama," xi. 21.

[6] "That any class of Hindus, save perhaps the Mānavas, at any time regarded the "Mānava Dharma Śāstra" as a law book of paramount authority, no person who has the most elementary knowledge of things Hindu can for a moment suppose."—Nelson, "View of Hindu Life," p. 12.

preserve their own habits and customs so long as they remained in a servile condition. When these non-Aryan folk became of social importance, or wealthy enough to demand recognition of their position, they themselves tended to rise to an Aryan status and amalgamate their customs, cults, and superstitions, on such terms as the Brāhmans were inclined, from prudence, to offer, with the laws and religions of the ruling class.[1]

On the Brāhman, as well as on the king, the whole moral welfare of the world was held to depend.[2] So the king chose as a "purohita" a Brāhman austere and righteous, and of a noble family.[3] The man who raised his hand against a Brāhman was declared to be shut out from Heaven for one hundred years.[4] If he struck a Brāhman he lost Heaven for one thousand years. The shedder of a Brāhman's blood was debarred from entering Heaven for the number of years to be counted by the particles of dust held together by the shed blood.[5]

According to Baudhāyana,[6] "the murderer of a Brāhman shall practise the following vow during twelve years: "Carrying a skull and the foot of a bedstead (instead of a staff); dressed in the hide of an ass; staying in the forest; making a dead man's skull his flag; he shall cause a hut to be built in a burial-ground and reside there; going to seven houses in order to beg food; while proclaiming his deed, he shall support life with what he gets there, and shall fast if he obtains nothing." Vasishta[7] held that the expiation for Brāhman murder was the burning by the murderer of his own body piecemeal. A milder penance[8]

[1] *See* Nesfield, "Caste Systems," pp. 171-2.

[2] "Gautama," viii. 1:—They "uphold the moral order in the world."

[3] *Ibid.*, xi. 12.

[4] *Ibid.*, xxi. 20-21.

[5] "Baudhâyana," iii. 1, 2, 3.

[6] *Ibid.*, ii. 1, 1, 3.

[7] "Vasishta," xx. 25-26.

[8] "Les rédacteurs des livres ont simplement soudé en ce système des faits isolés, plus ou moins exceptionnels qu'un idéal de perfection rarement réalisés." —Senart, "Castes dans l'Inde," p. 126.

set forth by the same law-giver for the murderer was: "Let him fight for the sake of the king or for the sake of the Brāhmans, and let him die in battle with his face turned to the foe."[1]

There are clear evidences, however, that between the four ideal classes no insurmountable barriers had grown up at the time of the earliest law-giver, Gautama,[2] who may be ascribed to before the sixth century. His laws lay down the rule that a Brāhman, in time of distress, might assume the occupation of a Kshatriya, Vaiśya,[3] or Sūdra,[4] though in no case should he mix with, or eat with, a Sūdra. The ordinary duties of a Brāhman were, however, held to be sacrificing for others, accepting gifts, and teaching.[5] Āpastamba[6] similarly allowed a Brāhman to trade, although, ordinarily, trade was not lawful for a Brāhman. Vasishta held, that those who were unable to live by their own occupations might adopt those of the lower classes, but never those of a higher class.

The one great permanent division between the Brāhmans, Kshatriyas, Vaiśyas, and Sūdras was the rite of initiation into the Aryan brotherhood. This was the consecration, in accordance with the texts of the "Veda," of a male who "is desirous of, and can make use of, sacred knowledge."[7] It was this initiation which made the three higher classes twice-born. It excluded Sūdras and women from ever taking part in the religious life of the Aryans; the knowledge sufficient for them was dancing, singing, and such arts.

The initiation for a Brahman took place from the age

[1] "Vasishta," xx. 27.

[2] "Āpastamba" is placed by Bühler (S.B.E., vol. ii. p. 43) two hundred years before the third century B.C.

[3] "Gautama," vii. 6-7.

[4] *Ibid.*, vii. 22-23; "Manu," x. 81; "Yajn.," iii. 35.

[5] "Vasishta," ii. 14.

[6] "Āpastamba," i. 7, 20, 10.

[7] *Ibid.* i. 1, 1, 8.

of eight to sixteen. He was then invested with the girdle of sacred grass and taught the holy verse to Sāvitrī. The age of initiation for a Kshatriya was from eleven to twenty, when he received a girdle made from a bow-string. The age for a Vaiśya was from twelve to twenty-two; his girdle was of wool. Before the initiation took place the neophyte was viewed as a Sūdra, and as such was presumed to act, speak, and eat as he felt inclined.[1] After the initiation the twice-born Aryan passed from the care of his father to the care of a teacher, or "guru," with whom he dwelt for the purpose of being instructed in his sacred duties, for as Āpastamba held: "Virtue and sin do not go about and say, 'Here we are;' nor do gods, Gandharvas, or Manes say, 'This is virtue, that is sin.' But that is virtue, the practice of which wise men of the three twice-born castes praise; what they blame is sin."[2]

Twelve years was the time fixed[3] for a student to remain under tutelage. This was the time required for learning by rote one of the "Vedas," so that if the four "Vedas" had to be learned, the time had to be extended to forty-eight years.[4] This rule was, no doubt, an injunction which it would be meritorious to obey. It was no doubt followed in many cases, yet, like nearly all the laws of the Brāhmanic order, it was an ideal counsel of perfection, to be modified according to circumstances; one law-giver declaring that studentship might last only so long as it was necessary to impart the sacred instruction. During his training the pupil should remain restrained in all his acts, be chaste, refrain from all spirituous liquor,[5] and live only on food obtained by begging.

The student, during his pupilage, was under the absolute

[1] "Gautama," ii. 1.

[2] "Āpastamba," i. 7, 20, 6, 8.

[3] "Gautama," ii. 45.

[4] "Āpastamba," i. 1, 2, 12; "Manu," iii. 1; "Gautama," ii. 46.

[5] "A Brāhman always, a Kshatriya and Vaiśya during studentship."—*Ibid.*, ii. 20 (*note*).

control of his Guru, who was to be revered and reverenced as holy. Āpastamba, while explaining that a Brāhman could alone be chosen as a teacher, clearly shows that no great rigidity of class distinction had taken place up to his time, for he allows that, in a matter of such great importance as that of choosing a spiritual preceptor, a Brāhman might, in times of distress, study under a Kshatriya or Vaiśya.[1] More striking still is the injunction that the Brāhman, "during his pupilship must walk behind such a teacher. Afterwards the Brāhman shall take precedence of his Kshatriya or Vaiśya teacher."

The course of study ended, the Guru received a fee, and the pupil underwent a new rite, that of ceremonial bathing, a ceremony that set him free to face the world. He then became a householder, and took to himself a wife. Three wives[2] were allowed for a Brāhman,[3] two for a Kshatriya, one for a Vaiśya.

By all Aryan householders there were forty great sacrifices to be performed, including the nineteen domestic ceremonies, the seven Pāka sacrifices, the seven Havir sacrifices, and the seven Soma sacrifices. Once the sacred fire was lighted in the householder's home,[4] his chief daily duty was to worship the gods, the *manes*, the goblins and sages of old, to daily recite such portions of the "Veda" as

[1] "Āpastamba," ii. 2, 4, 25-26.

[2] The wife should not belong to the same Gotra, nor be a Sapinda relative of his mother."—Gobhila, "Grihya Sūtras," iii. 4, 4, 5. "Gautama," xiv. 13; "Manu," v. 60, ii. 4, 5; Jolly, "Recht und Sitte," p. 62:—"Da diese exogamische Princip schon in den Grihyasūtras auftritt so besteht kein Grund an den hohen Alter desselben zu zweifeln wenn die Forderung hinsieht sich und erst allmählig gesteigert haben." The term "caste," as used in the "Census Report," p. 182, is defined as "the perpetuation of status or function by inheritance and endogamy."

[3] "The Census of India" (1891), p. 254, states of polygamy that "the extent to which it exists among the Brāhmanic section of the people must be very slight."

[4] "Gautama," v. 7.

he had learned from his Guru, and as far as possible perform the sacrifices. Yet, although he performed these duties, it was declared that, "all the four 'Vedas' together with the six Angas and sacrifices, bring no blessing to him who is deficient in good conduct."[1]

The whole forty sacrifices were vain if the Aryan householder was not endowed with the eight good qualities of the soul. These eight good qualities comparable to the Eightfold Path of Buddha are: Compassion on all creatures, forbearance, freedom from anger, purity, quietism, auspiciousness, freedom from avarice, and freedom from covetousness.[2] The path for the Aryan was made easy; he had but to take the place allotted to him by the Brāhmans and all would go well with him. "He, forsooth, who is sanctified by a few only of these forty sacraments, and whose soul is endowed with the eight excellent qualities, will be united with Brahmā, and will dwell in his Heaven."[3]

The guest was ever to be welcomed in the Aryan homestead, honour being first paid to old age, then to learning, after which followed in due order, birth, occupation, relations, and lastly, wealth. When life was drawing to its close[4] the householder passed out from amid his people to take upon himself the fourth stage of life, and prepare his soul for its final doom. He then became either a hermit (*vaikhānas*), living in the forest on roots and fruits, practising austerities,[5] yet still keeping up the sacred fire, and worshipping the gods, the Brāhmans, the forefathers, men and goblins, or else he passed at once into the last stage of all, that of the ascetic sage (*bhikshu*). The ascetic

[1] "Vasishta," vi. 4.

[2] *See* "Āpastamba," i. 8, 23, 6.

[3] *See* Hopkins, "Rel. of India," p. 255.

[4] "Gautama," iii. 1; "Vasishta," vii. 3; "Baudhāyana," ii. 10, 17, 2, for the student after his studentship directly assuming the life of a hermit or ascetic.

[5] "Baudhāyana," ii. 10, 17.

sage[1] was to be dead to all around him. He entered the haunts of men but to beg for food, and then only when all others had finished eating. He was merely to wear a rag to cover his nakedness, and to have no regard to either his temporal or spiritual welfare. For him the scene was ended and was fading into the dimness of the past.

So every man's lot in life was mapped out by the Brāhmans. Those enfolded within the twice-born Aryan ranks were stamped for all eternity as separated from the Sūdra[2] and far-removed alien races. Rules forbidding intermarriage, eating and drinking, or habits of social intercourse between the ever-increasing divisions among the people were, under Brāhmanic guidance, given the sanctity of Divine ordinances. As with the sacrificial rites, customs that had sprung from principles underlying all primitive social life became stereotyped and preserved for ever, as sacred and inviolable laws of caste.

The Aryans of Vedic times were divided into their tribes, and clans, and groups of families.[3] The great binding tie of the family was descent from some common ancestor. The sacrifice was alone for the benefit of the group that held together in the very closest bonds of descent from the same blood. No one outside of these bonds could partake of the sacrificial feast.[4] The feast became a sign of relationship, and the very act of eating—among primitive people restricted to the family for whom the food is laboriously

[1] "Gautama," iii.

[2] Zimmer, "Alt. Ind. Leben.," p. 204; Caldwell, "Gram. of Dravidian Languages," p. 112:—"Whatever may have been the origin of the word 'Sūdra,' it cannot be doubted that it was extended in course of time to all who occupied or were reduced to a dependent condition; whilst the name 'Dasyu' or 'Mleccha' came to be the appellation of the unsubdued non-Aryanised tribes."

[3] Baden-Powell, "Ind. Vill. Com.," 194, 206.

[4] "A Rome il suffit de la présence d'un étranger au sacrifice de la *gens* pour offenser les dieux."—Senart, "Castes dans l'Inde," p. 214.

acquired, and carried on with a reserve and secrecy which civilisation but slowly breaks down—became surrounded with greater importance and significance. It grew to be a sign of blood-fellowship. The drinking of water together typified a family union; the accepting of salt made the accepter, for the time, one with the sib of him from whom it was accepted. The prohibitions and restrictions that hemmed round intermarriage were founded on primitive customs. In savage life, in many cases, female infanticide is a common, if not a necessary, custom, when food is hard to obtain. From this cause it is difficult, if not impossible to find a wife within the clan or family;[1] one has to be stolen or bought from an outside group more favourably circumstanced. The group possessing female children naturally looked upon them as valuable articles of merchandise.

The tendency was to place strong restrictions on these females being acquired or married by young men of their own group. Robbery of a bride can only take place from a hostile tribe, the purchase of a bride in primitive society only by barter with a friendly tribe. The principle would thus be soon established that a marriage could only take place outside a specified group,[2] and within the limits of a .nore extended group.

These primitive restrictions as to communality and connubuism are at the very foundation of the divisions which separate the different castes in India from one another at the present day. They grew deeper as the racial and class divisions became of greater import in the

[1] "Au témoignage de Plutarque les Romains dans la période ancienne n'épousaient jamais de femmes de leur Sang."—Senart, "Castes dans l'Inde," p. 209.

[2] "Vielleicht ist die Exogamie uberhaupt zuerst bei den Rajputen (Kshattriyas) aufgekommen, bei denen sie sich, wie dies Sir A. Lyall anziehend schildert ('Asiatic Studies,' pp. 219-21) in Rajputana in verbindung mit den noch jetzt üblichen Schein raub und dem ehemaligen Frauenraub und der Geschlechter verfassung noch in ihren ursprünglichsten Form studieren lässt." —Jolly, "Recht und Sitte," p. 63.

social life of the people under the fostering care of the Brāhmanic hierarchy. In the books of law and domestic custom,[1] the limits within which the twice-born may marry within their own groups are restricted[2] more and more between those where no traces of common descent from accepted ancestors, saintly or heroic, can be recognised; just as among the lower races intermarriage is forbidden between those who trace their genealogy from the same animal, or totem.[3]

So in the present day, although marriage is forbidden between members of the varied groups into which the people of India have been subdivided under the persistent pressure of the hierarchial pretensions, yet, within these groups, marriage has its exogamous limits.[4]

In the metrical law book, ascribed to the fabled Manu, "First-born of the Creator," composed at a late date, probably about the commencement of the Christian era, the law of marriage within the caste is stated to be in the northern

[1] "Manu," iii. 5; "Āpastamba," ii. 5, 11, 15; "Gobhila," iii. 4, 3-5; "Vishnu," xxiv. 9; "Baudhāyana," I. 1, 2, 3. In "Recht und Sitte," Jolly gives the full reference to the literature of the subject. Grierson, "Bihar Peasant Life," § 1354.

[2] Hopkins, "Rel. of India," p. 270.

[3] Risley ("Caste Systems of N.W. Provinces and Oudh"), in discussing Nesfield's statement that "function, and function alone, has determined the formation of the endogamous groups which in India are called castes," propounds his theory, that "community of race, and not, as has been frequently argued, community of function, is the real determining principle, the true *causa causarum*, of the 'caste system'" (p. 254). "In Bengal proper, castes with a platyrhine index have totemistic exogamous divisions" (p. 253). "The Brāhmanical system which absolutely prohibits marriage within the gotra" (p. 245).

[4] "Differences of religious practice, within the limits of Hinduism, do not necessarily affect the *jus connubii*."—Risley, p. 241, *loc. cit.* "In Southern India differences of religion (Vaishnavism, Śaivism, etc.), and even narrower divisions, are a bar to marriage between members of what is strictly called the same caste."—Burnell, *note* to "Manu," iii. 12-13. *See* Grierson, "Bihar Peasant Life," § 1354, for the custom of the Soti Brāhmans of East Tirhut keeping registers of genealogical descent, and giving certificates of lawful marriage to show that "the patres are not within prohibited degrees of affinity."

country where the rules were in vogue as follows: "A damsel who is neither a Sapindā on the mother's side, nor belongs to the same family (*gotra*) on the father's side, is recommended to twice-born men for wedlock and conjugal union."[1] According to the two great commentators of Manu, Medhātithī and Kullūka, the bride must be one "between whose father's and the bridegroom's family no blood relationship is traceable."[2] Bühler further expands the meaning by stating that it is very probable that the full meaning of the text is, "that in the case of Brāhmanas, intermarriage between families descended from the same Rishi, and in case of other Aryans, between families bearing the same name or known to be connected, are forbidden." It is sufficiently clear that the people were subdividing up into groups, separated from each other by restrictions inevitably tending to prevent the creation of any national life or spirit, whereby social, sectarian, and racial distinctions might become obliterated or give place to higher ideals. From violation of the laws of marriage, from intermarriage or illicit union of members of the original four theoretical groups, that of Brāhmans, Kshatriyas, Vaiśyas, and Sūdras, it was held that the confusion of castes had arisen as the offspring had to be relegated to inferior positions, there to intermarry and form new sub-groups. The law book of Manu,[3] having described the baser castes which had been created from the abhorred irregular union between members of the four castes, proceeds to point out how to each caste there were specific functions. "These races," he declares, "which originate in a confusion of the castes, and have been described according to their fathers and mothers, may be known by their occupations, whether they conceal or

[1] "Manu," iii. 5 (S.B.E., vol. xxv.). *See*, as mentioned in the *note* to "Āpastamba," ii. 5, 11, 15-16; "Gautama," iv. 2-5; "Vasishta," viii. 1-2; "Baudhâyana," ii. 11, 37; "Yâjn.," i. 53.

[2] *Note* to "Manu," iii. 5 (S.B.E., vol. xxv.).

[3] *Ibid.*, x. 40.

openly show themselves." "Those who have been mentioned as the base-born offspring of Aryans, or as produced in consequence of a violation of the law, shall subsist by occupations reprehended by the twice-born."

It is, in fact, the life-history of a struggling group of foreigners shut out from aid, vainly fighting that their life's strength should not be slowly sucked from out them by parasitic growths.

The world is strewn with monuments of the past, and the saddest tomb the world has ever reared is the tomb of despairing Aryanism in India. Stone by stone, as the tomb is built, it tells its own story, and down through the pages of history the same story runs that, in conquering, the Aryan always succumbs.[1]

In India the Aryan threw round himself the bulwark which his genius told him could alone ward off final decay —the bulwark of caste. Down to the present day the Aryan has preserved much of his heritage from being entombed in the structure he has raised, and the great problem for England to face is whether she has brought aid to the beleaguered camp in time to infuse it with new life. If England has not succeeded in warming into vitality the latent spirit of Aryanism, in spreading new hope amid the cultured classes of India, that they may come out from their caste restrictions to aid her without fear of defeat in the crusade against superstition and ignorance, her mission is a failure and her past in the East must inevitably be entombed in the same grave as that over which she found Aryanism hovering on her advent into India. For this reason alone it is necessary to note the faintest light that breaks through the mists shrouding so much of the past history of India from our ken. So much remains steeped in the doubt that a Brāhmanic genius, keen enough to rise and respond to the beating mark of time

[1] Rendall, "Cradle of the Aryans."

would not have been equally subtle to screen its deeper movements from vulgar gaze. The suspicion of wilful reticence, of predesigned purpose, stays the mind as it ventures to trace the lines of Brāhmanic thought in the pages of its own literature.

A vague gleam of light from Western sources flickers for a moment over the social and political life of India during the few centuries preceding the Christian era. From the time when the Aryans first sang their victorious songs of praise, as they marched in their manhood and tribal strength, down to the days when the Brāhman theocracy strove to isolate the scattered fragments of the race from the contaminating influence of more uncivilised people, the unhappy remnant of the great Indo-European family remained closed off from all share in the heritage that had fallen to its brethren in the West. The fables that are told by Diodorus of the expeditions of Sesostris or Semiramis to the far East may serve to adorn a tale told in hopes of rousing the youthful interest in the past history of India, but nowhere can the sober historian, as he views the teak found in the city of Ur, the indigo or porcelain found in ancient Egypt, discern evidences that the east and west Aryan-speaking people had joined hands in these early days.[1] Herodotus shows that India was not unknown by repute to the West. He narrates[2] how Dareios, son of Hystaspes sent Skylax of Karyanda on an expedition of discovery down the Indus, and how Skylax reached the ocean and returned home by way of the Red Sea. Herodotus, in enumerating the possessions of Dareios, who had advanced his conquests as far as the Panjāb, states that India formed the twentieth satrapy of the Persian monarch whence he drew a tribute of three hundred and

[1] *See* M'Crindle, "Homeric Use of Kassiteros and Elephos," p. 3; Birdwood, *Athenæum*; Grünwedel, "Buddh. Kunst," p. 8; M'Crindle, "Ancient India as Described by Megasthenes and Arrian," p. 5.

[2] "Herodotus," book iii. 98.

sixty talents of gold dust, a tribute exceeding that paid by all other people.[1] Indian soldiers[2] marched with the Persian troops of Xerxes into Thessaly and fought under Mardonius[3] at Plataea.[4]

Ktēsias of Knidos, a physician who remained in Persia for seventeen years, from 416 B.C. to 398 B.C., learned there something of India, and the fragments of his "Indika," preserved by later historians,[5] give marvellous tales of the mysterious home of fables. They tell of a fountain from which could be drawn pitchers full of gold, fluid when drawn but soon solidifying. The sun appeared ten times larger in India than in other lands, and the sea, for four fingers in depth, was so hot that fish never came to the surface.

His fragments of history also give a graphic account of a man-eating monster living in India, with a face like a man, with double rows of teeth, with a tail like a scorpion's, a cubit long, from which it discharged darts capable of killing every animal save the elephant.

They are full of stories of burning mountains, miraculous lakes, and healing fountains, four-headed birds which guarded the gold of the desert, slaying all who came in quest of the precious metal that had to be sought for in the night-time by bands of men, one and two thousand strong. They also describe a race of pygmies less than two cubits high, and a tribe one hundred and twenty thousand in number, who are men, and yet have heads, teeth, and claws like those of dogs, their speech being carried on by barking and signs, yet they are, "like all the other Indians, extremely just men." The stories of Ktēsias are not unlike many which delight a credulous, wonder-loving public, who still believe that Yogis remain buried

[1] "Herodotus," iii. 94; M'Crindle, "Ancient India as Described by Ktesias, the Knidian."

[2] *Ibid.*, vii. 65. [3] *Ibid.*, viii. 113. [4] *Ibid.*, ix. 31. [5] *Ibid.*, iii. 94.

beneath the earth for long spaces of time, without food or nourishment; who believe that Mahātmas can rival the feats of Maskelyne and Cooke; that magicians can remain suspended in the air without support and make mango trees grow from out a juggler's bag; that scorpions sting themselves to death with their own poison; and that the mongoose when smitten by a cobra knows of a plant to free itself from death.

The remark of Strabo[1] that, "generally speaking, the men who have hitherto written on the affairs of India, were a set of liars," was harsh, for there was much of truth in the accounts he had before him. These accounts were derived from the description of the country by the trained historians who accompanied Alexander the Great in the first effort of the West to pierce through the mysteries that had so long separated it from the East. Alexander the Great, son of Philip of Macedon, found himself in 336 B.C., at the early age of twenty, King of Macedonia, with the fortunes of Greece at his disposal. Within one year he had curbed the Northern barbarians, put Attalos to death, reduced Thebes to submission, and stood prepared to set forth as the conqueror of the world, and fulfil the mission of his father as humbler of the proud Persian.

The Persian Empire, founded by Cyrus, stretched from the shores of the Aegæan and Levant to the far east Jaxartes and Indus. Its king, Dareios Kodomameos, however, lacked the power to hold beneath his sway the satraps who longed to have for themselves the provinces into which the kingdom had been divided, and over which they held a more or less independent rule. On the plains of Issos, the King Dareios fled in his chariot from before the new-risen Conqueror of the World, and left his treasures, his wife, children, and mother, at the mercy of the Macedonian king. Alexander turned aside for a season to reduce

[1] M'Crindle, p. 18.

Phœnicia, and crowned himself with glory by capturing the island fortress of Tyre, though he tarnished his fame by slaying and selling into captivity its inhabitants and merchant princes. In Egypt he founded Alexandria so that the commerce of the world should follow the path which he saw, with commanding genius, was marked out for it, and then turned again to follow his relentless purpose. On the field of battle known as Arbela,[1] Dareios fled in dismay to perish by the treachery of his own kinsman, the Satrap of Bactria. Into Babylon Alexander entered in triumph, gave back to the people their own gods, and restored to the priesthood the wealth they had enjoyed under their Assyrian kings.[2] At Susa[3] he found wealth greater than he had left behind him in Babylon, and as he passed on toward the far East, he left naught to tell of the wealth and power of the Persian nation save the burned ruins of Persepolis, and the rifled tomb of Cyrus.[4] A new Alexandria was built by him at the gateway of India, now known as Herat, whence he over-ran Bactria and Samarkhand, piercing to the Jaxartes, along the banks of which he established his own soldiers in fortified positions, in order to shut out from his possessions the Northern Scythian hordes.

Early in the year 327 B.C. his troops marched down on the plains of India. Crossing the river Indus near Attock, on a bridge of boats, he passed unopposed through the land of a Turanian people called the Taxilas, there being no one between the Indus and the Jhelum (Hydaspes) to combine the petty chieftains and tribes against the invading force. Beyond the modern battle-field of Chiliānwala, Alexander the Great crossed the Jhelum, and was there

[1] M'Crindle, p. 31. [2] *Ibid.*

[3] "The sums contained in the treasury amounted to 40,000 talents of uncoined gold and silver, and 9000 talents of coined gold, and there was other booty besides of immense value, including the spoils which Xerxes had carried off from Greece."—M'Crindle, p. 32.

[4] *See* Curzon, "Persia," vol. ii. p. 76.

met by Porus, a Paurava chieftain of the Lunar race, the first Indian prince to come forward and defend his dominions. In the battle that ensued Porus was wounded, his son slain, and his troops trampled down by his own elephants. With Alexander, the Indian chieftain made an alliance, and received back his territories. Near the battle-field Alexander founded a new city, and called it Bucephala, after his famed charger, Bucephalus, slain during the fight. He thence marched through the land of the Arashtra, made alliance with the king of the Sophytes, pierced as far as Amritsar, and then razed the city of the Kathians, who, in the history of Diodorus the Sicilian, are recorded to have possessed the custom that widows should be burned with their husbands, so that the men might not go in fear of being poisoned by their wives during their lifetime. Strange rumours soon reached the Macedonian camp of the desert lands and fierce tribes to the far East. Outcast adventurers, however, told Alexander the truth, that there was no chieftain powerful enough to stay his conquering the land as far as the Ganges. The Macedonian soldiers were laden with wealth and weary from travel; they longed to see their homes once again. On the banks of the Beas (Hyphasis), Alexander saw the visions he had dreamed—of piercing to the eastern seas, and enrolling the whole world under one sceptre—fade away as his troops refused to follow him further past the Sutlej, towards the broad Jumna and river-valleys of the Ganges.

The Conqueror of the World turned from the rich prize, and led his troops down the banks of the Indus towards the unknown ocean. In an impetuous assault at Multān, on the fortress of the fierce tribe of the Malloi, Alexander was wounded almost to death by an arrow, yet he founded another Alexandria at the modern Ucch, before he left India to commence his perilous journey across the sandy deserts of Gedrosia towards Babylon, where he died at the early age of thirty-two from fever and drink. The records of the historians and scientific men who accompanied the Macedonian king on his expedition into India have perished, and the accounts given of them by later writers, such as Arrian, Strabo, and Pliny, remain the only light that comes from the West regarding the social life of the people of India during the period.

While Alexander remained in the Panjāb, a base-born adventurer, one Chandragupta, destined to become the first Emperor of North India, is said[1] to have told the monarch how he might advance down the Ganges and spread his conquests over all the divided tribes and people. Chandragupta, finding his advice not taken, left the Macedonians and sought refuge in Magadha. There he offended the reigning Nanda king, and again returned to the Panjāb, where he found that the Greek governor, Eudemos, left by Alexander, had foully murdered Porus, and that the greater part of the Greek garrison had been withdrawn from the cities of the Panjāb to join in the dissensions that had broken out in the West on the death of Alexander. Chandragupta at once headed an uprising of the native tribes, and soon found himself in power as sole ruler over the Panjāb and lands of the lower Indus.

Remembering the weakness of the kingdoms in the valley of the Ganges, he returned to Magadha, and there by his intrigues secured for himself the throne by the assassination[2] of the last of the Nanda dynasty. India, for the first time, saw, in the low-caste Chandragupta,[3] a ruler whose empire extended from the Indus to the lower Ganges.

In the meantime, Seleukos Nikator, the successor to

[1] "Sandrakottos (Chandragupta) was of obscure birth, and from the remark of Plutarch that in his early years he had seen Alexander, we may infer that he was a native of the Panjāb."—M'Crindle, p. 405.

[2] The story is told in the "Mūdrarākshasa," by Viśākadattā, *see* p. 294 (post).

[3] His accession dates from 315 B.C., or 312 B.C.

the eastern dominions of Alexander, marched from Syria and Asia Minor to re-establish his power in Bactria and Western India. With the new Maurya Emperor of Northern India, Seleukos Nikator found it prudent to make an alliance. The Syrian king gave his daughter in marriage to Chandragupta, and sent his ambassador, Megasthenes, to reside at Pātaliputra, the city whose foundations Buddha had seen laid by the generals of Bimbisāra as a fortress to check the raids of the Wajjians. At Pātaliputra, Megasthenes resided for eight years, from 306 to 298 B.C. In what remains, in the writings[1] of later Greek and Roman writers, of the "Indika of Megasthenes," the Western world has preserved its only literary record of the condition of India, at a period of time when the Aryan race was approaching a doom from which it was, for a time, saved by the dread of the Macedonian soldiery to penetrate further into the East and raise the veil which the priestly chronicles have drawn over the political life of the times.

From Strabo[2] it is learned that Megasthenes held that no reliance could be placed on any previous Western account of India, for "its people he says never sent an expedition abroad, nor was their country ever invaded or conquered except by Herakles and Dionysus in old times, and by the Macedonians in our times."

The belief held by the Indians themselves evidently was that they were autochthonous, and for some reason, perhaps to gratify the pride of Megasthenes, they also asserted that their gods, myths, and philosophies were similar to those of Greece.

The history of Megasthenes was evidently founded on

[1] "'Ancient India as Described by Megasthenes and Arrian,' being a translation of the fragments of the 'Indika of Megasthenes,' collected by Dr Schwarbach, and of the first part of the 'Indika of Arrian'" (M'Crindle).

[2] Strabo, xv. 1, 6-8; M'Crindle, p. 107. *See* Pliny, "Hist. Nat.," vi., xxi. 4-5.

facts he had himself observed, or on the evidence of witnesses he deemed credible. The more it is examined the more it is found to be trustworthy, while the whole account of Indian social and political life falls in with what might have been imagined forth from the vague references of the sacred literature of India. Pātaliputra, the capital of Chandragupta, the walls of which have recently been unearthed 12 to 15 feet beneath the modern city of Patna, is described as the greatest city in all India, stretching 80 stadia along the river to a breadth of 15 stadia. The ditch surrounding its wooden palisades—for all cities near rivers were of wood, those on eminences alone being constructed of mud and brick—was 600 feet broad, and 30 cubits in depth, the walls of the city having sixty-four gates and five hundred and seventy towers. To the king there were six hundred thousand foot soldiers, thirty thousand cavalry, and nine thousand elephants. It would be difficult to enumerate all the different tribes scattered over India who were mentioned by the ambassador of Seleukos Nikator and of whom many cannot now be identified. It is evident that over the vast continent separate stable governments existed, many holding vast resources at their command. The King of Kalinga, although he was subject to Chandragupta, held independent possession of his own dominions along the eastern coast, while a branch of the race he ruled over seems[1] to have been the people of Lower Bengal, near the mouth of the Ganges. The capital of this great eastern viceroy was at Parthalis, and the army consisted of sixty thousand foot soldiers, one thousand horsemen, and seven hundred elephants.

The great Andhra kingdom between the Godavari and the Krishna, where the law books of Baudhāyana and Āpastamba were revered, stretched far and wide, having

[1] M'Crindle, "Alexander," p. 364; "Megasthenes," p. 155.

numerous villages,[1] thirty walled and defended towns, and a king having an army of one hundred thousand foot men, two thousand cavalry, and a thousand elephants.

On the west coast were varied tribes, now more or less identified, while in the basin of the Chambal were the Pandae, a branch of the famed Pandus,[2] "the only race in India ruled by women. They say that Herakles having but one daughter, who was, on that account, all the more beloved, endowed her with a noble kingdom. Her descendants ruled over three hundred cities,[3] and commanded an army of one hundred and fifty thousand foot, and five hundred elephants."

Many of the stories told by Megasthenes seem incredible, but then it would be unwise to stigmatise the historian as wilfully setting forth false statements. Some of the stories he relates were furnished by credulous narrators, and when these are eliminated there is generally a solid substratum of historic facts in the remaining portions of his writings. The danger into which a too incredulous reader might fall in rejecting everything as false, the evidence for which lies not on the surface, may be seen from a single example. Pliny narrates[4] that, according to Megasthenes, there lived a race in India whose feet were turned backwards. This palpably cannot be accepted as a true statement of fact. Nevertheless, the historian merely recorded statements he had heard from what he deemed reliable sources, and the very fact that he mentions this strange race shows that his sources of information must have been numerous and varied.

[1] M'Crindle, "Megasthenes," p. 138.

[2] *See Ibid.*, p. 147 (*note*).

[3] *Ibid.*, p. 147 :—"They further assert that Herakles was also born among them. They assign to him, like the Greeks, the club and the lion's skin. . . . Marrying many wives he left many sons, but one daughter only." *See* also p. 39 (*note*), "apparently Śiva is meant."

[4] Pliny, "Hist. Nat.," vii. 11, 14, 22.

This belief in the existence of spirits and witches who wander about with their feet turned backward is common not only in India but elsewhere.[1] The following account of one of this race of Churels, as they are called, is told by Mr Crooke, who has done much to probe the depths of primitive belief in India, and no doubt the Greek historian had heard somewhat similar stories on which he based his record. One of the race of Churels generally "assumes the form of a beautiful young woman and seduces youths at night, particularly those who are good-looking. She carries them off to some kingdom of her own, keeps them there till they lose their manly beauty, and then sends them back to the world grey-haired old men, who, like Rip Van Winkle, find all their friends dead long ago. I had a smart young butler at Etah, who once described to me vividly the narrow escape he had from the fascinations of a Churel who lived in a pipal tree near the cemetery. He saw her sitting on a wall in the dusk and entered into conversation with her, but he fortunately observed her tell-tale feet and escaped. He would never again go by that road at night without an escort."

The sources of information at the disposal of Megasthenes, and the accordance, for the greater part, of the facts narrated by him with what is known to have been the state of affairs at the period during which he visited India, make his statements of peculiar value for the purposes of adding reality to the hazy outline of the Brāhmanic texts.

The population of India is by him divided into seven main classes. At the head of all in dignity and importance were those whom he called the philosophers, easily recognised as the Brāhmans. They, according to Megasthenes,

[1] Crooke, "Popular Religion and Folk-lore in Northern India," p. 169; Tylor, "Primitive Culture," vol. i. p. 307.

are of great benefit to the people, for, "when gathered together at the beginning of the year, they forewarn the assembled multitudes about droughts and wet weather, and also about propitious winds, and diseases, and other topics capable of profiting the hearers."[1]

Should a philosopher make any error in his prognostications, he incurs "no other penalty than obloquy, and he then observes silence for the rest of his life." These philosophers not only confer great benefits on the people, they also "are believed to be next door to the gods, and to be most conversant with matters pertaining to Hades." They perform all sacrifices due by the people; they perform the funeral rites, and, in "requital of such services, they receive valuable gifts and privileges."

The philosophers, according to Megasthenes, were divided into two orders. First, the Brāhmans proper, who live as students for thirty-six years,[2] and then become householders, when "they eat flesh, but not that of animals employed in labour." "The Brāhmans keep their wives —and they had many wives—ignorant of all philosophy, for if women learned to look on pleasure and pain, life and death, philosophically, they would become depraved, or else no longer remain in subjection."[3] This statement is in accord with the teaching of the "Vedānta," which excludes all women from its scheme of salvation. The basis of much of Indian thought is contained in his summing-up of the Brāhmanic speculations of his time: "They consider nothing," he records, "that befalls man to be either good or bad; to suppose otherwise being a dream-like illusion."[4] Their views regarding the soul and creation were declared to be the same as the Greek, and "they wrap up their doctrines about immortality, and future judgment, and kindred topics, in allegories, after the manner of Plato."

[1] M'Crindle, "Megasthenes," p. 41.
[2] "Manu," iii. 1.
[3] *See* M'Crindle, "Megasthenes," p. 100.
[4] *Ibid.*, p. 100.

The second order of the Brāhmans was the Sarmanes, or "ascetics," of whom the most honoured were the Hylobioi,[1] who "live in the woods, where they subsist on leaves of trees and wild fruits, and wear garments made from the bark of trees."[2] Besides the orthodox Brāhmans,[3] there were numerous diviners and sorcerers living on the superstitions of the people, begging their way from village to village, and even women were said in some cases to "pursue philosophy."

The second class into which Megasthenes divided the population was that of husbandmen. They, as they do to-day, formed the gross mass of the population living in scattered villages.

The land, according to the Greek account, was the property of the king, to whom a land tribute was paid, as well as a fourth part of the produce raised by each cultivator. The husbandmen are depicted as remaining supremely indifferent to the change of their rulers, to the coming and going of new invaders: even in those days they were as they are to-day, when, "the Mogul, the Afghan, the Pindari, the Briton, and the mutinous Sepoy, with others, have swept to and fro, as the dust storm sweeps the land, but the corn must be grown, and the folk and cattle must be fed, and the cultivator waits with inflexible patience till the will of Heaven be accomplished, and he may turn again to the toil to which he is appointed."[4]

The picture of the agricultural labourer was much the same over two thousand years ago. The Greek historian

[1] Haradatta, in his *note* to "Gautama," iii. 2, says:—"The Vānaprastha is called the Vaikhānasa, because he lives according to the rule promulgated by Vikhanas;" and adds, "for that sage chiefly taught that order." *See* Bühler, "Manu," p. xxviii.; S.B.E., vol. xxv.

[2] M'Crindle, "Megasthenes," p. 102.

[3] "Among the Indians are those philosophers also who follow the precepts of Boutta, whom they honour as a god on account of his extraordinary sanctity."—M'Crindle, p. 105.

[4] Lockwood Kipling, "Man and Beast in India," p. 154.

narrates how, when soldiers fought their way to overlordship of the soil the cultivators remained silent spectators. "While the former are fighting and killing each other as they can, the latter may be seen close at hand tranquilly pursuing their work, perhaps ploughing or gathering in their crops, pruning the trees, or reaping the harvest."[1]

The shepherds, artisans, soldiers,[2] and overseers formed the next four classes into which the people were divided; the seventh and last being that of the councillors, or assessors, to whom belonged "the highest posts of government, the tribunals of justice, and the general administration of public affairs."[3]

The salient features of the system of caste division of the people into distinct groups, ranging from the Brāhman downwards,[4] is described in an extract from Megasthenes preserved by Arrian: "No one is allowed to marry out of his own caste, or to exchange one profession or trade for another, or to follow more than one business. An exception is made in favour of the philosopher, who, for his virtue, is allowed this privilege."[5]

The Indians, as a nation, are depicted as frugal and abstemious in their habits. Wine was only drunk at sacrifices. They seldom went to law. Theft was rare; houses and property were left unguarded. The women were purchased as wives for a yoke of oxen.[6] The care of

[1] M'Crindle, "Indika of Arrian," p. 210.

[2] "The fifth class consists of fighting men, who, when not engaged in active service, pass their time in idleness and drinking. They are maintained at the king's expense, and hence they are always ready, when occasion calls, to take the field, for they carry nothing of their own with them but their own bodies." —M'Crindle, p. 85.

[3] *Ibid.*, p. 85.

[4] *See* also *Ibid.*, p. 213:—"It is permitted that the sophist only be from any caste; for the life of the sophist is not an easy one but the hardest of all."

[5] *Ibid.*, p. 86.

[6] *Ibid.*, p. 70.

the king's person, in his palace and when hunting, was entrusted to female guards. Famine is affirmed never to have visited India. "The greater part of the soil, moreover, is under irrigation, and consequently bears two crops in the course of the year."[1]

Arrian, in his history, gives a realistic, matter-of-fact account of the form of marriage, so often poetically and prettily alluded to in the epics and drama as that of the Svāyamvara, or "choice by the bride of a bridegroom": "The women, as soon as they are marriageable, are brought forward by their fathers and exposed in public, to be selected by the victor in wrestling or boxing or running, or by some one who excels in any other manly exercise."[2] Differing from Strabo, who fixed the ordinary price of a bride at a yoke of oxen, Arrian says that there was no dowry given or taken.

The worship of the god Śiva, or his counterpart—a deity finding its birthplace among the fiercer Scythian tribes, and then accepted into Brāhmanism as a form of the Vedic Rudra—as well as the worship of Krishna, born amid shepherd folk, are both described by Megasthenes as having been fully incorporated into Brāhmanism.

Writing of the philosophers, Megasthenes records, that "such of them as live on the mountains are worshippers of Dionysos, showing, as proofs that he had come among them, the wild vine which grows in their country only, and the ivy, and the laurel, and the myrtle, and the box-tree, and other evergreens. . . . They observe also certain customs which are Bacchanalian. Thus they dress in muslin, wear the turban, use perfumes, array themselves in garments dyed of bright colours; and their kings, when they appear in public, are preceded by the music of drums and gongs. But the philosophers who live in the plains worship Herakles."[3]

[1] Diodorus, "Epitome of Megasthenes," ii. 36; M'Crindle, "Megasthenes," p. 31.

[2] *Ibid.*, p. 222.

[3] *Ibid.*, p. 97.

While these and other strange changes had crept into Brāhmanic orthodoxy, there was one task remaining for it to accomplish before it had to withdraw within the defences it had reared, and there await the attacks soon to be made against it, the last of which has come from all the forces at the command of a Western civilisation.

The enormous mass of sacred literature of the varied schools, the knowledge of which led towards Heaven, made it almost impossible that it could be all remembered, or serve as a guide through life.[1]

The special rules of the early "Sūtras" were more guiding principles of life than practical expositions of the civil and criminal law. Some authoritative statement of the practical relationship of the varied classes, and of the civic duties of each member of the Aryan community, had to be set forth with a prestige sufficient to inspire the allegiance of all. Father Manu was a name wherewith to conjure. It was a name held sacred throughout the pages of literature. From him all men had sprung. At the time of the Flood he had preserved in his own self the human race for re-creation. He was ruler of all law and order, father and revealer of the sacrifice, the author of Vedic Hymns, and the great legendary forefather and guide of all Aryan people.

Among the varied Brāhmanic schools for the preservation and teaching of Vedic texts, the ritual, and subsidiary branches of learning, there was one great school of the Mānavas—a branch of the Maitrāyanīya Black Yajur Veda school—whose founder became, in time, identified with the primeval Manu.

The ancient Sūtra law book of the school is lost.

[1] *See* the exhaustive and learned treatise on the whole subject prefixed by Bühler to his translation of "Manu" (S.B.E., vol. xxv. p. xlv.), under the four heads:—(1) What circumstances led to the substitution of a universally binding "Mânava Dharma Śâstra" for the manual of the Vedic school? (2) Why was so prominent a position assigned to the remodelled "Smriti"? (3) How was the conversion effected? (4) When did it probably take place

This was the text seized on by the Brāhmans, out of which they composed a systematic treatise[1] on law and order, free from sectarian strife, so that it might stand forth as a code of civil and criminal jurisdiction for all Aryan people. The well-known law book of Manu has thus obtained the sanction of an antiquity held to date back to primeval days, when the Divine decrees were revealed by Manu, the offspring of the Self-Existent,[2] the mythical progenitor of the human race. The date of the composition of the work can now be confidently placed somewhere near the commencement of the Christian era.[3]

Tradition, however, holds that the Creator, having created the universe, composed the law, and taught it to Manu, who taught it to the ancient seers. The work itself was for the Aryan community, for the use of those Brāhmans[4] who assisted kings and princes to administer the law. The peculiar customs of countries, peoples, and families lying outside the sphere of Brāhmanism were always acknowledged to have retained their own validity.[5] Not until much later did the idea grow up that local laws[6] should give place to Brāhmanic ideals, and not until English lawyers fell into the error of seeing in the law books of Manu the sacred and common source from which the habits and customs of the entire people of India had sprung, did it become the text by which disputes between people, who had never heard of its existence, were decided.

[1] In the easy metre of the late epic "Anushtubh Śloka."—Bühler, p. xix.

[2] "Yaska, Nirukta," iii. 4; Bühler, p. lxi.; "Manu," i. 102.

[3] Bühler, p. cxvii. :—"It certainly existed in the second century A.D., and seems to have been composed between that date and the second century B.C." Burnell, "Ordinances of Manu," p. xxiv.:—"Between about 1 A.D. and 500 A.D."

[4] "Manu," viii. 1.

[5] *Ibid.*, i. 118; Burnell, p. xxxvi. ; "Baudhāyana," i. 1, 2, 1-7; "Āpastamba," ii. 6, 15, 1; "Gautama," xi. 20-21.

[6] Burnell, p. xxxvii. *See* Lee Warner, W., "Jour. Soc. Arts" (February 1897), p. 170.

In the words of the late profound scholar and jurist, Dr Burnell, the result is that "we shall soon see 'Jack the Giant Killer' cited as an authority on the law of homicide."[1] The laws of Manu grew out of a natural development in the political and social life of Brāhmanic India. The ruder races, as they rose in the social scale, naturally fell under the influence of the system formulated by the learned and priestly classes, and modified their own usages and customs so that, as far as possible, they might conform to the ideals of the higher castes. It was the Brāhmans[2] alone who could expound the laws of Manu, and it was to the three higher castes alone that the right of studying them was given.[3]

All women, Sūdras, and tribes outside the Aryan pale, were excluded from "these Institutes" by the very words of the text.[4] The pretensions of the Brāhmans were rising higher, and signs of change are evident in the laws themselves. In one verse the ancient custom of the sale of women in marriage is condemned, for "no father who knows the law must take even the smallest gratuity for his daughter."[5]

The Greek historian narrated how brides were sold for a yoke of oxen, and Manu bears witness to the fact that the sale was in vogue, for "some call the cow and bull given at an Arsha wedding a 'gratuity,' but that is wrong, since the acceptance of a fee, be it small or great, is a sale of the daughter."[6]

Again the same want of consistency, showing how varied the local customs were, is seen from the fact that in the law book it is declared that not even a Sūdra[7] should sell his daughter, that such a custom had never been heard of in any creation. And again, in a different chapter,[8] treating

[1] Burnell, "Manu," p. xxxviii.
[2] *Ibid.*, i. 103.
[3] *Ibid.*, ii. 16.
[4] *Ibid.*, x. 126.
[5] *Ibid.*, iii. 51.
[6] *Ibid.*, iii. 53.
[7] *Ibid.*, ix. 98.
[8] *Ibid.*, viii. 204.

of the sale of chattels, the text lays down: "If after one damsel has been shown, another be given to the bridegroom, he may marry them both for the same price; that Manu ordained."

The confusion arose from the fact that the laws and customs of the people were changing in the course of time, and were varied among the different sections of the people. The Brāhmans, however, hoped to stereotype the conditions of life and society to which they owed their position, wealth, and power; and so far they have succeeded, for, from the time Warren Hastings drew from the Brāhmans their "Gentoo Code," down to the time when the Queen issued her proclamation after the Mutiny, declaring that the "ancient rights, usages, and customs of India" should be duly regarded, it has been held that "Manu" and later law books were codes wherein to find a sure and safe guide for the administration of civil law to all Hindus. There were Sūdras and Sūdra kings in India at the time of the compilation of the laws of Manu, who, according to its tenets, would have been excluded from its purpose, while the Kshatriyas and Vaiśyas, for whom it was compiled, find few or no representatives in India of to-day.[1] The Brāhmans sought but to frame laws for the preservation of the usages and customs of the people with whom they were concerned, and whom they recognised as within the sphere of Aryanism.[2]

These efforts of Brāhmanism have received a finality and sanction which not even Brāhmanism itself now would claim, or if it did, be powerful enough to sustain. The law but follows and recognises the changing course of social life. In accepting the Brāhmanic law books as final,

[1] Nelson, "Scientific Study of the Hindu Law," p. 5.

[2] "The authority of the inferior castes to make their own laws was early admitted" ("Baudhāyana," i. 1, 2, 1-7; "Gautama," xi. 20, 21; "Āpastamba," ii. 6, 15, 1). "Neither were the Sanskrit Brāhman laws forced on them, nor were their own customs ignored, as is now the case."—Burnell (Pref.), p. xxxvi.

the whole transition of the society from its ancient condition to that of an advancing civil community has been retarded, if not frustrated, while much of its progress has been reduced to a chaos, out of which few can see any possibility of restoring law and order.

CHAPTER IX.

THE FINAL RESTING-PLACE OF ARYAN THOUGHT.

THE Brāhmans had, with all the care and pains granted only to high genius, with all the insight bred of long hereditary training, striven manfully in the fight they had to fight—the fight for the consolidation and preservation of their own race, class, and power.

They were to abide immutably the intellectual guides of the people, for so Divine ordinance had decreed. Kings and warriors had their appointed places as upholders of the State, and favoured allies of the Brāhmanic might. The varied classes of those who were Aryan by descent, or had been admitted within the ranks of Aryanism, were one and all allotted their appointed place in life, and bid look for their spiritual welfare in obedience to the priestly dictates.

The very gods had come on earth to dwell personified as the Brāhmans. The Creator of the Universe had resigned his earthly sceptre to the high keeping of those whose hands and feet still show that their ancestors, for generations past, have never sullied themselves by submission to vulgar toil and labour, and whose features bear the stamp of conscious knowledge of their high calling. All alien races and tribes were the polluted offspring of those who had confounded the divinely-decreed divisions between class and class.

The Brāhmans based their claim to rule supreme solely on their traditional lineage from Vedic bards, on their high intellectual power and sacred calling. It was thought, not action, mind alone, not mind working out its ideals in dramatic, sculptured, or artistic forms, that enslaved the nation. The architect, the builder, or sculptor, were relegated to the lower classes, in common with all those who worked with their hands. No great architectural buildings, no temples, no works of sculpture, whose origin can be traced back to Brāhmanic genius, remain in India. The Aryan had set before him but one ideal, and that was to unravel the secret that set strife on earth as the stepping-stone to law and order, to solve the mystery of the seeming endless struggle wherein the evil and the strong men often prosper while the good and weak are swept away. It is a problem yet unsolved, a problem Nietsche has newly set forth with the all too-overpowering earnestness of one born into a world out of joint to set it right.

Even the weak, diseased, and contaminated are nurtured and left free to send their taint to future generations by civilisations which hold forth, as their highest ideals, sympathy towards the suffering, and protection towards the feeble. Yet these same civilisations take heed to stand armed at every point, straining every nerve to add to their strength, knowing well that speedy decay and dissolution await the nation not stern enough to fling its boasted shibboleths of peace and goodwill to the winds when assailed by stronger foes. India, subdued to her own ideals, fell, and so remains fallen. Before she fell, all that she held of intellect or genius had prepared her course down to a soothing resting-place. If she ever rises it will be because those before whom she fell will wake her from a peaceful sleep and send her forth to find new leaders, who no longer seek to see their fitting end in striving to reconcile man's ethical notions of right and wrong, justice and injustice, with the struggle and strife of life, but simply rest assured that, while they take their part in the battle of the world's strife, the lofty ideals they held aloft when Europe was plunged in barbarism will, in the appointed time, be fully realised, and until then can but be held as guiding hopes.

While Brāhmanism was cradling its wasted strength in the summit of the many-storeyed wicker-work edifice of caste, into which all outsiders might creep from below, and work their way upward from storey to storey, it sent abroad throughout the land those bright rays of thought which are the sole guiding stars to those who still in India love to tread the paths of old.

The cry, the incessant cry sent forth by Aryan India, was that life was pain—pain from the body, pain from the world, pain from the heavens, and the gods.[1]

The cry went up from Brāhmanism. The first answer philosophy had to give is ascribed to Kapila, said to be the founder of the Śānkhya philosophy. By him the Aryan people were directed to fix their gaze on two facts—the world as they saw it spread out before them, and their own souls. So far they knew and no more. The phenomenal world was self-evident. Kapila undertook to prove the existence of soul in five ways. Firstly, he held the soul to exist from an inverted doctrine of design.[2] If one beholds a bed, he naturally concludes there must be a sleeper; so, when one sees the world, he must conclude that there is soul to enjoy it. Secondly, soul is shown to exist because every one is conscious of something inside himself distinct from matter. Thirdly, soul must exist as a superintending

[1] *See* Garbe, "Śānkhya Philosophie," p. 133.

[2] Davies, "Hindu Philosophy," p. 46.

power. Fourthly, it must exist to enjoy; and fifthly, and lastly, because all men feel within themselves that the soul exists, yearning, striving to free itself from the contamination of matter. So far the existence of soul, soul transmigrating from birth to re-birth, having been proved, the connection between it and the world had to be traced, for in this connection lay pain and sorrow. Freed from matter the soul would remain isolated, inactive, and uncreative, unconsciously self-existent and self-contained. It would remain quiescent, placid as a lake on whose surface no ripples break. The Indian sage loves to brood, in a dreamy semi-hypnotic trance, over that calm resting-place to which the soul might take wing, having shaken off from itself all bonds that keep it fettered. The soul, however, is constrained to rouse itself from painless isolation. The allurements of the flesh and the evidences of the senses constrain it to lend its reluctant consent to join in the drama sent forth by matter. Primordial matter, unmanifested, is, according to Kapila, that which originally existed outside, and independent of, soul.[1] This matter, the primordial germ substance, eternal, indivisible, self-developed, ever invisible, had potentially to send forth real existence.[2] This primal matter has, as its nature, the three modes [3] of goodness, passion, and darkness. The system knows no idealistic monism; germ matter and soul remain distinct—the soul, when separated from matter, being self-existent, with no object of thought.

So far Kapila held forth before the astonished gaze the Prakriti, into which he had resolved all objective reality, and the inward light, the soul, having an existence of its

[1] The Prakriti or Pradhâna.

[2] "After all, what do we know of this terrible 'matter,' except as a name for the unknown and hypothetical cause of states of our own consciousness."—Huxley, "Lay Sermons," p. 142, quoted Davies (*note*), p. 19.

[3] These three modes, or gunas, are not to be taken as qualities of Prakriti; the clear distinction between substance and its qualities had not been marked out at this period. The three gunas are the very constituents of Prakriti.

own. From Prakriti he had to create a rival world wherein the soul would find its sorrow. With all the limitation of man's knowledge of time, and space, and cause, the Eastern Frankenstein had to set to work and evolve the spectral vision of a world, and then, haunted by the terror of the scene of woe and desolation, point out a means to mankind how they might escape from their brooding fears. A change had to take place in primordial matter, so that the different forms of matter might become manifest. Prakriti had, as its essential nature, but the three equipoised qualities of goodness, passion, and darkness. From the proximity of soul to matter a disturbance takes place in matter. The quality of passion is roused, matter no longer remains quiescent. She manifests herself to soul[1] so that soul may contemplate creation, and learn for itself the bliss of its primeval condition of isolated self-existence. In this action of Prakriti there is no intelligent design. The system knows of no Creator, matter is unintelligent. The favourite simile is that matter manifests itself unconsciously, without intelligence, just as milk is secreted without any design on the part of a cow.[2] Prakriti is blind, it cannot see; the soul is lame, it cannot act. So "it is that the soul may be able to contemplate Nature, and to become entirely separated from it, that the union of both is made, as of the halt and the blind, and through that (union) the universe is formed."[3]

In the tragedy evolved by unconscious Nature for the soul's training, the soul remains inactive, receiving as a sovereign all that is presented to it, yet preserving its freedom from contact with matter. Prakriti first sends forth intellect (*buddhi*) for the benefit of soul. From intellect, consciousness, or egoism, is evolved, and from

[1] "As the loadstone is attracted by iron merely by proximity, without resolving (either to act or to be acted upon), so by the mere juxtaposition of the soul, Nature (*Prakriti*) is changed."—Davies (*note*), p. 37; *see* Garbe, p. 222.

[2] *See* Davies, p. 93.

[3] *Ibid.*, p. 51.

consciousness the mind (*manas*).[1] The mind-matter receives from the senses such sensations as are to be passed on to consciousness, thence to the intellect, for presentation to the soul, so that the pulsating and heaving life may be viewed by Soul, as though all passed before it like objects seen in a mirror. From consciousness are evolved five subtle elements—sound, touch, odour, form, and taste.[2] From these five subtle principles proceed the five gross elements —ether, air, earth, light, and water. From consciousness also proceed the five organs of sense and the five organs of action. Intellect, consciousness, and mind, with the five subtle elements, form a subtle body,[3] which covers in the soul, and remains connected with it from transmigration to transmigration, passing in its course to celestial abodes, ranged in order of rewards for virtue or vice.[4] The soul is thus held in bondage, subject to imperfections, disease, decay, and transmigration. Until it sees the sadness of life spread out before it, in all its hopeless gloom, it is unconscious, with no object of thought, knowing nothing of the unfruitfulness of desire. To reach again this self-existent, unborn, and undying stage, it has but to gain knowledge of itself, of Prakriti, of intellect, consciousness, mind, the five subtle elements, the five gross elements, the five senses, and the five organs of action. The soul then becomes freed from pain, freed from the subtle body which sinks back into Prakriti; for "as a dancer, having exhibited herself on the stage, ceases to dance, so does Nature (Prakriti) cease (to produce) when she has made herself manifest to Soul."[5]

Such was the new-found solution held forth for man who, looking within himself, found there the problem raised which is the mission of all higher art, philosophies, and religion to present in one form or another.

[1] *See* Davies, p. 108. [2] *Ibid.*, p. 19. [3] The *linga sárira*.
[4] *See* Davies, p. 82. [5] *Ibid.*, p. 94.

The great aim for the Eastern sage was to obtain rest from transmigration, from re-birth, wherein the higher castes might descend to lower ranks, and thence into bestial and degraded forms. The problem was set forth, worked, and solved, in methods peculiarly Eastern, and therefore evasive in their subtle mysticism. Nature, or Prakriti, abstract and self-existent, was beyond the ken of the Śānkhyan sage. It could but be connoted by its triple gunas[1] of goodness, passion or energy, and darkness—the threefold essence afterwards personified in the triple gods, Vishnu, "The Preserver," Brahmā, "The Creator," and Śiva, "The Destroyer." The Eastern mind, trained from Vedic times to trace all creation from human analogy, could not escape the fatal step, and so Soul had to approach close to Nature, with the result that passion was aroused and creation ensued—a hazy generalisation that could only find its fitting place, not in a philosophy to be couched in occidental phraseology, but in the half-man, half-woman symbolic form in which the god Śiva came to be represented. The Eastern sage wandered on in *a priori* guesses, here and there betraying his trend of thought when he likens Nature to a female dancer who exposes her charms[2] that Soul may satiate itself, and then send forth the wail that its yearnings for the Infinite, the Ideal, the Absolute, have been mocked, with the result that Nature retires abashed, leaving Soul to its own loneliness.

The mystic charm is everywhere, gently persuading the mind to accept the analogy by which Nature is represented, retreating from the gaze of wearied Soul "as a modest maiden who may be surprised in *déshabillé* by a strange man, but takes good heed that another shall not behold her off her guard."[3]

[1] These gunas, or qualities, are taken as the actual substance of Prakriti. *See note* to p. 208.

[2] "Sankya Kar.," p. 59.

[3] Wilson, "Tattwa Kaumudi," p. 173.

The descent from the high idealistic beauty of the poet's dream is apparent in the setting of Śānkhyan fine-spun thought in terms of formal philosophy, as well as in the hazy speculations of the Eastern dreamer, who, in his hopes to cast a halo of reality about his visions, sends them forth as a guide towards the unknown, with the declaration: "He who knows the twenty-five principles, whatever order of life he may enter, and whether he wears braided hair, or a top knot only, or be shaven, he is free; of this there is no doubt."[1]

This doctrine was one too far removed from the yearning hopes of humanity to find acceptance outside the schools of esoteric thought. Its theological completion, however, found expression in a system by Patanjali, who in the second century B.C. compiled his "Yoga Sūtras," in which the idea of a Supreme Being is introduced. This Supreme Being, or Lord, is an Omniscient Soul, addressed as the mystic syllable "Om," infinite, directing and presiding over Nature, yet living far away, untouched by good or evil and their results. With this Divine Essence the individual soul hopes to gain union (*yoga*), and in it find absorption. By self-restraint, religious observances, by sitting in strange postures, by suppression of the breath, subduing the senses, fixing the mind by contemplation and meditation, the senses become stayed, the will falls into a mesmeric trance in which the soul is supposed to wander free with occult powers, finding nearness and ultimate union (*yoga*) with the Supreme Soul. The far-famed Yogīs[2] of India identify this Supreme Spirit with the dread god Śiva, and in their austerities and self-inflicted tortures give ample evidence of how slight the partition is 'twixt sanity and reason.

[1] Davies, p. 55.

[2] For Yogīs, astral bodies, Mahatmas, etc., *see* the interesting account in "Indian Life," by Professor Oman.

The great crown and glory of Indian thought is to be found in the tenets of the system known as the "Vedānta," or the summing-up of all the revealed knowledge of the Vedic literature.

Believers in, and expounders of, the "Vedānta" are to be found in every Hindu village. Of all philosophies of the East it is the only one which presents a seemingly unassailable front to metaphysic doubt, and at the same time extends its principles far enough to win the adherence of those who would seek some simple explanation of the lonely cravings of their soul for peace and rest in the moving changes of life. So the most learned admirer of the "Vedānta" in the West has recently declared, in the course of an address to the Bombay branch of the Royal Asiatic Society, that "the 'Vedānta,' in its unfalsified form, is the strongest support of pure morality, is the greatest consolation in the sufferings of life and death. Indians, keep to it."[1]

The full "Vedānta" doctrines were systematised and reduced to terse leading phrases in the "Brahma Sūtras" of Bādarāyana, which probably date from the fourth century B.C.[2] The full meaning of the "Sūtras" was commented on by various commentators, the greatest of whom was the renowned reformer of the eighth century, Śankara Āchārya.[3]

The first "Sūtra" of Bādarāyana gives the keynote to the system in the short rule: "Then, therefore, a desire to know Brahman." This rule as well as the remaining rules

[1] Deussen, "Elements of Metaphysics," p. 337.

[2] *See* Telang, "Bhagavad Gīta," p. 52; Max Müller ("Vedānta Philosophy," *note*, p. 29) assigns Bādarāyana to 400 A.D.

[3] It would be out of place to enter here upon the question as to whether Śankara Āchārya's interpretation of the "Sūtras" is most consistent with the framework of the system. His commentary sets forth the accepted view of at least 75 per cent. of Vedāntists in India, and though the system of Rāmānuja may be more in accordance with the letter of the "Sūtras," it is more to the purport of this history to accept the more advanced and typical rendering of Śankara. The four schools of Vedāntic teaching are known as Advaita, Viśishthādvaita, Dvaita, and Śuddhādwaita, having as their representatives Śankara, Rāmānuja, Mādhava, and Vallabha.

are to be carried in the memory; their full meaning must be expounded and explained by a competent teacher. Each word had to be commented on, and in course of time new commentaries and explanations arose. The word "then" denotes that something is antecedent to all enquiry into the "Vedānta." The person who desires to obtain the full benefit of the salvation promised by the system must, before he commences the enquiry, be in the frame of mind which the word "then" presupposes him to have acquired. This antecedent qualification draws the line closely round those select few who are competent to enter on the enquiry. It limits all enquiry, and resulting salvation, to those whose minds have been chastened by long training, to those who can claim the same heritage of refined thought and religious instincts that has fallen to the lot of the twice-born Aryans of India. The essential requisites are that the enquirer should discriminate between eternal and non-eternal; that he should be free from all desire for the reward of his acts here or hereafter; that he should be tranquil and self-restrained; that he should renounce the performance of all religious rites and ceremonies, and have patience in suffering, concentration of mind, and lastly, faith. These essentials are all the products of Eastern modes of life and thought; they strike at the basis on which are founded most of the great religious systems of the world. This much springs from the first word "then" of the "Brahma Sūtras." The word following is "therefore," on which depend equally important results. The whole of the teaching of the "Vedānta" is professedly founded on the sacred and revealed character of the Vedic literature in which were recorded all the past hopes and aspirations of the Aryan race, now called upon to venture on a hope of a higher salvation than that to be obtained from good deeds or burned offerings of the priesthood. The word "therefore" indicates that, as the revealed texts themselves declare, "as here on earth whatever has been acquired by action perishes, so perishes in the next world whatever is acquired by acts of religious duty."[1] There must be some higher aim for mankind. This highest aim is itself declared in one Upanishad to be the knowledge of Brahman, for "he who knows the Brahman attains the highest."[2] From this it "therefore" naturally follows that one has "a desire to know Brahman," and the object of the whole system is to show that the nature of Brahman is revealed in the sacred literature of India; and that he who knows the true nature of Brahman obtains release from the weary transmigration of Soul.

From the use of the word "Brahman" in the "Sūtra," it is intended that the derivation of the term from its verbal root *brih*, which indicates its chief attributes of pervading and eternal purity, will be brought to mind. It is further stated that there is "a desire" for a knowledge of Brahman. This implies that the desire will not be frustrated; that the nature of Brahman will be fully explained, and an exhaustive analysis made of all subjects necessary for its comprehension, so that ignorance may be removed and the soul be prepared to reach freedom from the causes leading on to transmigration. The second aphorism of the "Vedānta" is, shortly: "From which the origin, etc. of this." The expanded meaning is that Brahman is that from which the origin, stay, and decay of this world proceed. From out this aphorism springs the starting-point of cleavage between the varied schools holding diverse opinions as to the true interpretation of the Vedāntic teaching. In the system of Śankara Āchārya—a system of uncompromising monistic Advaita, or "non-duality"—Brahman is held to be sole entity, defined as[3]

[1] Thibaut, S.B.E., vol. xxxiv. p. 12; also "Ch. Up.," viii. 1, 6.

[2] "Taitt. Up.," ii. 1.

[3] S.B.E., "Vedānta," vol. xxxiv. p. 16.

"that omniscient, omnipotent cause from which proceeds the origin, subsistence, and dissolution of this world—which world is differentiated by names and forms, contains many agents and enjoyers, is the abode of the fruits of actions, these fruits having their definite places, times, and causes, and the nature of whose arrangement cannot even be conceived by the mind—that cause we say is Brahman." Still the question remains unanswered as to what is the nature of Brahman before the production of the world takes place, and what caused it to produce. According to Śankara, the above definition of Brahman applies to a Universal Being, of the nature of pure thought or intelligence as its sole constitution, beyond which nothing exists save an illusive principle called Māyā.[1] With this Māyā, Brahman is associated, and through it sends forth an imaged world, just as a magician produces illusive effects, or a man in sleep fashions forth appearances of animate and inanimate beings.[2]

Brahman, the Supreme Soul, which alone existed indivisible, in the beginning, as pure thought without any object of thought, had no desire nor purpose to create until Māyā produced the illusive appearance of divisibility, through which individual souls (*jīvas*) seem separated from the Supreme Soul. In its ignorance Soul knows not its true nature, which is veiled from its knowledge by Māyā, and the web of seeming reality which Māyā has woven. Not only is the creation unreal and delusive, but, moreover, it is a

[1] Avidyā, or "ignorance." The subject has been ably handled in the "Doctrine of Māyā: its Existence in the Vedāntic Sūtra, and Development in the Later Vedānta," by Raghunath N. Apte (Bombay, 1896). His conclusions are, that the doctrine of Māyā, although it had its germ in the "Upanishads," does not exist in the "Sūtras," and that it arose from the fourth century A.D. on a revival of Brāhmanism and vigorous speculation of Gaudapada and Śankara. "Gaudapada explained and formulated the doctrine, and Āchārya worked out its details."

[2] Thibaut, S.B.E., xxxiv. p. xxv.

profound error consequent on the action of Māyā. Once the individual soul holds for true its surrounding environment of mind, body, and organs of sense, it becomes a partaker in their merits and demerits, unable to shake itself clear from the necessity of birth and re-birth as the result of its acts. At the end of each period, or "kalpa," of creation, the Supreme Soul rests free from the power of Māyā, and all individual souls merge back into the pure Brahman. The great object of the "Vedānta" therefore is to teach the individual souls the true knowledge of Brahman and the delusive working of Māyā. From knowledge the individual soul recognises itself truly as Brahman—a knowledge which nullifies the delusion of Māyā and obtains for the soul immediate release and freedom, or union and identity with Brahman. The great cry of Vedāntic release from transmigration is : "*Tat twam asi*" ("Thou art That") ; or in Western phraseology, Thy soul is not merely Divine or God-like, it is Divine, it is God ; and there is no real existence anywhere save God and Soul which are identical. The world is a dream, presenting passing visions of sin and sorrow amid which the soul moves in lonely separation until it finds its safe abiding-place in eternal union with Brahman. The "Vedānta" further, according to Śankara, teaches a twofold knowledge. It teaches that there is a Lord, or "Īśvara," a lower Brahman, conditioned by attributes and related to the world so long as the delusive action of Māyā subsists. By following the practices of meditation and devotion, as laid down in the Vedic texts, which declare the nature of, and the conduct to be pursued in relation to, the lower Brahman, the individual gains his reward here and hereafter, and rises to higher and higher spheres of activity and enjoyment. Yet these are but preparations for the knowledge of the higher Brahman ; pure consciousness without any object to be conscious of ; pure joy without anything to rejoice over ; pure being without any second, which is taught also in Vedic texts, the expounding of which is the purport of the "Vedānta."[1]

Kant, followed by Schopenhauer, showed how the phenomenal world, as existing in space, and time, and moved throughout[2] by causality, is but a representation of these three innate perceptive forms of our intellect. So Śankara Āchārya held that the highest Brahman, being devoid of all these three innate perceptive forms of time, space, and cause, can only be defined by negation. The one loved answer to all enquiries as to the qualities of Brahman is, "No, no," for there is no power of mind that can fathom its true nature. Śankara simply held that the human intellect had not arrived at that stage of development in which it could postulate that its innate perceptive form of time, space, and causality were applicable in dealing with the nature of a Brahman and its manifestations, transcending, as these do, all finite limitations.[3] The world seen is but the shadowed-forth form of the subjective forms of intellect, and therefore but realised so far as the imperfectly-developed condition of the intellect permits it to be conceived. The man who dreams, and an organism imagined as moving in space of two dimensions, or even of one dimension, have as limited a knowledge of the true mysteries of life and existence as the man whom the Vedāntist holds to be bound by the spell of Māyā.

The "Sūtras"[4] themselves declare that, in the pursuit of knowledge, reasoning which disregards revelation is of no value. Śankara, in his interpretation of the "Sūtra," declares that arguments, ingenious in themselves, are but

[1] *Sad-cid-ānanda*, the triple constitution of Brahman, just as *satwas*, *raja*, *tamas* was the triple constitution of the Śankyan Prakriti.

[2] Deussen, "Metaphysics," p. 331.

[3] S.B.E., vol. xxxviii.; "Sūtras," iii. 2, 3:—"But the dream-world is mere illusion—Māyā, on account of its nature not manifesting itself with the totality of the attributes of reality."

[4] S.B.E., vol. xxxiv. 2, 1, 11.

advanced by clever men to be afterwards found fallacious by others more clever. He holds that "the true nature of the cause of the world, on which final emancipation depends, cannot, on account of its excessive abstruseness, even be thought of without the help of the holy texts."[1]

As sources of knowledge, the "Upanishads"[2] are held by Śankara to be the chief works, and as confirmation for their import, the "Smriti." The lower Brahman, as limited by attributes, and as seen by ignorance, is but an object of worship. "According as a man worships him that he becomes."[3] The highest Brahman, as free and pure, can be only an object of revealed knowledge. Yet remains the question as to why Brahman, through this association with Māyā, should be under any necessity to create the world, for it acts just as a "person when in a state of frenzy proceeds, owing to his mental aberration, to action without a motive."[4] The answer is that "Brahman's creative activity is mere sport, such as we see in ordinary life."[5] Even then comes in the question why the Creator has cruelly awarded merit and demerit indifferently. Eastern pessimism holds that the gods are happy, men less happy, and animals eminently unhappy; yet the Scriptures declare the Lord to be of essential goodness. The answer given is similar to that given by Hamlet, unable to explain to himself why he should be thrust into a world out of joint to set it right: "For if the sun bred maggots in a dead dog"—is that to be argued as against the purity of the sun? Śankara answers:[6] "The position of the Lord is to be looked upon as analogous to that of Parjanya, 'The Giver of Rain.' For as Parjanya is the common cause of the production of rice, barley, and other plants, while the

[1] *See* S.B.E., vol. xxxiv. p. 316.

[2] Not only the older "Upanishads," but also the later, as well as the "Mahābhārata" and "Bhagavad Gīta."

[3] S.B.E., vol. xxxiv; "Sūtra," i. 1, 11.

[4] *Ibid.*, ii. 1, 32.

[5] *Ibid.*, ii. 1, 33.

[6] *Ibid.*, p. 358.

difference between the various species is due to the various potentialities lying hid in the respective seeds, so the Lord is the common cause of the creation of gods, man, etc., while the differences between these classes of beings are due to the different merit belonging to the individual souls." If the enquirer ask further how the Lord came to be bound in His creation by a regard for past merit and demerit, the answer is, that it is known from the revelation of Vedic texts, that "a man becomes good by good work, bad by bad work."[1] And the "Gīta" declares in confirmation: "I serve men in the way in which they approved me."[2] The answer is, in fact, that the emanation of the transmigratory world is without a beginning, and that merit and demerit arise like seed and sprout, without which no one could come into existence.[3]

If the Brahman alone exists "without parts, without actions, tranquil, without fault, without taint,"[4] and his nature is only to be described by silence, or by the ever-repeated formula, "No, no,"[5] it may be asked how it, One only without a Second, can cause the creation of the world, which existed from before all time. The only answer is, that it is by a "peculiar constitution of its causal substance, as in the case of milk" which turns into curds,[6] or analogous to the manner in which the "female crane conceives without a male, and as the lotus wanders from one pool to another without any means of conveyance."[7] It is, in short, impossible, without the aid of Scripture, to conceive "the true nature of Brahman, with its powers unfathomable by thought."

If the objector answers that he cannot, from holy texts,

[1] "Brih.-Aran. Up.," iii. 2, 13; S.B.E., vol. xv.
[2] "Bhagavad Gīta," S.B.E., viii. iv. p. 59.
[3] S.B.E., vol. xxxiv. p. 360.
[4] "Svetâs. Up.," vi. 19.
[5] "Brih.-Aran. Up.," vi. 6, 15:—"That Self is to be described by No, no!"
[6] *Ibid.*, ii. 1, 24; "Vedânta Sûtras," S.B.E., vol. xxxiv. p. 346.
[7] "Brih.-Aran. Up.," ii. 1, 25; "Vedânta Sûtras," S.B.E., vol. xxxiv. p. 347.

understand what is apparently contradictory, the reply is that the apparent inconsistency is due to the fact that all these questions are mere matter of names and forms, for Brahman itself is raised above the world and the "element of plurality which is the fiction of nescience."

The individual soul remains, according to Śankara, ever eternal. Its essence is intelligence or knowledge. It is identical with Brahman, from which it is separated at the time of creation by its illusive connection with its adjuncts. "It is not born; it dies not; it is immortal. It is, indeed, Brahman."[1]

So long as the soul gains not freedom by knowledge of its true nature, it passes[2] to reap its reward for good deeds to the moon, and then descends to earth again.[3]

By meditation on Brahman, and by Divine knowledge, the soul "shakes off all evil as a horse shakes his hair, and shaking off the body as the moon frees herself from the mouth of Rahu, obtains, self-made and satisfied, the uncreated world of Brahman."[4]

The wise man who sees through the unreality of pain and sorrow, and recognises that this whole fabric of a vision will vanish as a dream, will find that "the fetter of the heart is all broken, doubts are solved, extinguished are all his works."[5] And yet again, "as water does not cling to a lotus leaf, so no evil deed clings to him who knows this."[6] The full sublimity of this freedom from the results of even past acts on the attainment of knowledge is shortly summed up as follows: "Brahman am I, hence I neither was an agent nor an enjoyer at any previous time, nor am I such at the present time, nor

[1] "Vedānta Sūtras," ii. iii. 17.

[2] Surrounded by subtle elements (*bhūta sukshma*), the abode of the eleven prānās (*buddhīndriyas, Karmedriyas, and the manas*).

[3] "Brihad. Up.," iii. 1, 8-10.

[4] "Ch. Up.," viii. 13.

[5] "Mandukya. Up.," ii. 28.

[6] "Ch. Up.," iv. 143.

shall I be such at any future time."[1] More definitely and tersely is summed up freedom from all results of good or evil deeds in the verse:[2] "If one should recognise the Soul saying, I am Brahman, desiring what, or for the love of whom should he trouble himself." As enunciated by Śankara, the crown and glory of his system is, that once Brahman is comprehended all duties come to an end, all work is over.

It is not meant here that the Vedāntic system is non-moral in its essence;[3] it simply means that when the soul becomes free from the delusion of belief in a world as set forth by Māyā, it is one with Brahman. It rests in sovereign isolation, untouched by the sin or sorrow of the world, "watching over all works, dwelling in all beings, the witness, the perceiver, the only one, free from all qualities."

The system of Śankara stands supreme as the loftiest height to which Eastern intuitive thought has reached. It has more influence in India than all other phases of thought. It is part of the life-blood of the nation. It is as natural to the land as the miasmic vapours which rise and permeate, with their heavy taint, the brain-matter of

[1] "Śankara Com.," p. 355; S.B.E., vol. xxxiv.

[2] "Brihad. Up.," iv. 4, 12.

[3] *See* Deussen, p. 433:—"Die Erlösung durch keine Art von Werk, auch nicht durch moralische Besserung, sondern allein durch die Erkenntniss—vollbracht wird." An objection to the teaching is given by Prof. R. K. Bhandarkar in his "Visit to the Vienna Congress" (J.R.A.S., Bombay, vol. xvii. p. 76), where he narrates a conversation he had on the subject with Prof. Max Müller:—"As I am not an admirer of the doctrine in the form in which it is taught by Śankara Āchārya, and which is now the prevalent form in India, I observed that though, according to his system, a man must rise to the knowledge, 'I am Brahma,' previous to his entering on the state of deliverance or of eternal bliss, still it is essential that the feeling of *me* or *egoism* should be destroyed as a necessary condition of entrance into that state. The *me* is the first fruit of ignorance, and it must be destroyed in the liberated condition. A soul has no individual consciousness when he is delivered, and in that state he cannot have the knowledge, 'I am Brahma.'"

the dwellers in the land where man has thought much that at times astounds for its deep and clear insight, and much that astounds for its lack of freedom from the trammels of a time-worn past. In the Vedāntic philosophy there lies one assumption—that of Māyā—which pervades and vitiates the whole philosophic purport of the teaching. Once accepted as a working hypothesis it solves the problem that Kant and Kapila had to take for granted —the objective reality of the perceptions of the senses. With this doctrine the school of Rāmānuja, who follows the more exoteric teaching of qualified non-duality, will have naught to do. Brahman, according to his rendering, is truly the deity Vishnu, or Nārāyana, who is endowed with all good qualities, intelligence being but its chief attribute. He is all-knowing, all-merciful, all-pervading, and all-powerful, matter and soul being the very essential elements of his nature, though in but a germinal state till creation occurs.[1] At the beginning of great "kalpas," or periods of creation, this Lord, by his own volition, acts on unevolved matter and non-manifest soul, so that the former becomes manifest, and souls acquire material bodies corresponding to their good or bad deeds in previous existences. According to this doctrine of modified non-duality, Vishnu, Brahmā, or the Lord, is, by nature, a personal deity, evolving the world and individual soul out from himself. The soul remains personally existent, and on its release from migration, passes into an undisturbed bliss in Heaven.

The systems of the "Śānkhya," "Yoga," "Vedānta," and that of the "Bhagavad Gīta," stand naturally together as seeking to free the soul from its ceaseless transmigration. Starting from the Śānkhya assumption that matter—Pradhāna, or Prakriti—is roused to action by the near proximity of Soul, just as a magnet, by its inherent nature, acts on the keeper brought close to it, the constant yearning

[1] Thibaut, S.B.E., vol. xxxiv. p. xxix.

of the Indian mind is to seek some means whereby the act of creation may be nullified, and the soul once more set free from the force which condemned it to conscious existences, compelling it to proceed from birth to birth, through long periods, or "kalpas," during which the initial force, set in action at the commencement of creation, continues its potentiality.

All these systems, down to that of the "Bhagavad Gīta," which takes a more strictly theological than philosophical view of the question, are allied as consecutive phases of investigation by the same order of mind, tied down by its environment, physical and climatic, to a mode of viewing life and reasoning thereon in a manner essentially Eastern.

Everywhere there is an exuberant play of fancy, as though the soul was but dreaming dim visions of a mirrored life, and the mind was not sternly laying down cold and logical facts concerning the injustice of God, and the deeps of despair into which His act has hurled the pleading soul. The whole treatment of the subject is mystic, unemotional, except in so far as the theoriser is concerned. The mind has reached, by the deepest intuitive stretch of thought that the history of the world's philosophy knows of, to an *a priori* solution of some of the profoundest problems before science of to-day. Nevertheless, when the mind turns back to trace the course by which it arrived at these conclusions, it is constrained to linger everywhere along the path, and lose itself in dreamy ponderings over some idea conjured up by the fancy or lose itself in play over its own marvellous guess-work.

Even when the whole subject has been reduced to dry and formal aphorism, it is the ingenuity, and the craft, and delicate manipulation and cunning whereby everything is so set, as in mosaic that no flaw is left to found thereon a hostile criticism, that remains as the chief charm, and constrains the admiration rather than the dignity of the subject-matter or importance of the facts set forth. Though a deeper ring of earnestness runs through the cogitations of the Indian philosopher than through the corresponding schools of Greek philosophy, yet this is purely subjective and not objective. Never could it pass beyond the observer, and become actively interested in the practical application of his methods. To the Vedāntist all nature is GOD; nothing truly exists except God. Man is God if man but chooses to recognise himself as such; yet all Sūdras, all women, all not twice-born, were absolutely shut out, after careful consideration, from participation in the knowledge of the "Vedānta," and from any hope of arriving at that knowledge.

Two schools of philosophy—those known as the Nyāya and Vaiśeshika—stand apart from the more orthodox schools as individual in themselves, and are more allied to the purely scientific order of thought that produced such works as the "Grammatical Aphorisms of Pānini," and those dealing with the subjects of medicine, geometry, or astronomy.

The "Nyāya of Gautama" deals not only with the general subjects of human knowledge, but also gives an analytical exposition of the laws of thought and reasoning.

The Vaiśeshika system of Kanada[1] obtains its name from the doctrine that the world is supposed to be formed from the aggregation of atoms, each atom having an eternal essence, Viśesha, of its own; the atoms, which are eternal and existing without a cause, uniting, form the

[1] Jacobi in tracing (S.B.E., vol. xlv. p. xxxiv.) the relative position of Jainism with reference to other systems, points out the unscientific phraseology of the "Vedānta" and "Śānkhya," arising from the confusion of the category of substance with that of the category of quality: "Things which we recognise as qualities are constantly mistaken for and mixed up with substance." Alluding to the more scientific and philosophic arrangement of the "Nyāya-Vaiśeshika," he further remarks that "the categories of substance and qualities had been already clearly distinguished for one another, and had been recognised as correlative terms . . . in the Vaiśeshika philosophy which defines substance as the substratum of quality, and quality as that which is inherent in substance."

world. Colebrooke describes the process of creation as follows:[1]—"Two earthly atoms concurring by an unseen peculiar virtue (*adrishta*) or by the will of God, or by time, or by other competent cause, constitute a double atom of earth; and by concourse of these binary atoms a tertiary atom is produced, and by concourse of four triple atoms a quaternary atom, and so on to a gross, grosser, or grossest man of earth, the great earth is produced."

By the side of this atomic theory is the theory of existence of eternal souls, and a Supreme Soul of the Universe. "The seat of knowledge is the Soul. It is two-fold—the living and the Supreme Soul. The Supreme Soul is Lord, omniscient, one only, subject to neither pleasure nor pain, infinite and eternal."

[1] Monier-Williams, "Indian Wisdom," p. 83.

CHAPTER X.

THE EPICS.

ONE great task remained in India for Brāhmanism to set its hand to. If in that task Brāhmanism may be said to have failed, the failure cannot be ascribed to lack of genius. In all spheres of higher art, genius is ever confined to working on the lines along which it is impelled by its own instincts. Outside these limits it may venture and attain to results that astound and compel admiration, but in those results there will be ever found wanting the true touch of that inspiration which demands the universal and abiding recognition of humanity that something has been produced that the world would not willingly let die.

India has sent forth work stamped with all the peculiar impress of its own genius—works such as the lyric outbursts of the "Vedas," the mystic ponderings of the "Upanishads" and "Vedānta," as well as the highly dramatic productions of Sūr Dās and Tulsi Dās in the later days of Akbar—which will ever demand a place in the very first ranks of the world's literature, but this place could never be claimed for the two great Herculean labours of Brāhmanism—the construction of the two Indian so-called epics, the "Mahābhārata," and "Rāmāyana." These two vast poems were compiled by Brāhmans for the purpose of giving sacerdotal recognition to the floating folk-lore and epic traditions of the people, which have thus been preserved in the only form that Aryan genius could have preserved them, and that is a form curtailed of nearly all that was realistically and dramatically essential to the true epic.

Side by side with the Vedic literature[1] there existed in India, from times that may stretch back to the mists of Indo-Germanic antiquity, the legends of tribal warriors and their heroic deeds. These were held among the people as their national folk-songs, and were sung from court to court, from homestead to homestead, by travelling bards. Even to-day the professional bard, with his store of songs, is known everywhere in India, from north to south, from east to west. Not only are the tales of Rājput chivalry and Marātha daring recited in the homes where those of Rājput or Marātha descent dwell, but even the wars, victories, and defeats of the French and English, in their conquests over the petty chieftains and great feudatories, are sung from village to village. All of these ruggedly-versed stories are instinct with dramatic power. With true epic genius they are more concerned in the characters than in the historic setting. It is impossible to generalise for a vast continent such as India, especially when there are no written records dealing with the subject, so it can only here be asserted that, so far as South India is concerned, where the author has listened to, and copied the songs, of many travelling bards, these narratives are of absorbing dramatic reality. So deeply do the bards enter into the moving scenes they so vividly picture forth, and, strange to say, their imagination seems to dwell more, so far as the West is concerned, on the exploits of French generals, such as Dupleix, Bussy, and Labourdonnais, than on the deeds of the English, that the emotions of the

[1] Holtzmann, "Mahâbhârata" :—„ Epos und Veda sind gleich alt."

reciters follow in quick, changing moods each scene and incident. So intensely are the feelings of these impulsive Eastern bards aroused, that as their tears fall, and their feelings rise at the most pathetic lines—such as those describing how the women of Bobbili sought death in the flames to escape from the French conquest, and their fighting men rushed forth to die, arms in hand—they, to conceal the deep hold the narrative has taken over them, often burst forth for a moment into a jingling verse of meaningless import, or even of ribald nonsense.

Throughout the two great compositions known as the "Mahābhārata" and "Rāmāyana," there lies a substratum of this old, true, epic narrative.

In the West, in the lands of the Kuru Panchālas, and in the East, in the land of the Kośālas, the local bards, from time unknown, had sung the heroic deeds of the tribal heroes and deities, mingling fact and fiction, natural and supernatural, into short and disconnected dramatic pictures, wherein the characters move free and life-like.[1] All these folk-songs and supernatural legends of local aboriginal deities were outside the stately purposes for which early Brāhmanism had set itself, in sovereign isolation, apart from the mass of the people. The time, however, came when it had to recognise the existence of traditions, thoughts, and aspirations, other than its own. Some compromise had to be made; a bond of friendship and alliance had to be entered into with the mass of local history, superstition, and religion, so that they might be assimilated into Brāhmanic literature, and pass as part of the armoury of priestcraft. The compromise was one of

[1] Professor Ker, in his "Epic and Romance," says that "to require of the poetry of an heroic age that it shall recognise the historical incoming and importance of the events in which it originates, and the persons whose names it uses, is entirely to mistake the nature of it. Its nature is to find or make some drama played by kings and heroes, and to let the historical framework take care of itself."

bondage ill-suited to the Aryan genius, and as a consequence, the traces of it are patent everywhere.[1]

The cultured and learned Brāhmans—the "Mahābhārata" is ascribed to one Vyāsa—accordingly wove into two colossal verse poems, one for the West of India, one for the East, all the floating mass of epic tradition, demonology, and local hero-worship, essaying, in the effort, to unite the whole into connected stories. So far as the epic portion was concerned, its movements were foreign to Brāhmanic instincts and genius. The Brāhmans were subtle dreamers and thinkers. They had drawn themselves apart from the warrior class and warrior ways, yet they now found themselves called upon to glorify and dramatise the acts of heroes, and to depict the stirring scenes of strife and bloodshed. So far as demonology and hero-worship were concerned, the Brāhmans had long since ceased to build up for themselves even the indistinct outlines of the Vedic gods, and yet they essayed to clothe the local heroes, demons, goblins, and fierce deities, with the cast-off armoury and attributes of their Indra, Sūrya, Rudra, and following train of Devas. The task[2] has been accomplished; the "Mahābhārata" runs to 20,000 lines in eighteen sections, and the "Rāmāyana" to no less than 48,000 lines.

In the "Rāmāyana" the legends of the hero Rāma, as sung by the Eastern bards in their vernaculars, were strung together in the classical Sanskrit verse by the Brāhman poet, Valmīki. Rāma, a local conquering warrior and deified

[1] Here I part altogether from Mr Dahlmann's theory that the union of epic and law is a chemical union and not a mechanical union. J. Dahlmann, "Das Mahābhārata als Epos und Rechtsbuch" (Berlin, 1895-98); *see* Bühler and Kirste, "Ind. Stud." (1892).

[2] "Not re-edited or re-published in the polished Sanskrit language till the adaptation of Sanskrit to profane literature somewhere about thirteenth century of our era."—Grierson, "Ind. Ant." (December 1894), p. 55. "It has been conclusively shown" (Bühler and Kirste, "Contribution to Study of Mahābhārata") "that the poem was recognised in 300 A.D., and by 500 A.D. was essentially the same as it now exists."

hero, rises in the "Rāmāyana" to be exemplar of all morality and duty, a descent on earth or incarnation of the god Vishnu for the repression of wrong and the inculcation of virtue. This didactic element is the Brāhmanic infusion which in the "Rāmāyana," as well as in the "Mahābhārata," strings the detached epic elements and disconnected episodes together, to the unavoidable weakening of the dramatic force and epic character of the narrative.

In the "Rāmāyana" the deeds of Rāma, the descendant of the Solar race of Ikshvaku, form the epic background. Rāma, the eldest son of Daśaratha, the fabled king of Ayodhya, or Oudh, was banished from his father's kingdom in consequence of Daśaratha's submission to Kaikeyī, the wicked mother of Rāma's younger brother Bhārata, for whom she longed to procure the crown. Rāma and his gentle wife, Sītā, departed from Ayodhya to spend their term of fourteen years' banishment in the southern forests. The unity of the narrative centres round the adventures in the forest and heroic deeds of Rāma to regain his wife, Sītā, who was forcibly borne away by a fierce ten-headed monster, Rāvana, King of Lanka, an island which some, forgetting the unhistorical motive of the early preservers of epic tradition, have identified with Ceylon. In the hands of Tulsi Dās, the Shakespeare of Akbar's time, the characters rise from out their didactic surroundings and live not in their lost original epic reality, but with a dramatic vividness that has raised them into romantic ideals. Whatever of interest for a study of the history of the Indian people is preserved in the ancient Sanskrit so-called epic, "Rāmāyana," will therefore be found in the much more popular vernacular rendering of Tulsi Dās, where it can be best considered.[1]

The "Mahābhārata" remains unaltered from its chaotic and early Sanskrit redaction. Whatever historic value it may

[1] *See* p. 367 (*post*).

have lies not in its scattered and subdued epic fragments,[1] loosely strung together by didactic teachings, irrelevant episodes, artificial battle scenes, and classic descriptions of scenery, but in the evidences it affords of the existence of beliefs and creeds that were aspiring to the patronage of Brāhmanism, with which they were to unite to form the popular religion, known as Hinduism, of the mass of Aryan and non-Aryan people classed as Hindus.

The central story of the epic revolves round the rivalries between the Kurus, the hundred sons of Dhritarāshtra, descendant of Bhārata of the Lunar dynasty, the fabled conqueror of all India north of Delhi, and the five Pāndava princes, said to be sons of Dhritarāshtra's[2] elder brother, the pale-skinned Pāndu. The "Mahābhārata" is thus made to represent a great contest between the descendants of Bhārata for the possession of North India, ever known as the land of Bhārata, or Bhārata Varsha.

The rivalries of the warrior heroes end in eighteen battles fought on the plain of Kurukshetra, in which the Kurus are exterminated and the Pāndavas gain the kingdom, perform the great horse sacrifice, denoting their universal sway, and finally, after a glorious reign, take their long and lonely journey towards Mount Meru, there to enter the Heaven of Indra. As in the "Rāmāyana" and "Iliad," the wrongs suffered by a woman supply the motive force to rouse the heroism of the warriors, for the true epic ever rises free above all the

[1] "I believe that the Hindu epic is ancient, as ancient in its origin as the earliest traditions of the nation."—Barth, "Ind. Ant." (1895), p. 71.

[2] Holtzmann ("Das Mahābhārata," i. 156; ii. 174) has advanced weighty reasons for concluding that Bhīshma, the uncle of the Pāndavas, was the real father of the five princes, having been appointed to marry his brother's wife. The Niyoga, similar to the Levirate, allowed the sonless widow to bear a child to her brother-in-law on her husband's death, so as to continue the family. In the early law books the custom was restricted by very definite directions. It was not until the time of the revised epic that the Brāhmans made efforts to become the chosen partners of sonless wives or widows. The meaning is quite obvious, and totally opposed to Mr Dahlmann's theory of the epic as a law book.

restraining facts of prosaic history. Draupadī, the common wife of the five Pāndava brothers is, in the "Mahābhārata," the cause of the great slaughter on the plain of Kurukshetra, where, as the narrator of the poem tells, "in that great battle of the Kurus came hundreds and thousands of monarchs for fighting against each other. The names of that innumerable host I am unable to recount even in ten thousand years." Kurukshetra, the scene of slaughter, where the ancient race of Kurus was defeated by a confederacy of hostile tribes, headed by a band of non-Aryan warriors, to whom Brāhmanic power was obliged to submit and assign a fictitious relationship with Aryan folk, became one of the holiest places of pilgrimage for all Hindus. This holy place of sacrifice, the plain on which Aryanism and Brāhmanism[1] suffered their first crushing defeat at the hands of the despised non-Aryan, probably Dravidian, races, was the very spot over which Brāhmanism sang its loudest songs of triumph, so that all record of the defeat might be passed over in the pages of history. The battle-field was lauded as so sacred that "he is freed from all sins who constantly sayeth, 'I will live in Kurukshetra.' The very dust of Kurukshetra, conveyed by the wind, leadeth a sinful man to a blessed course in after life. They that dwell in Kurukshetra, which lieth to the south of the Sarasvatī and the north of the Drishadvatī, are said to dwell in Heaven. O hero, one should reside there, O thou foremost of warriors, for a

[1] Even if this defeat be held not to be conclusively shown to have happened at the hands of an un-Aryan foe (*see* Jolly, "Recht und Sitte," p. 48), and even if it be contested that there is not sufficient evidence, though I do not see that the weight of the evidence does not establish it, that a custom such as polyandry may be no more than a family custom, still this does not affect the main point which it is here the object to lead up to, the intrusion of Krishna and Śiva worship into Brāhmanic circles. The whole history is doubtful and obscure. The view that presents itself as most plausible and readily understood is here accepted, though I am perfectly aware of the insecurity of the position. In the "Lalita Vistara" the Pāndavas are a rude tribe. *See* Weber, "Indian Literature," pp. 126-35.

month. Thou, O Lord of the earth, the gods with Brahmā at their head, the Rishis, the Siddhas, the Charanas, the Gandharvas, the Apsaras, the Yakshas, the Nāgas, often repair, O Bhārata, to the highly sacred Kurukshetra. O foremost of warriors, the sins of one that desireth to repair to Kurukshetra, even mentally, are all destroyed, and he finally goeth into the region of Brahmā." The "Mahābhārata" is steeped in exordiums such as this, inculcating sacred duties and expounding moral principles, all necessary for a Brāhmanic purpose ever desirous of extending its influence over established systems and supporting *de facto* principalities.

The Pāndavas are stated in the poem to have been instructed, at Hastinapur, in the use of arms and in warrior feats, along with their fictitious cousins, the Kuru princes, by Drona, a Brāhman preceptor. When the time came for Yuddhisthira, the leader ever firm in war, the eldest of the Pāndava brothers, to be crowned King of Hastinapur, he and his brothers were persuaded by the intrigues of the one hundred Kuru princes, to depart from the city on a visit to a town eight days' distance. The Pāndavas were thus removed from Hastinapur, where it was necessary, for the purpose of the poem—to give them a relationship with the Kurus—that they should spend their childhood. It was further necessary to account for the mode whereby they afterwards appeared as leaders of a great national movement against the exclusive system built up by Aryanism. The Pāndavas, as ultimately the winning side, are glorified as models of all virtue, law and justice. It has even been held that the whole poem is an allegory symbolising the ever-recurring strife between the might of righteousness and the evil of passion, between justice and injustice, between right and wrong,[1] justice being personi-

[1] Dahlmann, "Das Mahābhārata als Epos und Rechtsbuch" (Berlin, 1895-98). Although the theory of Dahlmann is ingeniously worked out, I am unable to accept it as in any sense setting forth the purport of the poem.

fied in Yuddhisthira, the leader of the Pāndavas, injustice being personified in Duryodhana, the eldest of the Kurus. It could not, however, have been until long after these events —until the Pāndavas, in fact, had won their cause, and established their position—that they were glorified by the Brāhmans as incarnations of divinity, and all evidence of their rude habits and alien descent obliterated as far as possible. The Pāndavas, with their mother, are represented as leaving Hastinapur for their pleasure-trip to the eight-days'-away town, amid the weeping and wailing of all the inhabitants. The Kurus, in the meantime, prepared for their reception a house, into the walls of which had been skilfully built "hemp, resin, heath, straw, and bamboo, all soaked in clarified butter." The Pāndavas found out the details of the plot laid against their lives and at once prepared to escape. They dug an underground passage from the house to the outside forest, and then enacted a part more fitting to rude savages than to incarnations of justice. They prepared a feast, "and desirous of obtaining food, there came, as if impelled by the fates, to that feast, in course of her wandering, a Nishāda woman, the mother of five children, accompanied by all her sons. And, O king, she and her children, intoxicated with the wine they drank, became incapable." The cunning of the Pāndavas had succeeded. They set the house on fire, and disappeared through the underground passage. The low-caste woman and her five children, whom Brāhmanic justice sees no moral wrong in slaying, were burned to death, and when their charred bodies were recovered, the rumour was spread abroad that the Pāndavas had vanished off the scene. The trick is one of stage melodrama. The Pāndavas were cut adrift from Hastinapur, and free to commence their true career. The entrance of the brethren on the new scene has a true epic touch, although it be in the uncertain realms of the supernatural. The figure of Bhīma, the fierce and savage warrior, the smasher, in the last great fight, of the thigh of Duryodhana, emerges from the underground passage, with all the avenging might of a demon foe let loose to pursue his relentless course. He was the fierce Vrikodara, the "Wolf Stomached," who hovered near his brethren endowed with more than human powers, and armed with magic missiles. The supernatural shrouds him round, but from it he rises clear and distinct, the life-like creation of true epic genius. The wooden hut is burning fiercely; the first links uniting Aryanism with its new fetters are being forged; while from out the darkness of the cavern arises Bhīma, "taking his mother on his shoulders, the twin-brothers, Nakula and Sahadeva, on both his arms, Vrikodara, of great energy and strength, and endowed with the velocity of the wind, commenced his march, breaking the trees with his breast, and pressing deep the earth with his steps."

The scene grows darker and gloomier. Brāhmanism has to watch the coming struggle, note its course, and side with the winning force. New ways and customs have to be temporised with, new gods accepted, and new superstitions made room for. The storm the Pāndavas and their allies were to raise was coming fast. The epic fades away as the Brāhmans set the story to a purpose. Bhīma hastens on, bearing his mother and his brothers, to seek the deep recesses of the forest, whence he and the Pāndavas emerge on their true career. "The twilight deepened, the cries of birds and beasts became fiercer; darkness surrounded everything from view, and an untimely wind began to blow that broke and laid low many a tree, large and small, and many a creeper with dry leaves and fruit."[1]

Brāhmanism had for long remained in sovereign isolation. As Bhīma cried out in his wrath against the Kurus: "He who hath no jealous and evil-minded relatives, liveth in

[1] "Adi Parva," § 153.

happiness in this world, like a single tree in a village. The tree that standeth single in a village with its leaves and fruits, from absence of others of the same species, becometh sacred and is worshipped and venerated by all."[1]

The first great friendship made in the forest by the Pāndavas, was with the sister of a demon Rākshasa. This Rākshasa was a cannibal, an eater of raw flesh, such as the early Aryans described their Dasyu foes to have been. This fierce dweller in the forest recesses, where dwelt the rude aboriginal races, "was now hungry and longing for human food."[2]

A long fight ensued between Bhīma and the fierce Rākshasa, until at length "the Rākshasa sent forth a terrible yell that filled the whole forest, and deep as the sound of a wet drum. Then the mighty Bhīma, holding the body with his hands, bent it double, and breaking it in the middle, greatly gratified his brothers."[3]

The sister of the demon stood by watching the fight, for, at the bidding of her brother, she had assumed the form of a fair woman to entice the Pāndavas into her brother's power, but had relented of her purpose on beholding the beauty of the fierce Bhīma. For one year she remained with Bhīma, and then her son was born, and named Ghatotkacha, or "pot-headed," for his head was bald. Ghatotkacha became the famed warrior, an incarnation of Indra, who fought in the foremost rank against the Kurus, only to be slain by Karna.[4]

The further allies of the Pāndavas had now to be accounted for. News came to them that Draupadī, the daughter of the King of the Panchālas, was about to hold her Svayamvāra. Draupadī is described as having "eyes like lotus leaves, and features that are faultless; endued with youth and intelligence, she is extremely beautiful."

[1] "Adi Parva," § 153. [2] *Ibid.*, p. 446. [3] *Ibid.*, p. 454.

[4] Son of Kuntī—the son miraculously conceived before her marriage with Pāndu.

She is "the slender-waisted Draupadī, of every feature perfectly faultless, and whose body emitteth a fragrance like unto that of a blue lotus full two miles round."[1]

To her Svayamvāra came monarchs and princes from various lands, and "from various countries, actors, and bards, singing the panegyrics of kings and dancers, and reciters of 'Purānas,' and heralds, and powerful athletes."[2]

All failed to bend a wondrous bow, the test of the skill and strength of the competing suitors. The five Pāndu princes advanced, disguised as Brāhmans, and Arjuna, the ideal type of manly heroism and knightly courtesy, drew the bow and pierced the mark, so that Draupadī became his prize, and the Pāndus won the alliance of the Panchālas. So far the poem is free from taint, but, unfortunately for Brāhmanic purposes, the early epic preserved the unfettered truth that the Pāndavas were of a polyandrous race, like many of the present aboriginal races of India. Draupadī, in the original epic, was the common wife of the five Pāndava brethren. This was a custom opposed to all Aryan habits, for, as the present poem itself contends, "it hath ever been directed that one man may have many wives, but it never hath been heard that one woman may have many husbands. O son of Kuntī, pure as thou art, and acquainted with the rules of morality, it behoveth thee not to commit an act that is sinful, and opposed to usage and the 'Vedas.'" This is the Brāhmanic objection urged by the father of Draupadī to Yuddhisthira, the eldest of the Pāndu brothers. The Pāndus and their polyandry, and all the aboriginal customs, superstitions, and tribal deities, had, nevertheless, to be brought within the fold of Brāhmanism. The marriage of Draupadī to the five brothers is explained away by the Brāhmanic apology that it arose out of a mistake. The Pāndus, when they brought Draupadī home to their mother, who resided in a potter's house, a

[1] "Adi Parva," p. 525.

[2] *Ibid.*, p. 528.

house in which a Brāhman may still take up his residence, are represented in the poem to have cried out that they had obtained alms that day. The mother, not understanding that her five sons referred to Draupadī, directed them to share together,[1] and as the command of a mother could not be recalled or broken, Draupadī had to consent to wed the five Pāndus. With their new-won allies the Pāndavas appeared again in Hastinapur and demanded their share in the kingdom. Their claim was compromised, and they received the land lying along the Jumna, where they laid the foundations of the ancient Delhi, known from of old as Indra-prastha.

At Indra-prastha the five princes measured out the limits of their new abode. There they cleared the forest, reclaimed the land, and raised the walls of India's great capital, "and surrounded it by a trench wide as the sea, and by walls reaching high into Heaven, and awhile, as the fleecy clouds or the rays of the moon, that foremost of cities rose adorned like the capital of the nether kingdom, encircled by the Nāgas. And it stood adorned with palatial mansions and numerous gates, each furnished with a couple of panels resembling the outstretched wings of Garuda. And the gateways that protected the town were high as the Mandara mountain, and massy as the clouds. And furnished with numerous weapons of attack, the

[1] "Adi Parva," ¶ 193. The whole accounts in the poem are disjointed and disconnected. Three solutions are set forth to explain the action of the five brothers, all equally evasive of the main issue. I fail to follow the fantastic theory of Dahlmann, that the united marriage of the five brothers symbolised the undivided unity of a joint family. The subject of the joint family, as well as of the Niyoga, have been so far carefully avoided. The whole evidence on the subject is fully in the hands of scholars, and as yet no historical treatise on the subject is forthcoming. The law books ("Gautama," xxvii. 4) show that division was favoured by the Brāhmans, as encouraging an increase of responsibility and rites. The undivided family exists in India down to the present day (*see* Jolly, "Tagore Law Lectures" (1883), p. 90). It is the one dividing line between Aryans and non-Aryans in India (*see* Baden-Powell, "Ind. Vill. Com." (1896).

missiles of the foe could not make the slightest impression on them. And the turrets along the walls were filled with armed men in course of training. And the walls were lined with numerous warriors along their whole length. And there were thousands of sharp hooks and machines slaying a century of warriors, and numerous other machines on the battlements. And there were also large iron wheels planted on them. And with all these was that foremost of cities adorned. And the streets were all wide, and laid out excellently. And there was no fear in them of accidents. And, decked with innumerable white mansions, the city became like unto Amarāvati, and came to be called Indra-prastha ('like unto Indra's city'). And in a delightful and auspicious part of the city rose the palace of the Pāndavas filled with every kind of wealth. And when the city was built, there came, O King, numerous Brāhmans well acquainted with all the 'Vedas' and conversant with every language, wishing to dwell there."[1]

As the Pāndavas reared their city, the gods whose aid they sought were not the Aryan gods of old, though they were to become the gods of the people, and the gods before whom Brāhmanism had to bow down. To fuse these new deified heroes and fierce deities into Brāhmanism, Arjuna is represented as going forth from Indra-prastha to seek their aid for the Pāndava brethren. The Brāhmanic poem tells its own tale.

"Then Arjuna, of immeasurable prowess, saw, one after another, all the regions of sacred waters and other holy places that were on the shores of the Western ocean, and then reached the sacred spot called Prabhasa."[2] Here Arjuna meets Krishna, the deified hero destined to become the loved deity whose name is heard in every village, at every festival, at every place of pilgrimage, throughout all India. "And Krishna and Arjuna met together, and,

[1] "Adi Parva," pp. 577-78. [2] *Ibid.*, p. 602.

embracing each other, enquired after each other's welfare. And those dear friends, who were none else than the Rishi Nāra, and Nārāyana of old, sat down."[1] The meeting ends with the establishment of a great fellowship between Krishna and Arjuna, the Pāndu prince ultimately falling in love with Krishna's sister. Arjuna told Krishna of his love, and the Western chieftain, whose love-adventures are the favourite themes of all Indian women, placed his experience at the disposal of his friend. "O thou bull amongst men, the Svayamvāra hath her ordained for the marriage of the Kshatriyas. But that is doubtful, as we do not know this girl's temper and disposition. In the case of Kshatriyas that are brave, a forcible abduction for purposes of marriage is applauded, as the learned have said. Therefore, carry away this, my beautiful sister, by force, for who knows what she may do in a Svayamvāra?"[2] This translation of the poem, by the pious and charitable Protap Chandra Roy, clearly shows how impossible it would be for a Western to attempt to understand the true spirit of the Brāhmanic redaction. It requires a simplicity, a directness, a firm faith in the perfect unison of the whole, to avoid the fatal error of so many Western adaptations in endeavouring to improve on the tone of the original. There is no attempt here to trifle with the loved personality of Krishna, the deity glorified as a very incarnation of the Vedic Vishnu, who strode through the three spaces, placing his last footstep over the heavens. In the poem itself Krishna takes his place as highest among the gods. When Yuddhisthira was finally established as sovereign over all known India, and had performed the great horse sacrifice, symbolic of his universal sway, he bowed down before Krishna as chief of all the gods. Krishna was then declared to be the first of all warriors, the regent of the universe, therefore "do we worship Krishna amongst the

[1] "Adi Parva," § 220. [2] *Ibid.*, p. 605.

best and the oldest and not others."[1] Krishna is he who "is the origin of the universe, and that in which the universe is to dissolve. Indeed, this universe of mobile and immobile creatures hath sprung into existence from Krishna alone. He is the unmanifest primal matter (*avyakta prakriti*), the Creator, the eternal, and beyond the ken of all creatures. Therefore doth he of unfailing glory deserve the highest worship."[2]

The legends and character of Krishna[3] stand out clear in the underlying epic. He was the son of Devakī, and was saved by his father, Vasu-deva, of the Lunar race, from the wrath of the King of Mathura, whose death had been foretold would take place at the hands of a descendant of Vasu-deva. In his youth he was sent to be nursed by Yaśodā, the wife of a cowherd of the Yādava race, in whose home he lived first at Gokula or Vraja, then at Vrindāvana, now the holy places of pilgrimage for all worshippers of Krishna.[4] There he loved the "gopis," or milkmaids, destroyed a great serpent, and held up the mountain Govardhana on his finger to save the "gopis" from the anger of Indra. There he also lived happy with Rādhā,[5] his favoured and often forsaken loved one, and it was from there that he took the inhabitants of Mathura to his holy city of Dvārakā[6]

[1] "Śabha Parva," p. 108. [2] *Ibid.*, p. 109.

[3] "The earlier legends represent Indra as created from a cow. . . . Krishna was probably the clan deity of some powerful confederacy of Rājput tribes. Cow-worship is thus closely connected with Indra and with Krishna in his forms as the 'herdman god' . . . and it is at least plausible to conjecture that the worship of the cow may have been due to the absorption of the animal as a tribal totem of the two races."—Crooke, "Religions and Folk-Lore of N. India," vol. ii. p. 229.

[4] Monier-Williams, "Ind. Wisdom," p. 334.

[5] *See* Hewitt, 1st Series, p. 450:—"Rādhā means the maker (*dhā*) of Rā, the darkness or chaotic void from which the sun-god of light was born, and is thus another form of Rāma, the darkness, the mother of Rā."

[6] "This story telling of the removal of the Yādavas to the sea-shore is the mythical form assumed by national history, when it told how the inland race of the sons of the tortoise had settled on the sea-shore and become a race of mariners."—Hewitt, 1st Series, p. 469.

in Guzarāt. Krishna had to win his way slowly to Brāhmanic recognition and favour. Even in the "Mahābhārata," Śiśupāla, King of Chedi, reviled him, asking how is it that they[1] "who are ripe in knowledge are eager to eulogize the cowherd who ought to be vilified even by the silliest of men. If in his childhood he slew Śakuni, or the horse and the bull who had no skill in fighting, what is the wonder? . . . If the mountain Govardhana, a mere anthill, was held up by him for seven days, I do not regard that as anything remarkable. . . . And it is no great miracle that he slew Kansa, King of Mathura, the powerful king whose food he had eaten." For this speech the King of Chedi had his head smitten off by Krishna with a discus, so that he "fell like a mountain smitten by a thunderbolt." To Krishna the place of honour at the Rājasuya, or "coronation ceremony," performed by Yuddhisthira, had been given, and before Krishna the Pāndava chief bowed down and claimed him as the one great deity of the people. "Owing to thy grace, O Gōvinda, have I accomplished the great sacrifice; and it is owing to thy grace that the whole Kshatriya world, having accepted my sway, have come hither with valuable tribute. O hero, without thee, my heart never feeleth any delight."[2] So the black, deified, hero of a shepherd clan, fabled king of Dvārakā, and chief of the Yādavas, became the adored incarnation of Vishnu, who came on earth to aid the Pāndavas and allied alien tribes in their struggle for supremacy, and in their demand for recognition of their cults and customs at Brāhmanic hands. The Pāndavas had to pass through sore tribulation and trial before they gained their ends. Yuddhisthira, the eldest brother among the Pāndavas, the righteous guide and apotheosis of all virtue, fell before the guile of the Kurus. A challenge to war or gambling was a challenge no warrior could with

[1] Muir, "Sanskrit Texts," vol. iv. p. 210. [2] "Śabha Parva," p. 126.

honour refuse, so Duryodhana, chief of the Kurus, challenged Yuddhisthira, chief of the Pāndavas, to show his skill with dice. The Kurus, over whom Brāhmanism had to pour forth its condemnation in its praises of the Pāndavas, are said to have played unfairly. At each fall of the dice Yuddhisthira lost to Duryodhana his wealth, his kingdom, his brothers one by one, and then himself. There remained but one more stake—the fair figure, trailing hair, beauty and love of Draupadī. The stroke was made, the dice rolled and fell, and Draupadī became the prize of the exulting Duryodhana. The scene, in its underlying pathos, is the finest picture of the poem. One can imagine the vivid reality of what must have been the original epic as sung in the vernacular by the rude and impulsive wandering bard. There the deep pathos of the reciter, as he told the shame and sorrow of the noblest type of womanhood that Indian literature knows, found its relief—in a manner seen constantly in Western drama—in rude and ribald jeers and gibes even against Draupadī herself. In the Brāhmanic poem, as we now possess it, pathos and obscenity all have been mingled together by the Brāhmanic redactor into the most repulsive, cold, and unrealistic description of suffering womanhood that the literature of any country has preserved. The scene has been described in English adaptations over and over again as typifying the Indian ideal of womanhood, and as showing from the manner in which her sufferings were respected, the high place she had acquired. This ideal probably did underlie the original epic story. The "Mahābhārata" version is untranslatable, unreadable, without feelings of horror. Draupadī has been degraded, according to all sane thought, by her Brāhmanic redactors to depths from which she never again can rise. She has become the centre figure of a scene, once realised from the Sanskrit, that could only be willingly forgotten for ever. If she is to be remembered it must be by striving to recreate her as she lived in the lost epic of the rough and ready minstrels, who first sung her moving story to crowds of simple folk. The god Krishna, in the preserved version, is drawn into the scene to clothe the outraged woman with numerous celestial robes, as her single raiment was torn repeatedly off her suffering body in the gambling room before the humbled Pāndavas and one hundred rejoicing sons of Kuru. There is some excuse for the horrors which follow. The fierce and raging Bhīma swore to hew the head of Duhśāsana—who dragged Draupadī, a woman who had never seen the sun, from her private apartments to the assembly—from off his body and drink his heart's blood, a vow he fulfilled on the plains of Kurukshetra. He also vowed that he would smash Duryodhana's thigh, and this he did by a foul stroke in the final fight, and left the vile Kuru to die amid his brethren on the avenging battle-field.

The Pāndavas had to wait long for their revenge. In the gambling hall, Dhritarāshtra, the aged and blind father of the Kurus, stayed the rising wrath of the assembled heroes. The Pāndavas were judged to have lost all, yet they were not to be treated as slaves. Draupadī they received back, but only on their promising that they would go with her for twelve years into exile, and then remain concealed for one year longer, when, if they were undiscovered, they should receive back their kingdom. The story of the exile is the crowning glory of the "Mahābhārata." Here, in the classic beauty of its language, in its depth of thought, and in its incident, and to an Eastern in its description of scenery and didactic teaching, the poem is unrivalled in the history of India's literature. All the beauty of the poem, however, pertains to the form of the literature itself and not to epic narrative, dramatic reality, or even the prosaic history told by that literature. Outside its form the "Mahābhārata" is only valuable[1] as showing the change from Vedic Brāhmanism towards the tangled growth of modern Hinduism. The older Vedic deities—Agni, and Sūrya, Vāyu, Varuna, and Indra—truly remain, but shorn of their ancient power and brilliancy. Indra still has his Heaven, the Valhalla of the warriors. Yama is no longer Death, but grows more akin to Justice.[2] The great Vedic sacrifices, and the occasional sacrifices, are performed, but by their side, equally sacred, are pilgrimages to holy places, sacred rivers and bathing in streams, the worship of snakes and trees, idolatry and bowing down before painted images.[3] The great deities of modern Hinduism rise distinct and clear as the sole personal objects of worship, in whom all the subsidiary deities of India merge, and are held to have their source. The Supreme Spirit[4] assumes the triple form of the personal Creator, Brahmā, the personal protector, Vishnu or Krishna, and the fierce Śiva, the potential destroyer.

Śiva, to the Brāhmanic mind, is the Rudra of the Vedas.[5] In the underlying epic of the "Mahābhārata," he was even greater than Krishna; he was the wild, fierce deity of an aboriginal folk, and the chief aid of the Pāndavas. When the five brethren stayed with their restored wife, Draupadī, in the forest, Arjuna was directed by Indra to go to the Himālayas and seek the aid of the fierce deity, Śiva. The abode of Śiva was in the Heaven, Kailāsa, where he was waited on by the Yākshas, once gods among men, and had as his consort, the goddess, Kāli, or, as she is otherwise known, Umā, the gracious, Devī, Durgā, Gaurī, Bhairavā, the various names, along with her many others, that still echo

[1] "Let the reader attach no value to the names which are mostly myths, or to the incidents which are mostly imaginary."—Dutt, "Ancient India," vol. i. p. 189.

[2] Hopkins, "Religions of India," p. 380 (*note* 2).

[3] *Ibid.*, p. 374.

[4] *See* Holtzmann, Z.D.M.G., xxxviii. p. 204; Hopkins, p. 412.

[5] Muir, "Sanskrit Texts," iv. p. 283.

from the weary bands of pilgrims who travel to her many shrines all over India. It was not until Arjuna saw and submitted to the might of Śiva that he obtained the divine missiles which were to scatter the Kuru force. The promise held out by Indra to Arjuna declared the rising sway of Śiva. "When thou art able to behold the three-eyed, trident-bearing Śiva, the lord of all creatures, it is then, O child, then I will give thee all the celestial weapons. Therefore, strive thou to obtain the sight of the highest of the gods, for it is only after thou hast seen him, O son of Kuntī, that thou wilt attain all thy wishes."

Arjuna set forth to seek the deity, and, being defeated in a fierce fight, acknowledged the power of Śiva, fell down before him, and sang the Brāhmanic song of recognition of the fierce god of his race.[1] "I am unable to declare the attributes of the wise Mahādeva, who is an all-prevailing god, yet is nowhere seen, who is the creator and the lord of Brahmā, Vishnu, and Indra, whom the gods from Brahmā to the demons worship, who transcends material natures as well as spirits, who is meditated upon by sages versed in contemplation (*yoga*) and possessing an insight into truth, who is the supreme, imperishable Brahman, that which is both non-existent, and at once existent and non-existent. He is the deity who has a girdle of serpents, and a sacrificial cord of serpents, in his hand he carries a discus, a trident, a club, a sword, and axe—the god whom even Krishna lauds as the supreme deity."

Deep as the worship of Śiva is steeped in the underlying epic, it fades away before the worship of Krishna, the incarnation of Vishnu, who led the Pāndavas to victory, and whose adoration is inculcated more than that of Śiva by the Brāhmanic framers of the "Mahābhārata."

The dark figure of Krishna hovers mysteriously in the background of early Indian history. In the "Mahābhārata"

[1] Muir, "Sanskrit Texts," vol. v. p. 187.

Krishna rises to such prominence, that it has been held that the whole poem must have been written to extend his worship, and establish it for ever as the true faith for all India. The entire conception of a religion, founded on a faith in the saving grace of Krishna, is declared by some[1] to be merely the Hindu mode of inculcating the doctrines of Christianity, which first reached India in the second and third centuries of our era.

It has been asserted that in the "Mahābhārata" itself, a clear reference is made to Christian doctrines and Christian worship in an account of a pilgrimage made to the White Country, or Svetadwipa.[2] In the White Country the pilgrims are said to have "beheld glistening men, white, appearing like the moon, adorned with all auspicious marks, with their palms ever joined in supplication, praying with their faces turned to the East. The prayer which is offered up by these great-hearted men is called the 'mental prayer.'"

The pilgrims further heard those who in the White Country offered oblations to the god, singing their song of praise. "Thou art victorious, O lotus-eyed one. Hail to thee, O Creator of the Universe! Hail to thee, thou first-born Supreme Being!"[3]

There is nothing to show that the worship of Krishna had not arisen in India as the natural outcome of the life and thought of the period immediately preceding, or

[1] Lorinser (1869); Weber, "Krishna Gebürts Fest.," p. 316; *see* Hopkins, "Religions of India," p. 429. The whole subject is luminously treated in J. M. Robertson's "Christ and Krishna" (Freethought Publishing Company, 1890).

[2] "The ancient Bhāgavata, Sātvata, or Pancharātra sect, devoted to the worship of Nārāyana and its deified teacher, Krishna Devakīputra, dates from a period long anterior to the rise of the Jains in the eighth century B.C." —Barth, "Ind. Ant.," p. 248 (September 1894). Krishna Devakīputra is referred to in "Ch. Up.," iii. 17, 6, though no effort is made afterwards to connect him with Krishna, the son of Vasu-deva. *See* "Śāndilya Sūtras" (*ed.* Ballantyne, *tr.* Cowell), p. 51; S.B.E., vol. i. p. 52 (*note*).

[3] *See* Hopkins, "Religions of India," p. 432.

subsequent to, the Christian era. Throughout all early thought in India there runs an individuality of its own, removing it far from all lines of thought with which it is so frequently compared. Fresh inspirations have, undoubtedly, for a time, acted in the past from outside, and influenced certain phases of Indian literature and art, but the Indian mind soon sinks back to its own accustomed mode of thought and expression, so that, when the first motive force of the new influences fades and dies away, little is left in the essential form that the keenest eye of the scholar or artist can detect as not truly native in its execution, genesis, or tendency. Resemblances between phases of Indian philosophic thought and those of the West, from the time of Xenophanes[1] down to that of Schopenhauer and Von Hartmann, have been sought, and though there are coincidences everywhere, none has been shown not to have been evolved by independent, though similar, orders of thought. The whole case, on the side of those who claim an Eastern source for certain Western forms, has been recently examined in connection with certain practices referred to in the Buddhist Canon, as settled in the Council at Pātaliputra, or Patna, in 259 B.C., by order of Asoka. Yet even here[2] failure has to be confessed: "If the celibacy of the clergy, if confessions, fasting, nay, even rosaries, were all enjoined in the Hīnāyana Canon,[3] it followed, of course, that they could not have been borrowed from Christian missionaries. On the contrary, if they were borrowed at all, the conclusion

[1] Garbe, "Śānkhya Philosophie"; Davies, "Hindu Philosophy," p. 143. Huxley ("Romanes Lecture," p. 19) comparing Buddha and Berkeley. Better would be a comparison with Hume.

[2] Max Müller, "Coincidences" (*Trans.* R.S.L.), vol. xviii. part 2, p. 16.

[3] "To avoid all controversy, we may be satisfied with the date of Vattagāmani, 88 to 76 B.C., during whose reign the Buddhist Canon was first reduced to writing."—Max Müller, *Ibid.*, p. 14.

would rather be that they were taken over by Christianity from Buddhism. I have always held that the possibility of such borrowing cannot be denied, though, at the same time, I have strongly insisted on the fact that the historical reality of such borrowing has never been established."

The form in which the worship of Krishna is set forth and inculcated in the "Mahābhārata" precludes any possibility of its historical connection with the West ever being established, if, indeed, there are any grounds why it should be suspected. The same doubts, the same efforts to seek for the soul a secret hiding-place from the injustices of the world, the same black pall of despairing pessimism that can only be rent by belief or faith in the teachings of revealed truths by a qualified preceptor, all are woven into the very texture of the "Mahābhārata," even more than they are throughout the fuller exposition of Indian thought as seen in the "Vedānta." In India of the past, humanity had to tread the path that leads through life to death, and mark, as it marched, how the road was narrow, and the pitfalls many, how those who wandered from the track sank deep and were for ever lost to human aid or help. The whole of the best of Indian thought was one ceaseless effort to mark each snare and pitfall, to map the line out clear and plain, so that the age might pass from off the scene with something of hope and certainty. The beacon lights that were set ablaze to direct the quivering soul in its flight through time may appear dim and uncertain to us of to-day, who stand listening wearily to the muffled sound that comes from the chambers of science, in vain expectation that it may break forth into a cry that the secret of the Universe has been disclosed and matter reigns supreme. Nevertheless, those beacon lights, that in India guided those now passed away, and still guide many, were all the outcome of the deep and earnest brooding thought of generations of devout and holy men, who placed on record in their literature the efforts they had made to direct all things for the best, although those efforts often bear the taint, as all human efforts must, of selfish interest.

The underlying current of Indian thought, leading naturally, as it does, through faith in the teachings of the "Vedas," "Upanishads," and "Vedānta," or in a spiritual preceptor, on to faith in the teachings of the divine Krishna, has its keynote fully set forth in the song of despair sung by Draupadī to Yuddhisthira when the Pāndava brethren lived in the forest, bereft of all hope or aid. Here Draupadī bewailed to her husband how he, the chief of the Pāndava brothers, the very incarnation of virtue, uprightness, and fair-dealing, was powerless against the will of the Creator, who had ordained all things, and in whose hands all are as playthings. All men, urged the despairing queen, are subject to the will of God, and not to their own desires.[1] "The humble and forgiving person is disregarded, while those that are fierce, persecute others. It seemeth that man can never attain prosperity in this world by virtue, gentleness, forgiveness, and straightforwardness. Like the shadow pursuing a man, thy heart, O tiger among men, with singleness of purpose, ever seeketh virtue. Yet virtue protecteth thee not. The Supreme Lord and Ordainer of all, ordaineth everything in respect of the weal and woe of all creatures, even prior to their births. O hero amongst men, as a wooden doll is made to move its limbs by the wire-puller, so are creatures made to work by the Lord of all. Like a bird tied with a string every creature is dependent on God. Like a pearl on its string, or a bull held fast by the cord passing through its nose, or a tree fallen from the bank into the middle of the stream, every creature followeth the command of the Creator.

[1] "Vana Parva," § 28, 30.

They go to Heaven or hell urged by God Himself. Like light straws dependent on strong winds, all creatures, O King, are dependent on God. The Supreme Lord, according to His pleasure, sporteth with His creatures, creating and destroying them like a child with his toy. Beholding superior, and well-behaved, and modest persons persecuted while the sinful are happy, I am sorely troubled. If the act done pursueth the doer and no one else, then, certainly, it is God Himself who is stained with the sin of every act."

The wail of condemnation of the Cosmos was here again raised. The Brāhmanic mind was framing, in its own mode, the expression of the people's thought. It remained for an answer to be given which all classes might recognise as consonant with their own religious conceptions, and yet one that blended in with the prevailing philosophic notions of the age. This answer is fully set forth in the divine song, the "Bhagavad Gīta," set, as a mosaic, in the "Bhīshma Parva" of the "Mahābhārata." It is here declared that those who worship whatever god they choose, or perform whatever rites they will, are all sure to gain the Heaven they long for. It is Krishna himself who makes their faith firm. It is Krishna alone who grants the desires of all, though the foolish, in their ignorance, worship other deities, and fail to recognise him as the Supreme Spirit, and understand not his saving help.[1] Krishna is the sole Lord, Divine, without a belief in whom all sacrifices are in vain.[2]

In the "Bhagavad Gīta," this doctrine of belief or faith in Krishna is distinctly declared to contain the whole sum of man's duty on earth. When the Pāndavas, with their allies from all quarters, crowded round the Kurus to claim back their kingdom, they sought the active aid of Krishna, as greater than all human aid, an aid sought also by Duryodhana, chief of the Kurus. To both Krishna

[1] Davies, "Bhagavad Gīta," vii. 20-5. [2] *Ibid.*, vii. 28.

gave the same answer. He would take no part in the coming fight; they could choose between him, as passive spectator, and a hundred million warriors he threw into the other scale. Arjuna chose Krishna, Duryodhana chose the warriors. On the plains of Kurukshetra, the great battle-field of India, the old and new met for the first time.

Krishna, though he would not fight, appeared as charioteer to Arjuna. When Arjuna saw the vast host of warriors drawn up in hostile array his heart failed. The cry once raised by Draupadī unnerved his arm. He prayed to Krishna to instruct him as to the meaning of the strange conflict between his innate conceptions of justice and the deeds of blood towards which fate had now drawn him near. Between Arjuna and Krishna question and answer followed, as told in the "Bhagavad Gīta."

The object of the poem might be shortly summed up, according to Western notions, as inculcating that it is best for man to do the duty that lies nearest to his hand, and to leave the rest in God's keeping. There the poem might be left, were it not that the whole guidance of India's future has been assumed by the English nation, and that this is a task doomed to failure unless the leading principles are understood which still holds India tied to its own past. Above all, the wide-spread faith in Krishna, the mystic broodings of the soul over a longed-for union with the Supreme Spirit, are factors that missionary enterprise in India must first probe down to their roots before it can be said that the ground, which it is sought to clear and prepare for the sowing of new seed, has even been surveyed. Were the task an easy one it would have been long ago accomplished. There is no more illusive phase of thought than that of Eastern mysticism. To the Western mind it is evanescent, and only perceived in the peculiar stage in which it passes from the ideal to the real and becomes impossible of recognition. In the "Bhagavad Gīta," where it finds its chief source, it is bound up with some of the most perplexing problems in the whole course of the history of Indian thought.[1]

To some it would appear that the "Bhagavad Gīta" preceded any formal system of Śānkhyan or Vedāntic philosophic thought,[2] while to others, with what appears a surer view, it presents an unscientific exposition of existing philosophies, simplified in order to make them readily intelligible to the mass of the people.

All these critical points fade away into insignificance when the true purport, and subsequent influence, of the teachings which the poem promulgates are fully realised. It is sufficient for all practical purposes to direct the attention to the words of the poem itself, and the doctrines therein laid down. The poem dates from some time before the Christian era, and holds its place in the imagination of the people down through the ages to the present day.

Not by knowledge of the true nature of matter and soul, as in the Śānkhyan system, not by piercing through the misty film of delusion which separates the individual soul

[1] "This much is certain, that the student of the 'Bhagavad Gīta' must, for the present, go without that reliable historical information touching the author of the work, the time at which it was composed, and even the place it occupies in literature, which one naturally desires when entering upon the study of any work."—Telang, S.B.E., vol. viii. p. 1.

[2] *See* Hopkins, "Religions of India," p. 400. The question of the date of the "Bhagavad Gīta," and the opinions of Dr Thibaut, Dr Bhandarkar, and Telang, are learnedly discussed in a small pamphlet of Prof. T. R. Amalnerkar's (Bombay Education Society's Press, 1895). With his opinion that the song is Post-Buddhistic, and after the time of the "Vedānta Sūtras," I agree. "The decay of philosophy, to which the 'Gīta' bears testimony, may be roughly estimated as having taken place in the second century B.C., which brings us to the end of the Sūtra period" (p. 7). *See* Davies, "Bhagavad Gīta," p. 194, fixing date "not earlier than third century B.C." *See* Telang, S.B.E., vol. viii. p. 34, for the opinion that "the latest date at which the 'Gīta' can have been composed must be earlier than the third century B.C." Weber and Lassen are of opinion that the song was not written before the third century B.C.

from its own true essence, the Supreme Soul, as taught by the Vedāntists, nor yet by pious meditation, as in the "Yoga," is deliverance from the bonds of transmigration to be found. The way is declared by Krishna, the charioteer to the warrior, Arjuna :[1]—

"Hear now once more my deep words, most hidden in their meaning. Firmly you are desired of Me, therefore I will declare that which is for your welfare.
"Fix your mind on Me, praise Me, sacrifice to Me, reverence Me.
"To Me only you shall come, truly to thee I promise, for dear you are to Me. All duties[2] having forsaken, to Me only for protection come.
"I will release you from all sins, do not sorrow."

This doctrine of salvation, by devotion to, and faith in, Krishna, finds its conclusion in the instruction :[3]—

"This doctrine is not to be declared to him who practises not austere rites, or who never worships, or who wishes not to hear, nor to one who reviles Me.
"He who shall teach this supreme mystery to those who worship Me, he, offering to Me this highest act of worship, shall doubtless come to Me.
"Nor is there any one among mankind who can do Me better service than he, nor shall any other on earth be more dear to Me than he.
"And by him who shall read this holy converse held by us, I may be sought through this sacrifice of knowledge. This is my decree. And the man who may hear it in faith, without reviling, shall attain, when freed from the body, to the happy region of the just."

[1] "Bhagavad Gita," xviii. 64-6.

[2] Telang, S.B.E., vol. viii. p. 129 (*note* 3):—"Of caste or order such as Agnihotra, and so forth." Davies, p. 176:—"All religious duties."

[3] The Eastern form of the poem is given in the translation by the late Kasinath Trimbak Telang in S.B.E., vol. viii. p. 129, and shows how a very different impression is left in the mind as to the relationship of the song to the New Testament:—"This (the 'Gīta') you should never declare to one who performs no penance, who is not a devotee, nor to one who does not wait on (some preceptor), nor yet to one who calumniates Me. He who, with the highest devotion to Me, will proclaim this supreme mystery among my devotees, will come to Me freed from all doubts. No one

Krishna further declares that, surrounded as he is by the delusion of his mystic power,[1] he is not manifest to all. "This deluded world knows me not, unborn and inexhaustible. I know, O Arjuna! the things which have been, those which are, and those which are to be. But Me nobody knows. All beings, O terror of your foes, are deluded at the time of birth by the delusion."[2] Krishna is represented as the Supreme Spirit, as Brahman, the indestructible spiritual essence, the origin and cause of men and gods. He is the indivisible energy pervading all life and the divisible forms of men and things, so that "he who leaves this body and departs from this world, remembering Me in his last moments, comes into my essence."[3]

The supreme object of mankind therefore should be devotion, and not action, just as meditation was the supreme state for the Yogin. The "Bhagavad Gīta" accordingly holds a strange casuistical doctrine respecting action. Krishna declares, "the truth regarding action is abstruse. The wise call him learned whose acts are all free from desires and fancies." Arjuna, as a warrior, was directed by Krishna to perform his duty as a soldier and fight, although by devotion alone was he to gain salvation. All acts must therefore be done without attachment to them. "He who, casting off all attachment, performs actions dedicating them to Brahman, is not tainted by sin, as the lotus leaf is not tainted by water."[4] The man is saved, according to the words of Krishna, "who sees Me in everything, and every-

among men is superior to him in doing what is dear to Me. And there will never be another on earth dearer to Me than he. And he who will study this holy dialogue of ours will, such is my opinion, have offered to Me the sacrifice of knowledge."

[1] "Yoga māyā samāvritah," vii. 28.

[2] S.B.E., vol. viii. p. 78.

[3] "Even if you are the most sinful of all sinful men, you will cross over all trespasses by means of the boat of knowledge alone."—*Ibid.*, p. 62.

[4] *Ibid.*, p. 64.

thing in me, I am never lost, and he is not lost in me." The reply of Arjuna pursues the question still further. "O Krishna, the mind is fickle, boisterous, strong, and obstinate, and I think that to restrain it is as difficult as to restrain the wind."[1] So Krishna continues his teaching regarding renunciation of attachment to works, at length weighing down all objection by the cry:—

"I am death, the destroyer of the worlds, fully developed, and I now am active about the overthrow of the worlds. Even without you the warriors, standing in the adverse hosts, shall all cease to be. Therefore, be up, enjoy glory, and, vanquishing your foes, obtain a prosperous kingdom. All these have been already killed by Me. Be only the instrument, O shooter, with the left as with the right hand."[2]

All action is, in short, tainted with evil, yet, by doing one's duty without attachment, one does not incur sin, so Krishna holds that one, "even performing all actions, always depending on Me, he, through my favour, obtains the imperishable and eternal seat." Arjuna, therefore, has to do his duty and fight. For the four castes the duties to be done are laid down in the following words:[3]—"Tranquillity, restraint of the senses, penance, purity, forgiveness, straightforwardness, also knowledge, experience, and belief in a future world, this is the natural duty of Brāhmans. Valour, glory, courage, dexterity, not slinking away from battle, gifts, exercise of lordly power, this is the natural duty of Kshatriyas. Agriculture, tending cattle, trade, this is the natural duty of Vaiśyas. And the natural duty of Sūdras consists in service. Every man intent on his own respective duties obtains perfection." The wise man, however, looks upon "a Brāhman possessing learning and humility, on a cow, an elephant, a dog, and a low-caste man as alike." Such are the teachings of the "Bhagavad Gīta,"

[1] S.B.E., vol. viii. p. 71. [2] *Ibid.*, p. 95. [3] *Ibid.*, p. 126.

as set forth by Krishna, who promises salvation to all who believe in his saving grace.

> "Devote thy heart to Me; worship Me, sacrifice to Me, bow down before Me; so shalt thou come to Me. I promise thee truly for thou art dear to me.
>
> "Forsaking all religious duties, come to Me as the only refuge. I will release thee from all thy sins; grieve not."[1]

[1] Davies, p. 176 (*trans.*).

CHAPTER XI.

THE ATTACK.

INDIA was fast marching towards its doom. The monarch who claimed universal sovereignty performed the horse sacrifice as symbolic of his sovereignty. For one year a horse was let loose to wander where it would; he who stayed its course was presumed to show he did not recognise the ruling right of the sovereign over the lands where the horse had strayed. Should the wanderings of the horse not be opposed, it was sacrificed with due rites. The Pāndava brethren were fabled in the epic to have performed a horse sacrifice, a custom in its origin essentially Turanian or Scythian.

With the Pāndavas, and all their surrounding fierce and heroic gods, superstitions, and aboriginal beliefs, Brāhmanism had to compromise; it could no longer stay their course. It had to recognise that the great mass of the people of India would never accept the abstract teachings of the "Upanishads" or "Vedānta" philosophies; they would ever follow their own ways and gods. Asoka, sprung as he was from the outcast Chandra Gupta, found it wise to embrace the Buddhist faith, so that his renown and sway might increase among the people by his standing forth as the supporter of a religious system recognising no distinction of caste or family name.

Brāhmanism had marked its descent from its lofty ideals

when it compromised with beliefs alien to its own true spirit. Asoka showed the signs of his empire's decay when he set forth as principles on which sovereignty should rest those inculcated by the Buddha, instead of those principles, symbolised by the rough and ready defiance of horse sacrifice, on which his rule could alone abide amid the dark days it had soon to face.

Although Asoka succeeded his father, Bimbisāra, son of Chandra Gupta, about 259 B.C., yet it was not until the twenty-ninth year[1] of his reign that he stood forth as the champion of Buddhism. From Kābul and Kandahar to Kalinga on the east coast, which he conquered in the ninth year of his reign,[2] from Kapilavastu in the north, to Mysore in the south, he had established his fame and sovereignty. All over this vast tract he gave orders that his edicts should be engraven on stone pillars, on the rocky sides of mountains, and in caves,[3] so that his ordinances should abide for ever. The inscriptions in the north, such as that at Kupardagiri, or Shāhbāzgahrī on the Afghan frontier, are all written from right to left in a character derived from a Phœnician source, known for long as Northern Asoka, or Arian, sometimes as Arian Pāli, Bactro Pāli, or Gandhārian, and now called Kharosthi. Those to the south, such as that at Girnār in Kāthīawār on the west coast of India, run from left to right, and were in what is known as the Southern Asoka, Indo Pāli, Mauriya writing, to which the name of Brāhmī is now applied.

The thirteenth edict states that Asoka sent missionaries to Antiochus II. of Syria, Ptolemy II. of Egypt, Antigonos

[1] "Epigraphia Indica," vol. ii. p. 246:—"His conversion to Buddhism fell . . . in the twenty-ninth year of his reign." Rhys Davids ("Buddhism," p. 222, 1894) says:—"After his conversion, which took place in the tenth year of his reign, he became a very zealous supporter of the new religion."

[2] Edict XIII.

[3] Hunter ("Indian Empire," p. 190) gives the sites of the fourteen rock and seventeen cave inscriptions as described by Cunningham.

Gonatas of Macedonia, Magas of Cyrene, and Alexander II. of Epirus.

On the historic ridge, near Delhi, a pillar, broken in four pieces by an earthquake, is inscribed with the most interesting of these inscriptions of Asoka.

The edicts[1] tell their own story of the king's efforts to frame rules of ideal governance for his kingdom.

EDICT I.—King Piyadasi, beloved of the gods, speaks thus :—"After I had been anointed twenty-six years I ordered this religious edict to be written. Happiness in this world and in the next is difficult to gain except by the greatest love of the sacred law, the greatest circumspection, the greatest obedience, the greatest fear, the greatest energy. . . . And my servants, the great ones, the lowly ones, and those of middle rank, being able to lead sinners back to their duty, obey and carry out (my orders) likewise also the wardens of the marches. Now the order is to protect according to the sacred law, to govern according to the sacred law, to give happiness in accordance with the sacred law, to guard according to the sacred law."

EDICT II.—King Piyadasi, beloved of the gods, speaks thus :—"(To fulfil) the law is meritorious. But what does (the fulfilment) of the law include? (It includes) sinlessness, many good works, compassion, liberality, truthfulness, purity. The gift of spiritual insight I have given (to men) in various ways; on two-footed and four-footed beings, on birds, and aquatic animals I have conferred benefits of many kinds, even the boon of life, and in other ways I have done much good. It is for this purpose that I have caused this religious edict to be written (*viz.*) that men may thus act accordingly, and that it may endure for a long time. And he who will act thus will perform a deed of merit."

EDICT III.—King Piyadasi, beloved of the gods, speaks thus :—"Man only sees his good deeds (*and says unto himself*), 'This good deed I have done.' But he sees in no wise his evil deeds (*and does* not say unto himself), 'This evil deed I have done; this is what is called sin.' But difficult, indeed, is this self-examination. Nevertheless, man ought to pay regard to the following (*and*

[1] Bühler, "Epigraphia Indica," vol. ii. pp. 248-254.

say unto himself), 'Such (*passions*) as rage, cruelty, anger, pride, jealousy (*are those*) called sinful; even through these I shall bring about my fall.' But man ought to mark most the following (*and say unto himself*), 'This conduces to my welfare in this world, that, at least, to my welfare in the next world.'"

EDICT IV.—King Piyadasi, beloved of the gods, speaks thus:—"After I had been anointed twenty-six years I ordered this religious edict to be written. My *Lajūkas* are established (*as rulers*) among the people, among many hundred thousand souls; I have made them independent in (*awarding*) both honours and punishments. Why? In order that the *Lajūkas* may do their work tranquilly and fearlessly, that they may give welfare and happiness to the people of the provinces, and may confer benefits (*on them*). They will know what gives happiness and what inflicts pain, and they will exhort the provincials in accordance with the principles of the sacred law. How? That they may gain for themselves happiness in this world and in the next. But the Lajūkas are eager to serve me. My (other) servants also, who know my will, will serve (*me*), and they, too, will exhort some (*men*) in order that the Lajūkas may strive to gain my favour. For as (*a man*) feels tranquil after making over his child to a clever nurse, saying unto himself, 'The clever nurse strives to bring up my child well,' even so I have acted with my Lajūkas for the welfare and happiness of the provincials, intending that, being fearless and feeling tranquil, they may do their work without perplexity. For this reason I have made the Lajūkas independent in (*awarding*) both honours and punishments. For the following is desirable. What? That there may be equity in official business, and equity in the award of punishments. And even so far goes my order, I have granted a respite of three days to prisoners on whom judgment has been passed, and who have been condemned to death. Their relatives will make some (*of them*) meditate deeply (and), in order to save the lives of those (men), or in order to make (the condemned) who is to be executed meditate deeply, they will give gifts with a view to the next world or will perform fasts! For my wish is that they (*the condemned*), even during their imprisonment, may thus gain bliss in the next world; and various religious practices, self-restraint, and liberality, will grow among the people."

In the year 246 B.C., the eleventh[1] year of Asoka's

[1] *See* Monier-Williams, "Buddhism," p. 59:—"Sixteenth or seventeenth year." Oldenberg, "Vinaya Pitakam" (Introd.), xxxi.; S.B.E., x., xxvi.-xxxix.

reign, the whole Buddhist Canon was fully recited at a Council of one thousand Buddhist monks, who assembled together at Pātaliputra. Missionaries were then sent to far-off lands to propagate the Buddhist faith.[1] Mahendra, the son of Asoka, carried the three "Pitakas," or "books of law," in the Pāli language to Ceylon, and was soon after followed by his sister, Sanghamitta, who brought a branch of the sacred bo-tree, under which Buddha had attained enlightenment, a branch planted at Anurādhapura, from which grew the famous tree, for long held to be the oldest historical tree in the world.[2]

The alliance made by Asoka with Buddhism brought to him no peace, nor to his empire security. His end was full of trouble and sorrow. He lived to see his own son's eyes put out by the woman he loved, and himself restrained in his pious gifts to the so-called Buddhist mendicants.

Buddhism, though it might tend to break down the racial and class distinctions of an enslaved people, and unite them into one nation, yet rose above all the practical considerations of real life. And so it remains in its ideals a dream for the philosopher, in its degraded form a refuge for the indolent, in its results a warning to the man of action. Those who truly joined the Order became celibate monks, recluses, men of thought, not action. When they were slain or driven from their monasteries by the later Muhammadan invaders, and possibly by the reforming Brāhmans, the religion died out in India, for the lay professors of the faith had no guides nor preceptors, no mendicant monks to feed, clothe, or endow with wealth. The more a temporal

[1] "Dipavamśa," chap. viii.; "Mahāvamśa," chap. xii.

[2] Tennent, "Ceylon," vol. ii. p. 613. In the reign of Vattagāmini (88-76 B.C.) the Buddhist Canon was reduced to writing, and in 450 A.D. the faith spread to Burma through the great Buddhist commentator, Buddha Ghosha. *See* Rhys Davids, "Buddhism," pp. 234, 237.

sovereign and his subjects drifted towards the ideals inculcated by Buddha, the more unfitted they became for the war and strife on which alone an empire could be founded and maintained, so long as alien foes pressed round, prepared and eager to carve out a kingdom and heritage for themselves and their own race. Asoka had framed an ideal state.[1] A minister of religion had been appointed, in the fourteenth year of his reign, to supervise morals; wells were dug, resting-groves and wayside avenues planted, medical aid provided for man and beast. All, Aryans and aborigines alike, were to be constrained to the ideals set forth by Buddha with gentleness and kindness, not by force. The picture is the most pathetic in the whole vista of the struggles of humanity to reach and realise the ethical ideal, regardless of the stern dictates that decree the victory to the best fitted, physically and mentally, to maintain his place in the strife of life. The ideal must remain for the real to strive towards and never attain.

Asoka strove to realise the ideals personified in the passive figure of the Buddha, just as many of to-day would urge England to do, and stay her stern career wherein she sets before herself no other ideal than that of justice, unswayed by sentiment or emotion.

In the days of Asoka there were rough and ready Northern hosts, even as there are to-day, should England fall back from her high mission, ready to break down from their Northern homes and win a heritage for themselves amid a people unprepared, and too disunited, to defend their own birthright.

On the death of Asoka, the great Empire of Magadha drifted to decay. Of his grandson and successor, Daśaratha, history knows but little except what is contained in a few inscriptions, of interest alone to

[1] Hunter, "Indian Empire," pp. 190-91.

archæologists.[1] New dynasties[2] arose, among which one monarch figured as the hero in Kālidāsa's well-known play Mālavikāgnimitra.[3] By the middle of the fifth century Pātaliputra,[4] the ancient capital of India, lost its importance, and was described by the Chinese pilgrim, Hiouen Tsang,[5] as "an old city, about 70 li round. Although it has been long deserted, its foundation walls still survive."

The history of India, from Asoka's time down to the dark days of Muhammadan raids, is, in fact, a history of a disunited people, ruled over by local chieftains, among whom one here and there rose to a more or less extended sovereignty, and of invasions from Northern foes.

When first the rapid, moving, hardy horsemen, known as Turanians, commenced their raids across the Jaxartes, nothing loth to leave their arid grazing-ground of Central Asia for the richer Southern lands, is a question still outside the limits of historic evidence. It has been held, and excavations at Kapilavastu may prove the surmise true, that the Sākya race, among whom Buddha was born, was an early incursive band of these Northern warrior tribes, whom history loosely classes together as Scythian. Alexander the Great, before he ventured to invade India, had established posts along the Jaxartes to hold these Northern barbarians in check. Two hundred years later, a Tartar tribe drove out the Greeks from Bactria, and by the first century B.C. a yellow race, described as of pink and white complexion, and known to the Chinese chroniclers as the

[1] "Mahāvamśa," cxx.; Miss Manning, "Ancient India," 316.

[2] Pushpamitra overthrew the Maurya dynasty, and established Śunga dynasty (178 B.C.). *See* Burgess, "Cave Temples of India," p. 25.

[3] Agnimitra, son of Pushpamitra, who fought against the Bactrian Greeks. *See* Shankar P. Pandit, "Mālavikāgnimitra" (Preface).

[4] V. A. Smith (J.R.A.S., p. 24, 1897) holds that Pātaliputra was the early capital of Samudra Gupta (345-380 A.D.). Fleet, "Gupta Inscrip.," p. 5; Bühler, "Origin of the Gupta and Valabhi Era," p. 13.

[5] Visited India 629-645 A.D.

Yueh-Chi,[1] came riding down into the Panjāb to take their place in the annals of Indian history.

In Kashmīr these Scythians established their rule. Of the Scythian monarchs little is known from the time they poured their fierce bowmen across the north-west mountain passes until they disappear at the close of the sixth century A.D. Vikramāditya, the enemy of the Scythians, stands out as the sole national hero of North India at this period, and round him is centred all that was glorious of the times which commenced with the new Indian era of 56 B.C.[2]

The greatest of all the Scythian conquerors was Kanishka,[3] who extended his rule beyond Kashmīr, as far south as Guzarāt, and east to Agra, founding for himself and his race an era known as the Sāka era, which dates from 78 A.D. Kanishka, in his new home, accepted Buddhism as his state religion. It is known that he summoned a great council of five hundred monks to a monastery at Jālandra in Kashmīr, and there formulated, in Sanskrit, the doctrines of Northern Buddhism, designated as those of the Mahāyāna, or "Great Vehicle," accepted by all Scythian races. The full record of this Council now lies buried beneath some vast mound of earth. The only guide left to direct the searcher after these lost treasures was given thirteen hundred years ago by the Chinese pilgrim, Hiouen Tsang as follows:[4]—

"Kanishka-rājā forthwith ordered these discourses to be engraven on sheets of red copper. He enclosed them in a

[1] For connection of the Yueh-Chi with the Goths, as well as with the Jāts of India, and the Rājputs, *see* Max Müller, "India: What Can It Teach Us?" p. 86. Also Hunter, "Indian Empire," chap. vii., where the whole intricate history is summed up. J.R.A.S., N.S., xiv. p. 47.

[2] *See* J. F. Fleet, "Corpus Inscriptionum Indicarum," vol. iii. p. 37.

[3] The "Rāja-Taranginī" gives as predecessors Hushka and Jushka. *See* Albiruni, "Sachau," ii. 11.

[4] Beal, "Buddhist Rec. of Western World," vol. i. p. 156.

stone receptacle, and having sealed them he raised over it a stūpa with the Scriptures in the middle."

The sheets of copper probably still remain beneath the mound where Kanishka deposited them, and fame and wealth awaits him who searches out the Scriptures, and reveals to the world the long-lost Canon of the Māhāyana of the Northern Buddhists. On the death of Kanishka his kingdom fell to pieces. Inscriptions and coins are all that tell of the fluctuating fortunes of various dynasties that rose to power and extended their sway during the succeeding centuries through which India passed, before it fell a prey to foreign conquest.

At Surashtrā, or Guzarāt, the Sena kings are traced by their coinage from 70 B.C. to 235 A.D., while in the east the Āndhras of the Deccan ruled over Magadha from 26 B.C. to 430 A.D. A long line of Gupta monarchs[1] is known to have held imperial sway all over North India and Kāthiāwār, from the middle of the fourth century A.D. until 530-33, when the empire passed to Yaśodharman[2] of West Mālwā, who held the whole north until it fell to a Varman dynasty, that ruled down to 585 A.D., from whom it passed to the Vardhana kings of Thaneswar and Kanauj.

Among the Vardhana chieftains, one monarch rose to supreme power, the great Harsha Vardhana, known as Sīlāditya II., ruler of Kanauj from 606 to 648 A.D.[3] Down to the time of the Arab raid into Sind, in the eighth century, the Vallabhis held rule in Guzarāt (480-722 A.D.) among

[1] Gupta, 320 A.D.; Ghatotkacha, 340; Candra Gupta I., 360; Samudra Gupta, 380 (345-380).—Vincent Smith, J.R.A.S. (1897), part 1, 19. Candra Gupta II., 400-414; Kumāra Gupta I., 415-454; Skanda Gupta, 455-468; Pura Gupta, 470; Narasimka Gupta, 485; Kumāra Gupta II., 530.—Hoernle, "Inscribed Seal of Kumāra Gupta," vol. lviii.; J.R.A.S. (Bengal), p. 88.

[2] Hoernle, *Ibid.*, 96, for connection with Hūnas.

[3] Cowell and Thomas, "Harsha Charita," p. x.; Bendall, "Catalogue Buddhist Sanskrit MSS.," xli.

whom a new supreme emperor, Sīlāditya III. held the imperial rule in 670 A.D.

How far these later Indian rulers consolidated their conquests, and held under their own sway the territories over which their sovereignty is recorded to have spread, would now be impossible to ascertain. So long as tribute was paid, local principalities and chieftains might hold and administer their own territories, though the suzerain counted them as subject states.

Samudra Gupta, who ruled first at Pātaliputra,[1] and then changed his capital westward, until it finally rested at Kanauj, is referred to in an inscription as "the restorer of the Aśvamedha sacrifice"[2]—the great horse sacrifice. In one inscription, still preserved on a pillar at Allahābād, the praises of Samudra Gupta are recited, and all his conquests set forth in order.[3]

Nine kings of Āryāvarta were "violently exterminated;" kings of forest countries became his slaves. Twelve kings, whose names are given in the inscription, were subdued and then set free. These included the King of Kānchī, or Conjeveram, near Madras, the King of all the Western Malabar coast, the King of Central India and Orissa, the King of Kōttarā in Coimbatore, in South India, as well as kings over lands in the present Godavari district, and south of the Krishna. From the kings of Lower Bengal, Nepal, and Assam, he is recorded to have exacted homage and tribute, as he also did from frontier tribes, while from foreign nations, and from Ceylon, he received services and presents. More astounding than this record of the Empire of Samudra Gupta, in the middle of the fourth century of our era, is the record of the conquests of his son and successor, Chandra Gupta II., who extended the Gupta Empire to its furthest limits. The pillar on

[1] V. A. Smith, J.R.A.S. (1897), p. 27 (*note* 1).
[2] *Ibid.*, p. 22 (*note* 2). [3] *Ibid.*, p. 27.

which the fame of Chandra Gupta is set forth, has remained for long one of the many strange marvels of the East. The pillar stands in the courtyard of a great mosque, built by Katb-ud-dīn, about 9 miles south of modern Delhi. The pillar rises 22 feet above the ground, there being 1 foot 8 inches below ground. The whole pillar is solid, of malleable iron, wrought and welded into a mass of over six tons' weight. The pillar was erected in or about the year 415 A.D., by order of Kumāra Gupta I., son and successor of Chandra Gupta II. The construction of such a pillar of wrought-iron at so early a date seems, even to the Western world, a feat almost beyond belief. "It is not many years since the production of such a pillar would have been an impossibility in the largest foundries of the world, and even now there are comparatively few where a similar mass of metal could be turned out."[1]

The inscription on the pillar has been translated by Mr Vincent Smith, in his valuable article on the "Ancient History of India from the Monuments":—

> "This lofty standard of the divine Vishnu was erected on Mount Vishnupada by King Candra, whose thoughts were devoted in faith to Vishnu. The beauty of that king's countenance was as that of the full moon (*candra*);—by him, with his own arm, sole worldwide dominion was acquired and long held;—and although, as if wearied, he has in bodily form quitted this earth, and passed to the other-world country won by his merit, yet, like the embers of a quenched fire in a great forest, the glow of his foe-destroying energy quits not the earth;—by the breezes of his prowess the southern ocean is still perfumed;—by him, having crossed the seven mouths of the Indus, were the Vāhlikas[2] vanquished in battle;—and when, warring in the Vanga countries,[3] he breasted and destroyed the enemies confederate against him, fame was inscribed on (their) arm by his sword."

[1] Valentine Ball, "Economic Geology of India," p. 338.

[2] Balkh or Balūchistān.

[3] Bengal Lower generally. Vincent Smith, J.R.A.S. (1897), p. 8.

These details of the reigns and deeds of the kings of the varied dynasties, who, in the first seven centuries of the Christian era strove, with a success never lasting long, to bend the various chieftains, races, and people of India into recognition of one central power, capable of swaying the destinies of an empire, are preserved in the evidence recorded on coins and inscriptions. The evidences are not such as to enable any vivid picture to be drawn that would present a life-like history of the period. Such results as may be obtained are of interest to the antiquarian and archæologist; they can never throw a clear light on the causes whereby India was advancing to her doom, as an easy prey to foreign conquerors.

The self-control of Buddhism, the intellectual supremacy demanded by Brāhmanism, the gross ignorance of superstitious Hinduism, were all but products of the life of the times. The centre fact that the historian longs to arrive at, is the clue to the subjection of the East to the West. The enervating influence of climate may afford a solution when a Southern race is debarred from recruiting its more active and ruder instincts by hardier immigrants from colder climes, as Mughal and Portuguese rule found to their cost, and the Aryan has ever found in his migrations south. This may explain the present condition of the people of India; and if it be so, then the prospect in the future, both for Bengal Sikh, border Pathān, and Southern Pariah, is one of submission to the dictates of Nature. In the early ages there is no evidence that in the north, at least, the barriers of India had ever been closed to new-comers.

Persian, Greek, and Scythian alike swarmed in and made their own settlements, without great show of opposition. The Scythian element has been traced far to the east, among the Jāts,[1] in Central India, and among

[1] Now four and a half millions in number. *See* Hunter, "Indian Empire," p. 226.

the Rājputs—a race that rose with all its chivalry and manhood to oppose Muhammadan fanaticism, at a time when in the land there were no other signs of any tendency towards national life and spirit. North of the Vindhya, each chieftain and petty king strove to secure his own position, increase his forces, raid the territories of his neighbours, and win for himself the favour and support of Brāhmanism or Buddhism as the times inclined him. South of the Vindhya, great and ancient dynasties —Rāshtrakūta, Chālukyan, Pallava, Chera, Chola, or Pāndyan—preserved and increased, as they could, the limits of their own kingdoms.

A welcome light is thrown across the history of this early period by the account of the Chinese Buddhist traveller, Hiouen Tsang. The great ruler of North India was then Śrī Harsha, or Harsha Vardhana, the King of Thaneswar and Kanauj. He is described by the Chinese traveller as wavering between Buddhism and Brāhmanism, one day setting high a statue of Buddha, the next that of the sun, or the great god, Śiva. The "believers in Buddha and the heretics"[1] were described as about equal in number, there being some hundred of monasteries, with ten thousand priests, studying both the Great and Little Vehicle, and two hundred Hindu temples. The king, in six years, according to Hiouen Tsang, conquered all the Five Indies, subdued all who were not obedient, and his army reached the number of one hundred thousand cavalry and sixty thousand war elephants.[2]

In one great assembly held by the king at Kanauj, or Kanyā Kubja, as it was then called, kings of twenty countries are described as forming part of the king's escort, as he marched in procession with a golden statue of Buddha, high as himself, carried in front. Not only does

[1] Beal, "Buddhist Rec. of Western World," vol. i. p. 207.

[2] For his defeat by Pulikeśin, *see Ibid.*, p. 213 (*note* 21).

the presence of the twenty kings indicate the divided authority of Harsha Vardhana, but a more serious element of disunion is apparent from the recorded fact that the Brāhmans, jealous of the wealth showered on the Buddhists, laid plots to take the king s life, so that "the king punished the chief of them and pardoned the rest. He banished the five hundred Brāhmans to the frontiers of India."[1]

This account of Hiouen Tsang is fortunately supplemented by a realistic description of the court and camp of Harsha Vardhana, by the contemporary poet, Bāna, whose work is the only romance of any historical importance in the literature of the period. The work, so far as it goes—for it is unfinished in the original—has happily recently appeared in an English translation, most skilfully rendered from the difficult Sanskrit of the original.[2] There is but one other book comparable to it, in the manner in which it lays bare the very facts that are of peculiar interest and value for realising the exact chances of success any of the early so-called monarchs of North India had of uniting the scattered principalities and races into a political entity, containing permanent elements of stability. The position of affairs is strikingly similar to the account left in the "Letters from a Marātha Camp," during the year 1809, by Colonel Broughton, who travelled with the predatory and irresponsible forces of Mahārāja Scindia, in the raids, or, as a native chronicler would describe them, victorious progress of a universal monarch, into the semi-feudatory state of Rājputāna.

The impression left by the two accounts—that by Bāna, contemporary in the seventh century with Harsha Vardhana, and that by the English resident at the court of Scindia, at the beginning of the nineteenth century—may be

[1] Beal, "Buddhist Rec. of Western World," vol. i. p. 221.

[2] "The Harsha Charita of Bāna," translated by Prof. Cowell and F. W. Thomas (Oriental Translation Fund, 1897).

summed up in the words of Sir M. E. Grant Duff, in his preface to the letters of Colonel Broughton :—

> "First, how far away seem the scenes which they describe . . . and secondly, how soon they would come back if the power which saved, and saves India from tearing her own vitals, were to be withdrawn for a single lustrum. . . . Who can doubt that all the jealousies, all the passions, all the superstitions, which are set forth . . . are still there ready to break forth at any moment?"

It seems almost sacrilege to tear from out their setting, in a work of beauty such as the "Harsha Charita" of Bāna, such few references as may serve to furnish facts for history.

Bāna wrote for a purely artistic purpose, his only effort being to combine in his narrative "a new subject, a diction not too homely, unlaboured double meaning, the sentiment easily understood, the language rich in sonorous words."[1] The motives that incited him to recount the deeds of his lord are plainly indicated, and were purely artistic. He tells how one dramatist[2] "gained as much splendour by his plays, with an introduction spoken by the manager, full of various characters, and furnished with startling episodes, as he would have done by the erection of temples, created by architects, adorned with several storeys, and decorated with banners"; and how all are delighted at "the beautiful expressions uttered by Kālidāsa, as at sprays of flowers wet with honey sweetness." Accordingly his narrative is merely to be viewed as "like a bed, which is to wake up its occupant happily refreshed," and how it has been "set off by its well-chosen words, like feet, luminous with the clever joinings of harmonious letters." It would be well if the narrative could be left in the beauty of its own repose, for "a return of the mind to itself from seeking fact after fact,

[1] Introductory verse, p. 2 (Cowell's Translation).

[2] Bhāsā. *See* Weber, "History of Indian Literature," p. 205 (*note* 213).

and law after law, in the objective world; a recognition that the mind itself is an end to itself, and its own law."[1]

This is the proper realm of all Sanskrit literature, indeed, of all Indian life and thought—a realm far more seductive in its pleasant paths than that furnished by unending research in the objective reality of the world's phenomena. The whole of Bāna's narrative must therefore be taken in its own setting, if the true spirit of its composition is to be properly judged. Bāna commenced his story by pointing out, to those whom he addressed, his limitation: "What man could possibly, even in a hundred of men's lives, depict his story in full? If, however, you care for a part, I am ready."

The descent of Harsha Vardhana is first traced down to that of his father, Prabhākara Vardhana, King of Thaneswar, who was "famed far and wide under a second name, Pratāpacīla, a lion to the Hūna deer, a burning fever to the King of Indus land, a troubler to the sleep of Guzarāt, a bilious plague to that scent elephant, the lord of Gāndhāra, a looter to the lawlessness of the Jāts, an axe to the creeper of Mālwā's glory."[2] To Yasovatī, wife of this monarch, two sons were born, Rājyavardhana and Harsha, the hero of the story. There was also one daughter, Rājya Śrī, who married Grahavarman, son of a Mukhara King of Kanyā Kubja, or Kanauj.[3]

Prabhākara Vardhana is described as being a sun-worshipper. "Day by day at sunrise he bathed, arrayed himself in white silk, wrapped his head in a white cloth, and kneeling eastwards upon the ground, in a circle measured with saffron paste, presented for an offering a bunch of red lotuses, set in a pure vessel of ruby, and tinged, like his own heart, with the sun's hue."[4]

On the birth of the king's second son, Harsha, the

[1] W. P. Ker, "Essays in Philosophical Criticism," p. 173; quoted in "The Philosophy of the Beautiful," by William Knight (1891).

[2] "Harsha Charita," p. 101.

[3] *See Ibid.* (Introd.), p. xii.

[4] *Ibid.*, p. 104.

capital held high revel. A weird light is thrown on the scene, where the populace are depicted as having lost their sense with joy:—

> "Entrance to the harem in no wise criminal; master and servants reduced to a level; young and old confounded; learned and unlearned on one footing; drunk and sober not to be distinguished; noble maidens and harlots equally merry. The whole population of the capital set a-dancing."[1]

As the young princes grew up, the king appointed, as their companion, Kumāra Gupta and Mādhavā Gupta, sons of the king of Mālwā. When Rājya Śri, the king's daughter, came of age, it was determined that she should be married to Grahavarman, the son of the Mukhara King of Kanyā Kubja, for, "now at the head of all royal houses stands the Mukharas, worshipped, like Śiva's footprint, by all the world."[2]

The political struggles of the time now commenced. When Rājyavardhana, the king's eldest son, grew old enough to wear armour, he was sent "at the head of an immense force, attended by ancient advisers and devoted feudatories, towards the north to attack the Hūnas."[3]

During the prince's absence, the king, Prabhākara, was seized with illness, resulting in his death. Harsha, who had accompanied his brother towards the Himālayas to encounter the Hūnas, hastened back to the capital where the people were plunged in grief. Rarely has a more fearful description of Hindu superstition been summed up in a few lines than in the words describing the appearance of the grief-smitten city. "There young nobles were burning themselves with lamps to propitiate the mothers. In one place a Dravidian was ready to solicit the Vampire with the offering of a skull. In another an Āndhra man was holding up his arms like a rampart to conciliate Chandī. Elsewhere distressed young

[1] "Harsha Charita," p. 111. [2] *Ibid.*, p. 122. [3] *Ibid.*, p. 132.

servants were pacifying Mahākāla by holding melting gum on their heads. In another place a group of relatives was intent on an oblation of their own flesh, which they severed with keen knives. Elsewhere again young courtiers were openly resorting to the sale of human flesh."[1]

The panorama referred to in the drama of the "Mudra Rākshasa" is also described as being displayed. The showman displays his painted canvas, whereon is depicted Yama, "the Lord of Death," seated on his dreaded buffalo, while he recites his verses to the assembled crowd:[2] "Mothers and fathers in thousands, in hundreds children and wives, age after age have passed away, whose are they, and whose art thou?"[3]

The whole narrative, in fact the whole romance, in its perfect translation by Professor Cowell and Mr Thomas, gives more real information respecting the inner life of the people than any other work relating to India. From every page new life dawns, and in every sentence some unexpected beauty lies half-concealed.

On the king's death, Harsha Vardhana's grief was assuaged by "Brāhmans versed in 'Śrūti,' 'Smriti,' and 'Itihāsas,' anointed counsellors of royal rank, endowed with learning, birth, and character; approved ascetics, well-trained in the doctrine of the Self; sages indifferent to pain and pleasure; Vedāntists skilled in expounding the nothingness of the fleeting world; mythologists expert in allaying sorrow."[4]

In the midst of the city's grief, news arrived that Grahavarman had been slain by the King of Mālwā, and Rājya Śri cast into fetters. Rājyavardhana, the elder brother, who had returned to the capital after driving

[1] "Harsha Charita," p. 136. *See* also p. 222:—"Yet a seller of human flesh."

[2] Kipling, Lockwood, "Man and Beast in India," p. 123:—"God looks out of the window of Heaven and keeps account."

[3] "Harsha Charita," p. 136 (*trans.*). [4] *Ibid.*, p. 162.

back the Scythian Hūnas from the north-west, set forth with a mighty army, and defeated the King of Mālwā only to fall a victim to the intrigues of the King of Gauda. Harsha Vardhana now steps forth, as the true hero of the romance, to avenge the ill fate of his race. Before starting on his avenging expedition he vowed that he would establish his supremacy as sole monarch. "By the dust of my honoured lord's feet I swear that, unless in a limited number of days I clear this earth of Gaudas, and make it resound with fetters on the feet of all kings who are excited to insolence by the elasticity of their bows, then will I hurl my sinful self, like a moth, into an oil-fed flame."[1]

Harsha Vardhana started on his conquering career amid the beat of drums, the bray of trumpets, the bustle of an Eastern camp, and general lack of all system or controlling authority over the semi-independent chieftains who joined in the foray. "Elephant keepers, assaulted with clods by people starting from hovels which had been crushed by the animals' feet, called the bystanders to witness the assaults. Wretched families fled from grass cabins ruined by collisions. Despairing merchants saw the oxen, bearing their wealth, flee before the onset of the tumult. A troop of seraglio elephants advanced where the press of people gave way before the glare of their runners' torches."[2] Looting of the standing crop goes on at all sides. The cries of the rabble are heard: "Quick, slave, with a knife, cut a mouthful of fodder from this bean field. Who can tell the fate of his crop when we are gone?" The picture is dramatically true to life. "There poor unattended nobles, overwhelmed with the toil and worry of conveying their provisions upon fainting oxen, provided by wretched village householders, and obtained with difficulty, themselves grasped their domestic appurtenances, grumbling as follows:—'Only let this one

[1] "Harsha Charita," p. 187. [2] *Ibid.*, p. 201.

expedition be gone and done with.' 'Let it go to the bottom of hell.' 'An end to this world of thirst.'"[1]

On all sides the peaceful villagers fled, "others, despondent at the plunder of their ripe grain, had come forth, wives and all, to bemoan their estates, and to the imminent risk of their lives, grief dismissing fear, had begun to censure their sovereign, crying: 'Where's the king?' 'What right has he to be king?' 'What a king!'"[2]

The king on his march turned aside to save his sister, Rājya Śri, from burning herself to death, and vowed that he and she would both join the Buddhist order when all his designs had been accomplished.

The narrative ends before Harsha Vardhana finally overthrew all his opponents, and established himself as one of the few monarchs who essayed to build up an empire from out the shifting interests of rival creeds and divided principalities.

The extent of India was, however, too vast; the incongruous race-elements it held too diverse and scattered; the caste restrictions too firmly planted; the religious divisions too deeply founded in the life-history of the people, to give hope in those early ages that India from the Himālayas to the Vindhyas, much less to Cape Comorin, from Dvārakā to Kālighāt, would ever throb with the one great racial feeling and purpose that makes a Fatherland. It remains for the future to watch and mark how the dividing lines of old are breaking down, and how, where race and caste and creed no longer hold the people asunder, they may combine to demand the ruling of their own national life.

In the midst of the changing scene Aryanism and Brāhmanism remained unmoved, watching all and noting all from their own safe retreat, heedless of kings and warriors, battles and contests, greed for empire and the coming

[1] "Harsha Charita," p. 207. [2] *Ibid.*, p. 209.

storm, the tramp of passing bands of fighting men, the flames of burning towns, the wreck of principalities, the aggrandisement of new conquerors, and the submission of the people, all of which were but the crude factors wherewith poets and dreamers might fashion their drama of the world's history.

The classic beauties of the early drama, the romances and lyrics are all that later Aryanism has left us, from which may be shadowed out something of the "very age and body of the time."

CHAPTER XII.

THE DRAMA.

To understand the full significance of the influence Aryanism had on the language and literature of India as a whole, somewhat must be realised of the actual results attained, and the elements on which these influences had to work.

From the last Census returns[1] the population of India, excluding Burma, was numbered at nearly 295,000,000 of people; Indo-Aryan vernaculars were spoken by 210,000,000; the Dravidian languages by only 53,000,000, the rest of the populace speaking other languages.

While in the literature of India the Vedic Sanskrit became modified into the later classical language, more or less artificial in its structure, it further, from about some five hundred years before Christ, broke down into a vernacular known as "Prakrit,"[2] which existed up to about 1000 A.D.

The Eastern branch of this Prakrit was the Māgadhī, spoken in Magadha, or South Behar, while the Western branch was the Sauraseni, spoken in the lands lying between the Ganges and Jumna. Intermediate between these two distinctive homes of the Aryan culture lay the land, the vernacular of whose people showed traces of connection

[1] Census of 1891.

[2] Grierson, "Indo-Aryan Vernaculars," *Calcutta Review* (October 1895).

with both the Māgadhī and the Saurasenī, so that it was called the Ardha Māgadhī, or Half Māgadhī.

Outside these three distinctive branches of the Aryan vernacular, the spoken language of the North-Western district was known as the "Apabramśa," or decayed language. From these four vernaculars all the modern Aryan vernaculars of India have descended, as shown in the following table taken from Mr Grierson's article in the *Calcutta Review*, to which reference has been already made.

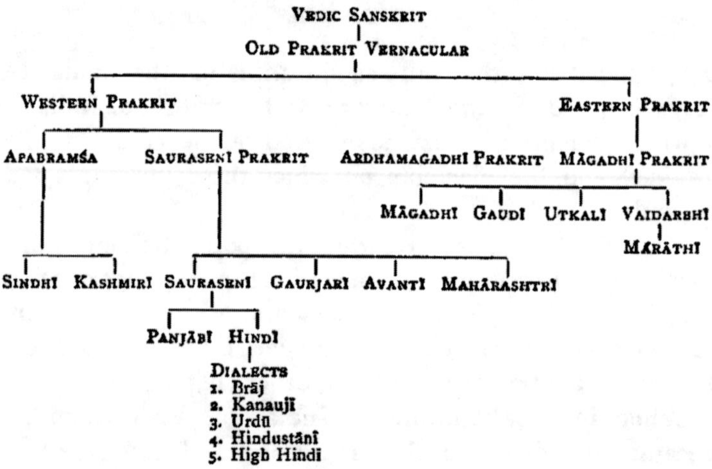

The term Hindī is here used by Mr Grierson, not as including the dialects of Rājputāna, the Baiswāri of Oudh, and the distinct dialect of Behar, but more scientifically to connote all the dialects of the North-West Provinces from Cawnpur westwards.[1] The Brāj dialect is that of the Gangetic Doab, south to Agra, northward to Multān and Delhi, thence beyond the Sivālik Hills. Kanaujī runs down the lower Doab to the south-east of Cawnpur towards Allahābād, where it merges into Baiswarī.

Urdū is the mixed language that grew up in the camp

[1] Grierson, "Indo-Aryan Vernaculars," p. 264.

of the Mughal invaders of India who used the local grammar, chiefly that of Brāj, to cement together a vocabulary mainly composed of Indian and foreign words. When used for literary purposes by the Mussalmans, the vocabulary employed was mainly Persian or Arabic. When used as a *lingua franca* for the people speaking the varied dialects of Hindustān, the vocabulary is mainly composed of the common words of the market-place, and the language itself called Hindustānī is readily intelligible to Hindus and Muhammadans alike. High Hindī is purely a book language evolved under the influence of the English, who induced native writers to compose works for general use in a form of Hindustānī, in which all the words of Arabic or Persian origin were omitted, Sanskrit words being employed in their place.

Great as has been the spread of languages finding their source in Aryan Sanskrit, still greater has been the classic influence of the Aryan literature itself on the whole thought and mode of expression of the great mass of the population with which Aryanism has come in contact. Everywhere, even to the remotest South, the Aryan literature of India spread, and became the model for all classic composition, and the means for the education and advancement of the people towards trained and ordered thought. The drama here exercised its own influence.

There is a vast difference between the stately repose of the cultured though somewhat artificial early Sanskrit dramas, and the primitive revel of dance and song, to be seen in every Indian village, when the temple deity is led forth on its high and costly decorated car, and the dancing-girls,[1] with measured step and mystic gestures, march in front, singing the deeds the god has done, and the joys of which its worshippers partake. In every step, and every motion, in every sign of the upheld hands and movement

[1] "Rig Veda," i. 10, 1, 1, 924; "Atharva-veda," xii. 1, 41.

of the dancing-girl's swaying body, the dramatic gestures and rhythmic movements all denote an advance in reasoned thought far beyond the fierce dances of the wild untamed tribesmen, who still live in the hill tracks in their barbaric freedom.

In their remote mountainous and fever-smitten homes the savage folk in their tribal war dances love to rehearse their fierce fights and the slaying of their enemies, or sometimes in their gentler moods to imitate the dancing and cooing of birds, peacocks, or jungle-fowl. Even in these forest tracks, it may be seen how the play instincts of the rude untutored races are even to-day being trained to higher purposes.

To the chance traveller in these tracks, perhaps nothing may be visible but these imitative dances of the savage folk. In the half-frenzied dance the warriors still revel in their mimic combats; every now and then some aged chief falls into an ecstatic trance, and his gesticulations show that he believes himself possessed by some evil spirit or some god whose commands or decrees he pours forth in wild cries that rush incoherently from his foaming lips. The savage expresses in his own way the instincts and superstitious fears his reason has not yet restrained. Animism rules the people who fancy that each burning hill, haunted grove, and fever-laden rill is endowed with spirit life.

These are the factors Brāhmanism has to work on and mould to its own purpose.

As the forests are cleared from the mountain's side, and the land prepared for permanent cultivation, Brāhmans and lowland traders take up their abode among the ruder indigenous races, and Hinduism slowly works its way towards its own advancement. The Brāhmans to be found in such districts may be schoolmasters, village merchants, land-owners, or agents for some overlord, to outward appearance coldly indifferent to the ways and beliefs of the rude hill folk from whom they hold aloof in their pride of learning and pride of birth. The influence of the Brāhman, and the spell of Hinduism, is, nevertheless, ever at work in its tendency to turn the people from their more savage rites, and bring them within the fold of Hinduism, with all its gods and class restrictions.

The stranger may move among the villages and mark somewhat of outward change. The elder people are becoming more settled ; their axes may perhaps be losing their ancient form, and changing gradually to forms suited for agricultural purposes. The belt of cultivated land is extending deeper into the surrounding forest, and a school perhaps has been established. Should the stranger desire to see how the Brāhman schoolmaster trains the village children, he can note how these children sit for hours learning to make letters and figures, by using their fingers to write in the dust, and to read, reckon, and recite by repeating all together sentence after sentence their simple lessons. There is, however, the legendary history of the god honoured by the preceptor to be learned, and so much as is necessary of the myths and fables, on which popular Hinduism is based.

Here the drama plays its part. In Vedic literature, in the temple dances, and in the wild, savage war dances and uncouth revels of the aboriginal folk, its past origin can be traced, but nowhere can its course of development into the form in which it first appears, full grown in the masterpieces of classic Sanskrit times, be followed. The form in which it is found among the people themselves can be best seen by asking the Brāhman preceptor to bid his pupils perform an act or two of some drama he has taught them. No preparations are necessary. The play will take place in the centre of the village or near the traveller's tents. There in the evening time the villagers will assemble, seat themselves in rows, all sedate and grave, unnoticing the clear starlit canopy of Heaven above, and ring of fire that, running along the distant mountain side, clears the fevered jungles.

In the centre of the front rank will be seated the stranger; at his side, sitting on a rug, will be the few Brāhmans the village contains—it may be only the Brāhman preceptor—the village traders, and officials. Behind, the ruder folk and aboriginal tribesmen stand or sit on their heels in native fashion.

There is no scenery. Two torch-bearers stand to right and left, their flaring torches dripping burning oil on to the ground. To one side sit the musicians, both incessantly and untiringly beating with their fingers a hide-covered drum. The actors stand at first behind one of the torch-bearers. Many are the disputes as to the setting of the piece and arraying of the boy actors. All, audience, actors, and torch-bearers, talk in high tones, yet all goes pleasantly.

Slowly from among the actors one boy moves forward, with feet shuffling along the ground in unison with the beat of the drum. He wears a high head-dress covered with tinsel and coloured glass, which sparkle now and then as the torches flare up; his face is fixed in an immoveable stare; his hands are held still, the palms turned towards the audience. His part he recites in prose and verse, his voice ever in rhythm with the music. The spectators are wrapped in dreamy bliss; they glance furtively at the foreigner to see if he is pleased, yet they no more than the foreigner understand one word of what is said, for the opening lines are in Sanskrit verse, composed by the preceptor. The audience merely knows the purport of the story represented.

As the chief actor plays his part the others move to and

fro as they will. Until the time arrives for them to take part in the action they hold a white or coloured shawl in front of them, to let the audience understand that they are not supposed to be seen.

They now drop their screen and commence their part. They are five in number, all dressed as girls. In the meantime, the first actor, with his shawl concealing him, is hoisted by some attendants, with much talking, on to the top of a post, and held there, seated on a cross-piece of wood. A light at last dawns on the spectators. The first actor is the god Krishna in his youth, the five others are the five milkmaids who have come to bathe in the river Jumna, not knowing that the god is watching them. The play goes on; the five milkmaids lay their outer white robes on the ground and pretend to bathe, singing songs in the local vernacular, mingled with praise of Krishna, all now more or less intelligible to the audience. Krishna descends from the tree, creeps near where the girls are supposed to be talking, steals their clothes, and then is hoisted back to the cross-piece on the top of the pole. The milkmaids discover their loss and come wailing to Krishna, declare their love and devotion, and beg the return of their garments.

For hours the play continues. The people never weary of the monotonous cadence of the actors' voices, relieved now and then by the local jokes and coarse allusions of the buffoon, generally represented as a Brāhman.

Beneath the whole performance can be seen the effort to represent, as it were, in the guise of a mystery play, the deeds of Krishna and the joy of those who worship him, for though "some knew him and sought him as a son, some as a friend, some as an enemy, some as a lover; in the end all obtained the blessing of deliverance and emancipation."[1]

[1] Wilkins, "Hindu Mythology," p. 176.

It is impossible to trace any connection between representations such as these or other dramatic forms found among the people, and the artificial drama of classic Sanskrit. This classic drama appears in India perfected and formed, affording no conclusive evidence as to whether it arose indigenously, or derived its classic impress from outside sources. The derivation of the terms "nātyā" and "nātaka," applied to dramatic representations,[1] from a root "nat," a corruption of "nrit," "to dance," brings no fresh light to bear on the subject. The no doubt striking resemblances between the best known Sanskrit plays and those of Terence and Plautus have been held to justify the assumption that the Indian classic drama borrowed its form from Grecian and Roman sources.[2] The question, so far, has received no final answer.[3]

The drama that may be taken as most typical of the earliest form of the classic school, and as giving a picture of Indian life about the commencement of the Christian era, more life-like and less artificial than any other known Indian drama, is the play of the "Mud Cart," the "Mricchakatīkā," of unknown date and author.[4]

The play itself has movement enough and is sufficiently realistic to be easily adapted to ensure a favourable

[1] Wilson, "Theatre of the Hindus," p. xix.

[2] Lassen, "Indische Altertumskunde," ii. 507.

[3] *See* Lévi, "Théatre Indien," for the connection between (1) the "vidūsaka" and "servus currens" (p. 358); (2) the "vīta" and "parasitus edax" (p. 360); (3) the "sakāra" and "miles gloriosus" (p. 360); (4) the Indian curtain, or "yavanika" as derived from "yavana"; the recognition ring, prologue, division into acts, etc. (p. 348). As the subject relates to literature, it is not further referred to here. It still remains for those who assert foreign influence to prove it more conclusively than up to the present has been done. *See*, especially, "Græco-Roman Influence on the Civilisation of Ancient India" (J.R.A.S., Bengal, No. III. 1889).

[4] Ascribed to Dandin of the sixth century A.D., by Pischel. *See* Col. Jacob, "Notes on Alankāra Literature," J.R.A.S. (1897), p. 284. From internal evidence I should, if discussing the work from a literary standpoint, place it before the time of Kālidāsa.

reception in an English theatre. It was played only a few years ago at the Royal Court Theatre in Berlin, as well as at the Court Theatre at Munich, where it roused enthusiasm sufficient to recall the actors eight times before the curtain. The play as there acted was adapted for the stage from the well-known and accurate German translation of Böhtlingk. For the English student of literature, or for the lover of the drama, there is a translation by Horace Hayman Wilson, which, meritorious and skilful though it be, fails to preserve the form of the original.

The play is in Sanskrit, mingled with the Prakrits, eleven of the characters speaking Saurasenī, two Avantī, one Pracīya, six Māgadhī, the king's brother-in-law, the keeper of the gambling-house, the low caste Chāndālas and acolytes speaking Apabramśa. The play opens with a benediction to Śiva, the dread god, whose blue neck, when encircled with the clinging arm of his wife, Parvatī, gleams like a dark cloud crossed by a running line of lightning.

The "Sūtradhāra,"[1] or stage-manager, first enters, and speaks in praise of the play and its author. The play, he states, is to treat of love and real life. The name of the author is declared to be Sūdraka, "first of warriors," with the walk of a noble elephant, the eye of a chakora bird, the face of a full moon, who, though a king, became a poet of unfathomable learning. He knew well the "Rig and Sama Vedas," mathematics, the art of singing, dancing, and wanton dalliance, and the management of elephants. The stage-manager then narrates how this kingly author lost his eyesight, had it restored to him by the favour of Śiva, then placed his son on the throne, performed the great horse sacrifice, and, at the age of one hundred years and ten days, ended his life by entering the fire. By this Sūdraka the play was written to tell how, in the town of

[1] Wilson, "Theatre of the Hindus," vol. i. p. xxxv.

Avanti, a young but poor Brāhman, Charudatta, was loved by Vasantasenā, a wanton like unto the goddess of Spring, and how from that pleasant love-feast arose in the course of fate the triumph of right conduct over the wickedness of judicial enquiry and the behaviour of the bad. The place of action of the drama is in the wealthy city of Avanti, or Ujjain. The time of opening is a day of festival. The streets are decorated; girls grind paint to adorn the house fronts; flowers are being strung to form festoons; from the houses comes the scent of savoury cooking. The giver of the feast but waits for a worthy Brāhman to partake first of the viands so that the feast may commence. This gives opportunity for the mention of Charudatta's name, for no actor may appear until his name is introduced. Charudatta then at length appears, dejected and downcast, sighing deeply as he presents an offering before the threshold of his house to the household gods. As he scatters the scanty store he sighs, and looking upward recites in Sanskrit verse his lament:—

"The ample offering to this, the threshold of my home, was quickly, in former days, borne away by swans and cranes; now it falls but a mere handful on the half-grown grass to be sought out by worms."

[His friend Maitreya, a Brāhman, the "Vidūshaka," or familiar companion of the hero, then enters and presents Charudatta with a jasmine-scented robe, sent by the giver of the feast. As Charudatta receives the robe, he remains plunged in thought.]

"Bho!" cries Maitreya, "why should you now ponder?"

"Alas, my friend," answers Charudatta, "happiness to one plunged in sorrows gleams but as the glimmer of a lamp amid deep darkness. The man who sinks from wealth to poverty is dead indeed; he lives but bound to the body."

MAITREYA [*asks*].—"Is then death to be preferred to poverty?" And quickly comes the answer:

"Death is by me preferred to poverty. Death is but fleeting pain, poverty is unending sorrow."

MAITREYA.—Nay, in you, your wealth all bestowed on loved friends, your poverty is to be admired, just as is the glory of the waning moon when its full brightness is snatched away by the immortal gods.

CHARUDATTA.—Friend! Truly I take no heed of my lost wealth. By the course of fate riches come and go. One thought burns me, and that is how the world falls off from friendship with one whose wealth has fled. Then from poverty flows shame; wrapped round by shame one's fame is lost; devoid of fame one is despised; then come deep despondency and grief. The mind then sunk in sorrow grows weak, the man sinks low. Wealth once gone, all other losses follow.

MAITREYA.—Cease lamenting, friend. Wealth is but a trivial thing.

CHARUDATTA.—Friend! Poverty overwhelms one with thought. Sneered at by strangers and the true strength of our enemies, it is the jest of friends and cause of scorn of one's own relations. It makes one long for the solitude of the forest, there to be free from the reproach of one's own wife. The fire of sorrow lingers in the heart, it burns not out. Friend, go, the offerings to the household deities have now been made; go, offer them to the Mothers at the cross-roads.

MAITREYA.—I go not.

CHARUDATTA.—Why?

MAITREYA.—Why should one honour the gods? By you they have been long honoured, yet they are not favourable.

CHARUDATTA.—Friend! Not so, not so. Where the gods are worshipped by holy men with offering, penance, mind and words, they are ever pleased. Consider, bear the offerings to the Mothers.

MAITREYA.—Bho! I shall not go. Send some one else. For me everything appears turned the wrong way round; right is left, and left right, just like an image seen in a mirror. Besides this, at this time of night on the high road dancing-girls, lewd men, servants and relations of the king wander about, and I might be seized just as the mouse was by the black serpent on the look-out for a frog. What shall you do seated here?

CHARUDATTA.—So be it. Stay then, and I shall engage myself in religious meditation.

[*Voice is heard behind the screen*].—Stay, Vasantasenā, stay.

[Then enters Vasantasenā, followed by the king's brother-in-law, his companion a lewd parasite and a servant.]

THE COMPANION.—Vasantasenā! stay, stay! Why, from fear, your gentle grace abandoned, your feet ever gleaming in the dance, thrown here and there, your eyes throwing out side glances, anxious and trembling, do you fly like a deer startled by the pursuing hunter.

KING'S BROTHER-IN-LAW, THE PRINCE.—Stay, dear Vasantasenā, stay. Why are you going? Why do you run? Why fly stumbling? Gentle one, be quieted, you shall not die, therefore stay. My heart with love is burning like flesh fallen on the burning coal.

ATTENDANT.—Stay, honoured lady, stay. Frightened, you go, sister mine, like a hot weather pea-hen with spread-out tail, while my respected master quickly follows like a young hound in the forest.

ATTENDANT.—Vasantasenā! stay, stay. Why do you go shaking like the young plantain tree, the edge of your red robe fluttering in the wind, scattering forth the opening buds from the masses of red lotuses, just like a cave of red ochre burst in pieces by an axe.

PRINCE.—Stay, Vasantasenā, stay! Inflaming my love, born of the bodiless god of love, cruelly driving sleep from my couch by night, you fly, stricken with fear, stumbling and slipping, you have fallen into my possession, as Kuntī into that of Rāvana.

ATTENDANT.—Vasantasenā! Why do you with your steps exceed mine? Like a snake dreading the king of birds you speed away. But I outstrip the rushing wind. In seizing you, O best of limbed, there is to me no effort.

PRINCE.—Sir, Sir! I have called her the scourge of money-stealers, the fish-eater, the wanton, no-nosed, destroyer of families, unowned, the treasure-casket of Cupid, a keeper of lewd houses, an adorned post, a parrot, a harlot; by me these ten names have been made for her, yet she loves me not.

ATTENDANT.—Why do you fly disturbed by fear? With your cheeks beaten by your swaying earrings, just as the Vīna struck by a Vita with the finger-nails.

PRINCE.—Why do you fly, like Draupadī[1] from Rāma, all your ornaments jingling as you go?

ATTENDANT.—Take now the king's brother-in-law, and you shall eat fish and flesh. Dogs wait not in a dead man's house in search of these. Honoured Vasantasenā, why do you fly overcome with fear, bearing on your hip your garland of many folds, gleaming with speckled stars like pearls, with your face deep dyed with red paint, like the city goddess?

[1] The speaker here, as elsewhere, makes humorous blunders.

PRINCE.—You are now being closely followed by us, as in the forest the fox by dogs; you fly quickly, hurrying with speed, bearing my heart with its covering.

[*Vasantasenā cries for help*].

PRINCE [*in fear*].—Sir, Sir! There are men.

ATTENDANT.—Fear not, fear not.

VASANTASENĀ.—Madanikā! Madanikā!

ATTENDANT [*laughing*].—Fool, she summons her attendants.

PRINCE.—Sir, Sir! She seeks women.

ATTENDANT.—Then what?

PRINCE.—I am a hero. I can kill a hundred women.

VASANTASENĀ [*seeing no one*].—Alas, alas! Even my attendants have disappeared. I must indeed protect myself.

ATTENDANT.—Search! search!

PRINCE.—Dear Vasantasenā! Cry, cry out for aid. Who can help you, followed by me? I, myself, having seized you by the hair of the head. Now see, now see, the sword is sharp and the head ready. We cut off the head or we slay. There is enough of your running away. One who is about to die does not truly live.

VASANTASENĀ.—Sir, I am but a woman.

ATTENDANT.—For that alone you will be preserved.

PRINCE.—For that alone you will not die.

VASANTASENĀ [*aside*].—How even his very courtesy engenders fear. Let it be so then [*aloud*]—Then you desire some jewels.

ATTENDANT.—Forfend us, Lady Vasantasenā. The gardener desires not to steal flowers. Therefore there is no fear for your jewels.

VASANTASENĀ.—Then what indeed now?

PRINCE.—That I, a god-like hero, a man, an incarnation of wealth, am to be loved.

VASANTASENĀ [*with anger*].—Shame! Shame! you speak unworthily.

PRINCE [*clapping his hands and laughing gently, mistaking the exclamation Shame!* (Sānta) for "śrānta" (*weary*)].—Noble sir, see now, how courteous is this young dancing-girl, since she asks me, Are you weary, are you tired. I have gone to no other village nor town. Lady, I swear by your head, and by my feet, that by following close on you I have become weary and tired.

ATTENDANT.—The fool imagines the girl says "be rested," when she cries "forfend us!" Vasantasenā, your house is that of a dancing-girl, open to all. You, a wanton, are like the wayside creeper swayed equally by peacock and crow.

VASANTASENĀ.—Merit and not power is truly the only cause of love.

PRINCE.—She is a dancing-girl from her birth. From the day she first saw Charudatta in the temple of the God of Love, she has become enamoured of him, and will not bend to my will. Take care, his house is near, see that she escape not from our hands.

ATTENDANT ON PRINCE [*aside*].—What! the fool blurts out what he should hide. Vasantasenā in love with Charudatta! then truly pearls match pearls. Let the fool go. I shall aid Vasantasenā. [*Aloud*] Hullo! all in deep darkness. The house of Charudatta is to the left. [*In a whisper*] Vasantasenā, conceal yourself in the evening darkness like lightning shut in by heavy clouds; let not the perfume from your garlands nor sound of your jewels betray you.

[Vasantasenā removes her garlands and jewels, and feels her way by the side wall of Charudatta's house. Charudatta is seen inside his house with Maitreya and a female servant.]

CHARUDATTA.—My prayers are now ended. Go, present the offerings to the Mothers.

MAITREYA.—I go not.

CHARUDATTA.—Alas! From poverty of a man, even his friends heed not his words. His power is laughed at; none desires his acquaintance, nor speaks to him with respect. Truly poverty is the sixth great sin.

MAITREYA.—O friend, if I must go, then let the servant go with me as a companion.

CHARUDATTA.—Be it so.

[As the servant takes a light, Maitreya opens the side door, near which stands Vasantasenā, who, as the servant approaches, blows out the light with the end of her garment.]

MAITREYA [*exclaims*].—Ah! by the opening of the door the light has been extinguished. Pass out, servant, while I go again inside to relight the lamp.

[The servant goes into the street, where she is seized by the prince and his attendant. She cries out.]

THE PRINCE.—See, see, I have seized Vasantasenā. Recognising her flying by the perfume of her garland I have seized her by the hair of her head. Now let her cry, weep, and rage on all the gods.

[The servant cries out, and Maitreya returns with an upraised stick.]

MAITREYA.—Shame! a dog in his own house would be outraged by this violence. How much more I, a Brāhman? With this knotted stick, rough as our fate, I shall grind like dried-up reeds your heads with blows. [*Seeing the prince*] Are, Are, bad man, this is not fit. If the honoured Charudatta be poor, what then? Has he not made all Ujjayin renowned by his merits. Why, then, is there this disgrace of strangers entering his house?

ATTENDANT ON PRINCE.—Great Brāhman, stay, stay, we came not through insolence; one loved by us was sought.

MAITREYA.—Who? This servant?

ATTENDANT.—Avert the sin. No, one who is as fire. She is now lost. By our mistake this insolence has occurred. Take now this sword, and let all be yours [*offering sword and falling at Maitreya's feet.*]

THE PRINCE.—Of whom are you afraid? Who is this Charudatta who has no food in his house? Who is he? slave from his birth, and son of a slave from her birth. Is he a renowned warrior or one of the heroes of old?

ATTENDANT [*rising*].—Fool! he is the noble Charudatta. The tree of plenty to the poor, bowed down by its own good fruits. He is the support of all good people, the model of all training, the touchstone of good behâviour, the boundary shore of decorum, the doer of good, the despiser of none, a mine of manly merit, courteous, gentle, and strong. He alone is worthy of praise. He alone lives, others merely breathe. Let us go.

PRINCE.—What! without Vasantasenā? I shall not go until I get her.

ATTENDANT.—An elephant may be held by a rope, a horse by a bridle, but have you not heard that a woman can only be held by her heart? Let us go [*departs by himself.*]

PRINCE [*turning to Maitreya*].—Hold! you crow-foot headed fool. Tell that beggar, Charudatta, that since the day Vasantasenā saw him in the temple of the God of Love she has become enamoured of him. As I sought to seize her by force she has now entered his house. If now he deliver her into my hands he wins my firm affection, if not, my deadly hatred. Go in and tell him this, else I shall chaw your head like a nut crunched beneath a door [*departs.*]

[Maitreya commands the servant to say nothing of the affray to Charudatta, so as not to increase the distress of his ill-fate.

Charudatta in his house mistakes Vasantasenā, who has entered in the darkness, for his servant, and holds out to her the jasmine robe, directing her to take it to his child, Rohasena, as the night is cold.]

VASANTASENĀ [*aside*].—He conceives that I am one of his servants [*taking the robe.*] Strange, the robe is scented with the perfume of jasmine flowers. Then he is not yet indifferent to everything.

[Charudatta, on discovering his mistake, apologises. Vasantasenā asks permission to leave her casket of jewels at his house; Charudatta consents, and the first act ends by her being escorted home by Charudatta and Maitreya.]

The second act introduces the home of Vasantasenà, both the inside of the house being seen and also a street with a small, empty temple.

A servant plys Vasantasenā with questions concerning Charudatta. A cry is heard from the street, announcing that a gambler has fled from a gaming-house without having paid ten gold pieces which he had lost. The keeper of the gaming-house and other gamblers are pursuing him to make him pay his debts. The gambler appears, bemoaning his bad luck and passion for gambling. Seeing the temple empty he enters, and stands there as if he were the image of the god. The pursuers sit down before the temple and proceed to play. The first gambler, unable to listen to the rattle of the dice, rushes from his place in the temple to join in the game. He is seized and beaten; a riot occurs, during which he escapes and flies for safety into the house of Vasantasenā, who, on hearing that he had been in the service of Charudatta, sends out to the keeper of the gambling-house and his associates a bracelet in payment of the debt. The gambler, overcome by his disgrace, departs, declaring his intention of becoming a Buddhist mendicant.

In the third act a dissipated Brāhman, in love with an attendant of Vasantasenā, steals the jewel casket confided by Vasantasenā to the care of Charudatta. The midnight scene, depicting the cutting through of the wall of Charudatta's house, the entry and seizure of the casket, is a most subtle picture of Hindu ingenuity. It is too long and minute in its descriptions for Western ideas, but in the East, where every restless want is soon satiated, an audience gladly luxuriates in these subdued effects.

When Charudatta's wife hears of the loss, she sends all that remains of her wealth—a wondrous string of pearls—to her husband, telling him to save his honour by forwarding them to Vasantasenā in exchange for the lost casket.

The fourth act shows Vasantasenā's house. The burglar of the night before brings the casket of jewels to his mistress, the attendant of Vasantasenā, by whom the casket is restored to Vasantasenā, who rewards her servant by giving her in marriage to the now reformed Brāhman robber.

So far the imagery throws a vivid light on the people, their thoughts and mode of life. The unity of action is now broken by introducing into the main plot a second plot, in which is well depicted the petty intrigues surrounding the downfall of a local chieftain and uprising of a new dynasty.

As the Brāhman robber and his wife depart from the house of Vasantasenā a herald's cry is heard :—

"Ho! ho! there, Bho! The king's brother-in-law hereby proclaims. It has been prophesied that one Āryaka, a cow-herd, shall yet become king. Now let each one hear and remain content in his own place, for the King Pālaka has taken the cow-herd Āryaka and placed him in a deep dungeon."

THE BRĀHMAN ROBBER.—Alas! the King Pālaka has bound my dear friend Āryaka, and I am about to marry. Ah, fate! In this world two things are very dear to a man, a friend, and a wife. Better, however, than even one hundred fair girls is one dear friend. I go not home.

[The Brāhman at once sends his new wife to his home, and hastens himself to raise a band to release Āryaka from the violence of the reigning king, Pālaka. Maitreya next enters Vasantasenā's house, and tells her of the loss of the casket. He presents to her the string of pearls in exchange, and she smilingly announces her intention of visiting Charudatta.]

The fifth act ushers in the tempestuous suddenness of a

tropical storm preluding the love of Charudatta and Vasantasenā. Charudatta is seated in his pleasure-garden, awaiting the visit of Vasantasenā, who hastens to his side, defying all the evil omens that hover round.

"Let the clouds fall in torrents, thunder roar,
And Heaven's red bolt dart fiery to the ground.
The dauntless damsel faithful love inspires
Treads boldly on nor dreads the maddening storm."[1]

[Charudatta receives her gently, and prays her not to revile the cloud:]

"Reprove it not, for let the rain descend,
The heavens still lour and wide the lightnings launch
A hundred flames; they have befriended me,
And given me her for whom I sighed in vain."[2]

In the sixth act Vasantasenā awakens in the house of Charudatta to find that he has gone to a neighbouring pleasure-garden, having left a message that she is to follow. Her carriage awaits her. Before she enters, the driver discovers that he has forgotten the cushions, and drives off to fetch them. In his absence, the carriage of the king's brother-in-law passes down the street. In the press of the traffic its driver stays it at the door of Charudatta's house, and descends to clear the road. Vasantasenā, taking it for her own, ascends, and is driven away.

The rebel Āryaka now appears on the stage. He is fettered, having escaped from the king's dungeon. He bewails his lot, and, seeing Vasantasenā's empty carriage, ascends it, and is driven to the pleasure-garden, where he is met by Charudatta, who, pitying his condition, removes his fetters, gives him a sword, and directs him to escape from the town.

The seventh act takes place in the same pleasure-garden. The gambler, who has turned a Buddhist mendicant,

[1] Wilson, "Theatre of the Hindus," vol. i. p. 97. [2] *Ibid.*, p. 280.

appeąrs, and is met by the king's brother-in-law. In fear he cries out :—

"Alas ! here comes the king's brother-in-law. We know that he was once insulted by a mendicant, and now he slits the nose of every Buddhist beggar he sees, and drives him forth. Where shall I unprotected fly? The lord Buddha is now my only refuge."

[As the Buddhist conceals himself, Vasantasenā arrives, and as she alights the king's brother-in-law falls at her feet and pleads his false love] :

"Mother, sister, hear my prayer. Here, O large-eyed one, at your feet I fall. With upraised hands I pray you, O fair-limbed one, to forgive the fault that in my passion I may have committed."

[Vasantasenā spurns him with her foot, and upbraids him for his ignoble behaviour. In his rage he drags her by the hair of her head from the carriage, and calls on the driver of the carriage by threats and bribes to slay her. The driver cries in horror that Vasantasenā has done no wrong; she is young, the ornament of the whole town. Should she be slain, the four quarters would bear witness to the deed, as would the sylvan gods, the Moon, the Sun with its bright rays, Justice and the Wind, the Inward Self, the Earth, the true witnesses of Right and Wrong.

[The king's brother-in-law beats the driver, who flies from the garden. An attendant alone remains concealed close at hand. The prince again pleads his suit, and Vasantasenā answers] :[1]

"I spurn you ;
Nor can you tempt me, abject wretch with gold.
Though soiled the leaves, the bees fly not the lotus,
Nor shall my heart prove traitor to the homage
It pays to merit though its lord be poor."

[The enraged Prince taunts her for still remembering Charudatta, and she replies] :

"Why should I not remember that which is planted in my heart."

PRINCE.—Then that which is planted in your heart, and you also, lover of a mean, wealth-forsaken Brāhman, I shall slay. Stay, stay.

VASANTASENĀ.—Speak again those words, for they flatter me.

[1] Wilson, "Theatre of the Hindus," vol. i. p. 135.

PRINCE.—Let then that Charudatta, son of a dancing-girl, now protect you.

VASANTASENĀ.—He would protect me if he could but see me.

[*Prince seizes her.*]

VASANTASENĀ—Ho! mother, where are you! Ha, noble Charudatta! The vile wretch slays me even before my wish has been accomplished. Yet I shall not cry out. No, that were shame should Vasantasenā's cry be heard. Let there be only this: salutation to the noble Charudatta!

PRINCE.—Again, the slave from her birth, uses the name of Charudatta [*seizes her by the throat*]. Remember, slave from your birth, remember.

VASANTASENĀ.—Salutation to the noble Charudatta [*falls senseless*].

PRINCE.—Now, at last, this bamboo box of wickedness, this abiding place of incivility, who came to meet her lover Charudatta, has met her death.

[The prince covers Vasantasenā with leaves, and then departs. The Buddhist mendicant appears, and discovers Vasantasenā. He pours water over her, and she revives. Fearing to touch a woman, he bends down a branch of a neighbouring tree, so that Vasantasenā may seize it, and rise. They depart for a neighbouring convent, where dwells a holy sister, the Buddhist mendicant reciting his lay that the man whose acts, and thoughts, and senses are subdued, has naught to do with affairs of the world, for he holds in his grasp the next world firm.]

The ninth act gives the only picture of a Court of Justice in Indian literature. There the prince carries all before him. Charudatta is accused of the crime, condemned, and led forth to execution sorrowfully lamenting:—

"Alas, my poor friend!
Had due investigation been allowed me,
Or any test proposed, water or poison,
The scales or scorching fire, and I had failed
The proof, then might the law have been fulfilled
And I deservedly received my doom.
But this will be avenged, and for the sentence
That dooms a Brāhman's death, on the mere charge
Of a malicious foe, the bitter portion
That waits for thee, and all thy line, O king,
Is Hell—proceed—I am prepared."[1]

[1] Wilson, "Theatre of the Hindus," vol. i. p. 159.

The tenth act occurs at the place of execution. At the last moment the truth is made known, and Charudatta is released. The news is then announced that the king Pālaka has been slain, and Āryaka placed on the throne. Charudatta is raised to high office, and signalises his accession to power by ordering the immediate release of the prince, whom the mob would have torn to pieces. The Buddhist mendicant is made chief of all the Buddhist monasteries in the land. Charudatta is restored to his wife, and the last words of the play are uttered :—

> "Fate views the world,
> A scene of mutual and perpetual struggle
> For some are raised to affluence, some depressed
> In want, while some are borne awhile aloft,
> And some hurled down to wretchedness and woe."[1]

The play differs essentially from all other plays of the classic period. In its dramatic interest, in its realistic view of life, in its humour and raciness, it is unique in the whole literary history of India. Many of the scenes are undoubtedly filled in with all the exuberance and artificiality of an Eastern poet's imagination, which makes it rash to assert that the whole play is the work of one hand. Nevertheless, to any one acquainted with the inner life of India, especially that phase of it dealt with in the "Mud Cart," the position of the dancing-girl, the surroundings and associates of a debauched Indian prince, the life of the merchant Brāhman, Charudatta, the behaviour of the officers of the household guard, of whom two are depicted in the play as falling to fisticuffs over the escape of Āryaka, the condition of affairs, and appearance of effeminate men, in the pleasure-garden of Vasantasenā, are all life-like, and founded on what must have been facts at the period treated of. The great value of the play is contained in the side-light it throws on the history of the people, revealing them, not as

[1] Wilson, "Theatre of the Hindus," vol. i. p. 180.

seen in the ideal descriptions of the law books and more recondite literature, but as types well known to the audience for whom the play was prepared. Although the simplicity of the style and structure of the language afford no conclusive evidence respecting the age of the play, still it may, in the absence of any reliable evidence to the contrary, be accepted as giving a poetic description, drawn from life, of the manners of the country where it was produced, at or about the commencement of the Christian era.

The difficulties in the way of ascertaining the dates of any of the earlier Sanskrit dramas seem to be almost as insurmountable as those for arriving at any unanimous opinion regarding the genesis of their form. While Kālidāsa is universally accepted as the Shakespeare of the Indian drama, it must be remembered that this is merely meant to indicate that his plays represent the purest and—according to Eastern ideals—highest artistic form of the classic drama.

Any natural tendency of the classic drama to recognise and assimilate to itself the common life-history of the people, and their modes of thought and expression, was unfortunately checked by foreign conquest. Kālidāsa,[1]

[1] Peterson, J.R.A.S. (Bombay), vol. xviii. p. 110:—"For it is certain now that Kālidāsa must be put earlier than has lately been very generally supposed. He stands near the beginning of our era, if indeed he does not overtop it, and dates from the year one of Vikrama's era." *See* more particularly G. R. Nandargikar, "Meghaduta of Kālidāsa" (Bombay, 1894), p. 84:—"And it is also probable, nay almost certain, that Kālidāsa, the Virgil of the Hindus, may have lived some forty years before the beginning of the Christian era, and may also have been a poet in the imperial court of Vikramāditya, who began to reign from 57 B.C."

To Miss Duff I am indebted for the following note:—"The Jaina poet Ravikīrti flourished 610 A.D., being contemporary with Pulikeśin II., 'Early Chālukya.' He was the composer of Pulikeśin's Aihole Meguti inscription, in which he claims equality with the poets Kālidāsa and Bhāravi, thus incidentally proved to have flourished before this time. No definite date can, as yet, be fixed for Kālidāsa, but, according to Kielhorn, he cannot be placed later than 472 A.D., the date of Kumāra Gupta's Mandasor inscriptions, a verse of therefore, remains the sole, unrivalled exponent of the pure, classic mode of representing life and thought in the early ages.

While with Wilson it may be said that "it is impossible to conceive language so beautifully musical and so magnificently grand as that of many of the verses of Bhavabhuti and Kālidāsa," the two great dramatists of classical India, it must be remembered that these dramas are studied compositions, the Sanskrit portions being intended exclusively as an intellectual feast for the learned. So much of the life of the period as is shadowed forth in the dramas of Kālidāsa can only be fully understood in the form in which the poet's mind conceived it in the original Sanskrit. Bereft of this, the vision is blurred and indistinct, lifeless facts alone remaining in any translation, however perfect. In the Sanskrit alone can the lines be traced on which the poet's fancy modelled a form such as grew to life in "Sakuntalā," who spoke in a music, each note of which was skilfully attuned to her own gentle grace.

The play itself is a true Nātaka, considered the highest form of Indian dramatic art, having for its object the representation of heroic or god-like characters, and the presentation of good deeds. The play does not profess to give a realistic picture of the life of the people. It is idealistic in its conception, full of lofty sentiment, artificial and wilfully elaborate in its diction, the Sanskrit portions being unintelligible to the greater part of the audience which heard the play.

The play opens with the appearance of the legendary king, Dushyanta, of the Lunar Race, descendant of Puru.

which so closely resembles Kālidāsa's 'Ritusanhāra' as to justify[1] the inference that this work was in existence when the inscription was incised. Similarly the Buddha Gayā inscription of Mahāvārnam contains a passage closely resembling one in the 'Raghuvanśa.'"—B.D., 59, vol. iii. 121*ff*; "Ind. Ant.," xix. 285; xx. 190; J.B.R.A.S., xix. 35.

[1] I fail to see that there are any grounds for the conclusion

He is seated in his chariot and is armed with bow and arrow. The absence of stage properties gives opportunity for the description of the scenery. The king's horses are being urged in pursuit of a flying deer. As Dushyanta gains on the deer he prepares to shoot an arrow, when a voice is heard, declaring that he is trespassing on a sacred hermitage, south of Hastinapur, the dwelling of the sage Kanva and his disciples.

Sakuntalā, the daughter of a heavenly nymph sent from Heaven by Indra to allure the ascetic sage Visvamitra from his penances, dwells in the hermitage under the care of her foster-father Kanva. Her lips gleam with the gleam of the young bud, her arms are twining like the tender creeper, while over all her limbs youth glows as in the blossom of a flower. The king stands in the midst of the hermitage, the peace of which he has so rudely broken. The hermits move quietly to and fro ; the smoke of sacrifice rises here and there in the sacred grove, lingering amid the foliage of the variegated forest trees ; fawns graze fearless on the sacred grass ; water led in channels flows throughout the grove ; parrots flit from out the hollow trunks of trees ; the garments made of bark for the sage's pupils hang here and there. Kanva, the sage, is absent from the hermitage, having gone on a pilgrimage to the sea-coast near Gujarāt.

As Sakuntalā appears on the scene the king stands watching her, wondering if he, a warrior, can ever hope to win one whom he takes to be the daughter of a Brāhman.

Though the king knows that among hermits, whose only treasure is their store of forbearance, there lies deep hidden a burning and passionate wrath which may blaze forth against those who oppose their sacred calling, still he knows that though the maiden is in the charge of the ascetic sage, his heart cannot turn back from her, no more than water can from the low land. The same is true of Sakuntalā.

Gentler, more winning in her grace, more youthful than Gretchen or Juliet, she has a deeper note, a more human charm than either. Eastern, subtle, evasive, throbbing with love, veiled with reserve, there yet grows within her a passionate and seething love for the king, which she tries to stifle, but from which she can find no peace. The king learns the secret of her descent from the warrior sage Visvamitra, and so all impediment to their union is removed. No adaptation, however skilful, no wealth of scenery, however gorgeous, could ever prevent the play from being laughed off an English stage. The languor of the movement as the love scenes subtly blend the whole ascetic grove into throbbing sympathy with the drama of life woven out by the poet is too essentially Eastern to stay the quick eagerness of Western thought.

The king and Sakuntalā twine their lives together, according to the Gandharva[1] form of marriage, a simple plighted troth, by which, as Dushyanta urges, other daughters of great sages have been led away, unblamed by their fathers. Dushyanta has soon to leave Sakuntalā, on an urgent summons to return to his kingdom. To Sakuntalā he leaves as sign of future recognition his token ring. She, dreaming of her departed husband, neglects to receive with due rites of hospitality a great sage, whose anger and imprecations were so feared that even the gods went in dread of him. This fierce sage, enraged by the neglect, cursed Sakuntalā, declaring that the king would never more recollect her face. He afterwards relented in so far as to declare that the king's memory would be restored on sight of the token ring.

The remainder of the play is the working out of the result of the sage's curse. Sakuntalā lost the ring when bathing, and it was swallowed by a fish. The king disowned her when she arrived at the court with her child,

[1] "Manu," iii. 32.

the famed Bhārata. The plays ends with the recovery of the ring by two fishermen, the restoration of the king's memory, and the recognition of Sakuntalā as queen, and of her son Bhārata as heir to the kingdom.

The second great drama of Kālidāsa, the "Vikramorvasī," or " Urvasī, Won by Valour," depicts in five short acts the adventures of a heavenly nymph, Urvasī, who was rescued from a demon by her lover, the heroic king, Purūravas.

The third play deals with history. It is the story of Agnimitra, the son of Pushpamitra, who having put to death the last of the Maurya monarchs, founded the Sunga dynasty of Magadha. In spite of the opposition of his two queens, Agnimitra falls in love with a girl of his court, Mālavikā, and ultimately succeeds in marrying her, and in having her recognised by her rivals.

The second great romantic dramatist of India was Bhavabhūti, who flourished at the end of the seventh century of our era. To him three plays are ascribed, the "Mālatī Mādhava," the "Mahā-vīra-Charitra," and the " Uttara-Rāma-Charitra."

The over-elaborated and fantastic style of Bhavabhūti, especially in the "Mālatī Mādhava," has produced a result so artificial and purely literary, that Mr Grierson declares: "I do not believe that there ever was even a pandit in India who could have understood, say, the more difficult passages of Bhavabhūti at first hearing, without previous study."

The poet in his opening prologue shows that he wrote his play with no attempt to appeal to any but scholars and learned pandits. " How little do they know," he wrote, " who speak of us with censure. The entertainment is not for them. Possibly some one exists, or will exist, of similar tastes with myself, for time is boundless, and the world is wide."

Notwithstanding the extreme artificiality of much of the

style of the "Mālatī Mādhava," it is invaluable for the strong light it throws on certain phases of the more obscure superstitious rites of Hinduism. In order to produce his effects, the dramatist conjures up scenes that seize the imagination, with a reality more vivid and a spell more weird and uncanny than even the witch's scene in Macbeth, or the Walpurgis Night in Faust. In the play, Mālatī is the daughter of the minister of Ujjayin, and Mādhava, the son of the chief minister of the state of Viderbha or Berar. Mālatī is nursed by a Buddhist nun at Ujjayin. There Mādhava is also sent, for, as the drama declares, it was customary in these days for students to crowd to the schools of the Buddhists to learn logic. The King of Ujjayin demands Mālatī in marriage for a favourite of his own. The chief value of the story, as a revelation of Indian thought, consists not only in the evidence it affords as to the position of Buddhism at the period, but also in the light it throws on later Hindu beliefs and practices.

In the more important eighteen "Purānas" a full account is given of Hinduism, so far as it is concerned with the worship of Brahmā, Vishnu, and Śiva, while in the numerous "Tantras," the tenets of the Śaktas, or worshippers of the Śakti, the active, creative side of each deity, personified as a female energy, bearing the Śānkhya relationship of the Prakriti to Purusha, are detailed in all their forbidding reality.

In the drama of Bhavabhūti, these Tantric practices are pictured forth in scenes which never could have been imagined unless they were based on a substratum of fact. Though these practices are reprobated in the text, and set forth in their more unholy aspect as fit only for outcasts and heretics, yet there is ample evidence that they were not uncommon.

The goddess whose worship is described in the "Mālatī Mādhava," is Chāmundā, a form of Durgā, the consort of

Śiva. Her high priest has vowed to present to the dread goddess a chaste virgin as a sacrifice, and the choice falls on Mālatī. The maiden is led by sorcery to the temple of the goddess, there to be slain. Kapāla Kundalā,[1] the serving priestess, sings the praise of the goddess, the personification of divine energy. The scene takes place in a burning ground, near which stands the temple of the dread deity. Inside the temple Mālatī lies bound. In the midst of the horrible scene, the most horrible that genius has ever made sublime, Mādhava enters. Determined to call in the aid of foul demons and sorcery to win Mālatī for his bride, he has come to put the unholy Tantric rites into practice on the very ground where stands the temple of Chāmundā. He is unaware of the fact that Mālatī has been entrapped, and lies bound near at hand. The darkest aspect of Indian superstition is now revealed in the play:—

> "Now wake the terrors of the place, beset
> With crowding and malignant fiends ; the flames
> From funeral pyres scarce lend their sullen light
> Clogged with their fleshy prey to dissipate
> The fearful gloom that hems them in. Pale ghosts
> Spirit with foul goblins, and their dissonant mirth
> In shrill respondent shrieks is echoed round."[2]

Mādhava enters bearing the flesh of man, "untouched by trenchant steel," to present to the fell demons and unholy spirits, and so gain their aid.

The priestess enters, "in a heavenly car, and in a hideous garb" to disclose the means whereby, some have imagined, the Yogīs of India acquire mystic powers :—

> "Glory to Saktināth, upon whose steps,
> The mighty goddesses attend, whom seek
> Successfully alone the firm of thought.
> He crowns the lofty aims of those who know
> And hold his form, as the pervading spirit,

[1] The title chosen for one of Bankim Chandra Chatterji's novels.

[2] Wilson, "Theatre of the Hindus," vol. ii. p. 55.

> That, one with their own essence, makes his seat
> The heart, the lotus centre of the sphere
> Sixfold by ten nerves circled. Such am I.
> Freed from all perishable bonds, I view
> The eternal soul embodied as the God,
> Forced by my spells to tread the mystic labyrinth,
> And rise in splendour throned upon my heart.
> Hence through the many channelled veins I draw
> The grosser elements of this mortal body,
> And soar unwearied through the air, dividing
> The water-shedding clouds. Upon my flight,
> Horrific honours wait ;—the hollow skulls,
> That low descending from my neck depend,
> Emit fierce music as they clash together,
> Or strike the trembling plates that gird my loins."[1]

The scene that follows is horribly revolting. To those before whom it will bring up memories of the true records of the Aghoris, or human flesh-eating religious maniacs of recent days in India, it is a scene of extreme interest, as well as to all students of Indian thought, who cannot neglect anything that tends to throw light on a subject which is ever fascinating—the strange diversity of the wanderings of Eastern beliefs. Mādhava shakes off the demon host and unclean spirits :—

> "Race dastardly as hideous. All is plunged
> In utter gloom. The river flows before me,
> The boundary of the funeral ground that winds
> Through mouldering bones its interrupted way.
> Wild raves the torrent as it rushes past,
> And rends its crumbling banks, the wailing owl
> Hoots through its skirting groves, and to the sounds
> The loud, long moaning jackal yells reply."[2]

Within the temple the human-sacrificing priest dances his Tantric dance around his victims, invoking the goddess :—

> "Hail ! hail ! Chāmundā, mighty goddess, hail !
> I glorify thy sport, when in the dance
> That fills the court of Śiva with delight,
> Thy foot descending spurns the earthly globe
> . . . .

[1] Wilson, "Theatre of the Hindus," vol. ii. p. 53. [2] *Ibid.*, p. 56.

"The elephant hide that robes thee, to thy steps
Swings to and fro: the whirling talons rend
The crescent on thy brow; from the torn orb
The trickling nectar falls, and every skull
That gems thy necklace laughs with horrid life."[1]

Mādhava breaks in upon the scene. He slays the priest and rescues Mālatī, happily ending one of the most awe-inspiring pictures that the history of the literature of any nation could fashion from real life, and clothe in the brilliant colours so typical of all the work of Bhavabhūti. The play moves on through many more incidents, the most interesting being the appearance of a Buddhist priestess towards the end of the drama, who, by practising all the principles laid down in the "Yoga," has arrived at a command over sorcery even greater than that reached by a Bodhisattva.

The second great play of Bhavabhūti, the "Mahāvīra-Charitra," dramatises the first six books of the "Rāmāyana," detailing the story of Rāma, who rescues from the grasp of the ten-headed monster, Rāvana, the King of Lanka (Ceylon), his wife, Sītā, the loved of all Indian women.

In the "Uttara-Rāma-Charitra," the third play of Bhavabhūti, the seventh book of the "Rāmāyana" is dramatised, in which the chastity of Sītā is questioned, and she is for a time divorced from Rāma, to be reunited after many trials:—

"'Tis Sītā: mark,
How lovely through her tresses dark
And floating loose, her face appears
Though pale and wan and wet with tears.
She moves along like Tenderness
Invested with a mortal dress."[2]

In the "Uttara-Rāma-Charitra" is introduced the strange

[1] Wilson, "Theatre of the Hindus," vol. ii. p. 58.
[2] *Ibid.*, vol. i. p. 327.

story of Sambūka, a Sūdra, who was slain by Rāma for that he, being a Sūdra, dared to engage in pious penances.

To Rāma—

> ". . . There came a voice from Heaven
> Commanding him go forth and seek Sambūka,
> One of an outcast origin, engaged
> In pious penance ; he must fall by Rāma."

In Manu[1] the duty of a Sūdra is distinctly laid down as meekly serving the three higher castes. In the "Raghuvamsa"[2] of Kālidāsa the same story of Sambūka is repeated. Here Rāma finds the Sūdra practising penance by hanging, head downwards, from a tree, his eyes full of smoke. On Rāma questioning the Sūdra, the "drinker of smoke," as he is called, replied that he desired to attain the position of a god, whereon Rāma cut off his head as a punishment for overstepping the duties of his caste and engaging in penance. In both these cases the Sūdra obtained the heavenly reward,[3] not because of his penance, but because he had been slain by the deified hero, Rāma.

By some the legend of this punishment of the Sūdra Sambūka is held to contain a reference to Christian influences on the west coast of India.[4]

The "Nāgānanda" is remarkable as being the only Buddhist drama known. It is often ascribed to the king, Śilāditya II., whom Hiouen Tsang, the Chinese pilgrim, found as King of Kanauj in the seventh century when he visited India, but it was more probably the work of a poet Dhāvaka.[5] The two last acts of the play are laid in the western Ghāts, where the Garuda, the king of birds, is engaged in daily devouring a Nāga, a man-like snake.

The hero of the drama, Jimūtavāhana, gives his own

[1] "Manu," i. 91. [2] "Raghuvamsa," 15, 50.

[3] "Satāmgatim, 15, 53; "Raghuvamsa."

[4] *See* V. A. Smith, "Civilisation of Ancient India," J.B.R.A.S., vol. lxi. part 1, p. 76.

[5] *See* Cowell's Introduction to Boyd's translation.

body to be devoured, so as to save the Nāga race from desecration. The Garuda, recognising him as a Bodhisattva, exclaims :—

> "What a terrible sin have I committed! In a word, this is a Bodhisattva whom I have slain."

Jimūtavāhana revives and expounds to the Garuda the Buddhist doctrine of respect for all life.

> "Cease for ever from destroying life; repent of thy former deeds; labour to gather together an unbroken chain of good actions by inspiring confidence in all living beings."

The "Mudra Rākshasa," ascribed to one Visākadatta, a play of the twelfth century, is based on the revolution that placed Chandra Gupta, the Sandrakottos of Megasthenes, on the throne of Pātaliputra, in the commencement of the fourth century B.C., by the aid of the crafty Brāhman minister, Chānakya, who slew the reigning Nanda king.[1]

The plot is, for the most part, the winning over of Rākshasa, the minister of the deposed monarch, to the party of the new king, Chandra Gupta I., of the Maurya dynasty. The play opens with Chānakya devising means to secure the kingdom he had won for Chandra Gupta against all future intrigues.

> "'Tis known to all the world,
> I vowed the death of Nanda and I slew him.
> The current of a vow will work its way
> And cannot be resisted. What is done
> Is spread abroad, and I no more have power
> To stop the tale. Why should I? Be it known,
> The fires of my wrath alone expire
> Like the fierce conflagration of a forest
> From lack of fuel, not from weariness."[2]

The rumour has been spread throughout the city that the murder of Nanda had been perpetrated by

[1] The story of Nanda, as given in the "Brihad Kathā" of Vararuchi, is detailed in Wilson's "Theatre of the Hindus," vol. ii. pp. 138-41.

[2] Wilson's translation, vol. ii. p. 157.

Rākshasa, the late minister, and the cunning craft of Chānakya has now to work to gain Rākshasa to the winning side. So Chānakya soliloquises how to effect his purpose :—

> "I have my spies abroad—they roam the realm
> In various garb disguised, in various tongues
> And manners skilled, and prompt to wear the show
> Of zeal to either party, as needs serve."[1]

One of the spies is depicted as wandering through the country with a panorama,[2] describing the terrors of hell, and the tortures there suffered by the wicked. The same travelling show[3] is common in India to-day, and is also alluded to in the "Harsha Charita" of Bāna, showing how slowly changes take place in habits and customs.

This showman in his travels, while displaying his panorama and singing his ballads, enters the house of one, Chandana Dās, where the wife of Rākshasa is concealed. The spy observes her, manages to secure the signet ring she wears, and bring it to Chānakya, who recognises it as that of Rākshasa. The wily minister has obtained the clue he sought, and lays his plans accordingly. Chandana Dās is cast into prison, there to await his death for refusing to declare where he has hidden the wife of Rākshasa. The news of his friend's danger is brought to Rākshasa by a spy of his own, a snake-charmer, who obtains entrance into the houses he wishes to inspect by his cry: "Tame snakes, your honour, by which I get my living. Would you wish to see them? Those who are skilled in charms and potent signs, may handle fearlessly the fiercest snakes." In the conference between the snake-charmer and Rākshasa, the former refers to the late revolt,

[1] Wilson, "Theatre of the Hindus," vol. ii. p. 159.

[2] Wilson, in his footnote, p. 160, confesses his ignorance of the meaning of the text. "The person and his accompaniments is now unknown," is his remark.

[3] The panorama is described in the "Harsha Charita."

in which Chandra Gupta advanced against the city, accompanied by a wild multitude

> "Of Sakas, Yavanas, and mountaineers ;
> The fierce Kambogas, with the tribes who dwell
> Beyond the western streams, and Persia's hosts,
> Poured on us like a deluge."

Rākshasa still longs to revive the hopes of the ancient dynasty, but against his plans the subtle brain of Chānakya has devised counter-plans. These plans Chānakya works out himself. The opponents of Chandra Gupta are driven to quit the city, so that inside no intrigues may be fomented, and Rākshasa remains alone and unsupported. Even the king Chandra Gupta is ignorant of his minister's intrigues, and when he ventures to question the haughty Chānakya, the answer given shows the proud consciousness of intellectual superiority of the Brāhman :—

> "What I have done,
> Is done by virtue of the state I hold ;
> And to enquire of me why I did it,
> Is but to call my judgment or authority
> In question, and designedly offend me."

The moral to be drawn is clear ; without Brāhmanic aid the warrior-might, even of a monarch such as Chandra Gupta, could be of no avail. Chandra Gupta attempts to rule unaided. He defies the Brāhmanic power, and in his anger at feeling himself a puppet in the hands of the minister, dismisses Chānakya. He does so, however, in fear and trembling for the result. As he watches the angry face of the Brāhman, he wonders in doubt :—

> "Is he indeed incensed? methinks the earth
> Shakes apprehensive of his tread, recalling
> The trampling dance of Rudra, from his eye,
> Embrowned with lowering wrath, the angry drops
> Bedew the trembling lashes, and the brows
> Above are curved into a withering frown." [1]

[1] Wilson, "Theatre of the Hindus," vol. ii. p. 203.

He has, however, made his choice, and the third act closes in with his dejected forebodings :—

> " My mind is ill at ease
> Oh, how can those who have indeed provoked
> The awful anger of their sacred guide,
> Survive the terrors of such dread displeasure."

The king's fears are soon to be realised. The son of the late king approaches Pātaliputra, with a hostile force to avenge his father's death. The intrigues of Chānakya work out their purpose. Dissension and distrust are sown in the camp of the advancing prince. Spies spread the falsehood that Rākshasa, not Chānakya, had murdered the late king, and insinuate that Rākshasa was now luring the last of the Nanda race to his doom.

Rākshasa, in disgrace, is driven from the cause of the Nanda dynasty he has so long and faithfully supported, and no course remains open to him except that prepared by Chānakya, the saving of his friend, Chandana Dās, who is condemned to death for sheltering his wife and family. A scene similar to the execution scene in the " Mud Cart," opens the seventh act. As Chandana Dās is led forth, followed by his wife and children, to be impaled, Rākshasa rushes forward, demanding that the penalty should fall on him alone. He is brought before Chānakya, and there acknowledges how he and the Nanda cause have fallen before the subtler brain and power of Chānakya.

> " Mine ancient faith
> And grief for Nanda's race, still closely cling,
> And freshly, to my heart ; and yet perforce
> I must become the servant of their foes!"

Chānakya declares to Rākshasa and to Chandra Gupta the intrigues whereby the designs of the discontented within the city were frustrated, and the advancing host from outside broken to pieces by a cunningly devised stratagem. Chandra Gupta bows before the Brāhmanic keenness of Chānakya's intellect :—

> "And yet what need of prowess, whilst alert,
> My holy patron's genius is alone
> Able to bend the world to my dominion?
> Tutor and guide, accept my lowly reverence." [1]

The whole drama ends with the strangest and most impressive strokes of genius that Brāhmanism could ever have evolved. Chānakya had firmly established the rule of the new monarch Chandra Gupta, won the allegiance of Rākshasa, the hereditary minister of the ancient dynasty, but the crowning master-touch still was wanting. Above all personal considerations, Chandra Gupta, as fount of all honour and support of the Brāhmanic power, has to be planted firm. Chānakya accordingly resigns to his rival, Rākshasa, the right to remain sole minister, so that all friends and upholders of old and new might be reconciled, and the State dwell in unison.

From Vedic times down to the dark days of the Mutiny, the Brāhman power never failed to work its way, and never lost its cunning. To-day it moves on in subtle paths, for the Brāhman is still prepared, before all his hopes fade away, to watch unmoved—

> "From numerous pyres, and undisturbed, the smoke
> Spread a long veil of clouds beneath the sky,
> And blurr the light of day, expectant flights
> Of vultures hover o'er the darkness, and clap
> Their wings with hope."

[1] Wilson, "Theatre of the Hindus," vol. ii. p. 248.

So the Brāhman will yet remain as determined, proud, and cunning as the crafty Chānakya.

> " Rather let me own,
> The wise Chānakya ; an exhaustless mine
> Of learning—a deep ocean stored with gems
> Of richest excellence. Let not my envy
> Deny his merits."[1]

[1] Wilson, " Theatre of the Hindus," vol. ii. p. 247.

CHAPTER XIII.

SOUTH INDIA.

THE land claimed by the Aryans had for its extreme northern boundary the Himālayan range of mountains stretching from extreme East to West as far as from the mouth of the Thames to the Caspian Sea. In the centre of this vast tract were the districts now known as the North-West Provinces and Oudh, with an area equal to that of Italy, and a present population nearly as large as that of the German Empire. Bengal to the east has now a population almost equal to that of the United States and Mexico, while its extent rivals that of the whole United Kingdom. Aryanism had, however, to extend its conquests still further until they spread down to Cape Comorin, and embraced the whole of India, a continent equal in area to all Europe, leaving out Russia, and with a present population of about one-fifth of the human race. As a result of Aryan influence in the North, almost [1] two hundred millions of people in India to-day speak languages based on Sanskrit, while even more [2] designate themselves as Brāhmanic by religion. Besides Aryanism, powerful though its influence has been, there are other factors to be considered in dealing with the problem of the history of the Indian people.

[1] 195,463,807. [2] 307,731,727.

One-fifth of the entire population class themselves as Muhammadan, and look back to Mecca and Muhammad as their guiding lights.

Again, over seven millions of the people speak languages known as Tibeto-Burman. These Tibeto-Burman-speaking races are the descendants of early invaders, who pressed in through the North-East passes and found abiding-places in the higher slopes of the Himālayas, along the upper reaches of the Brahmaputra, or in Burma. Nearly[1] three millions of the population speak languages classed as Kolarian. The ancestors of these so-called Kolarians are held to have entered India through the North-East, at some unknown period, and to have fallen back from the plain country and river-valleys before more vigorous and civilised invaders. At present they dwell in isolated and detached groups, in the more inaccessible hill-tracts, preserving traces of a common origin in speaking dialects which, from linguistic similarities, must be classed as having originally sprung from one parent stock. Of these the Santāls dwell along the Eastern edges of the central plateau, where it slopes down to the Ganges, while allied tribes, such as the Kūrkū,[2] Mundas, Kharrias, and Bhunjias, carry the Kolarian speech across India, until it almost reaches the sea-coast on the West, where it is spoken by the Bhils. Far away from their own Kolarian kinsmen are found, in the hill-tracts of Orissa and Ganjam on the East coast, the still almost uncivilised Juangs, Savaras, and Gadabas.

All these rude races, as well as the great mass of the labouring population of India, find the natural expression of their thoughts and feelings more in the local folk-songs and folk-lore than in any formulated writings or records that can be classed as literature. There is thus a whole life-history of a large proportion of the people which must remain untold. For the greater part, the literary history

[1] 2,959,006. [2] "Census Report," p. 147.

of the people of India must be an effort to note and mark the culminating waves of thought that rise on the great stream of Aryan literature that flows from Vedic times down to our own days.

There still remains to be noted the wave of thought that swept across the central range of mountains to rouse the Dravidian people of South India to new ideals and lead them to claim the gods of the Hindu Pantheon as their own.

From Vedic times, down to late Brāhmanic days, the South was shut off from the Aryans of the North by the lofty range of mountains known as the Vindhyas. This range is the second great barrier to all invaders from the Northward, a barrier that up to the advent of the English had effectually prevented even an Aurangzīb from consolidating his rule from the South to "Far-off Delhi."

To the Aryans, all beyond the Vindhyas was for long an impenetrable forest. It was held to have been the abode of Rākshasas, fierce demons and ape-like men. It was the Dakshina, or "southern" part, a Sanskrit word that in the Prakrit, or broken vernaculars, became corrupted into "Dakkhina," thence into the modern Dekkan or Deccan, now used to designate the centre table-land lying between the Eastern and Western mountain ranges. By the people of South India the tradition still is held that the sage Āgastya was the first to cross the Vindhyas and bring the Northern language, grammar, and religions, to Dravidian homes. At Āgastya's bidding the mountains, once loftier than the Himālayan peaks, are said to have bowed down, so that the sage might cross them. As Āgastya passed on, he bade the range remain bowed down until his returning, but as he remained in the South, the Vindhyas still have their heads lower than the Northern range.

The Dravidians, however, probably once had possession of the whole of India, long before the arrival of the fair-skinned Aryans, and still retain their own languages and civilisation in the South. North of the Vindhyas almost all traces of their former existence have faded away before the stronger forces of Aryan speech and culture. The long pause given to the fair-skinned invaders, who found their course and progress stayed by the forest and central mountain ranges, preserved the indigenous languages, customs, and forms of land tenure of the South, free from the dominating force of the Northern influence. So the Aryans, when at length they reached the South, found the Dravidian speech too well established and the literature too formed to accomplish more than to enrich them with words from the new vocabulary, and mould them to Sanskrit forms of thought, rules of prosody and metre.[1]

Down to the present day the Dravidian languages, such as Telugu, Tamil, Canarese, and Malayālam, have accordingly preserved a rich literature of their own. Long before Aryan influences commenced to work, the Southern people sang their own songs of love and war, had their own sacrificial rites and cults, and worshipped their own tribal gods, akin to the deities the Aryans had in the North accepted from the aborigines and included in the Hindu Pantheon as forms of Vishnu, Krishna, or Śiva. Like the Dravidians of to-day, they were, as can be ascertained from linguistic evidences, skilled potters, weavers, and dyers. They were builders of ships, and traded far and wide from their coast villages, known then as now, as "patnams" or "pattanams" (villages), seen in the native termination of so many towns, such as Cennapatnam[2] (Madras), and Masulipatam, Fish Village.

[1] The Śentamil or classic Tamil has, however, preserved its own structure and alliterative form of metre free from any foreign mixture. *See* especially Senāthi Rājā, "Pre-Sanskrit Element in Ancient Tamil Literature," J.R.A.S., vol. xix. p. 558.

[2] For suggestion that it may mean Chinatown, *see* Burnell and Yule, "Glossary of Anglo-Indian Words."

The great mass of the people were skilled agriculturists, cultivators of rice, and builders of the vast tanks and works of irrigation, still used and preserved under British rule. Each cultivator held and cultivated his own clearing, as is done to-day under the form of tenure known as the "Raiatwari," or individual holding, of the Madras Presidency. The agricultural population crowded together in well-watered tracts, where their town bore the common Dravidian termination "ūr," or village, a term often seen still in some places as Nellore, Tanjore, Coimbatore, and Mangalore. The most noted town in the South was Madura, or Mūdur, the old town. The same form may, perhaps, be traced in the Northern Mathura,[1] the home of Krishna, the dark deity, who finds his counterpart and probable prototype in the Dravidian deity still worshipped by the simpler folk of the South, as Karuppan, or "dark one."[2]

The management of the external policy and internal economy of such villages fell naturally into the hands of the oldest or most renowned member of the community, who became known as the "Kiravan," or "Pāndiyan,"[3] both terms having the common meaning of "elder," or "old man."

When robber bands came sweeping down on the rich villages the sturdy retainers of the land-owners beat their rude drums, or "parrais," to summon the villagers forth to man the mud-walls that enclosed the settlement. Down to our own days the servile classes of South India are known as the Parriyars, or "beaters of drums," though their caste name has become a term of abuse to Western ears long

[1] *See* Madura, "Glossary of Anglo-Indian Words," where Mathurā of North is said to have its name "modified after Tamil pronunciation."

[2] Senāthī Rājā, J.R.A.S., vol. xix. p. 578, note 3.

[3] For connection with the Northern Pāndavas, *see* Caldwell, "Gram. Dravidian Languages," p. 16; and "Senāthī Rājā," p. 577.

accustomed to hear the pariahs, or "servile workers with their hands," reviled by those who live on their labours. As time rolled on the forests around the parent villages were cleared, and new lands were brought into cultivation. Hamlets and new villages (*Perūr*) were established, which all looked back to the old village (*Mūdūr*) and its Pāndiyan as their ancient home and chieftain. So from earliest times history holds record of a Pāndiyan or Pāndya chieftain ruling the far South from his capital at Madura. Other chieftains claimed for themselves the open land along the eastern and western sea-coast. The Cheras, or Keralas, held the power in Malabar and South Mysore. Another dynasty—that of the Cholas—had, from the second century, their capital at the ancient town of Uraiyur, changed in the seventh century for Combaconam, and then in the tenth century for Tanjore.[1] The Cholas held the land to the north and east of the Pāndiyans, leaving the land north of Conjeveram to fall to the dynasty known as that of the Pallavas.

It was long before the Aryans of North India penetrated to these Southern villages, there to work their way to power and spread abroad their civilising influence. The "Rāmāyana," according to tradition, is the allegorical story of the Aryan conquest of South India. Sītā, the loved wife of the hero Rāma, is, according to this view, the "field furrow" sung of in the Vedic Hymns. As she advanced South, Rāma, the incarnation of Vishnu, followed and established the worship of the Hindu gods. The monkey army, who aided him against the fierce demon Rāvana, represented the wild races of the South, while Lanka, the island home where Sītā was kept bound, has, without any support from the epic, been held to represent Ceylon. The "Mahābhārata," however, shows a greater knowledge of the Southern region than even the "Rāmāyana."[2]

[1] Sewell, "Lists of Antiquities in Madras," vol. ii. p. 154.
[2] Bhandarkar, "History of the Dekkan" (1895), p. 10.

The latter epic, although it mentions the Cholas and Keralas, and refers to the golden gates, adorned with jewels, of the Pāndya city,[1] only knows the whole country south of the Vindhyas as the Great Southern Forest, or "Dandakāranya," where Rāma lived in his hermitage, Pancavati, on the banks of the Godavari.

The "Mahābhārata," on the other hand, mentions many places in the Deccan as then well known.[2] To both poems the land of the King of Vidarbha, or modern Berar, was known, as it had been early entered by Aryans who advanced along the eastern coast.

In the "Aitareya Brāhmana," the Āndhras, or Telugu-speaking Dravidians of the Northern Circars, probably then dwelling near the mouths of the Godavari, are referred to as the people to whom the fifty sons of Visvamitra were banished, so that "the Āndhras, Pundras, Śabaras, Pulindas, and Mūtibas, and the descendants of Visvamitra, formed a large portion of the Dasyus."[3] It is clear that in the seventh century B.C., this country of the Āndhras and the east coast, or Kalinga, were known in North India. They are mentioned by the grammarian, Pānini, who makes no reference to the existence of the Southern kingdoms of the Pāndyans, Cheras, and Cholas, although, in the sixth century B.C., these kingdoms were so famed for their importance and wealth that a king, Vijaya, is recorded[4] to have been sent from Magadha in the north to Ceylon, and to have married a daughter of a Pāndya monarch.

[1] "Rāmāyana," iii. 13, 13.

[2] Foulkes, "Civilisation of the Dekkan."

[3] "Ait. Brāh.," vii. 18; Bhandarkar, "History of Dekkan," p. 6.

[4] Caldwell, p. 15, quoting Mahāvamśa; Turnour, pp. 55-57. Vijaya of Magadha is supposed, on authority of Dipavamśa and Mahāvamśa, to have conquered Ceylon in 543 B.C. *See* "Ind. Ant." (October 1872) for Burnell's view that the Dravidian people held aloof from Aryan influence, until at least the advent of Kumārila, who reached the South on his mission of Brāhmanic reform in the eighth century of our era.

The first clear literary references to the kingdoms of South India occur in the first half of the fourth century B.C., in the "Vārtikas,"[1] or explanation to the rules of Pānini by the commentator, Kātyāyana, who adds to the examples given by the earlier grammarians, for the formation of the names of tribes and kings, the two instances of the Pāndyas and Cholas, showing that he knew the Southern kingdoms then extending from the modern district of Tanjore to Madura.

By the middle of the third century B.C., Asoka, in his second and thirteenth edicts, mentions the Āndhras, Cheras, Cholas, and Pāndyas, as well as Mahārashtra along the Godavari, then governed by the Rattas and Bhojas. One hundred years later, in 150 B.C., the grammarian, Patanjali, shows his knowledge of Behar, Conjeveram, and Kerala or Malabar. From this time forth the political history of South India has to be pieced together from inscriptions on rocks, temples, and in caves, from copper-plate grants, local traditions, and the uncertain evidence afforded by later Purānic accounts of kings and principalities. South of the Vindhyas, in the northern Deccan, a dynasty, known as that of the Buddhist Āndhrabrityas, ruled for a period extending from 73 A.D. to 218 A.D., during which the Buddhist mound at Amrāvati was built.[2]

Local chieftains succeeded until, in the sixth century, a new dynasty, known as that of the Chālukyas, arrived from Ayodhya, or Oudh, and held sway up to the middle of the eighth century (747 A.D.). Under the rule of this new-formed dynasty Buddhism gave way to Jainism, and a revival of the Brāhmanic sacrificial system, along with a worship of the Hindu deities, chief among whom was Śiva. The greatest of all the early Chālukyan monarchs was "He with the Lion Locks," or Pulikeśin II., whose rule, from 611 to 634 A.D., forms a landmark in the early political and literary history of India. Some idea of

[1] "Pānini," iv. 1, 168. *See* Bhandarkar, p. 7.

[2] *See* Sewell, "Lists of Antiquities of Madras," vol. ii. p. 141.

the divided rule of the various dynasties and principalities of India, at the period when this Chālukyan monarch rose to paramount power, and Jainism and Brāhmanism gained new life and influence, can be obtained from the inscriptions setting forth the conquests of this great Southern monarch, Pulikeśin II. He is recorded to have subdued the prince of the Ganga family, who ruled over the Chera kingdom, then extending over the modern province of Mysore, as well as the chieftain who held the Malabar coast. "With a fleet of hundreds of ships he attacked Purī, which was the mistress of the western sea, and reduced it." The kings of Lāta, Mālava, and Gūrjara were conquered, and became his dependents.

Harshavardhana, King of Kanauj, then endeavoured to extend his power to the south of the Narmadā, but was opposed by Pulikeśin, who killed many of his elephants and defeated his army. Thenceforward, Pulikeśin received, or assumed, the title of "Parameśvara," or lord paramount. This achievement was considered so important by the later kings of the dynasty, that it alone is mentioned in such of their copper-plate grants as record the deeds of Pulikeśin II.

"Pulikeśin appears to have kept a strong force on the banks of the Narmadā to guard the frontiers. Thus, by his policy as well as valour, he became the supreme lord of the three countries called Mahārāshtrakas, containing ninety-nine thousand villages. The kings of Kośāla and Kalinga trembled at his approach and surrendered. After some time he marched with a large army against the King of Kānchipura, or Conjeveram, and laid siege to the town. He then crossed the Kāverī and invaded the country of the Cholas, the Pāndyas, and the Keralas. But these appear to have become his allies. After having, in this manner, established his supremacy throughout the South, he entered his capital and reigned in peace."[1]

[1] From Bhandarkar, "History of the Dekkan," p. 51.

The newly-founded kingdom of the Chālukyas fell to pieces in 747 A.D. Local Kshatriya warriors, the Rāshtrākūtas, then held sway for some two hundred and fifty years.[1]

A new and later Chālukyan line again rose to power, and kept a divided rule down to the end of the twelfth century, during which Buddhism and Jainism disappeared before Brāhmanism and the rise of the sect of Lingāyatas.[2]

The Hoyśala Ballālas, Yādavas of Halibīd in Mysore, succeeded and ruled the whole Deccan, contending with the remaining dynasties of the South, the Pāndiyas and Cholas,[3] down to the year 1318, when the Muhammadans invaded the country from Delhi, captured Devagiri, the Southern capital, and flayed alive the last Hindu monarch, Harapāla. A Vijayanagar chieftain at length succeeded in driving out the Muhammadans, and his successors maintained native independence down to the time when it fell, to rise no more, on the fatal field of Talikota in 1565.

So far history traces the fluctuating fortunes of the rulers who in the early ages held the sovereign power south of the Vindhyas. The literature of the South, like that of the North, takes but little note of the political history of the times.

Before Brāhmanism, Jainism, and Buddhism came from Aryan homes to Dravidian villages, there exist no evidences in literature from which the previous religious notions of the people can be ascertained. The Dravidian languages show that there was a word for a god, and a word for a temple, still, all the great temples of South India are later than the days of Aryan influence, and are dedicated to the Hindu gods, Vishnu, and Śiva. From folk-lore, from a study of the primitive beliefs of the more uncivilised Dravidian people of to-day, as well as from noting the sacrificial customs, the gods, demons, or godlings worshipped

[1] Kielhorn in "Epigraphia Indica," vol. iii. p. 268, gives nineteen Rāshtrākūta kings.

[2] Bhandarkar, "Dekkan," p. 96.

[3] Sewell, "Antiquities of Madras," vol. ii. p. 142.

by the wild hill races, some clue may be gained as to the religious ideas of the Dravidian people in pre-Aryan days. From such sources, however, little more can be culled than is to be found in all primitive life, that is, superstition, animism, demon-worship and devil-dancing, human sacrifices and offerings to local deities. Amid the numerous deities worshipped in pre-Aryan times by the Dravidians there may have been prototypes of such gods as Śiva, and his son Skanda, and Krishna or the Black One, introduced in the "Mahābhārata" by the Pāndus into Brāhmanism.

Brāhman priests, Buddhist monks, and Jaina ascetics must have reached the land before the Christian era, and established themselves at the court of ruling princes, where they founded schools of learning, and exercised their influence on the thought of the times. The local gods, national deified heroes, and sacrificial cults of the people became in time absorbed into Brāhmanism. At the same time the local literature and poetry were assimilated to Sanskrit models and forms, so that the new ideas might be disseminated among the Dravidian races. The oldest Tamil grammars[1] cite treatises evidently compiled on the Sanskrit system of Vyākarana, or Grammar. The ancient classic Tamil poetry, in which the epics and folk-songs of the people were composed, had, however, sufficient vitality of its own to resist the foreign influence, and so it retains down to the present day, alone of the Dravidian languages, its own peculiar forms of alliterative metre and rhythm.

The infusion of Aryan thought and learning among the Southern people soon produced its effect in the awakening of Dravidian literature to proclaim the new message it had received from Northern lands. It was through the fostering care of the Jainas,[2] that the South first seems to

[1] For the "Tolkāppiyan," *see* J.R.A.S., vol. xix. p. 550.

[2] Rice ("Early History of Kannada Literature," J.R.A.S., vol. xxii. p. 249) holds that in the first half of the second century the Jaina poet, Samantabhadra, preached from Kānchi in the south to Pātaliputra, Benares, Ujjayini, Mālwā,

have been inspired with new ideals, and its literature enriched with new forms of expression.

In the words of the veteran Dravidian scholar, Dr Pope, the "Jain compositions were clever, pointed, elegant, full of satire, of worldly wisdom, epigrammatic, but not religious."[1]

Jainism has faded away in South India of to-day, and the worship of Śiva remains the prevailing faith of all Tamil-speaking people. This worship of Śiva is also prevalent, in a bigoted form, among the Canarese-speaking Vīra Śaivas, or Lingāyatas, and recognised by the Smarta sect of Brāhmans;[2] in the West, however, it is popularly considered as degrading in its outward forms, and revolting in its rites and practices.

The phase of thought which inculcates a devout faith in the saving grace of this deity, Śiva, contains much that is worthy of study, not only by the student of humanity and by the missionary, but also by the administrator.

India can never be severed from its own past or be drilled into entirely new modes of thought. Her past must be studied and understood before a commencement can be made in training her genius into directions in which its tendencies can alone attain results beneficial to the world at large. Mills and factories, science and matter-of-fact realities are products of the West. To hope to transplant them into the enervating plains of South India, with the prospect of attaining the advancement they should court amongst races to whom they are more congenial, would be a hope as visionary as to expect that the oak could thrive in the East, overgrow and dwarf the

and Panjāb in the north. Fleet, J. F., in his exhaustive "Dynasties of the Kanarese Districts" (Bombay, 1896), p. 320, places the authenticated evidences for the earliest Western Gangas after about 750 A.D.; vol. xv. pp. 3-4. *See* Pope, Introd. to "Nalādiyar," p. x., also xiii.

[1] "History of Mānikka Vāśagar" (paper read at Victorian Institute, May 17, 1897).

[2] Sundaram Pillai, "Some Milestones in Tamil Literature," p. 1.

drooping grace of the palm-tree. If Christianity can be said to have failed in awakening the mass of the people of India, it is because Christianity has been, for the greater part, presented to them by those who had not grasped the secret of their thoughts and feelings, which can alone be read in the literature they have handed down to the ages as a record of their deepest aspirations.

In the West there are patent evidences that the thoughts of many are swinging back from realism, and the hastily-raised hopes that the misunderstood aims of science were to solve the ultimate truth of all things, to old-world dreams of spiritualism and supernaturalism, mysticism, idealism, and their ancient faiths. In this movement the thought of India has had no small influence. Eastern Buddhism, mysticism, spiritualism, and Vedāntism have all played their part in America, India, and France, affecting their art, literature, and emotions. Strong as this influence is, and will continue to be, the movements in India itself have drifted between an Eastern mode of idealisation and assimilation of Christianity and a reaction towards Vedism, Vedāntism, and supernaturalism.

To the missionary who is unacquainted with the "Vedānta," with the spirit of the true mysticism underlying the worship of Krishna, with the "Rāmāyana" of Tulsi Dās, with the quatrains of the "Nalādiyar," the task set before him is one that must always lack somewhat of its full promise of success. He cannot throw aside literature such as the Indian people love and cherish as though it were nothing but folly and superstition. Of the best of the Dravidian, as well as the Aryan, literature it can be said, in the words of the learned scholar and missionary, who has assimilated the language and the thought of the people of the South as though they were his own, that "there seems to be a strong sense of moral obligation, an earnest aspiration after righteousness, a fervent and unselfish charity, and generally, a loftiness of aim, that are very impressive."[1]

These words refer specially to the "Nalādiyar," still taught in every vernacular Tamil school. It consists of four hundred quatrains of moral and didactic sayings, each one composed, according to tradition, by a Jaina ascetic. The story goes[2] that eight thousand Jains came in time of famine to a monarch of the Pāndiya kingdom, who strove to retain them when the famine had departed, so that he might add an additional lustre by their presence to his kingdom. They, however, departed in secret, leaving each a verse behind. The indignant king threw all the verses into the river, when, to his surprise, four hundred of them floated against the current, and, in consequence of this miraculous event, were preserved and formed into the present collection, dating, according to native belief, from some two thousand years before our era. The whole of the verses, however, treat of topics familiar to a student of Sanskrit literature, the misery of transmigration, the effects of Karma, and the joy of release from bondage and re-birth.[3] The unconnected four hundred verses of the "Nalādiyar" present no definite philosophic or religious teaching, although generally they have a didactic tendency. Each aphorism is lighted up with a brilliant play of fancy and revels in an Eastern love for soothing sounds, apt and startling similes, quaint conceits, and sensuous imagery. The poem deals with the three great objects of life—virtue, wealth, and pleasure; each subject being treated in typical Eastern modes of thought so skilfully rendered in Dr Pope's

[1] Pope, "Nalādiyar," p. xii.

[2] *See* Rev. G. U. Pope, Introd. to "The Nalādiyar," p. x. *See* also Rice, "Early Kannada Authors," J.R.A.S., vol. xv. p. 295:—"That an extensive old literature exists in the Kannada (or so-called Canarese) language is admitted by more than one eminent writer on Oriental subjects, but of the nature and history of that literature little or nothing is known, beyond the fact that it was of Jaina origin."

[3] *See* Introd. to "Nalādiyar," p. xl.

translation here quoted. Before all things, the poet declares, let virtue be practised by man, even as if Death had already seized him by the hairs of the head:—

> "Like a cloud that wanders over the hills, the body here appears, and abides not; it departs and leaves no trace behind."

Youth fades away, love dies, beauty sinks to decrepitude, and losses crowd round as man prepares to leave the scene wherein his part was played:—

> "Then look within and say what profit is there in this joyous life of thine? The cry comes up as from a sinking ship."

The fancy plays round the same pessimistic wail of the soul's unsatisfied longings.

> "Youth decays. Desire not her whose eyes gleam bright as darts. Full soon, she too will walk bent down with a staff to aid her dim sight."[1]

. . . .

> "Considering that all things are transient as the dewdrop on the tip of a blade of grass, now, now at once, do virtuous deeds. 'Even now he stood, he sat, he fell, while his kindred cried aloud he died.' Such is man's history."[2]

. . . .

> "Though worthless men untaught should fret my soul, and rave of teeth like jasmine buds and pearls, shall I forego my fixed resolve, who have seen in the burning ground those bones—the fallen teeth strewn round for all to see."[3]

. . . .

> "Lord of the sea's cool shore, where amid the wave swans sport, tearing to shreds the Adamba flowers. When those whose hearts are sore with urgent need stand begging, and wander through the long street in sight of all, this is the fruit of former deeds."[4]

. . . .

> "They went to bathe in the great sea, but cried, 'We will wait till all its roar is hushed, then bathe.' Such is their worth who say, 'We will get rid of all our household toils and cares, and then we will practise virtue and be wise.'"[5]

[1] Pope, "Nalādiyar," 17. [2] *Ibid.*, 29. [3] *Ibid.*, 45.
[4] *Ibid.*, 107. [5] *Ibid.*, 332.

The following verse brings up a vision worthy to form the subject of an artist's picture:—

> "She of enticing beauty, adorned with choice jewels, said forsooth, 'I will leap with you down the steep precipice;' but on the very brow of the precipice, because I had no money, she, weeping, and pointing to her aching feet, withdrew and left me alone."[1]

The same three subjects of virtue, wealth, and pleasure, are further exhaustively dealt with in the two thousand six hundred and sixty short couplets of the "Kurral," the universally acknowledged masterpiece of South Indian genius. These verses were composed for the Támil people by Tiruvalluvar, a pariah weaver, who lived on the sea-coast in a suburb of Madras named St Thomé, in memory of the doubting Apostle, St Thomas, who, for very long, was supposed to have suffered death at the hands of a fowler, who, legend and tradition hold, accidentally shot the Apostle when he was engaged in prayer. As told in the "Acts of Thomas," the Apostle declared to the Saviour, who appeared before him in the night-time: "Wheresoever Thou wishest to send me, send me elsewhere, for to the Indies I am not going." There can be no doubt that St Thomas never did go to India.[2]

That the weaver pariah, who lived within sound of the ceaseless swell and break of the waves along the sandy shore near Mayilāpūr, or St Thomé, may have heard of the teachings of Christianity is not impossible, though there is no evidence of any Christian influence or doctrines in his verses.[3] Every Hindu sect, including the Jains, claims that the poet designed to set forth in his work, the dogmas of their special creeds. The teaching of Tiruvalluvar is,

[1] Pope, "Nalādiyar," 372.

[2] *See* Geo. Milne Rae, "The Syrian Church in India" (1892), p. 24:—"In short, we look in vain among the writings and monuments of the first five centuries for any attestation of the existence of the 'South Indian Church.'"

[3] *See* Pope, "The Sared Kurral," p. iv.

however, purely eclectic, and inculcates such principles as are common to all systems of morality. The first couplet of the "Kurral" gives the poet's eclectic view of the deity called Bhagavan, the Lord who stands first in all the world, just as the letter "A" stands first in all speech. As in the "Bhagavad Gīta," they who have faith in this deity, "they who dwell in the true praise of this Lord,"

> "Affects not then the fruit of deeds done ill or well."

The poet, having thus first enunciated the cardinal dogma of faith in a primal deity, proceeds to build up an entire system of an ideal state, treating of Virtue under its different aspects—in domestic life, in ascetic renunciation, and in the effects of fate or former deeds. Wealth, or property, is viewed as it relates to royalty, to ministers of the king, to the State itself, and the individual. The third object of enquiry, Love, is subdivided into two chapters—the first treating of concealed love, the second of wedded love. Domestic virtue is inculcated in a string of short epigrammatic verses, rivalling, in their crisp and cutting vigour, the soft languid grace of the aphorisms of the "Nalādiyar:"—

> "In Nature's way who spends his calm domestic days,
> 'Mid all that strive for virtue's crown hath foremost place."[1]

The patient Griselda of the household stands out in all her plaintiveness, finding, in adoration of her husband, her sole faith:—

> "No god adoring, low she bends before her lord;
> Then rising serves: the rain falls instant at her word."[2]

In describing, under the division Wealth, the qualities of a great king, a plea is set forward for what now would be called the unrestricted liberty of the Press:—

[1] Pope, "Kurral," 47. [2] *Ibid.*, 55.

> "The king of worth, who can words bitter to his ear endure,
> Beneath the shadow of his power the world abides secure."[1]

The minister of state is provided with some salutary advice, which might be accepted with advantage by not a few modern politicians:—

> "Though knowing all that books can teach, 'tis truest tact,
> To follow common-sense of men in act."[2]

The following hint, if judiciously acted on, might serve to establish the reputation of a man as wise in council:—

> "Speak out your speech, when once 'tis past dispute
> That none can utter speech that shall your speech refute."[3]

Although it is full one thousand years since Tiruvalluvar composed the following aphorism, it has a strange homely truth for us of to-day:—

> "Who have not skill ten faultless words to utter plain,
> Their tongues will itch with thousand words men's ears to pain."[4]

The full power of Tiruvalluvar to compress into the intricate setting of the Vempa, the most difficult metre in his language, some of the most perfect combinations of sound, set to the most delicate play of fancy, is to be best seen in his verses on love. The intimate and perfect acquaintance of Dr Pope with the people and their language, has enabled him to preserve, in an unrivalled manner, the form of the Eastern setting. Every verse is perfect in the original:—

> "A sea of love, 'tis true, I see stretched out before,
> But not the trusty barque that wafts to yonder shore."[5]

> "The pangs that evening brings I never knew,
> Till he, my wedded spouse, from me withdrew."[6]

> "My grief at morn a bud, all day an opening flower,
> Full-blown expands in evening hour."[7]

[1] Pope, "Kurral," 389. [2] *Ibid.*, 637. [3] *Ibid.*, 645. [4] *Ibid.*, 649.
[5] *Ibid.*, 1164. [6] *Ibid.*, 1226. [7] *Ibid.*, 1227.

> "Or bid thy love, or bid thy shame depart;
> For me, I cannot bear them both, my worthy heart."[1]

The short sayings of the "Kurral" end with what may have been the poet's own experience of the subject he treats so gracefully:—

> "Though free from fault, from loved one's tender arms
> To be estranged awhile hath its own special charms."[2]
>
> . . . .
>
> "In lover quarrels, 'tis the one that first gives way
> That in reunion's joy is seen to win the day."[3]
>
> . . . .
>
> "Let her whose jewels brightly shine, aversion feign.
> That I may still plead on, O night, prolong thy reign."[4]

Unfortunately, no certain date can be ascribed to these early outbursts of song, the first sign of the awakening of the Dravidian genius after contact with Aryan civilisation. They are fabled to have been issued from the Sangan, or College of Madura, where the Pāndiyan monarch assembled learned Jaina and Buddhist monks. Tradition holds that this famed seminary of learning at Madura ceased to exist when its chief members drowned themselves in despair, on the miraculous preservation of the despised "Kurral" of the low-caste Tiruvalluvar.[5]

However that may be, the early Brāhmanic influence soon reasserted itself, and led to the downfall of both Jainism and Buddhism, which virtually disappeared from the Tamil country by the eleventh century of our era. The first great sign of the coming change was seen in the revival of the worship of Śiva, the deity early accepted by the South as the Brāhmanic representation of the ancient

[1] Pope, "Kurral," 1247. [2] *Ibid.*, 1325. [3] *Ibid.*, 1327. [4] *Ibid.*, 1329.

[5] *See* Caldwell, "Gram. of Dravidian Languages," p. 130:—"We should not be warranted in placing the date of the 'Kurral' later than the tenth century A.D." *See* also p. 122:—"There is no proof of Dravidian literature, such as we now have it, having originated much before Kumārila's time (700 A.D.), and its earliest cultivators appear to have been Jainas."

Dravidian god,[1] or gods. This revolt, from the dominating agnosticism of the times, found its earliest literary expression in the "Tiru Vāśakam," or "Holy Word," composed by Mānikka Vāśagar,[2] who turned the thoughts of the people once more to the weary quest of the suffering soul for rest in a union with a personal deity.

This fierce opponent of the heretical Jains and Buddhists was born near Madura, where his father was a Brāhman at the court of the Pāndya monarch, Arimarttanar, "The Crusher of Foes." The poet is said to have acquired all the Sanskrit learning by the age of sixteen, when he was made prime minister at Madura. The dread god, Śiva, with rosary round his neck, his body smeared with ashes, with a third eye in his forehead, is said to have appeared before the sage, while on a journey, and revealed his true nature, as the Divine Essence, in knowledge of which there is alone enlightenment and salvation. The poet at once bowed down before the deity, whose worship was to spread all over South India, and in whose honour the great Śaivite temples were built, and in many cases covered over with plates of gold.

The longings of the poet's soul had found no answer in the agnosticism of Buddhism or Jainism. The answer had come to the henceforth bitter opponent of the dominant Jains, and to Śiva he poured forth his prayer:[3] "Henceforth I renounce all desires of worldly wealth and splendour. To me, thy servant, viler than a dog, who worships at thy

[1] Probably the earlier form was Skanda. *See* Senāthi Rājā, "Pre-Sanskrit El. in Ancient Tamil Lit.," J.R.A.S., vol. xix. p. 376 (*note* 1).

[2] *See* Pope, "History of Mānikka Vāśagar," p. 3 (*note*):—"The date here given for the poet is 1030 A.D., reckoning two hundred years before Sundara Pāndiyan's time and Sambhanda's time. If the date of Sambhanda be, however, taken as the middle of the sixth century, then Tiru Vāśagar must be placed in the fourth century, along with the Śaivite revival. As these dates depends largely on the 'Tiru Vilaiyādal Purāna' and 'Periya Purāna,' no certainty can be claimed for them." *See*, however, P. Sundaram Pillai's article quoted later.

[3] *See* Pope, *Ibid.*, p. 7.

feet, grant emancipation from corporeal bonds. Take me as thy slave, O King of my Soul!"

No finer picture could be given of an Eastern enthusiast, stirred by emotions that are as deep in India to-day as they were when the soul of Manikka Vāśagar was roused to preach a salvation through a faith in Śiva, than that sketched forth of the converted sage in the earnest words of Dr Pope:[1]—

"From his head depends the braided lock of the Śiva devotee, one hand grasps the staff, and the other the mendicant's bowl: he has for ever renounced the world—all the worlds, save Śivan's self. And he is faithful henceforward, even to the end. In the whole legendary history of this sage, whatever we may think of the accuracy of many of its details, and whatever deductions we are compelled to make for the exaggerations that have grown up around the obscurity of the original facts, there stands out a character which seems to be a mixture of that of St Paul and of St Francis of Assisi. Under other circumstances what an apostle of the East might he have become! This is his conversion as South India believes it; and in almost every poem he alludes to it, pouring forth his gratitude in ecstasies of thanksgiving, and again and again repeating the words, 'I am Thine, save me!' His poetry lives in all Tamil hearts, and, in the main and true essence of it, deserves so to live!"

Persecutors of the new reformer now succeeded, and, as is usual in all Eastern biographies, miracles, more or less absurd and meaningless, are recorded to have been worked. The news of the revived faith in Śiva was preached by the reformer in the land of the Cholas, and in Cithambaram, where he is still held as the patron saint. To Cithambaram the King of Ceylon is said to have come, and there with all his court, to have been converted from Buddhism to Śaivism, by the sage's argument which showed that, according to the heretic monks, there can be "neither god, nor soul, nor salvation."[2]

The poems of Mānikka Vāśagar are held to have been

[1] *See* Pope, "Mānikka Vāśagar," p. 7.

[2] *Ibid.*, p. 16.

transcribed in one thousand verses by the god Śiva himself. They still "are sung throughout the whole Tamil country with tears of rapture, and committed to memory in every temple by the people, amongst whom it is a traditional saying that 'he whose heart is not melted by the "Tiru Vāśagam" must have a heart of stone.'"[1]

To learned and unlearned alike, these mystic raptures, in perfect verse, over the soul's faith in the deity are sacred treasures, and have a deep importance to all who would seek to read the spirit of the best of Indian religious thought. Happily these are soon to be published in an English translation by the Oxford Professor of Tamil. They are all but unknown to the West, yet a careful and wide-read scholar, in whose native language the poems are written, states:[2] "There are, indeed, but few poems in any language that can surpass 'Tiru Vāśagam,' or the 'Holy Word' of Mānikka Vāśagar, in profundity of thought and earnestness of feeling, or in that simple, child-like trust in which the struggling human soul, with its burdens of intellectual and moral puzzles, finally finds shelter."

The whole essence of the teachings of the new reformer, who did so much to rouse an active opposition to the debased Buddhism then in vogue, and whose followers inaugurated the temple-building era in South India, has been summed up as follows:[3]—

> "He taught the people that there was one supreme personal God, no mere metaphysical abstraction, but the Lord of Gods and men. He also taught that it was the gracious will of Śiva to assume humanity, to come to earth as a *guru*, and to make disciples of those who sought him with adequate preparation. He announced that this way of salvation was open to all classes of the

[1] Pope, "History of Mānikka Vāśagar," p. 17.

[2] P. Sundaram Pillai, M.A., M.R.A.S., Fellow of the Madras University, and Professor of Philosophy, "Some Milestones in the History of Tamil Literature," p. 3. (The news of the early death of this able scholar was received after the above was written.)

[3] Pope, "Mānikka Vāśagar," p. 18.

community. He also taught very emphatically the immortality of the released soul—its conscious immortality—as he said that the virtual death of the soul which Buddhism teaches is not its release. It will be seen how very near in some not unimportant respects the Śaiva system approximates to Christianity; and yet, in some of the corruptions to which it has led, by what almost seems a necessity, are amongst the most deplorable superstitions anywhere to be found."

How popular are these lyric raptures of a soul tossed in doubt, yet still seeking some answer to its wail of loneliness, may be judged from the fact that a whole series of them is still sung as a rhythmic accompaniment to a game, played by six girls sitting in a circle, who toss balls or pebbles from one to the other. The forthcoming translation of the poem will, it is hoped, give these verses; at present it must suffice to quote one verse as sung by the six girls in chorus as they play their game, known as "Ammanāy":—

"While bracelets tinkling sound, while earrings wave, while jetty locks
Dishevelled fall, while honey flows and beetles hum,
The Ruddy One, who wears the ashes white, whose home
None reach or know, Who dwells in every place, to loving ones
The true, The Sage Whom hearts untrue still deem untrue,
Who in Ai Ārru[1] dwells, sing and praise, Ammanāy see!"[2]

Many personal details of the poet's own life are scattered through his poems. The allurements of earthly love, which drag the soul from its calm repose, are fought against in verses that tell of the bitter grief of a lapse from high ideals:—

"Flames in forest glade, Sense-fires burn fierce with smoky glare.
I burn! Lo, thou'st forsaken me! O Conquering King of Heaven,
The garlands on Whose braided locks drip honey, while the bees
Hum softly 'mid Mandāram buds, whence fragrant sweetness breathes."

[1] A shrine near Tanjore, lit. "The Five Rivers."

[2] For this and the following verses I am indebted to the great kindness of the Rev. Dr Pope.

And again :—

"Sole help, whilst thou wert near I wandered, wanton deeds my help.
Thou hast forsaken me, Thou Helper of my guilty soul;
The source of all my being's bliss; Treasure that never fails.
I can't one instant bear this grievous body's mighty net."

The same theme is sung again, ending with the prayer for faith :—

"Choice gems they wore, those softly-smiling maids; I failed, I fell.
Lo, thou'st forsaken me. Thou gav'st me place 'midst Saints who wept,
Their beings fill'd with rapturous joys; in grace did'st make me Thine!
Show me thy feet, even yet to sense revealed, O Spotless One."

The monistic essence of the deity, Śiva, is summed up in one verse :—

"O King, my joy, mean as I am, who know not any path!
O Light, Thou hast forsaken me,
Thou the true Vedic Lord,
Thou art the First, the Last!
Thou art this universal Whole."

These poems of the earliest exponent of pure Vedāntic teachings were included in a renowned collection of Hymns which forms the "Vedas," "Upanishads," and "Purānas" for the great mass of Śaivas of South India. The first three books of this Śaiva Bible contain the three hundred and eighty-four hymns of a virulent opponent of all heretic Buddhist and Jaina monks—the renowned patron saint and impromptu lyric poet of the Tamil people, the sage, Tiru Nāna Sambandha,[1] whose fame in the South is so renowned that there is scarcely a Śiva temple in the

[1] An interesting contribution towards the elucidation of the literary history of South India has been recently made by P. Sundaram Pillai in his Essay, "Some Milestones in the History of Tamil Literature," in which he has advanced very strong proof that Sambandha must have lived before Śankara Āchārya, *i.e.* in the seventh century A.D.

Tamil country where his image is not daily worshipped. In most of them special annual feasts are held in his name, when the leading events of his life are dramatically represented for the instruction of the masses.[1] As is usual in the case of poets, the life of Sambandha begins with miraculous events and ends in mystery. Born, as there is no reason to doubt, of Brāhman parents in the Chola country, a few miles south of Chidambaram, he is said to have composed, when a child, his earliest lyric hymns of praise to Śiva which were set to a music, now lost, and played on an instrument, the form of which is now no longer remembered. To account for his unrivalled mastery over form and verse, tradition holds that, when as a child Sambandha was left alone, the local goddess appeared and nourished him herself, whereon the child recited the first of his inspired hymns and received the name of Tiru Nāna Sambandha, or "He who is united to the deity through wisdom." In all, three hundred and eighty-four hymns were composed by this poet, who, with his disciples,[2] strove vehemently to uproot the Jaina faith and establish the worship of Śiva. The reigning Pāndiyan king was led by Sambandha to renounce Jainism, and soon the people of the Tamil land forsook Buddhism, or at least the debased form of it then existing, though the cult did not finally become extinct until the eleventh century. The tenth verse of each hymn of Sambandha was launched against Buddhists and Jains alike, though there is no certainty as to why these heretics had aroused the hate of

[1] *See* also "Epigraphia Indica," vol. iii. pp. 277-78:—"The two great Śaiva devotees, Tirunāvukkarayar (or Appar), 573 A.D., and Tirunāna Sambandha . . . were contemporaries of the two Pallava kings, Mahendravarman I. and Narasimhavarman I." "Tirunāna Sambandhar was a contemporary of a general of the Pallava king, Narasimhavarman I., whose enemy was the Western Chālukya king, Pulikeśin II."

[2] *See* Caldwell, "Dravidian Grammar," p. 138. *See* P. Sundaram Pillai, "Milestones in Tamil Literature," p. 7 (*note* 1), for the six companions of Sambandha, who accompanied his impromptu lyric songs with music.

the Śaivite sage. With the passing-away of Sambandha and his disciples, a new era dawned in South India. Temples to Śiva and Vishnu took the place of Buddhist monasteries, while a series of Āchāryas, or theological teachers, spread far and wide in one form or another the philosophic doctrines of the "Vedānta" until the close of the twelfth century, when darkness settled down over the whole literary history of the people with the advent of the Muhammadans.

It would have been strange if the extension and revival of Brāhmanism and downfall of Jainism and Buddhism had not inspired those who stood forward as victors with a new-awakened fire of enthusiasm for the cause they championed.

So it came that Śankara Āchārya, the greatest revivalist of Aryanism, and the greatest commentator that India has known, arose in the South, and that at a period when he might have been expected—the period round which centres the "Kurral" and Brāhmanic revival, towards the eighth century of our era.[1]

This greatest of all great ascetic sages[2] bears a name revered by every learned Hindu, all over the land where he preached and taught from his monastery of Badrināth in the south to that of Sringiri in the north, from Dvārakā, the city of Krishna, in the west, to Jagannāth, once the Buddhist place of worship, now the common ground of assembly for all Hindus, on the coast of Orissa in the east. All sects claim him[3] as their own patron saint.

[1] "It is certainly inadvisable to assail Śankara's date (*i.e.* 788-820 A.D.), which is given most circumstantially by his own followers."—Yajñeśvar Sāstrī, "Āryavidyā Sudhākara," p. 226, etc. etc.; Bühler, "Ind. Ant.," xiv. 64. Other references are:—"Ind. Ant.," xiv. 185 (*note* 13); xi. 174; xiii. 95*ff.*; xvi. 42, 160; J.B.R.A.S., xviii. 88*ff.*, 218, 233; W.L., 51; Bhandarkar, Report, 1882-3, 15. *See* Pathak, J.R.A.S. (Bombay, 1891), xviii. p. 88; also Barth, "Ind. Ant." (1895), p. 35.

[2] For Kumārila Bhatta, *see* Hunter, "Indian Empire" 240, 259, 388; Cowell and Gough, "Sarva Darśana Sangraha."

[3] Monier-Williams, "Brāhmanism and Hinduism," p. 58; Wilson, "Rel. of Hindus," vol. i. p. 28.

All scholars, Eastern and Western, honour his learning and scholarship. He seems to have risen as an inspired genius to throw a quick, bright light, like to the momentary after-glow of an Indian sunset before darkness descends over the land, on the fading glories of Aryanism before they sink into the dimness of the drear days of Hinduism. Of his life almost nothing is known. In legendary lore he appears everywhere in India; now persecuting the Buddhists, now vehemently denouncing the sectarian differences whereby Hinduism was being divided against itself, so that it could not abide. Again he appears as the miraculously-born son of a Brāhman woman, his father being the dread god, Śiva, and as finally departing from the world no one knows how.

The "Great Conquest,"[1] or life of Śankara Āchārya, was told in a work supposed to have been composed in the ninth or tenth century, while the sage's "Great Conquest of the Quarters"[2] was written by the second great commentator of South India, Mādhava Āchārya, in the fourteenth century.

From these accounts and others, no safe historical facts can be deduced. At most, it may be held that Śankara was born in Malabar in the eighth century of our era, and that he died at Kedernath, in the Himālayas, at the early age of thirty-two, after having enriched, in the short course of his life, the literature of India by commentaries on most of its later sacred texts. He is popularly held to have been an incarnation of Śiva. The Smārta sect of Brāhmans, recognisable by wearing on their foreheads one or three horizontal lines of sandal paste, with a red or black spot in the middle, hold him to have been the founder of their Order. These Smārtas look upon Śiva as the Unconscious

[1] "This spurious work."—*See* Barth, "Ind. Ant.," vol. xxiv. (February 1895).

[2] *See* Telang, "Ind. Ant.," vol. v. p. 287, who places it before the fourteenth century.

Spirit of the Universe, with which the soul unites to realise its ideals.

According to the teachings of Śankara, the entire system of Vedāntic thought finds its natural culmination in an uncompromising declaration that the sole object of the sacred literature of India was to reveal the delusive appearance of what appeals to the senses as reality and the doctrine of non-duality.

The evidences of the senses are wiped away as merely delusive. The question of metaphysic is solved, not as Kant resolved it, by referring all objective reality to perceptions of the intellect where he sought a solution, but in endeavouring to pierce, in the manner of Plato, and Parmenides, beyond the reality itself. This objective form was held by Śankara to be but the mode in which the delusion of life was mirrored forth. This phase of idealistic monism which is ably expounded in Śankara's commentary on the "Vedānta Sūtras," finds a popular exposition in a song that can be obtained from any travelling pedlar of books in South India for about one twelfth of a farthing.

The song itself contains but twelve verses, said to have been addressed by Śankara to a learned Brāhman, whom he found studying the rules of Sanskrit grammar outside a Hindu temple. One or other of these verses is constantly recited with a smile or a sigh by educated Hindus of the South. The refrain all through is, "Bhaja Govinda!" or "Praise the Lord!" It means to a Hindu what "Praise God" means to a Salvationist. There is a yawning gulf of thought and feeling, bred of race and climate, between the two modes of expression of the aspirations of those who in East and West use the words.

The verses of Śankara are so terse, hold so much the sense in the sound, that it is impossible to give their meaning in a translation. As they are unknown in the

West, and so often quoted in the East, their meaning is here given as true to the original as possible.

The sage stands before the Brāhman, who has paused in his studies, and declares the truth of the emptiness of the vain dream of life, and its struggles after wealth and fame.

"Give up this greed," is the sad reproof, "for storing wealth, O Fool! place in your mind the thirst for knowledge of the Existent, satisfied with what each day brings forth."

"As the water drop lies trembling on the lotus leaf, so rests our fleeting life. The world is full of sorrow, seized by pain and pride of self. Gain wealth, and then your friends cling near; sink low, and then no one seeks news. When well in health, they ask your welfare in the house; when the breath of life goes forth, then the loving wife shrinks from that body. Gain leads but to loss; in wealth there is no lasting happiness; in childhood we are attached to play; in youth we turn to love; in old age care fills the mind. Towards (para Brahman) God alone no one is inclined. As the soul moves from birth to birth, who remains the wife, the son, the daughter, who you, or whence? Think truly, this life is but an unreal dream."

"With mind fixed on truth, one becomes free from attachment. To one freed from attachment, there is no delusion; undeluded, the soul springs clear to light freed from all bondage. When youth goes, who is moved by love? When wealth goes, who then follows? When the great truth, that the Soul and Brahman are One is known, what then is this passing show? Day and night, morning and evening, Spring and Winter come and go, time plays and age goes, yet desire for life passeth not. Take no pride in youth, friends, or riches, they all pass away in the twinkling of an eye. Give up all this made of Māyā, gain true knowledge, and enter on the path to Brahman."

Such has ever been the incessant cry of cultured Brāhmanic thought, and of much of Western pessimism. It was the cry with which was to be met the fierce fanaticism of Muhammadanism, soon to burst forth in relentless warfare against all idolaters and unbelievers in God and Muhammad as His sole Prophet.

Though the darkness of desolation, unrest, rapine, and war was to settle over the land, the Brāhmans of the South could hold on to the even tenor of their ways, and proclaim that the moans of the suffering, the gleam of the sword, the lust of conquerors, and the rule of the foreigner, were but the unreal visions of a passing dream, woven out by the fictitious power of Māyā.

The strict Advaita doctrines of Śankara Āchārya were no doubt useful in their own way, as opposing the heretic agnosticism of Buddhism. In their inculcation of idealistic non-duality, and of non-reality of the intuition of perception, they had also their own charm for the dreamer and religious mystic who turns away from a crude materialism.

An intermediate resting-place had, however, to be found for the mass of the people who placed their faith in the saving grace of a personal deity. In the system of Śankara, this was supplied by the sectarian schools, which hold that the god Śiva was a personal manifestation of the Unconscious Spirit of the Universe, and claim that, by a worship of this deity, the soul finds its salvation.

The true revolt from the teachings of Śankara, and the drifting of the thought of India back to its more orthodox beliefs, came in the reformation led by the second great commentator of South India, the Brāhman Rāmānuja, born at the beginning of the eleventh century.[1] Rāmānuja held the doctrine of qualified non-duality, according to which the

[1] Monier-Williams, "Brāhmanism and Hinduism," p. 119:—"Born 1017 A.D. at Parambattur."

Supreme Spirit is both the cause of the visible world and the material from which it is created. He further proclaimed the adoration of the god Vishnu, as representative of the Supreme Spirit, so that the Heaven of the god might be ultimately gained, and freedom from re-birth obtained. Until this consummation was arrived at, when the separate spirits are reunited with the Supreme Spirit, re-birth occurs in its incessant round, there being a plurality of form continued in respect of that which is Soul, and that which is non-Soul.[1]

The final step was taken by Mādhava, the last of the Southern Teachers, a renowned Brāhman of the Kanarese country in South India, who died towards the close of the twelfth century.[2] By him the worship of Vishnu, or Hari, was preached as the worship of one Supreme God, eternally existent, the world subsisting as his form, on Whom the souls of men are dependent, though abiding themselves distinct. So the thought of India, North and South, remained divided between a salvation, from transmigration, by a faith in Krishna, or by a worship of Vishnu, or Śiva; the aspiration of the soul ever being to find a closer union with, or knowledge of, the Supreme Cause that manifested itself in the works of Creation.

Vedism, and the gods of the Vedas, had passed away from the memories of the people; the South had found the exponents of its intellectual life in the persons of the great scholars, Śankara, Rāmānuja, and Mādhava. The deep moral tendencies of the age were preserved in the "Nalādiyar," and "Kurral" of Tiruvalluvar, and the Devāran Hymns of Sambandha and his disciples. The crude superstitions, lusts, and ignorance of the mass of the people who passed from the scene, leaving no literary record

[1] "Sarva Darśana Sangraha," p. 75.

[2] Died 1198 A.D. P. Sundaram Pillai, "Some Milestones in Tamil Literature," p. 27 (*note* 1).

behind them, were satisfied with worship of the village godlings, ghosts, and demons, with foul and obscene carnivals of Tantric orgies, and with stray and furtive visits and offerings to the great temples of the Hindu deities. New conquerors had come to guide the destinies of the land and leave the people to work out their own ideas.

CHAPTER XIV.

THE FOREIGNER IN THE LAND.

WHEN in 631 of our era Muhammad proclaimed war against the civilised world, he had first given to all idolaters the choice between the Koran and the sword. All Jews and Christians who would not accept a belief in the unity of God, and in Muhammad as the Prophet of that God, were to be subdued and made to pay tribute. The creed of the Prophet known as Islām, or "submission to the will of God," was outwardly simple—simple enough to ensure for it an early and speedy success. The creed is shortly: "There is no God but God, and Muhammad is His Prophet."

There are further five daily prayers, fastings in due season, giving of alms, and a pilgrimage to Mecca, the birthplace of the Prophet.

The fanatics of the Arabian desert, inspired by the wild rhetoric of the new Prophet who denounced idolatry, licentiousness, infanticide, drunkenness, and gambling, came swarming from their tents, drunk with zeal, to propagate the creed and to revel in the slaughter and plunder of their opposing foes.[1]

[1] *See* an article by Sir Roland K. Wilson in the *Indian Magazine and Review* (December 1896), p. 634, criticising Mr Arnold's statement in "The Preaching of Islām," that "it is due to the Muhammadan legists and commentators that

Against the Western frontier of India, from Sind to Peshāwar, the Muhammadan wave of conquest flowed and ebbed for four hundred years.[1] In Sind the Rājput garrisons, unable to hold their strongholds against the fierce Arabs, placed their women and children on the funeral pyre there to find in death safety from dishonour, and fell themselves in one last despairing and avenging onslaught on their enemies. From Lahore the Hindu chieftains chased back, through the passes of Afghānistān, the raiding Turks of Ghaznī only to court their own avenging fate.

The full wave of desolation spread over the north-west when, in 1002 A.D., Muhammad of Ghaznī, born of a Turkī father and a Persian mother, burst down on Lahore, that ancient meeting-place of many races. Its wealth was carried back to Ghaznī, and its chieftain, the twice-defeated Jaipāl, mounted the funeral pyre, according to the stern dictates of his Hindu subjects. For twenty-five years Muhammad of Ghaznī continued, year by year, his raids. From the holy city of Thaneswar, not far from Delhi, he carried off to his Afghān home the riches of its great temples, and two hundred thousand of its inhabitants he made slaves to his soldiery. At Kanauj, north of Cawnpur,

jihād comes to be interpreted as a religious war against unbelievers, who might be attacked even though they were not the aggressors. . . . But though some Muhammadan legists have maintained the righteousness of unprovoked war against unbelievers, none (as far as I am aware) have ventured to justify compulsory conversion, but have always vindicated, for the conquered, the right of retaining their own faith on payment of *jizyah*." He writes: "*What Mr Arnold will find it difficult to disprove is, that the intimate companions and immediate successors of Mohamet considered, without a shadow of doubt, that they had ample warrant in the Koran, and in the example of their master, for extirpating idolatry and enforcing the whole law of Islām* throughout Arabia at the cost of a most sanguinary struggle, and for pushing hostilities against the two neighbouring empires far beyond any possible requirements of self-defence—in fact, without any other limit than the enemy's power of resistance." Sir Roland Wilson, however, continues: "We are willing to allow that mediæval Islām was, by one degree, less tolerant than mediæval Christendom."

[1] From 647 to 1030, the death of Muhammad of Ghaznī.

he received the submission of its garrison, said to have consisted of eighty thousand men in armour, fifty thousand cavalry, and five hundred thousand foot men. With the wealth of Muttra—the rubies, sapphires, and pearls of its idols—he raised Ghaznī from a hovel of mud huts to a city of marble palaces, mosques, domes, and pillared halls. From the ocean-beaten temple of Somnāth in Guzarāt, with its vast array of Brāhman priests and dancing-girls, he carried away the massive gates, twelve phallic emblems,[1] and a vast store of treasure, and left nothing behind him but the slain garrison and dejected priesthood.

Aryanism in India was about to realise what, happily in the West, remained but the shadow of a passing danger. The fate that overtook the East was one visioned forth for the West in the words of Freeman: "If Constantinople had been taken by the Muhammadans before the nations of Western Europe had at all grown up, it would seem as if the Christian religion and European civilisation must have been swept away from the earth."

Spared from Muhammadan dominion, a Sivajī, or a Ranjīt Singh might have arisen in India and founded a more lasting native rule than even that of Chandra Gupta, Asoka, or Harsha Vardhana. Even had that been so, it seems impossible that Marāthā could ever have coalesced with Sikh or Rājput to bend the distant Easterns and far-off Southerns to yield obedience to the supremacy of any one indigenous dynasty. Even had a Hindu Akbar, or Aurangzīb sprung up and extended his rule over Marāthā, Rājput, Sikh, Bengali, and the clansmen of South India, the sceptre would soon have passed from the hands of one or other of his degenerate descendants, and the land been plunged in anarchy such as that from which the Mughal

[1] R. P. Karkaria, *Calcutta Review* (October 1895), p. 411:—"It is clear from Albiruni that the idol of Somnāth was merely a solid piece of stone, having no hollow in which jewels and precious stones could be concealed to reward the pious zeal of an iconoclast."

Aurangzīb, with his army of three hundred thousand horse and four hundred thousand men, could not for long preserve it. As it was, the rivalries between the Rājput Prithivi Rājā,[1] the last great Chauhān king of Delhi and Ajmere, and the Rāhtor prince of Kanauj led, before the close of the twelfth century, to the defeat and overthrow of both by the Afghāns of Ghor. The new Muhammadan Emperor raided the country as far as Benares and Gwalior, while his generals drove out (1203) the distant Sen king of Bengal from the ancient capital at Nadiyā.[2]

This very lack of unity and central authority, however, saved Brāhmanism from disappearing before the attacks of a rival creed or foreign rulers. The whole fabric of Buddhism disappeared, for when once its mendicant and celibate monks were slain, and their monasteries burned, it fell to decay. The idols and temples of the Hindus were shattered to pieces, and their wealth carried off to Ghaznī and Ghor; the Brāhmans were slain in Kanauj, Muttra, Benares, and at distant Somnāth. Nevertheless, the roots of Brāhmanism remained firmly fixed in the very structure of Indian life, social observances, and in its undecaying literature. For three hundred years the Muhammadan rule in India strove in vain to hold the outlying nationalities subject to its sway. The early Muhammadan invaders of India swarmed into the land in the double rôle of religious enthusiasts with a mission to root out unbelief in the teachings of the Koran, and of roving bands of adventurers eager to seize the wealth of the Hindu temples. Disunited

[1] Prithī Rājā-Rāyasā of Chand. Tod in his "Rajasthān" (vol. i. p. 254, *note*) states he had translated thirty thousand stanzas. Grierson ("Literature of Hindustān," p. 3) gives an account of the work done on this history; but in the "Padumawati Bib. Ind." (Calcutta, 1894, Introd.), he states that the genuineness of this work is doubtful. *See* also J.B.R.A.S. (1868), vol. xxxvii. p. 119; vol. xxxviii. p. 1.

[2] The Rājput clans of North India departed to the desert east of the Indus, where they established their chieftainship over their new homes, still known as Rājputāna.

among themselves as these raiders were, they were for long unable to gain a resting-place east of the Indus, and when at length they came in numbers sufficient to force their way to Delhi, and there establish a permanent centre for revenue exactions, they were ever menaced with the swarming-down of new robber bands from central Asia; while the basis on which Muhammadanism was founded precluded their compromising with, or conciliating of, the Hindu people in order to gain their aid or support in repelling new invaders. The Rājputs might be driven to the deserts of Rājputāna, their proud reserve survived not only to defy the august power of Akbar, but for the best of their chivalry and manhood to come forth and parade the London streets and grace the triumph of their sovereign lady, the Queen-Empress of India.

Though the unwarlike people of Bengal were obliged to submit, in 1203, to Bkhtiyār Khiljī, the general of Muhammad of Ghor, the lower province soon became independent of the distant authority of the Delhi emperor, and in 1340 set up an independent ruler of its own, in the person of the local governor, Fakīr-ud-dīn, who was succeeded by a line of twenty sovereigns until Akbar, in 1576, reconquered the revolted province.

Muhammad of Ghor, who may be classed as the first Muhammadan ruler of India, fell before a fierce attack of a body of hill Gakkars, from the Sewālik hills, who crept into the monarch's tent and, as he lay sleeping, stabbed him to death with no less than twenty-two wounds, before the gaze of his petrified attendants.[1] On his death, Katb-ud-dīn, a Turkī slave—whose name is remembered by the great mosque he built at Delhi, and the majestic minar, rivalling in finish and moulding, though not in height, the Campanile at Florence—proclaimed himself, at Delhi, monarch of all India. His dynasty, which lasted until 1290, continued the ceaseless contest against Rājput princes, fierce hill

[1] *See* Syed Mahomed Latif, "History of the Panjāb," p. 94.

tribes, revolting Hindu principalities, and incursive bands of warlike Mughals, who rode down to pillage the plain-country east of the Indus. The Khiljī and Tughlak dynasties followed, until at length, in 1393, the lame Timur, or Tamerlane, named by Ferishta "The Firebrand of the Universe," collected together his wild horsemen, swept down through the north-west passes of Afghānistān, and marched towards Delhi. "My principal object in coming to Hindustān," says Timur, "and in undergoing all this toil and hardship, was to accomplish two things. The first was to war with infidels, the enemies of the Muhammadan religion, and by this religious warfare to acquire some claim to reward in the life to come. The other was a worldly object, that the army of Islām might gain something by plundering the wealth of the infidels: plunder in war is as lawful as their mother's milk to Mussulmans who fight for their faith, and the consuming of that which is lawful is a means of grace."[1]

The famed city of Delhi was captured by a ruse, and for five days the newly-proclaimed emperor sat in the mosque, constructed by Firoz Tughlak, giving praise to God that the idolaters had submitted like "sheep to the slaughter," and that the Hindus lay dead in heaps so that the streets were impassable. The fabulous wealth of Delhi was borne away; a hundred thousand Hindu prisoners were slain "with the sword of holy war"; the women were dragged into slavery, and the stone masons and workers in marble were driven across the wasted land of the Panjāb, and beyond the bleak passes of Afghānistān, to build, for the new conqueror of the world—from Delhi in the south to Siberia in the north, from Syria in the west to China in the east—a mosque at Samarkhand. His descendants were to found the great Mughal Empire of India, and point the lesson which Timur had learned before he ventured on his rapid

[1] Holden, E., "Mughal Emperors," p. 52.

raids into the country. The lesson was plainly taught to Timur in the answer given by those of his court whom he consulted on the enterprise: "If we tarry in that land our posterity will be lost, and our children and our grandchildren will degenerate from the vigour of their forefathers and become speakers of the language of Hind."[1]

For over a century after the passing-away of Timur, weak dynasties, Sayyid and Lodi, held a feeble rule around Delhi and Agra until the so-called Mughal invasion of Bābar.

During the early centuries of Muhammadan raids and rule, the intellectual life of Northern India seems to have been seized with a paralysis that crept even as far to the east as Mithilā or North Behar, which had remained the great centre of philosophic thought since the days of Janaka, King of the Videhas. It was a palsy under which Mithilā sank to decrepitude.

In the eighteenth century the great logician of India, Raghunath, had to turn to where vitality alone remained—to the land where the torch of learning has been kept burning down to the present day—to Bengal, where he established, at Navadvīp, the most renowned school of logic in all India. It was Bengal that saw almost a second Buddha appear in the ecstatic dreamer and revivalist, Chaitanya, in the fifteenth century, and not, as might have been expected, in Magadha or South Behar. Here Kullaka Bhatta wrote his famous commentary on "Manu" in the fourteenth century, almost five centuries after Mithilā had had learning enough to send forth Medātithi, the second great commentator of the same sacred law book of the Hindus. It was in Bengal also that Jimūtavāhana wrote, in the fourteenth century, the "Dāyabhāga," a work which has become there the recognised law book on Hindu succession and inheritance,

[1] "Institutes, Political and Military, written originally in the Mogul Language by the Great Timour," published, Clarendon Press (1783), by J. White, B.D., p. 131.

a task that Vijnānesvara had done in his "Mitākshara," or "Commentary on the Law Book of Yājnavalkya," in the eleventh century for Behar and the West.

Bengal had, however, produced for itself a poet as early as the twelfth century. Set to the sweetest music of sound and of moving rhythm of which the Sanskrit language has been found capable, Jaya Deva had sung the theme that became, in one form or another, universal in subsequent Indian literature. It was the mystic theme of the longing of the soul to find union with, or absorption into, the Divine Essence, personified in one or other of the Hindu deities, Rāma or Krishna. There is no direct evidence that the poem itself was written with any religious purport. It simply tells of the longings and laments of Rādhā, the favourite of Krishna, for her lord and lover. Still, all Vaishnavites take the poem as the mystic rendering of the longing of the soul for the Divine.[1] Jaya Deva[2] was born in the Bīrbhūm district of Bengal, in the twelfth century.

The poem opens with the customary reverence to Ganeśa, the opposing deity of all good efforts. The praises of Vishnu are then sung, and the deeds recited done during his descent on earth in various forms, in which he still retained his Divine Essence. His first descent was as the Fish that bore to a resting-place, on the northern mountains, the ship in which Manu escaped from the Flood. The second form in which Vishnu appeared was as a Tortoise, on whose back was suspended the mountain Mandara, round which was wound the huge serpent Śesha, to form a rope that the gods and demons might churn the waters of the flood, and bring to the surface the fourteen precious treasures lost during the deluge. The last of

[1] Weber, "History of Indian Literature," p. 210.

[2] Monier-Williams, "Hinduism," p. 139. The Nimbārkas, a Vaishnavite sect, without a literature, who worship Krishna and Rādhā, claim Jaya Deva as a follower of their founder, Nimbārka, or Nimbāditya, of the twelfth century.

these lost treasures was the poison which would have destroyed humanity had it not been drunk by Śiva, whose neck it burned so badly that he still bears the mark—the symbol of the sufferings he bore for man—and is therefore called "The Blue-throated God."

Again Vishnu descended in the form of a Boar, to raise the earth from below the waters and hold it firm. As the Man-Lion, Vishnu came on earth to tear to pieces the monster, Hiranya Kāsipa, whom the god Brahmā had given security from mortal injury. The fifth incarnation the poet reverences is that of the Dwarf, the form in which Vishnu appeared before the demon, Balī, who had usurped dominion over the three worlds. Balī, in jest, offered the Dwarf so much of the worlds as he could stride over in three steps, whereon, in three strides, the deity re-annexed the three worlds. The sixth incarnation is that of Parasu Rāma, or "Rāma with the Axe," who came to extirpate the warrior caste, and re-establish Brāhmanical might. The seventh was that of Rāma Chandra, "The Moon-like Rāma," whose victory over Rāvana is told in the "Rāmāyana." The eighth form was that of Krishna, "The Dark God," the chief of the Yādus, the charioteer to Arjuna when the Pāndavas fought against the Kurus. The ninth incarnation was that of Buddha, who came to free the land from Vedic sacrifices of animals. The last incarnation, one yet to come, is that of Kalki, who will appear seated on a white horse, bearing a sword to slay all those who in the Kāli, or "depraved age," do wrong and work unrighteousness. The Kāli, or "present age," is that described in the "Vishnu Purāna":[1]—

"The observance of caste, order, and institutes will not prevail in the Kāli Age, nor will that of the ceremonial enjoined by the 'Sāma,' 'Rik,' and 'Yajur Vedas.' Marriages, in this Age, will not be conformable to the ritual, nor will the rules that connect the

[1] Wilson, H. H., "Vishnu Pūrana," pp. 622-23.

spiritual preceptor and his disciple be in force. The laws that regulate the conduct of husband and wife will be disregarded, and oblations to the gods with fire no longer be offered. In whatever family he may be born, a powerful and rich man will be held entitled to espouse maidens of every tribe. A regenerate man will be initiated in any way whatever, and such acts of penance as may be performed will be unattended by any results. Every text will be Scripture that people choose to think so: all gods will be gods to them that worship them, and all orders of life will be common alike to all persons. In the Kāli Age, fasting, austerity, liberality, practised according to the pleasure of those by whom they are observed, will constitute righteousness. Pride of wealth will be inspired by very insignificant possessions. Pride of beauty will be prompted by (no other personal charm than fine) hair. Gold, jewels, diamonds, clothes, will all have perished, and then hair will be the only ornament with which women can decorate themselves. Wives will desert their husbands when they lose their property; and they only who are wealthy will be considered by women as their lords. He who gives away much money will be the master of men, and family descent will no longer be a title of supremacy. Accumulated treasures will be expended on (ostentatious) dwellings. The minds of men will be wholly occupied in acquiring wealth, and wealth will be spent solely on selfish gratifications. Women will follow their inclinations, and be ever fond of pleasure. Men will fix their desires upon riches even though dishonestly acquired. No man will part with the smallest fraction of the smallest coin, though entreated by a friend. Men of all degrees will conceit themselves to be equal with Brāhmans. Cows will be held in esteem only as they supply milk. The people will be almost always in dread of dearth, and apprehensive of scarcity, and will hence ever be watching the appearances of the sky; they will all live, like anchorets, upon leaves, and roots, and fruit, and put a period to their lives through fear of famine and want. In truth, there will never be abundance in the Kāli Age, and men will never enjoy pleasure and happiness. They will take their food without previous ablution, and without worshipping fire, gods, or guests, or offering obsequial libations to their progenitors. The women will be fickle, short of stature, gluttonous; they will have many children and little means. Scratching their heads with both hands, they will pay no attention to the commands of their husbands or parents. They will be selfish, abject, and slatternly; they will be scolds and liars; they will be indecent and immoral in their conduct, and will ever attach themselves to dissolute men. Youths, although disregarding the rules of studentship, will study the 'Vedas.' Householders will neither sacrifice nor practise becoming liberality. Anchorets will subsist upon food accepted from rustics, and mendicants will be influenced by regard for friends and associates. Princes, instead of protecting, will plunder their subjects, and under the pretext of levying customs, will rob merchants of their property."

The poet, having duly honoured Vishnu, commences the special subject of the poem, the love of Rādhā for the dark god Krishna.

With all the sensuous languor of an Eastern mind, the loves of the gopis, or shepherd girls, who woo the god, are set to the gentle music and soft sound to which the Bengali poet has moulded the sounding Sanskrit. As the love-sick shepherdesses flit round the god, Rādhā, the favourite of Krishna, remains apart pouring forth her longings for the near presence of her lover. She conjures up to herself memories of his might and majesty, his once-whispered words of love, when she alone was his loved bride.

The love of Rādhā is also remembered by Krishna when he has freed himself from the allurements of the five shepherdesses—perhaps allegorical of the five senses. The form of Rādhā rises up before him; he prays her to return, to fear no more, for he no longer bears the form of the fierce god who roams with ash-besmeared and matted locks. He has covered himself with the dust of the sweet sandal-wood, and wears a dark lotus leaf to conceal the blue stain his throat bears. The words of Rādhā are then borne to Krishna. The messenger tells how she sits beneath the moonbeams weeping over her deep sorrow, and the separation of her soul from that of her beloved. The soft south wind, as it steals round her limbs, soothes her no longer; it is as though it had crept through sandal trees where it had received the taint of the poisoned breath of serpents. She is languid and weary; she pants to be once more near to her beloved in whom alone her hopes are centred. Krishna cries for her to come, but as she approaches, adorned with all her ornaments, her steps falter. She weeps, she cries on Hari, her lord, to come and support her failing feet; she sinks to the ground, to embrace, to kiss the shadow of the passing dark blue cloud, imagining that it is Krishna who approaches near. Her strength fails to bear her further. She weeps, she wails, for in her fancy she sees the lips of a rival touching those of her lord, the rival's long black hair trailing over the dark god's face, like to evening clouds sweeping past the clear moon; the rival twines white flowers in his dark locks. Rādhā's companion prays her to tarry not, to hasten to the god, for she has teeth with the gleam of the moon; she has but to fall at her lord's feet and claim his love with gentle words of faith.

Let the lyric raptures of the poem be taken as they may, either as an allegory of the soul striving to pierce through the bondage of the sense and find rest, or else as a love song, too sensuous and unrestrained for Western ideas, it is a poem that found its way to the hearts of the myriads of pilgrims who have, for centuries past, journeyed to the birthplace of Jaya Deva, crying out the praises of Vishnu, Krishna, Hari, Lord of the Braided Locks, Lord of the World. Although portions of the poem are untranslatable from the poet's unrestraint, yet his artistic reserve saved him from the gross lewdness which is too often, especially in Bengal, the besetting sin of so many of his imitators and successors. The poem of Jaya Deva marks the gradual development in the twelfth century of the doctrine of faith (*bhakti*), of devotion, and personal love towards a deity in human form. The Krishna of the "Gīta Govinda" is now usually taken by all the Vaishnavites as an incarnation of the Divine Essence. In the poem itself there is no direct indication that its object was to found any phase of religion based on the saving grace of a faith in Krishna. One verse is often quoted in proof of the poem's mystic and religious significance. Krishna, in despair at the anger of Rādhā, is represented as kneeling down, and praying her to place her feet on his head. Later tradition holds that the poet could never have so far forgotten the divine nature of Krishna as to represent him thus addressing Rādhā, and asserts that Krishna himself wrote these words. The story is that, in the absence of Jaya Deva, the god entered his house and inserted these words in a half-finished line. The poet had commenced the line with the words: "On my head as an ornament," and then, pausing, had gone out to consider how he could possibly represent the god as having a foot placed on his head. In his absence, Krishna, in the form of Jaya Deva, appeared and finished the line, so that it now reads: "On my head as an ornament place thy beauteous feet."

This doctrine of "bhakti," or faith, so often ascribed to Christian influence, became from its inculcation in the "Bhagavad Gīta," and fuller exposition in the "Bhagavad Purāna," and "Bhakti Sūtrā" of Śāndilya in the twelfth century, the almost pervading theme of Indian literature. It passed from the system of Yoga, or attainment of absorption of the Soul into the essence of the deity in whom faith is placed, to its final development in the hope of salvation, following from a faith or absolute belief in the words and doctrines of the great teachers, such as Śankara Āchārya, Rāmānuja, Ramānand, Bassava, Vallabha Āchārya and the Sikh gurus.[1]

From the commencement of the fourteenth century, almost coincident with the disappearance of Tamerlane, with his blood-stained horsemen across the passes to the

[1] For erotic literature, *see* Beames, J., "Ind. Ant.," i. 215; "Vishnu Purāna," xiv. (Preface); Wilson, "Select Works," vol. i. 161. Muir, "Metrical Trans." (Introd.), gives full account of connection between Christianity and Hinduism.

north-west, when the Muhammadan Sayyid[1] and Lodi[2] dynasties ruled from Delhi with what feeble power they possessed until the arrival of the Mughal Bābar, the Gangetic valley and the East saw a great literary revival centring itself around the doctrines of Vaishnavism. Rāmānand[3] early heralded in the worship of Vishnu, as incarnated in Rāma, the hero of the "Rāmāyana," and in the lands where he sang his songs, especially near Agra, his sects, the Rāmavats, or Rāmānandīs,[4] still form a large community.

The most famous of all Rāmānand's early disciples was one Kabīr,[5] a weaver of Benares, reputed[6] to have been the son of a virgin Brāhman woman. His writings, especially the "Sukh Nidhān," are quoted widely at the present day, and mark the tendency of the time, under the stress of contact with Muhammadanism, to break free from the exclusive bondage to Hindu sacred literature, and rise above the restrictions of caste, sect, and the bowing-down to idols. In place of these there was inculcated faith in one Vedāntic[7] conception of a deity addressed as "Ali" by the Muhammadans, and "Rāma" by Hindus. To this was added a belief in the guidance of a guru, or spiritual preceptor, the principle that in time welded the religious sect of Sikhs, or disciples of Nānak, into a political power under the tenth Panjāb guru, Govind Singh.

In the "Śabdābalī," or "One Thousand Sayings of Kabīr," the Vedāntic doctrine of Māyā, the Jaina, Buddhistic, and Brāhmanic doctrines of compassion towards all life were

[1] 1414-50. [2] 1450-1526.

[3] Grierson, "Modern Literature of Hindustān," p. 7:—"I have collected hymns written by, or purporting to have been written by him, as far east as Mithilā."

[4] Wilson, H. H., "Religious Sects," p. 67.

[5] Hunter, "Indian Empire," p. 269 (1380-1420).

[6] In the "Bhakta Mālā." [7] Barth, "Rel. of India," 239.

brought side by side with the monotheistic conception of Vishnu:[1]—

"To Ali and Rāma we owe our existence, and should therefore show similar tenderness to all that live. Of what avail is it to shave your head, prostrate yourself on the ground, or immerse your body in the stream, whilst you shed blood you call yourself pure and boast of virtues that you never display. Of what benefit is cleaning your mouth, counting your beads, performing ablution, and bowing yourself in temples, when, whilst you mutter your prayers, or journey to Mecca and Medina, deceitfulness is in your heart? The Hindu fasts every eleventh day, the Mussulman during the Ramazān. Who formed the remaining months and days that you should venerate but one? If the Creator dwells in Tabernacles, whose residence is the universe? Who has beheld Rāma seated amongst images, or found him at the shrine to which the Pilgrim has directed his steps? . . . Behold but one in all things, it is the second that leads you astray. Every man and woman that has ever been born is of the same nature with yourself."

On the death of Kabīr, the Hindus and Muhammadans are represented by tradition as disputing over their respective rights to claim the body of the teacher. The Muhammadans, according to their custom, desired to bury it, the Hindus to burn it. Kabīr, it is said, appeared in the midst of the disputants and directed both Hindus and Muhammadans to raise the cloth covering his supposed remains. Beneath the cloth they found nothing but a heap of flowers. In the holy city of Benares half of the flowers were burnt by the Hindus, and there the ashes were kept as sacred relics; half were claimed by the Muhammadans, who buried them beneath a tomb near Gorakhpur.[2]

All over the land the loves of Sītā for Rāma, of Rādhā for Krishna, were sung in more or less realistic or mystic significance. As all hopes of a national

[1] Wilson, H. H., "Religious Sects," "Sabda," lvi. p. 81.

[2] Flourished in 1400 A.D.

existence were further fading away, the people seemed in their loneliness to be wailing forth their despairing cry for the sympathy of a human or Divine love or aid.

To the East, in Behar, Bidyāpati Thākur told in his passionate and never-imitated sonnets, in the Maithili dialect, the longings of the Soul for God, in the allegorical form of the love of Rādhā for Krishna. In the songs of Chandīdās, the imitator of Bidyāpati in Bengal, a deeper note, though not so sweet, is given of the same phase of thought which sent the intellectual life of the time in on itself to brood over a love of God for humanity, and humanity for God, in times when Mughal raids had, for their rallying cry, the Prophet's declaration of a Divine revelation: "Slay the unbeliever and infidel where he may be found."[1]

Chandidās sang the same wail of love in which the Soul, personified as Rādhā, pours forth her love for the Divine, as incarnate in Krishna.

This surrender of the Soul and the Self, as dreamed of in all the true mystic symbolism of Jaya Deva, reached its tenderest, though perhaps not its truest, depths in the vision of Mira Bai,[2] of Mewar, in the West of Hindustān, in the fifteenth century, as it did in the sixteenth century in Spain in the ecstasies of Santa Theresa.[3] Mira Bai's commentary on the "Gīta Govinda" shows her passionate devotion to the form of Krishna she worshipped, while songs of her own composition[4] are sung far and wide, from Dvārāka to Mithilā. Tradition loves to tell how, as she worshipped the image of Krishna, pouring forth her impassioned appeal for its love, the image opened and

[1] Timur, "Designs and Enterprises," p. 2.

[2] Wilson, H. H., "Sects of the Hindus," p. 138; Grierson, "Modern Literature of Hindustan," p. 12.

[3] G. C. Cunningham, "Santa Theresa: Her Life and Times," *Edinburgh Review* (October 1896).

[4] Tod, J., "Rajasthan," vol. i. p. 289.

closed around her so that she for ever disappeared from earth.[1] The piety of Mira Bai, the devoted follower of Krishna, and founder of the Mira Bai sect, did not save her from scandal and from persecution by her family. The theme she sang had its own fascinations and dangers. The mystic brooding over the longings of the Soul which found expression in the burning terms of human love used by Jaya Deva in the twelfth century in India, and by San Juan de la Cruz[2] in the West, tottered on the verge of a steep precipice.

In the soft, relaxing lowlands of Bengal the step was early taken that sped mysticism down to realism. The safeguard of spiritualism once abandoned, all was lost on which the theme could preserve itself free from the contaminating taint of the earth and earthly. The tendency of the whole literature was to sink lower and lower into the abyss of lewd imaginings and sensuous fancies. The outward and popular expression of the same realistic tendency took the form of foul Tantric orgies, until at length literature and religion dragged down in their fall all the best on which they were founded.

Both phases of thought, the realistic and spiritualistic, found their fullest expression and glorification in the writings, teachings, and influence of two great founders of distinct Vaishnava sects—the one, Vallabha Āchārya, still having numerous followers in Central India, Bombay, and Gujarāt, the other, Chaitanya, a name familiar in every household of Bengal.

Vallabha Āchārya, the founder of the Swāmi Vallabha sect, is held to have been an embodiment of a portion of the Divine Essence of Krishna, and numerous are the stories current of his superhuman intelligence and power. His great work was a commentary on the "Bhāgavata Purāna."

[1] Tod, J., "Rajasthan," vol. ii. p. 760.

[2] Lewis, D., "St John of the Cross: Life and Works."

According to his teachings, the human soul, though separated from the Divine Essence of Krishna, is identical with it, and, as such, is as though it were a divine spark of the Supreme Spirit itself. The body, as the abode of this portion of the Divine Essence of Krishna, should be honoured and revered, not subjected to asceticism, but nourished with every luxury in the way of eating, drinking, and enjoyment. The doctrine was one destined to attract a numerous following. The personality and undoubted genius of Vallabha secured for it the recognition of the wealthy and influential members of the community who were shut out from all national life or political power. These Epicureans of India might be passed over in silence, along with all the worshippers of Śakti, or "force personified as a goddess," and followers of Tantric rites, inasmuch as they show no strife against the more debasing factors of human nature, were it not that the most remarkable libel case that could ever have arisen in a Court of Justice respecting the privileges of a priesthood was heard in 1862 before the Supreme Court of Bombay, when a charge was brought against the Mahārājas, or modern successors of Vallabha, that they claimed, as actual manifestations of Krishna, to be entitled to receive from their disciples not only adoration, expressed by submission of mind and outpourings of wealth, but also by dedication of the bodies of their female worshippers to probably the most eccentric whims the depraved imaginings of a sect, working out perverted ideals, could evolve.

Chaitanya, held to have been an absolute incarnation of Krishna, and a worker of many miracles, represents to the mystic-loving East what Luther represents to the West.

Born at Nadiyā (Navadvīp) in 1485 A.D., this enthusiastic reformer and preacher, Chaitanya, gave expression in Bengal to the peculiar mode in which its life and thought had become modelled under climatic and political pressure, just as Kabīr before him had proclaimed the form the religious thought of the people was taking in North India.

Of all the varied phases of Indian thought arising within the lull that preceded the final conquests of the Mughals, that phase which it was the mission of Chaitanya to proclaim, with all the power of his eloquence and mesmeric influence of his presence, shows most clearly how deeply the time was moved by a faith or devotion in a deity, with whom, as a consummation, complete union is sought. Chaitanya, first inspired at Buddha Gayā by the universal sympathy of the Buddhist sage, and then roused to enthusiasm by the memories of the thought of past ages as they swept round the temple of Jagannāth, went forth from his wife and child as an enthusiast, to proclaim the love for, and of, Krishna, at a time when Luther was preparing to rouse Europe by his preaching. Five hundred years have passed away since the time Chaitanya spread a faith in the saving grace of Krishna throughout the land, nevertheless, down to the present day, the same spirit that inspired Chaitanya continues still to dwell among his followers.

In an interesting account of the life and precepts of Chaitanya,[1] lately[2] published by his devout and aged follower, Śri Kedar Nath Dutt, Blakti Vinod, it can be read how this spirit preserves its vitality undiminished amid the changes that are sweeping over the land. This exponent of the hopes of the present followers of the teachings of Chaitanya declares his firm faith that, from a devoted love to Krishna, a love like that of a girl for a loved one, shown by constant repetition of his name, by ecstatic raptures, singing, calm contemplation and fervour, a movement will yet take place to draw to the future church of the world "all classes of men, without distinction of caste or clan to the highest cultivation of the spirit. This church, it appears, will extend all over the world, and

[1] The standard life is that of Krishna Das Kavi Raj. [2] 1895.

take the place of all sectarian churches, which exclude outsiders from the precincts of the mosque, church, or temple."[1]

The spirit that is to animate this new church is to be founded on the principle that "spiritual cultivation is the main object of life. Do everything that keeps it, and abstain from doing anything which thwarts the cultivation of the spirit." A devoted love to Krishna is to be the guiding light, as preached by Chaitanya: "Have a strong faith that Krishna alone protects you, and none else. Admit him as your only guardian. Do everything which you know Krishna wishes you to do, and never think that you do a thing independent of the holy wish of Krishna. Do all you do with humility. Always remember that you are a sojourner in the world, and you must be prepared for your own home."[2]

The simple piety of this latest preacher of the teachings of Chaitanya holds that Chaitanya "showed in his character, and preached to the world, the purest morality as an accompaniment of spiritual improvement. Morality, as a matter of course, will grace the character of a bhakta (one who has faith)."[3]

The perplexing question of idolatry receives its usual explanation in the following manner: "Those who say that God has no form, either material or spiritual, and again imagine a false form for worship, are certainly idolatrous. But those who see the spiritual form of the deity in their soul's eye, carry that impression as far as possible to the mind, and then frame an emblem for the satisfaction of the material eye, for continual study of the higher feelings are by no means idolatrous."[4]

The words seem as if they pointed to the images Chaitanya in his trances used to vision up before him of the deity and the shepherdesses. In one of these trances, Chaitanya is

[1] Dutt, K. N., "Chaitanya: His Life and Precepts," p. 60.
[2] *Ibid.*, p. 57. [3] *Ibid.*, p. 58. [4] *Ibid.*, p. 47.

held by tradition to have seen a vision of Krishna and the shepherdesses, sporting in the glistening waters of the sea near Pūri, in Orissa, and, as he walked out towards them, passed away forever from the world, having gained the heaven of Vaikuntha in 1527 A.D., at the age of forty-two.

While Chaitanya in Bengal, moved by the same spirit that had inspired the sonnets of Bidyāpati in Behar, the ecstatic trances of Mira Bai in Mewar, and the languid and enervated sensualism of Vallabha Āchārya in Benares, was pouring forth his mystic raptures over the loves of Rādhā and Krishna, a new line of conquerors, whose song was the "Song of the Sword," and whose love was a love for plunder and the firebrand, was biding its time until all things were prepared for the raid on Hindustān, and capture of Agra, where all of the army were to gain presents in silver and gold, in cloth, in jewels, and in captive slaves.[1]

In 1526, Bābar, "The Lion," fifth in descent from Timur, or Tamerlane who had conquered Kābul in 1504, received an invitation from the contending rulers of the north-west to enter India with his Turkī hordes, and proclaim himself Emperor of Hindustān.

Bābar and his hardy troops soon swarmed down through the Khaibar Pass, and on the fatal field of Panipat broke in pieces the forces of the last king of the Lodi dynasty. The new emperor, in his "Memoirs," narrates how this, his fifth invasion, was crowned with success :—

"In consideration of my confidence in Divine Aid, the most High God did not suffer the distress and hardships I had undergone to be thrown away, but defeated my formidable enemy and made me the conqueror of the noble country of Hindustān. This success I do not ascribe to my own strength, nor did this good fortune flow from my own efforts, but from the fountain of the favour and mercy of God."[2]

Though the rule of Bābar and his descendants is known

[1] Holden, E., "Mughal Emperors," p. 87.
[2] Leyden, John, "Memoirs of Bābar," p. 310.

as that of the Mughals, Bābar himself, as descended from Tamerlane, was a Turk, and, although his mother was a Mughal, he speaks of that race with disdain and contempt, as composed of wretches who plundered foes and allies alike :—

> "If the Mughal race were a race of angels, it is a bad race.
> And were the name Mughal written in gold, it would be odious.
> Take care not to pluck one ear of corn from a Mughal's harvest.
> The Mughal seed is such that whatever is sown with it is execrable." [1]

Bābar, having overthrown the power of the Lodi king, found that, beyond the immediate neighbourhood of Delhi, Hindu princes and Afghān governors and garrisons held independent rule over such lands as yielded revenue, while the outlying tracts were left at the mercy of marauding bands, and of such petty chieftains as were capable of raising themselves to power. Thus, when in 1526 Bābar reached the Chenab, he recorded how

> "Every time that I have entered Hindustān, the Jāts (of the Panjāb) and the Gujyars have regularly poured down in prodigious numbers from their hills and wilds in order to carry off oxen and buffaloes. These were the wretches that really inflicted the chief hardships, and were guilty of the severest oppression on the country. These districts, in former times, had been in a state of revolt and yielded very little revenue that could be come at. On the present occasion, when I had reduced the whole of the neighbouring districts to subjection, they began to repeat their practices. As my poor people were on their way from Siālkot to the camp, hungry and naked, indigent and in distress, they were fallen upon by the road, with loud shouts, and plundered." [2]

Bābar's own views of the country, its religions and people, show how he and his race came to the land as much foreigners as the succeeding European adventurers. His

[1] Leyden, J. "Memoirs of Bâbar," p. 93.
[2] *Ibid.*, p. 294.

accounts read almost as though they were the superficial observations of some stray traveller of to-day :[1]—

"Most of the natives of Hindustān are Pagans. They call the Pagan inhabitants of Hindustān, Hindus. Most of the Hindus hold the doctrine of transmigration. The officers of revenue, merchants, and work-people, are all Hindus. In our native countries, the tribes that inhabit the plains and deserts have all names, according to their respective families; but here everybody, whether they live in the country or in villages, have names according to their families. Again, every tradesman has received his trade from his forefathers, who for generations have all practised the same trade. Hindustān is a country that has few pleasures to recommend it. The people are not handsome. They have no idea of the charms of friendly society, of frankly mixing together, or of familiar intercourse. They have no genius, no comprehension of mind, no politeness of manner, no kindness or fellow-feeling, no ingenuity or mechanical invention in planning or executing their handicraft works, no skill or knowledge in design or architecture; they have no good horses, no good flesh, no grapes or musk-melons, no good fruits, no ice or cold water, no good food or bread in their bazars, no baths or colleges, no candles, no torches, not a candlestick."

His "Memoirs" give a vivid picture of the times in his famed siege of Chānderi, one hundred and thirty-five miles south of Agra. He describes the despairing valour of the garrison in words which recall the incident so proudly sung of in the Rājput ballads :—

The troops likewise scaled the walls in two or three places. In a short time the Pagans, in a state of complete nudity, rushed out to attack us, put numbers of my people to flight, and leaped over the ramparts. Some of our people were attacked furiously and put to the sword. The reason of this desperate sally from their works was, that on giving up the place for lost, they had put to death the whole of their wives and women, and having resolved to perish, had stripped themselves naked, in which condition they had rushed out to the fight, and engaging with ungovernable desperation, drove our people along the ramparts. Two or three hundred Pagans . . . slew each other

[1] Leyden, J., "Memoirs of Bābar," pp. 332-33.

in the following manner: One person took his stand with a sword in his hand, while the others, one by one, crowded in and stretched out their necks, eager to die. In this way many went to hell; and by the favour of God, in the space of two or three hours, I gained this celebrated fort.'[1]

One short couplet of Bābar sums up the sentiments that inspired the fierce valour of the new-come, hardy Northern warriors, in their contests with the gentler and less physically capable Hindus of the East and South.

> "Let the sword of the world be brandished as it may,
> It cannot cut one vein without the permission of God."[2]

His remark to his son on the subject of style in letter-writing, shows how much sympathy Bābar himself would have had for the sensuous languor, the musical cadence of word and rhythm, the use of brilliant metaphor and startling allegory so loved by all Hindu poets. In writing to his son, Humāyūn, Bābar records with all the frankness and unpleasing truth of a Cobbett: "You certainly do not excel in letter-writing, and fail chiefly because you have too great a desire to show your acquirements. For the future you should write unaffectedly, with clearness, using plain words which would cost less trouble, both to the writer and reader."[3]

Bābar had but short time to do more than extend his rule from Multān to Behar. He died in 1530, leaving an empire which extended from "the River Amu in Central Asia, to the borders of the Gangetic delta in Lower Bengal."[4] His son Humāyūn, after a troubled reign, from 1530 to 1556, during which he was driven from India by the previous Afghān settlers under Sher Shāh, the Governor of Bengal, left the task of founding and consolidating the Mughal rule to his son and successor, Akbar.

During the long and glorious reign of Akbar (1556-1605), coinciding almost with that of Elizabeth in England, India, for the first time, saw hopes that her varied peoples,

[1] Leyden, J., "Memoirs of Bābar," p. 377. [2] *Ibid.*, p. 415.
[3] *Ibid.*, p. 392. [4] Hunter, "Indian Empire," p. 344.

divided as they were one from the other by race, language, creed, and customs, might, under one sole ruler, tolerant of all beliefs, and setting forth as his ideal the principle that "every class of the community enjoys prosperity,"[1] lay aside their differences, unite and acknowledge "the suzerainty of one prince who would protect and not persecute."[2]

From first to last the endeavour of Akbar, with the aid of his friend and biographer, Abul Fazl, was to reconcile the contending claims of rival creeds and of varied races that clamoured for recognition in the body politic. Hindus and Muhammadans were employed alike. To win the allegiance of the Rājput princes he intermarried with their daughters. No one was persecuted for conscience sake, and India obtained what it had never before possessed, some hope that union, peace, and prosperity might be secured within its borders. Akbar, in the words of one of the most brilliant historians of India, "had convinced his own mind that the old methods were obsolete; that to hold India by maintaining standing armies in the several provinces, and to take no account of the feelings, the traditions, the longings, the aspirations of the children of the soil—of all the races in the world the most inclined to poetry and sentiment, and attracted by the strongest ties that can appeal to mankind to the traditions of their forefathers—would be impossible."[3]

He early abolished the poll tax imposed by former Muhammadan rulers on those of their subjects who did not follow the faith of Muhammad. In the same year he put an end to the inland tolls which each semi-independent local governor had levied on the confines of the separate provinces. He further relinquished a lucrative source of revenue by refusing to continue the imposition of the pilgrim tax on Hindus whose religion necessitated the

[1] "Ain-i-Akbari," quoted in Holden's "Mogul Emperors."

[2] Malleson, "Akbar" (Ruler of India Series), p. 98.

[3] *Ibid.*, p. 154.

performance of pilgrimages to holy shrines, temples, and sacred bathing-places.

There were, however, Hindu customs and ancient rites which Akbar, tolerant as he was, refused to recognise. These he strove vehemently to suppress, and by his efforts and laws forestalled the British Government in some of the most important enactments by which its administration has been signalised. He put an end to the time-honoured custom of making slaves of those captured during war. He made the re-marriage of widows legal, forbade infant marriage, and prohibited, unless the act was voluntary on the woman's part, the practice of Satī, or the burning of a widow on her husband's death.

In his efforts to form a state religion, wide enough to be acceptable to all his subjects, he was actuated by the spirit that had already given rise to the teaching of Kabīr, and was to infuse the army of the Khālsā with a bond of Sikh unionism.

He directed his "king of poets," and friend Faizī,[1] the brother of Abul Fazl, to prepare a translation of the New Testament into Persian, and his historian, Abul Kādir Badaunī, the author of the "Tarikh-i-Badaunī," to translate the "Rāmāyana," and part of the "Mahābhārata."

To strict Muhammadans Akbar was an apostate from the true dictates of his own religion. In his efforts to frame a religion eclectic enough for both Muhammadans and Hindus, he went so far as to erase the name of Muhammad from the creed, "There is but one God, and Muhammad is His Prophet." He himself was to be the declarer of the more merciful decrees of the one God, and he was to be the sole arbitrator in religious matters and the source of all legislation.

[1] Raja Birbāl was the Hindu Poet Laureate, and Faizī, the Persian Laureate.—Blochmann, "Ain-i-Akbari," p. 404 (*note* 1). "Faizī also translated the 'Līlāwatī,' and Abul Fazl the 'Kalīlah Damnah.'"—*Ibid.*, p. xvii.

The full meaning and result of this design of Akbar is set forth in the introduction to Blochmann's translation of the "Ain-i-Akbari, or Account of the Religion, Politics, and Administration of the Times," by Abul Fazl:—

> "If Akbar felt the necessity of this new law, Abul Fazl enunciated it and fought for it with his pen; and if the Khān Khānāns gained the victories, the new policy reconciled the people to the foreign rule; and whilst Akbar's apostasy from Islām is all but forgotten, no emperor of the Mughal dynasty has come nearer to the ideal of a father of his people than he. The reversion, on the other hand, in later times to the policy of religious intoleration, whilst it has surrounded, in the eyes of the Moslems, the memory of Aurangzīb with the halo of sanctity, and still inclines the pious to utter a 'May God have mercy on him,' when his name is mentioned, was also the beginning of the breaking-up of the empire."[1]

Although Akbar encouraged Brāhmans, Mussalmans, Jews, Parsis, and Christians, to proclaim freely before him their creeds, beliefs, and faiths, and although tradition tells, though perhaps on no strong evidence, that one of his wives was a Christian, still the task to which he had set his hand was one impossible to accomplish. His desire to see good in every religion and good in every man, his very tolerance and efforts to extract the best from every faith, left him indifferent to the carping distinctions of dogmas and creeds.

For himself he fashioned forth an eclectic creed of his own. Not only did he bow down before the Sun, as the representative and ruler of the Universe, but he claimed for himself the homage and adoration of his subjects—a worship which strict Muhammadans held to be due to God alone. As a result, the bigotry of Muhammadanism led to the assassination of Abul Fazl, and, on the death of Akbar, the contending interests of rival religions and races broke forth afresh with a vigour and animosity renewed from their long slumber.

[1] Blochmann, "Ain-i-Akbari," p. xxix. (Introd.).

Akbar's own Poet Laureate Birbāl, was a Brāhman Bhāt, or minstrel of Kālpī, whose wise sayings and *bon-mots* are still remembered in North India.[1] In 1583 Birbāl was sent to fight against the Yūsufzaīs, and there, to the grief of his devoted friend, Akbar, met his death. The poet gained the lasting hate of all orthodox Muhammadans for the part he was supposed to have taken in influencing the emperor to forsake Islām.

Badauni, the historian, in recording the defeat of the army, the severest defeat suffered by Akbar, grimly says:—

> "Nearly eight thousand men, perhaps even more, were killed. Birbāl also, who had fled from fear of his life, was slain, and entered the row of the dogs in hell, and thus got something for the abominable deeds he had done during his life-time."[2]

The same historian, while narrating the events of the year 1588, mentions:—

> "Among the silly lies—they border on absurdities—which, during this year, were spread over the country, was the rumour that Birbāl, the accursed, was still alive, though in reality he had then for some time been burning in the seventh hell. The Hindus, by whom His Majesty is surrounded, saw how sad and sorry he was for Birbāl's loss, and invented the story that Birbāl had been seen in the hills of Nagarkot, walking about with Jogīs and Sannāsīs. His Majesty believed the rumour, thinking that Birbāl was ashamed to come to court on account of the defeat which he had suffered at the hands of the Yusūfzaīs; and it was, besides, quite probable that he should have been seen with Jogīs, inasmuch as he had never cared for the world."[3]

What shape the course of Indian history might have taken had the Mughal dynasty produced a successor worthy of Akbar is now impossible to foresee. He himself, it is said, had designed his tomb to be crowned with a dome.[4] Perhaps he foresaw in the early death of

[1] Blochmann, "Ain-i-Akbari" p. 404; Grierson, "Literature of Hindustān," p. 35.

[2] *Ibid.*, p. 204.

[3] *Ibid.*, p. 404.

[4] Purchas, "His Pilgrims," vol. i. p. 440, quoted by Fergusson, p. 587.

his sons, and the debaucheries of the heir-apparent, Prince Salīm, who had instigated the assassination of Abul Fazl, the speedy decay of the empire, and left his design uncompleted, dreaming, as he is pictured by the late Poet Laureate:—

> "I watch'd my son
> And those that follow'd, loosen stone from stone
> All my fair work; and from the ruin arose
> The shriek and curse of trampled millions, even
> As in times before; but while I groan'd
> From out the sunset poured an alien race
> Who fitted stone to stone again, and Truth,
> Peace, Love, and Justice came and dwelt therein."

There is no evidence that the hopes of Akbar would have been realised even if his work had been continued by successors gifted with a genius equal to his own. The rule of the earlier Muhammadan emperors had shown how impossible it was to keep the land from being turned into a battle-field whereon the rival claims of divided chieftains, princes, and robber bands should be for ever contested and never finally placed at rest.

Guzarāt, in the West, had thrown off the authority of the Delhi Sultan, and remained an independent kingdom, from 1371 to 1573, gaining strength to include, in 1531, within its dominions the territories of the adjoining ruler of Mālwā. Even the independent Muhammadan state of Jaunpur, which included Benares, the sacred city of the Hindus, continued independent from 1393 to 1478. In the South the kingdom of Vijayanagar, until overthrown at the battle of Talikot, in the middle of the sixteenth century by the Muhammadan rulers of the Deccan, held independent rule from its ancient capital, whose ruins now lie scattered along the banks of the Tangabhadra, and the last of its kings had authority enough to grant the site of Madras to the English in 1639.

More convincing still of the impossibility of a native central authority being able to preserve touch with all the outlying states of India, and to conquer and compel the allegiance of, or to conciliate, the varied races and nationalities, is the fact that, on the break up of the great Bahmani dynasty, which exercised independent rule over the Deccan from the middle of the fourteenth century to the end of the sixteenth century, the five great Muhammadan governorships, with their capitals at Bijāpur, Golconda, Bīdar, Ahmadnagar, and Ellichpur, founded dynasties known as those of the Adil Shāhī, Katb Shāhī, Barīd Shāhī, Nizām Shāhī, and Imad Shāhī, and preserved sovereign independence until overthrown, the first four by Aurangzīb, and the last two, which had united in 1572, by Shāh Jahān in 1636.

The whole of the difficulties of the situation are indicated in the summing-up, by Sir W. Wilson Hunter,[1] of the results attained by the early Muhammadan rulers at Delhi, where he shows how "they completely failed to conquer many of the great Hindu kingdoms, or even to weld the Indian Muhammadan state into a united Muhammadan empire."[2]

By the time of the death of Bābar, Muhammadan rule had shown no sign of obtaining a permanent abiding-place in India. In 1541, Humāyūn was a fugitive in Sind, and returned not to Delhi until 1554, and then only for a few months' reign.

Four years later, when Akbar came to the throne, Benares, Behar, and Bengal were independent, and India, South and West, was beyond the limits of his empire. It was not until he had reigned almost twenty years, that all

[1] "Indian Empire," p. 343.

[2] In the fourteenth century Muhammad Tughlak had conquered the Deccan, but at his death the Afghān dynasty of the Bahmani kings, whose possessions, at the close of the fifteenth century, were divided into the five kingdoms of the Deccan, assumed possession.

India north of the Vindhyas, and Orissa, acknowledged his sway. After subduing Berar and capturing Ahmadnagar in the Deccan, he had to be content with tribute and vows of friendship from the kings of Bījapur and Golconda.

The spirit of Akbar's time and genius has its memorial written imperishably in stone, in the tomb built for him at Sikandra. In itself, it typifies the limit reached by Muhammadan and Hindu compromise.[1]

The tomb, like Akbar's eclectic religion, represents the conception his master-mind had worked out, of a reconciliation of all racial and religious difference, so that the best that India held of valour and genius might unite to rule the land for the benefit of all, and evolve in peace and rest new ideals of law and order.

The early Muhammadan architecture, like its rule, was essentially foreign to the people, and to the soil of India. The dynasty of Ghor built its mosques with high front walls, overlapping courses and ogee-pointed arches. The dynasty of Khiljī lapsed into horse-shoe arches and elaborate decoration, while the house of Tughlak stamped the impress of its heavy hand on its great sloping walls, plastered dome, and pointed stucco arches. The commencement of the rule of the Mughals was marked by their own peculiar style, as seen in the tall Persian domes and glazed tiles of the tomb of Humāyūn. During the long reign of Akbar, the compromise with the Hindu architecture ran parallel with the development of Akbar's eclectic religion and philosophic systems, the Hindu bracket and horizontal style of building leading gradually to the disappearance of the arch. The great fort and palace at Agra, and the

[1] "A design borrowed, as I believe, from a Hindu or, more correctly, Buddhist model."—Fergusson, "Ind. Architecture," p. 583. "The consequence is a mixture throughout all his works of two styles, often more picturesque than correct, which might, in the course of another half century, have been blended into a completely new style if persevered in."—Fergusson, p. 574.

magnificent ruins at Fatehpur Sīkri tell the spirit of Akbar's reign as distinctly as do the "Ain-i-Akbari" of Abul Fazl, the history of Badaunī, or the "Tabākat-i-Akbari" of Nizām-ud-dīn-Ahmad.

The builders of the Mosque of Katb-ud-dīn at Delhi had razed the Hindu temples to the ground, hewn the idolatrous decorations from the stately pillars, and then used them as supports for their own arched colonnades. The tombs of the Ghori Altamsh and his son, the great majestic south gateway of the Katb Mosque, the Tughlak Mosque of Khān Jahān at Delhi, and the later Afghān Kila Kona Mosque at Indrapat, as well as the tall, domed tomb of Humāyūn, all stand forth uncompromising, in their stern severity and strict adhesion to their own ideals and purposes. The palaces of Akbar, the ruins of his buildings at Fatehpur Sīkri, and his own tomb, show, step by step, the weakening of the vigour, and simplicity of the foreign influence, the drooping of the fanaticism and intolerant spirit of Muhammadanism, until, finally, the palaces and tombs, with their pictured mosaics and lavish decorations, of the luxurious and pleasure-loving sensualist, Shāh Jahān, tell not of a tolerance, but of an indifference and submission to the bondage of climatic influence, which all the bigotry and fanatic Muhammadanism of Aurangzīb could not strive against. There were elements of danger and decay underlying the whole of this spirit of toleration. The climate was quickly producing its enervating effect on the rude and rough soldiers who had won Bābar his empire. From beyond the frontiers no new recruits were coming to preserve the pristine vigour of the ancestors of Aurangzīb. Bījapur and Golconda had yet to be conquered. The Marāthas, in their mountain homes, were a race waiting to rise to power, defy the whole army of Aurangzīb, and sorely try the valour of British troops. The proud Rājputs would support an Akbar who respected their chivalry and honour, yet their aid could easily be turned into defiance. The great general of Akbar, Bhagavan Dās, the Rāja of Jaipur, gave his daughter to the Mughal Emperor, and bears a name among the Rājputs which is still "held in execration, as the first who sullied Rājput purity by matrimonial alliance with the Islāmite."[1] The successor of Akbar, born the son of a Rājput princess, continued more from indifference than toleration the policy of his father, a policy followed by Shāh Jahān, also the son of a Rājput princess, daughter of the Rājā of Marwar. The intolerance and bigotry of Aurangzīb, however, roused the Rājputs to rebellion, and Hinduism showed its power and strength when the stiff-necked Aurangzīb imposed again the odious poll tax, and gave orders "to all governors of provinces to destroy, with a willing hand, the schools and temples of the infidels, and . . . to put an entire stop to the teaching and practising of idolatrous forms of worship."[2] The effete Mughals were left to continue their work of the conquest of the South, with new forces rising around them on all sides, threatening to sweep away the structure already undermined and sapped of its strength.

Brāhmanism remained with its undying vitality of intellectual life to continue its own course unmoved. The glorious reign of Akbar had seen an outbreak of native genius that, in its own lines, rivals that seen in England in Elizabethan times. In his days, his great finance minister, Todar Mal, a Kshatriya of Oudh, not only wrote vernacular poems himself on morals (*nīti*),[3] but translated the "Bhagavata Purāna" into Persian, to induce the Hindus to learn that language, in which he ordered that all government accounts should be kept, a

[1] Malleson, "Akbar," p. 182, quoting Tod's "Rajasthan."
[2] Quoted in S. Lane-Poole's "Aurangzīb," p. 135.
[3] Grierson, "Vernac. Lit. of Hindustān," p. 35.

determination that soon gave rise to the new Urdū dialect.

Typical of the time is the story of Hari Nāth, a poet who, having received one lakh of rupees from Mān Singh for one verse, and two lakhs from another prince for two verses, met, on his way home, "a mendicant of the Nāgā sect, who recited a śloka to him, at which he was so pleased that he gave the beggar all the presents he had collected and returned home empty-handed."[1]

The two poets who stand forth as shining stars of the period were the blind bard, Sūr Dās, and the greater poet, Tulsi Dās, whose life and work extended into the reign of Jahangīr. Mr Grierson, whose every word in criticism is weighed and uttered after a thorough and unique mastery of his subject in all its bearings, classes the master-pieces of Sūr Dās and Tulsi Dās as not far behind the work of Spenser and Shakespeare. These two names in themselves would have made the reign of Akbar the most renowned in the history of Indian literature since the days of Kālidāsa. Sūr Dās, the blind bard of Agra, sang of the faith in Krishna, in his "Sūr Sagar,"—said to contain sixty thousand verses[2]—as the deity to whom he was devoted, and who, according to popular tradition, appeared and wrote down the verses as the blind poet spoke them. The story goes that the poet, finding that his amanuensis wrote faster than his own thoughts flew, seized the deity by the hand and was thrust away, on which the poet wrote a verse declaring that none but the deity himself could tear the love of Krishna from his heart:—

> "Thou thrustest away my hand and departest, knowing that I am weak, pretending that thou art but a man,
> But not till thou depart from my heart will I confess thee to be a mortal."[3]

[1] Grierson, "Literature of Hindustān," p. 39. [2] *Ibid.*, p. 24 (*note* 3).
[3] *Ibid.*, p. 24 (*note* 4).

Referring to verses[1] of the later poet, Bihārī Lāl, who sang, in his incomparable seven hundred lyric couplets in the Braj Bāshā, near Mathurā, the same mystic raptures over the loves of Rādhā and Krishna as did Sūr Dās, Mr Grierson[2] has happily expressed himself, with no uncertain meaning, as to the importance of a correct appreciation of Eastern mysticism within its proper limitations. Dealing first with the Christian expression of love to God, and the answering love of God for his creatures, the Eastern mode of thought is then fearlessly put forward in words that must be weighed by all who would read the native mind:—

> "Hence the soul's devotion to the deity is pictured by Rādhā's self-abandonment to her beloved Krishna, and all the hot blood of Oriental passion is encouraged to pour forth one mighty flood of praise and prayer to the Infinite Creator, who waits with loving, outstretched arms to receive the worshipper into his bosom, and to convey him safely to eternal rest across the seemingly shoreless Ocean of Existence. . . . Yet I am persuaded that no indecent thought entered their minds when they wrote these burning words; and to those who would protest, as I have often heard the protest made, against using the images of the lupunar in dealing with the most sacred mysteries of the soul, I can only answer:—
>
> 'Wer den Dichter will verstehen
> Muss in Dichters Lande gehen.'"[3]

A deeper, though less mystic, expression of the deep religious broodings of the people was given by Tulsi Dās in his rendering of Valmikī's "Rāmāyana," a work in which he showed the latent powers of Eastern dramatic genius.

The drifting of the soul and self into a mystic dream of ecstatic union with the throbbing life that beats throughout the universe had found in India a congenial resting-place

[1] For 1617-1667. For the "Sapta Śatikā" of Hāla, *see* Von Schrader, "Ind. Literature," 575.

[2] The remarks of Mr Grierson in his Introduction to the edition of the "Satsaiya of Bihari," by Śri Lallu Lal Kavi (Calcutta, 1896), were unfortunately received too late for more than reference here.

[3] Grierson, "Satsaiya" (Introd.), p. 8.

in the spiritualising by Jaya Deva of the pastoral loves of Rādhā and Krishna. This phase of thought rose to its culminating point in the raptures of such great mystics of the Middle Ages as Vallabhā, Mira Bai, and Bidyāpāti, and the greater poets of Akbar's days such as Krishna Dās and the blind bard, Sūr Dās. A love and faith in Rāma, a more human and heroic figure than that of Krishna, and the love of Sītā, a more perfect and womanly love than that of Rādhā, were the themes that inspired Ramānand, Kabīr, and the great master poet of North India, Tulsi Dās.

The Western mode of estimating the value and influence of the work is given in the words of Mr Grierson:—"Pandits may talk of 'Vedas' and of the 'Upanishads,' and a few may even study them; others may say they pin their faith on the 'Purānas,' but to the vast majority of the people of Hindustān, learned and unlearned alike, their sole norm of conduct is the so-called 'Tulsi krit-Rāmāyan.'"[1]

The real title of the famed work is the "Rāma Charit Mānas," or "Sea of Wanderings of Rāma." It was commenced in 1574, but the date of its completion is unknown. Tulsi Dās, however, died in 1624 A.D. Rāma represents the Supreme Being, through faith in whom all intuition of Self fades away, leaving the soul in a trance-like ecstasy to sink into placid oneness with the deity's own true nature, the Universal Essence from which proceeded all Creation.

The poem of Tulsi Dās was founded on the story of Rāma and Sitā, as told in the second great epic of India, the "Rāmāyana" of Vālmīki. In the well-known "Bhaktā Mālā," or "Legends of the Saints," by Nābhā Dās, giving, in a hundred and eight verses, a short account of the Vaishnavite poets who flourished in the sixteenth and seventeenth centuries in Hindustān, one verse being given to each poet, it is declared that the pronunciation of a

[1] Grierson, "Literature of Hindustān," p. 43.

single letter of the "Rāmāyana" of Vālmīki, written as it was in the Treta Age for the salvation of mankind, would suffice to save from all sin, even that of Brāhman murder. In the same "Legends of the Saints," Vālmīki is said to have appeared again on earth, in this the vile Kāli Age, in the person of Tulsi Dās, so that a new "Rāmāyana" might be constructed to lead mankind, as if in a boat, across the ocean of endless births and re-births.

In the "Rāmāyana" of Vālmiki, Rāma was the son of Daśaratha, King of Ayodhya of the Solar dynasty. As the king for long had no son, a great horse sacrifice was performed, and the gods thus propitiated. Rāma was born to the king's first wife, Kauśālyā, Bhārata to the second wife, Kaikeyī, and Lakshmana and Śatrughna to the third wife, Sumitrā.

Rāma, who possessed in the epic half the essence of Vishnu, while still a youth, bent the wondrous bow of Śiva, kept by Janaka, King of Videha, and, by doing so, won as his reward the king's daughter, Sītā, the type of ideal love and womanly grace. Through the intrigues of Kaikeyī, who desired the kingdom for her son, Bhārata, Rāma was banished by his father, King Daśaratha, from Ayodhya. During the sojourn of Rāma and Sītā in the forest retreat, Rāvana, the demon king of Lanka, bore off Sītā to his island home where he in vain sought to win her love. The recovery of Sītā by Rāma and his ally, Sugrīva, King of the Monkeys, who built the bridge of Rāma and burned down the stronghold of the demon, Rāvana, has been held as the metaphorical rendering of the Aryan conquest of South India and Ceylon, the monkeys representing the aboriginal inhabitants. The epic finds its fitting close in the return of Rāma and Sītā to Ayodhya, and their coronation as king and queen.

The story, however, is continued in a seventh book, dramatised by Bhavabhūti in his "Uttara-Rāma-Charitra," where Rāma hears of the lying rumour spread among his subjects of Sitā's submission to the love of Rāvana. Rāma, though he knew the falseness of the rumour, held that a king's first duty was the care of his subjects, so he banished Sītā from his kingdom, loth to have her share his throne until all suspicion had been set at rest. In the end he and Sītā found once more reunion and passed to final rest.

The rendering of the epic story in the "Sea of Wanderings of Rāma," by Tulsi Dās, stands as an abiding landmark in the literary history of North India, for not only did it spread far and wide the doctrines of Rāmānand, and of a faith in Vishnu, but saved the people by the influence of its chastened style and purity of sentiment and thought from falling into the depths of that lewdness and obscenity towards which the realistic rendering of the mystic and spiritual loves of Rādhā and Krishna was ever tending, and reached in Tantric and Śaivite orgies.

The mission of Tulsi Dās was simply to set before the people of North India, in their own vernacular, the figure of Rāma as a personification of the underlying Essence of the Universe, as a revelation beyond the senses and reason, to be received with faith, and cherished with love and piety. In the commencement of his poem, Tulsi Dās deplores, in the orthodox manner, his own want of ability, genius, or even capacity, for the theme he has undertaken. He, however, proceeds with the task from the belief that even an enemy would turn from censure if so exalted a theme be told in clear style.[1]

In terms of mysticism he then calls on the reader to repeat and ponder over the name of Rāma, as symbolising more than mere form, as connoting all that shadows forth the path along which the soul must be led before every semblance of the material is spiritualised. By thus

[1] Growse, F. S., "Rāmāyana," p. 10.

fixing the thoughts, the soul "enjoys the incomparable felicity of God, who is unspeakable, unblemished, without either name or form."[1] In the first age of the world the poet declared that salvation was to be found in contemplation; in the second age, in sacrifices; in the third, Dvāpara Age, in worship in temples, "but in this vile and impure Iron Age, where the soul of man floats like a fish in an ocean of sin, in these fearful times, the name is the only tree of life, and by meditating on it, all commotion is stilled. In these evil days neither good deeds, nor piety, nor spiritual wisdom is of any avail, but only the name of Rāma."[2]

The deep sincerity of Tulsi Dās, the purest of all the poets of his day, in seeking this refuge for the longings of his soul, breaks forth in the words of Janaka, King of Videha, whose daughter, Sītā, is won by the warrior Rāma:—

> "O Rāma how can I tell thy praise, swan of the Mānas lake of the Saints and Mahādeva's soul, for whose sake ascetics practise their asceticism, devoid of anger, infatuation, selfishness, and pride; the all-pervading Brahman, the invisible, the immortal, the Supreme Spirit, at once the sum and negation of all qualities, whom neither words nor fancy can portray, whom all philosophy fails to expound, whose greatness the divine oracles declare unutterable, and who remainest the self-same in all times, past, present, or future. Source of every joy, thou hast revealed thyself to my material vision; for nothing in the world is beyond the reach of him to whom God is propitious."[3]

The true power of Tulsi Dās as a descriptive poet is shown in his treatment of the intriguing and crafty hunchback maid of Kaikeyī, the mother of Bhārata, who is led to demand, on the day when Rāma was to be installed as heir to his father's kingdom, the fulfilment of a vow made to her by the king, that her own son, Bhārata, should receive the inheritance, and that Rāma should be banished from

[1] Growse, F. S., "Rāmāyana," p. 15. [2] *Ibid.*, p. 18. [3] *Ibid.*, p. 167.

the kingdom for fourteen years. The whole poem must be read if any conception is to be obtained of its artistic unity and dramatic power—a power unequalled in the whole history of Indian literature.

The translation of Mr Growse happily preserves the spirit and the form of this almost new Indian mode of thought.

The handmaid of the queen Kaikeyī thus prepares the motive for the poem:[1]—

> "Taking Kaikeyī as a victim for the slaughter, the Humpback whetted the knife of treachery on her heart of stone, and the queen, like a sacrificial beast that nibbles the green sward, saw not the approaching danger. Pleasant to hear, but disastrous in their results, her words were like honey mingled with deadly poison. Says the handmaid: 'Do you or do you not, my lady, remember the story you once told me of the two boons promised you by the king? Ask for them now, and relieve your soul: the kingdom for your son, banishment to the woods for Rāma. Thus shall you triumph over all your rivals. But ask not till the king has sworn by Rāma, so that he may not go back from his word. If you let this night pass it will be too late; give heed to my words with all your heart.' . . . The queen thought Humpback her best friend, and again and again extolled her cleverness, saying: 'I have no such friend as you in the whole world; I had been swept away by the Flood but for your support. To-morrow, if God will fulfil my desire, I will cherish you, my dear, as the apple of mine eye.' Thus lavishing every term of endearment on her handmaid, Kaikeyī went to the dark room. Her evil temper being the soil in which the servant-girl, like the rains, had sown the seed of calamity which, watered by treachery, took root and sprouted with the two boons as its leaves, and in the end ruin for its fruit. Gathering about her every token of resentment, she undid her reign by her evil counsel. But meanwhile, the palace and city were given over to rejoicing, for no one knew of these wicked practices."

Rāma, with his wife Sītā, and his brother Lakshmana,

[1] Growse, F. S., "Rāmāyana," p. 191.

go for fourteen years as hermits to abide in the forests, where Rāma is represented as a mere man, yet, by his wisdom and heroic virtues, pointing out the path of duty and virtue by which such of his devotees, as might realise him as truly Divine, should pass over the sea of transmigration as if by a bridge. Lakshmana, as he watches Rāma and Sītā sleeping in the forest on their bed of leaves, declares the lesson to illustrate which the poem has been composed. The doctrine of the delusive unreality of all external form and appearance is first expounded, and then Lakshmana continues :—

> "Reasoning thus, be not angry with any one, nor vainly attribute blame to any. All are sleepers in a night of delusion, and see many kinds of dreams. In this world of darkness they only are awake who detach themselves from the material, and are absorbed in contemplation of the Supreme, nor can any soul be regarded as aroused from slumber till it has renounced every sensual enjoyment. Then ensues spiritual enlightenment and escape from the errors of delusion, and finally, devotion to Rāma. This . . . is man's highest good—to be devoted to Rāma in thought, word, and deed. Rāma is God, the totality of good, imperishable, invisible, uncreated, incomparable, void of all change, indivisible, whom the 'Veda' declares it cannot define. In his mercy he has taken the form of a man, and performs human actions out of the love he bears to his faithful people, and to earth, and the Brāhmans, and cows, and gods." [1]

Again, when the pilgrims visit Vālmīki [2] in his retreat in the forest, the ascetic sage declares that Rāma alone is lord over all gods; that man is but a puppet, playing the part allotted to him in the dream of life, not knowing the eternal truth until Rāma, by his grace, bestows knowledge so that all may become united with the deity, with Rāma himself, pure joy and bliss. This grace is only vouchsafed to those who simply love Rāma, and not to those who beg for favours. The love for Rāma is summed up in the

[1] Growse, F. S., "Rāmāyana," p. 223. [2] *Ibid.*, p. 238.

words: "Perish property, house, fortune, friends, parents kinsmen, and all that does not help to bring one to Rāma."[1]

The universal salvation held out by faith in Rāma to all classes of the people, irrespective of caste, is set forth in the words:—

> "Even a dog-keeper, the savage hill people, a stupid foreigner, an outcast, by repeating the name of Rāma becomes holy and renowned throughout the world[2] . . . for he is omniscient, full of meekness, tenderness, and compassion."[3]

The best of all that Hinduism holds is sublimely rendered in one grand hymn to Rāma:[4]—

> "I reverence thee, the lover of the devout, the merciful, the tender-hearted; I worship thy lotus feet which bestow upon the unsensual thine own abode in heaven. I adore thee, the wondrously dark and beautiful; the Mount Mandar to churn the ocean of existence; with eyes like the full-blown lotus; the dispeller of pride and every other vice; the long-armed hero of immeasurable power and glory, the mighty Lord of the three spheres, equipped with quiver, and bow, and arrows; the ornament of the Solar race; the breaker of Śiva's bow; the delight of the greatest sages and saints; the destroyer of all the enemies of the gods; the adored of Kāmadeva's foe (*i.e.* of Śiva); the reverenced of Brahmā and the other divinities; the home of enlightened intelligence; the dispeller of all error; Lakshmi's lord; the mine of felicity; the salvation of the saints. I worship thee with thy spouse and thy brother, thyself the younger brother of Sachi's lord. Men who unselfishly worship thy holy feet sink not in the ocean of existence, tost with the billows of controversy. They who, in the hope of salvation, with subdued passions, ever delightedly worship thee, having discarded every object of sense, are advanced to thy own sphere in Heaven. I worship thee, the one, the mysterious Lord, the unchangeable and omnipresent power, the eternal governor of the world, the one absolute and universal spirit; the joy of all men day after day. I reverently adore thee, the king of incomparable beauty, the lord of the earth-born Sītā; be gracious to me and grant me devotion to thy lotus feet."

[1] Growse, F. S., "Rāmāyana," 264. [2] *Ibid.*, 268.
[3] *Ibid.*, 271. [4] *Ibid.*, 335.

Under the indifferent tolerance of Jahangīr, the able, though drunken and debauched, son and successor of Akbar, this faith in the saving aid of Rāma was taught by Tulsi Dās in North India, by the disciples of Dādū,[1] a cotton cleaner of Ahmadabad, throughout Ajmere and Rājputāna.

The long and peaceful thirty years' reign of Shāh Jahān left to the country prosperity, and to the emperor, in his later days, wealth and leisure to build, at Delhi, his great fort and palace, and the stately Juma Musjid, or "Great Mosque." At Agra, the chastened beauties of the Gem and Pearl Mosques, the magnificence, pomp, and splendour of the palaces, long the wonder of the world for their mosaics set in precious stones, depicting flowers, and fruits, and birds, even human faces and figures, some the work of Italian or Florentine artists, the stories left by travellers of the Peacock Throne and its inlaid sapphires, rubies, pearls, and emeralds, all give evidence of the easy luxury of the times. The Tāj built by Shāh Jahān to his devoted wife, Muntāj Mahal, the mother of his fourteen children, remains, for the Mughals, the great memorial of how their fierce wrath and lust for war and plunder fell on gentle sleep in the soothing plains of India. On the death of Shāh Jahān, his vast treasures and empire fell to his third son, Aurangzīb, the ascetic saint and bigoted adherent of Islām. The new emperor, in his fanatic zeal for the Sunni faith, changed the Deccan from a Dār-al-Hab to a Dār-al-Islām, and by his poll tax on all Hindus, whose idolatry he hated, turned the Rājputs from supporters of his throne to sullen foes. The Sikhs he changed from caste followers of the meek and humble precepts of the "Ādi Granth" of their first Guru, Nānak, to a race of fiercest fighting men, who gave up all claim to caste,

[1] Founder of the Dādū Panthi sect, who worship Rāma from a Vedāntic standpoint.

so that, under their tenth Guru, Gōvind Singh, they might unite "to wreak bloody revenge on the murderers of his father, to subvert totally the Muhammadan power and to found a new empire upon its ruins."[1] By his cold contempt for Sivajī, "the Mountain Rat," he allowed the wily chieftain —the protector of all "Brāhmans and cows"—to weld the Marātha peasantry into roving bands of predatory soldiers with a burning religious zeal and hatred of Muhammadanism, until they grew into a power capable of exacting a tribute of one-fourth of all the revenue up to the limits of the English factory at Surāt,[2] away to the "Marātha ditch," which had to be dug around Calcutta as a defence against their raids.

While Aurangzīb wasted his strength and resources in futile efforts to reduce the last two strongholds of independent rule in South India, held by the representatives of the Katb Shāhi dynasty at Golconda, and the Adil Shāhi dynasty at Bījapur, the people of the Panjāb had welded themselves into a bond of the fiercest warriors the English ever met in India, while the Marāthas were laughing at the feeble efforts of the emperor to follow their quick course.

Nānak, the founder of the religious faith of the Sikhs, was born of Hindu peasant parents in the year 1469, at a village named Talvandī, on the banks of the Ravī, not far from Lahore. Following close on the lines of his predecessor Kabīr, a large number of whose verses are included in the "Ādi Granth," the first utterances of Nānak which stirred the fanatic fury of both Hindu and Muhammadans against him were: "There is no Hindū and no Musalman."[3] Of his real life but little is known. He is said to have visited Ceylon, thence returned home

[1] Trumpp, Ernest, "Ādi Granth," p. xc.

[2] Burned as far as the English factory by Sivajī in 1664.

[3] Trumpp, Ernest, "Ādi Granth," p. iv.

performed miracles, and to have been captured by the troops of Bābar, on the conquest of the Panjāb in 1524, and then to have been released.[1] Before his death, in 1538 A.D., he appointed his servant and disciple, Lahana, to succeed him as Guru in his teachings, though it was not until the time of the fifth Guru, Arjuna, that the writings of Nānak and his successors were collected into the "Sikh Ādi Granth," or Scriptures, held to be of Divine revelation. The system inculcated by Nānak, the first Sikh, was, in its essentials, that taught by the "Bhagavad Gīta," by Kabīr, and by Vedāntism.

It was the worship of One Supreme Being, manifesting itself in a plurality of forms, under the power of Māyā, or delusion, which produces the fallacious appearance of duality. To the Sikh, this Supreme Being was known as "Brahm, the Supreme Brahm, Paramesur, 'the Supreme Lord,' and especially Hari, Rām, Gōvind."[2]

> "All is Gōvind, all is Gōvind ; without Gōvind there is no other.
> As in one string there are seven thousand beads (so), is that Lord lengthwise and crosswise.
> A wave of water, froth, and bubble, do not become separate from the water.
> This world is the sport of the Supreme Brahm, playing about he does not become another."[3]

Like all Vedāntic and Eastern Pantheistic teaching the system of Nānak had no quarrel with Hindu idolatry and the gods of the Hindu Pantheon. The various forms in which the Supreme Being manifests itself as sport, through the delusion of Māyā, were, however, not to be mistaken for the real, uncreated, invisible, incomprehensible, and indescribable Essence:—

[1] Trumpp, "Ādi Granth," p. v.
[2] *Ibid.*, p. xcviii.
[3] *Ibid.*, p. xcix.

"Kabīr says: A stone is made the Lord, the whole world worships it.
Who remains in reliance on this, is drowned in the black stream."[1]

The position has been clearly put by Ernest Trumpp, the late learned translator of the "Ādi Granth"—a work no Sikh Guru could read until he had first prepared a grammar and dictionary of the old Hindu dialect, for, as he records, "the Sikhs, in consequence of their former warlike manner of life, and the troublous times, had lost all learning."[2] According to his view

"It is a mistake if Nānak is represented as having endeavoured to unite the Hindu and Muhammadan idea about God. Nānak remained a thorough Hindu, according to all his views, and if he had communionship with Musalmans, and many of these even became his disciples, it was owing to the fact that Sūfism, which all these Muhammadans were professing, was, in reality, nothing but a Pantheism, derived directly from Hindu sources, and only outwardly adapted to the forms of the Islām. Hindu and Muslim Pantheists could well unite together as they entertained essentially the same ideas about the Supreme; the Hindu mythology was not pressed on the Musalmans, as the Hindu philosophers themselves laid no particular stress upon it. On these grounds tolerance between Hindus and Turks is often advocated in the 'Granth,' and intolerance on the part of the Turks rebuked."[3]

The Nirvāna, or absorption of the Soul into the Supreme Essence, was to be obtained by meditation on, and repeating of, the name and qualities of the Supreme Being, Hari, which must be taught by the Sikh Guru:—

"After the true Guru is found, no wandering (in transmigration) takes place, the pain of birth and death ceases.
From the perfect word all knowledge is obtained, he (the disciple) remains absorbed in the name of Hari."[4]

[1] Trumpp, "Ādi Granth," p. cl.
[2] *Ibid.* (Preface), p. vi.
[3] *Ibid.*, p. ci.
[4] *Ibid.*, p. 95.

Devotion to the Guru and faith in his teachings, lead to the true knowledge of Brahman and the power of Māyā, whence flows freedom from all delusion of duality:—

> "In whose heart there is faith in the Guru:
> Into that man's mind comes Hari, the Lord.
> That devotee is heard of in the three worlds,
> In whose heart the One is.
> True is his work, true his conduct,
> In whose heart the True One is, who utters the True One with his mouth.
> True is his look, true his impression,
> That the True One exists, that his expansion is true.
> Who considers the Supreme Brahm as true:
> That man is absorbed in the True One, says Nānak."[1]

Though Nānak received all men without respect of caste, and claimed for himself no divinity, no sanctity of learning, the power placed in the hands of the Gurus soon led to their very deification as the form of the Supreme Being itself.

In the days (1581-1606) of the fifth Guru, Arjuna, the verses of Nānak, and the later saints and Gurus, were collected in the "Ādi Granth," as the guide to the people, whose hitherto voluntary contributions to the Guru were reduced to a form of regulated taxation. Arjuna himself grew in wealth; the Sikh faith spread fast throughout the Jāt population of the Panjāb, until at length the fears of Jahangīr were roused. The Guru was arrested, imprisoned at Lahore, and there, it is said, he died from torture and ill-treatment. Guru Har Gōvind (1606-1638), the son of Arjuna, roused the Sikh disciples to arms against the murderers of his father, and sent them forth to blackmail the local governors of the Mughal emperor, Shāh Jahān, and retaliate for the insults levied on the Sikh Gurus. The ninth Guru, Teg Bahādur (1664-1675), was seized by the fanatic, Aurangzīb, at Delhi, cast into prison, and there

[1] "Ādi Granth," p. 407.

cruelly tortured along with some Brāhmans, in hopes that they might consent to embrace the Muhammadan faith. The Guru in despair, and wearied of his tortures, bowed his head before the keen sword of a Sikh disciple, his companion in misfortune, sending word to his son, Gōvind Singh, the tenth and last Guru, to avenge his death:—

> "My strength is exhausted, fetters have fallen upon me, there is no means of escape left;
> Nānak says: Now Hari is my refuge, like an elephant he will become my helper."[1]

Guru Gōvind Singh first summoned from Benares some Brāhmans to prepare him for the course he had set before him—a religious war against Muhammadanism and Aurangzīb. The aid of Durgā, the blood-loving wife of Śiva, the favourite deity worshipped by Gōvind Singh, had first to be gained. One of his disciples offered himself as a sacrifice to Durgā, and on his head being presented to the goddess, it is fabled that she appeared and promised success to the sect of the Sikhs. Five more disciples offered themselves as further sacrifices. Sherbet, stirred by a two-edged dagger, was given them to drink. The Guru drank himself, his disciples followed, and all were thus initiated as the first members of the Khālsā, or "special property of the Guru." To every disciple the name of Singh, or "Lion," was given. Their vows were: Not to cut their hair, to carry a comb, a knife, and sword, and to wear breeches reaching to the knee. To gather in all the people into one united body opposed to Muhammadans, Gōvind Singh abolished caste, and wrote for his followers a "Granth" of his own to "rouse their military valour and inflame them to deeds of courage."[2]

Sivajī, the welder of the Marāthas of the Deccan and

[1] A couplet in the "Granth," written by Teg Bahādur, quoted by Thornton in J.R.A.S., vol. xvii. p. 393.

[2] "Ādi Granth," p. xci.

West Coast into a band of robbers and fierce fighting men, was wise enough to use the same power of religious enthusiasm for his own purposes. Crafty, fierce, and determined, he had early taken as his Guru the Brāhman Rāmadās, so that he might be the acknowledged champion of Brāhmanism against Islām.

For long the Marāthas had slumbered in peace, tilled their fields, and worshipped their idol, Vithobā,[1] whose praises the great emotional poet of the Marāthas, Tukā Rāma,[2] a Sūdra of Poona, sang in his five thousand hymns:—

> "Sing the song with earnestness, making pure the heart;
> If you would attain God, then this is an easy way.
> Make your heart lowly, touch the feet of saints,
> Of others do not hear the good or bad quality, nor think of them.
> Tukā says: Be it much or little, do good to others."[3]

The policy of Sivajī was not wholly the outcome of his cunning. Like all Hindus, he had his own strong religious convictions, and these inspired many of his actions. His power he professedly held as the gift of his Guru, Rāmadās. All his wealth and kingdom he placed at the feet of the Brāhman, and would only receive it back as a gift, holding himself as the disciple and servant of his Guru, a position indicated by the flag his horsemen carried, the "red ochre-coloured cloth worn by Sanyāsīs."[4] To Tukā Rāma, the Sūdra poet of the Marātha nation, he sent a message, accompanied by a retinue of servants, elephants, horses, and the state umbrella, begging the favour of a visit, only to receive back the answer from

[1] Dr Murray Mitchell, "Hinduism," p. 170, for an account of the deity who derives his name from standing on a brick, and described by Tukā as "beautiful is that object, upright on the brick, resting his hand on his loin."

[2] "Poems of Tukā Rāma," edited by Vishnu Parashurām Shāstrī Pandit (Bombay, 1869).

[3] Quoted from Sir A. Grant's translation in *Fortnightly Review* (1867).

[4] "Poems of Tukā Rāma," p. 16.

the preacher of a salvation to the Marātha nation, through a faith in Krishna, worshipped under the form of Vithoba :—

"Brahmā has created this Universe, making it the scene of his diversion and skill.
I observe an amiableness in thy letter which proves thee
A child of skilfulness, devout in faith and wise, with a heart devotedly loving thy spiritual guide.
The holy name 'Śiva' was rightly given thee, since thou art the throned monarch of the people, the holder of the strings of their destiny.

. . . .

What pleasure is there in paying a visit? The days of life are fleeting past.
Having known one or two duties which are the real Essence, I shall now live in my own delusion.
The meaning of the whole which will do thee good is this—God is the all-pervading soul in every created object.
Live with thy mind unforgetful of the all-pervading soul, and witness thyself in Rāmadāsa.
Blessed is thy existence on earth, O king, thy fame and praise extend over the three worlds."

Like all great reformers Tukā Rāma had to suffer bitter persecution :—

"It was well, O God, that I became bankrupt ; it was well that famine afflicted me.
The deep sorrow which they produced kept in me the recollection of thee, and made worldly pursuits nauseating to me.
It was well, O God, that my wife was a vixen ; it was well that I came to such a miserable plight among the people.
It was well that I was dishonoured in the world ; it was well that I lost my money and cattle.
It was well that I did not feel worldly shame ; it was well that I surrendered myself to thee, O God.
It was well that I made thy temple my abode, neglecting children and wife."

Being a Sūdra, Tukā Rāma had to win his way against Brāhmanic opposition, and by his preaching, singing, and simple life rouse the slumbering spirit of the Marātha nation. The potential force of such a movement is too often lost sight of by those who judge Indian life from a Western standpoint.

In the life of the poet[1] by a native scholar accustomed to Western modes of thought, and trained to a Western respect for historic accuracy, the living power of a force exercised by such a character as Tukā Rāma is clearly indicated by the estimation given of his influence on the movements of the time :—

> "By that inherent force of truth to triumph, and to outlive, and by that unforeseen and unexpected succour which the truly faithful and sincere receive from quarters unknown, call it miracle or anything else, Tukā Rāma and his poems outlived his persecutors and inculcated in the Marātha nation the great doctrine of 'Salvation by Faith.'"

It was Marātha daring, Rājput chivalry, and the stubborn heroism of Sikh soldiery that England had to meet before it conquered India, and the West may rest assured that the awakening of a spirit of revolt in India will be first presaged by a wide-spread religious movement, broad enough in its basis, and popular enough in its forms, to enrol the sympathies of the mass of the people. All other movements must fall to pieces for want of strength, unity, or cohesion, or motive power.[2]

When the unloved and worn-out king crept back to Ahmadnagar to die in 1707, after twenty-six years' weary efforts to hold the Deccan free from Marātha raids, he wailed forth, in a letter to his son, Azīm,[3] the sad downfall of all his hopes and the wreck of his empire :—

> "I am grown very old and weak, and my limbs are feeble. Many were around me when I was born, but now I am going alone.

[1] By Jānārdan Sakhārām Gādgil, B.A., prefixed to the "Poems of Tukā Rāma" (1869), p. 12.

[2] This was written before the Marātha outrages of Poona, towards the end of June. Much uneasiness might have been assuaged, and much hasty counsel ignored, if a wider insight into Indian life and history was more prevalent than it seems to be at present.

[3] Quoted in S. Lane-Poole's "Aurangzīb," p. 203.

I know not why I am, or wherefore I came into the world. I bewail the moments which I have spent forgetful of God's worship. I have not done well by the country or its people. My years have gone by profitless. God has been in my heart, yet my darkened eyes have not recognised His light. The army is confounded, and without heart or help even as I am. . . . Come what will, I have launched my bark upon the waters. Farewell!"

Not one hundred years later the English took from out the keeping of his Marātha captors, the blind Shāh Alam, "King of the World," and the feeble remnant of Mughal supremacy passed under British power. The tragedy was well played out. The relentless sword of Bābar was sheathed by Akbar, its handle set with precious gems, and the scabbard cased in velvet by Shāh Jahān. When Aurangzīb once more drew the blade to proclaim a Jihād, or "Holy War," against all infidels, he found that the fanatic faith that fired his soul would call on God in vain to brighten up the blade and steel the edge, for the might that clove a way for Bābar's Mughal hosts was not the arm of God, but the fierce Northern strength of race and clime that had long since passed away from the debauched and effeminate nobles and followers of Aurangzīb, who were left in their vain crusade without hope or help. India fell not from Mughal sway to the divided rule and contending claims of Rājput, Marātha, or Sikh; it fell to a power able to hold all North India, from Calcutta to Bombay, and all south of the Vindhya range, secure from inward strife of race, religion, caste, or sect; powerful enough to protect it from all foreign invasion, and wise enough never to allow its manhood to decay by long residence or settlement in a clime where race after race of Northern conquerors, Aryan, Pathān, Mughal, Turk, and Portuguese have sunk to soothing rest in the sun-steeped plains.

CHAPTER XV.

THE FUSING POINT OF OLD AND NEW.

EVERY ten years the Government of India presents to the House of Commons a statement of the "Moral and Material Progress and Condition of India" during the nine preceding years. A similar statement, presented annually, shows the progress and change made during the year under review.

These statements give a graphic description of the frontiers and protected states. They contain a detailed account of the administration, of the laws, legislation, litigation, and crime. They give full information regarding the sources of revenue, trade, commerce, and manufactures, the outlay on, and income from, public works, vital statistics, and sanitation, and include tables of net revenue and expenditure, as well as a short account of public instruction, literature, and the Press. The statements set forth the salient features of the administrative machinery working for the advancement of the material improvement of the community. It, however, remains a task outside the scope and limits of a Blue Book to discern and chronicle in how far a Western civilisation has wrought changes of a permanent character in the religious or moral feeling of the people, or infused a new intellectual life into the traditional modes of thought that had satisfied the brooding spirit of Brāhmanical and indigenous genius, so long overwhelmed by the sea of Muhammadan conquest.

In how far, it might be asked, would the people of India, if left to govern themselves, undisturbed by foreign invasion or internal anarchy, carry out the ideals of a progressive civilisation, working for the amelioration of the lot of mankind? Would commerce thrive, or would it drift into a condition where none of the agricultural produce would be forthcoming for exportation, in exchange for the manufactures, metals, hardware, etc., of the West? Would India submit to religious intolerance, and a corrupt administration, after having been accustomed to the impartiality and justice of a British rule? Would the great works of irrigation be neglected and allowed to fall into decay? Would railways, and all efforts for sanitary improvement be abandoned if bereft of Western control? Would famine be allowed to devastate the land, and no efforts be made for a widespread organised relief, or medical skill be no more forthcoming to combat the ravages of pestilence and disease? Would caste once again forge its bonds, and enslave the people? Would superstition regain its old sway, and customs, abhorrent to humanity, be honoured as in days of old? Would India, in fact, drift back into a stationary condition of society as the final outcome of three hundred years of Western effort for its moral and material progress, or has she had implanted in her anything of the vital principles of energetic strife for advance in the history of the nations of the world? It may be laid down as a truism, that nothing of permanent good that has once been brought into contact with the East will be wholly thrown away or rejected. The subtle brain of the Eastern will patiently, all too slowly for unimaginative and hasty

Westerns, sift everything, assimilate what it finally discerns to be best suited for its own purposes, ultimately accreting nothing to itself, which with its own unfailing instinct it feels to be antagonistic to the conditions whereby it has its own existence.

Difficult as the task must always be, even if for the greater part it be not altogether impossible, to ascertain in how far the literature, architecture, science, and religions of India have been moulded or impressed by foreign influences—Accadian, Macedonian, Scythian, Muhammadan, Mughal, or Portuguese—still more difficult is it to discriminate in how far British rule in India has worked towards implanting new ideals destined to advance the moral and intellectual condition of the people. At the present day the evidence is so evasive and slight, so localised and difficult to discern, that it must remain more a matter of opinion [1] and feeling, than of proof, as to how far the people of India have been influenced by the new world of thought opened up to the educated natives through the medium of English education. The surest evidence is to be found in the literature which the thought of the time has produced. If the best of that literature indicates that new modes of thought and expression have been created, it may with confidence be expected that such a literature is yet destined, not only to remain an inalienable possession of the people, but also to abide as an influence for furthering the intellectual and moral advancement of the community. The means taken by the British Government to advance the intellectual life of the people, and what has been recorded as a result in the literature of the country, can only be summarised and indicated. It must remain for the future

[1] Sir Alfred Lyall has recently held that: "To no foreign observer, therefore, are sufficient materials available for making any sure and comprehensive estimate of the general movement or direction of ideas during the last forty years." —*Nineteenth Century* (June 1897).

to disclose whether, as claimed by the natives themselves,

> "We are just accommodating ourselves to environment that has hitherto been so unfavourable to the development of creative power. Within a quarter of a century more we shall be quite at home in our surroundings. Our future is a glorious one. Let *nil desperandum* be our motto, and we shall yet show to the civilised world that we are not only apt and *facile* imitators, but that we have genius for original intellectual work, and that we can produce results that will even excel the past splendours of Hindu literature and art."[1]

or whether, as has been urged, the Indian genius is effete, and no signs have as yet come to show that an infusion of new life and thought has had any power to rouse it to creative purposes.

The world presents no problem more interesting or more momentous. On its solution depends in history the final judgment on the success of England's mission in the East. The entire industrial resources of modern scientific days, the best of the intellectual heritage handed down from Semitic, Grecian, and Roman genius, are borne to India from the West, and yet the result of all these forces seems to remain within the realm of doubt and controversy. The forces are those on which the future hopes of the world are founded, and India can no more refuse to bend before them, than the West can refuse to recognise and accept the returning gift of her long record of how humanity, in its rest and quiet, has wearily turned from all that Nature can bestow, and probably all that she can disclose of her deepest mysteries to the intelligence of man, for some solution of the problem that lies nearest and dearest to him—that of himself, and of his aspirations towards some ideal completeness of life.

As yet the long past that has culminated in a Western

[1] S. Satthianadhan, M.A., LL.D. (Cantab.), "What has English Education done for India?" *Indian Magazine and Review* (November 1896).

civilisation, still on its rapid progress towards strange changes, has but clashed with the dead inertia of an Eastern civilisation that drags its heavy weight of tradition, time-worn philosophies, creeds, and customs behind it, restraining all its best endeavours for progress and advance.

Only one hundred years ago, in 1797, Charles Grant presented to the Court of Directors a treatise, written in 1792, in which he laid down the truth that "although in theory it never can have been denied that the welfare of our Asiatic subjects ought to be the object of our solicitude, yet, in practice, this acknowledged truth has been but slowly followed up."[1] He further states that "we have been satisfied with the apparent submissiveness of the people, and have attended chiefly to the maintenance of our authority over the country, and the augmentation of our commerce and revenues, but have never, with a view to the promotion of their happiness, looked thoroughly into their internal state." He proposed a scheme for future guidance which included the gradual instruction of the people in English and their education, "let not the idea hastily excite derision, *progressively* with the simple elements of our arts, our philosophy, and religions." By the introduction of English into the business of Government, "wherein Persian is now used," it was hoped that the use of the language would by degrees become general; that habits of correct reasoning on natural phenomena would be inculcated, natural philosophy diffused, the art of invention promoted, and finally, Christianity would triumph over superstition, idolatry, and the universal depravity of the native population.

In 1781 Warren Hastings had given evidence of his statesmanship by founding the Calcutta Madrissa, or Muhammadan College, for the purpose of promoting the

[1] Syed Mahmoud, "Observations on the State of Society among the Asiatic Subjects of Great Britain, etc.," p. 11.

study of Arabic and Persian and the Muhammadan law, so as to educate natives for the Courts of Justice.[1]

Three years later Sir William Jones gave the inaugural discourse at a meeting of thirty gentlemen, called in Calcutta for the purpose of instituting a society for enquiring into the history, civil and natural, the antiquities, arts, sciences, and literature of Asia—a society established under the name of the "Asiatic Society." Warren Hastings was invited to be the first president, an honour he declined, whereon the office fell to Sir William Jones, who remained president down to his death, in 1794. In 1791, Mr Jonathan Duncan, Resident at Benares, endowed the Sanskrit College at Benares for the teaching of Hindu law, as well as Hindu literature.

The two Lithuanian and Danish Lutheran missionaries, Ziegenbalg and Plutschau, both sent out from the University of Halle in 1706 to the Danish Settlement at Tranquebar, had translated the Gospel of St Matthew into the dialect of Malabar as early as 1714.[2] The efforts of these missions were largely supported by the Society for Promoting Christian Knowledge, under whom Schwartz worked in Tanjore, founding the Tinnevelly Mission, from his arrival in 1750.

More important in its effects were the efforts made by the Baptists, whose first missionary, William Carey, landed in Bengal in 1794,[3] to be followed in 1799 by the two famed Baptist missionaries, Marshman and Ward, who

[1] "Previous to the enunciation of this view, Warren Hastings had, in 1773, summoned eleven Brāhmans to Calcutta, and directed them to compile a text comprising all the customs of the Hindus, so that it might be translated into Persian for the use of the Court, and he appointed Hindu and Muhammadan advisers to the European judges to expound the laws and customs of the people, the first movement for an intellectual understanding of the literature of India by the Company."—"Papers relating to the affairs of India" (General Appendix I.: Public, 1832).

[2] The translation of the Bible into Tamil was completed in 1725 by Schultze, the successor of Ziegenbalg.

[3] Hunter, "Indian Empire," p. 313.

found a safe refuge from the East India Company at the Danish Settlement at Serampūr, fifteen miles from Calcutta.[1] There their endeavours for the conversion and education of the natives in the vernaculars of the country continued in spite of the Despatch of the Court of Directors in 1808 (7th December), declaring their policy of strict neutrality in all matters religious, and in spite of the contempt thrown on their efforts at home.

In England[2] it was feared that any efforts at conversion would lead to insurrection and a risk to the Empire. It was also urged that if once the Hindu faith was undermined, no fresh principles of faith would be engrafted on the converted natives, who would become merely nominal Christians. In spite of all these discouragements Carey and Marshman cast their own type, and, in 1822, started the first vernacular newspaper in India, the *Samāchār Darpan*, the first[3] English newspaper, *Hicky's Gazetteer* having appeared in 1780.

The Bible was soon printed in twenty-six vernaculars, including Bengalī, Marāthī, and Tamil, and in 1801 Carey was appointed, by Lord Wellesley, Professor of Bengalī, Marāthī, and Sanskrit at the new college of Fort St William. There he continued his work, issuing numerous books from the press, including an edition of the "Rāmāyana" in three volumes, the "Mahābhārata," and a Bengalī newspaper, while at the same time he established upwards of twenty schools for the education of native children.[4]

[1] It was at this time also that H. J. Colebrooke, who had landed in 1782 as a writer in the Company's service in Bengal, commenced his series of contributions to the "Researches" of the Asiatic Society towards Oriental learning. In 1794 he produced his treatise on the duties of a "Faithful Hindu Widow," in connection with the controversy on Satī, followed in 1798 by his "Digest of Hindu Law," and in 1805 by his "Grammar," founded on the rules of Pānini.

[2] *Edinburgh Review*, 1808.

[3] *Contemporary Review*, vol. xxxvii. 458.

[4] R. C. Dutt, "History of the Literature of Bengal," p. 136.

The clear and patent evidence that a new spirit was working among the people was the appearance of the first great reformer and apostle of modern India. Ram Mohun Roy, who lived and died a Brāhman, was born in 1774 at Rādhānagar, in the district of Hughli. In his own village he read Persian, proceeded to Patna to learn Arabic, and thence to Benares to study, in Sanskrit, the "Upanishads," and "Vedānta." In 1790, at the age of sixteen, he produced—probably as much under Muhammadan influence as any other—a treatise antagonistic to the idolatrous religion of the Hindus,[1] in which he laid the first foundations of a prose literature in his own vernacular, that of Bengalī. As Ram Mohun Roy wrote himself:—

> "After my father's death I opposed the advocates of idolatry with still greater boldness. Availing myself of the art of printing, now established in India, I published various works and pamphlets against their (the advocates of idolatry) errors, in the native and foreign languages. . . . I endeavoured to show that the idolatry of the Brāhmans was contrary to the practice of their ancestors, and the principles of their ancient books."[2]

After three years spent in Thibet to study Buddhism, he returned home and commenced the study of English, a language he afterwards wrote with a grace, ease, and precision that led Jeremy Bentham to declare that he wished that the style of James Mill had been equal to it.[3]

In other phases of thought the unrest, the waking-up to face the increasing pressure of the West, was equally apparent and no less real. The literature of India at the commencement of the nineteenth century was, for the most part, religious, devoted to mystic raptures over Rāma and Krishna. What may be called a new impulse was given

[1] Max Müller, in "Biographical Essays," p. 15, doubts the authenticity of the book (*see note* 1).

[2] Carpenter, M., "Last Days in England of Ram Mohun Roy," p. 19.

[3] Dutt, R. C., "History of the Literature of Bengal," p. 149.

by the introduction of printing into India, about the beginning of the nineteenth century.

In 1803, Lallu Jī Lāl, by the advice of Dr John Gilchrist, wrote his "Prem Sāgar," printed in 1809, in a new language, Hindi, in which the Urdū of the camp[1] was taken as the model, with all its Persian and Arabic words omitted, their place being supplied by Sanskrit words, so that it could be used for prose of a literary character but not for poetry.

In Bengal, Ram Mohun Roy used the vernacular Bengalī for his prose writings, commencing in 1790 with his early essay against idolatry, but neither in this nor in his later writings on the "Vedānta," translations of the "Upanishads," in 1816 and 1817, and subsequent polemics on the subject of widow-burning, did the language show any adaptability for becoming a medium to express his views so clearly and gracefully as he was enabled to express them in his Sanskrit and English writings. He but showed that the vernaculars were capable of being used for literary prose purposes, for, before his time, they had been used merely for poetic effusions.

When Ram Mohun Roy commenced to write, few Europeans, and probably fewer natives in Bengal outside the Brāhman caste, knew anything of the ancient Vedic texts. Ram Mohun Roy wrote, in 1816, regarding the universal system of idolatry:—

> "Hindus of the present age, with very few exceptions, have not the least idea that it is to the attributes of the Supreme Being, as figuratively represented by shapes corresponding to the nature

[1] Urdū itself is the camp language, with its structure and grammar framed on that of the North Indian dialects; most of the substantives are foreign words, which were mostly Persian or Arabic when the language was used by the Muhammadans for literary purposes. When this Urdū is deleted of most of its foreign words, and words of common use from the local vernaculars are inserted, the *lingua franca* of all India, the Hindustāni is arrived at, a language of common use for speaking all over North India, and also largely in the South.—*See* Grierson, *Calcutta Review* (October 1895), p. 265.

of these attributes, they offer adoration and worship under the denomination of god and goddess."[1]

His mission was a wide one and ably he filled it. He had first to create a new prose literature, to raise his own vernacular to the dignity of a medium for inculcating among the uninstructed mass of the people not only what he found suited to his own national instincts in the learning of the West, but what he deemed worthy of preservation in the sacred writings of his own race.

The work of perfecting the use of Bengalī for literary purposes was carried on by Isvara Chandra Gupta, who started the monthly *Sambad Prabhakar* in 1830, a journal in which his own poetry, not of a very high order, as well as his prose translations from the Sanskrit, and lives of Bengali poets, appeared from time to time, along with the writings of a class of rising authors. In a Minute of 1811 Lord Minto had drawn public attention to the deplorable decay of literature in India, due to a want of patronage from either the princes, chieftains, rich natives, or the Government itself, and advised the establishment of colleges in various places for the restoration of Hindu science, and literature, and Muhammadan learning. At the renewal of the Company's Charter in 1814, for a further period of twenty years, it was enacted by Act 53, Geo. III. c. 155, that a sum of £10,000 should be allotted for "the revival and improvement of literature, and the encouragement of the learned natives of India, and for the introduction and promotion of the knowledge of the sciences among the inhabitants of the British territories in India."

[1] "That the early growth of the native Press was but slow, can be judged from the fact that, in 1850, after twenty-eight years of existence, there were but twenty-eight vernacular papers in existence in all North India, with an annual circulation of about sixty copies, while in 1878 there were ninety-seven vernacular papers in active circulation, and in 1880 there were two hundred and thirty, with a circulation of 150,000. The first vernacular newspaper was printed in 1818, at Serampūr. In 1890-91 there were four hundred and sixty-three vernacular papers."—*Contemporary Review*, vol. xxxvii. p. 461.

In 1815 Ram Mohun Roy published a work on Vedānta philosophy in Bengali, and a treatise on it in English, and in the following year his translation of several "Upanishads." The first decided step taken to further English education was initiated, strange to say, by a watchmaker in Calcutta, Mr David Hare, who, in conjunction with Ram Mohun Roy, inaugurated, in 1816, the Hindu College of Calcutta, with its famed teachers, Richardson and Derozia, which gradually, in spite of many disheartening failures, increased its number of pupils from twenty, in 1817, its first opening, to four hundred and thirty-six in 1820,[1] when the subjects taught were Natural Science, History, Geography, with Milton and Shakespeare.

The name of Jognarain Ghosal of Benares deserves also to be remembered, for having founded a school at Benares for the teaching of English, Persian, Hindustāni, and Bengalī. The management of this school was entrusted to the Rev. D. Corrie of the Calcutta Church Missionary Society, and it was endowed with a sum of 20,000 Rs., and the revenues of certain lands. Another institution started for the moral and intellectual improvement of the natives was the Calcutta School Book Society, founded in 1817, which received an annual grant of 6000 Rs. from the Government in 1821, after it had published 126,446 copies of useful works.

The full force of these influences was soon apparent. In 1816, Ram Mohun Roy had, with his friend Dvāraka Nāth Tagore, founded a society for spiritual improvement called the Ātmīya Sabhā. In 1820, he published, in Bengal, his "Precepts of Jesus: a Guide to Peace and Happiness," and raised a storm of controversy over, what his chief opponent, Dr Marshman, termed, his "heathen" adaptation of Christian doctrines to Eastern modes of thought.[2]

[1] Syed Mahmoud, "History of English Education in India," p. 26.

[2] Ram Mohun Roy replied with a first and second Appeal, but the Baptist

In his preface Ram Mohun Roy declares :—

"This simple code of religion and morality is so admirably calculated to elevate man's ideas to high and liberal notions of One God, who has equally subjected all living creatures, without distinction of caste, rank, or wealth, to change, disappointment, pain, and death, and has equally admitted all to be partakers of the bountiful mercies which He has lavished over Nature ; and is also so well fitted to regulate the conduct of the human race in the discharge of their various duties to God, to themselves, and society, that I cannot but hope the best effects from its promulgation in the present form."[1]

The new religion has been called Unitarianism. Its monotheism, however, was not that of the West. The Brāhman, Ram Mohun Roy, went back to the Unconscious Essence, to the Brahman of the "Vedānta" for his Supreme Deity. It was to found an eclectic system of practical and universal morality that the apostle of the new religion published his "Precepts of Jesus," from which were eliminated all abstruse doctrines and miraculous relations of the New Testament.

Ram Mohun Roy indeed acknowledged: "that I have found the doctrines of Christ more conducive to moral principles, and better adapted for the use of rational beings than any other which have come to my knowledge."[2] Yet the tendency of the school of thought, out of which arose his new religion, was his statement in his final Appeal,[3] that "whatever arguments can be adduced against a plurality of Gods, strike with equal force against the doctrine of a plurality of persons of the Godhead ; and on the other hand, whatever excuse may be pleaded in favour of a plurality of persons of the Deity can be offered with equal propriety in defence of polytheism."

Press refused to publish his last Appeal, the third, so he had to start a press of his own and print his own works, which, however, the Unitarian Society republished in 1824.

[1] Max Müller, "Biographical Essays," p. 22.

[2] Monier-Williams, "Brāhmanism and Hinduism," p. 483.

[3] *Ibid.*, p. 484.

The real commencement of the struggle, to decide the general lines on which the future of the moral and intellectual development of the natives of India was to be carried out, commenced from the year 1823, when the General Committee of Public Instruction received the lac of rupees allotted by the Act of Geo. III. of 1813 for education. As a matter of fact, the average expenditure during the twenty years, from 1813 to 1830, exceeded two lacs of rupees. The keynote to the situation was struck in the year 1823, when Ram Mohun Roy addressed a letter to Lord Amherst expressing his lively hopes that the amount which Parliament had directed should be applied to the instruction of the natives, might be "laid out in employing English gentlemen of talents and education to instruct the natives of India in mathematics, natural philosophy, chemistry, anatomy, and other useful sciences,"[1] for "the Sanskrit system of education would be the best calculated to keep this country in darkness." In a few sentences, extolled by Bishop Heber for their good English, good sense, force, and thought, he drew a dismal picture of the waste of time spent over what he described as "the puerilities of Sanskrit grammar, the viciousness of the doctrines of Māyā and Ignorance, as expounded by the Vedāntic philosophy, the inherent uselessness of the 'Mīmāmśa,' and the lack of all improvement to the mind in the study of the 'Nyāya.'"

The Court of Directors had, however, made up their own minds on the subject. In their Despatch of 1824, they informed the Committee of Public Education that, "in professing to establish seminaries for the purpose of teaching mere Hindu or mere Muhammadan literature, you bound yourself to teach a good deal of what was frivolous, not a little of what was purely mischievous, and a small remainder, indeed, in which utility was not in any way

[1] Trevelyan, "Education of the People of India," pp. 55-71.

concerned." In their opinion, if there were any documents of historical importance to be found in Oriental languages, they could be best translated by Europeans. The great objects to be aimed at were the teaching of useful learning, and the introduction of reforms in the course of study, anything being retained that might be found of use in native literature.

To this the Committee pointed out that, with the exception of those natives who studied English for the purpose of obtaining a livelihood, the people, both learned and unlearned, held "European literature and science in very slight estimation," and that, in the Committee's opinion, "metaphysical science was as well worthy of being studied in Arabic and Sanskrit as in any other language, as were also arithmetic, algebra, Euclid, law, and literature." Western education and European ideas had, however, permeated deeper than even the Committee seem to have noted. The Brāhma[1] Samāj, or "The Society of the Believers in Brahman, the Supreme Spirit," or, as it is called, the Hindu Unitarian Church, was inaugurated, in 1828, by Ram Mohun Roy, and finally established at a house in Chitpore Road, Calcutta, in 1830.

This was the first outward sign of the change brought about through the influence and spread of Western literature among the educated natives of India. Not only had Ram Mohun Roy studied the "Veda" in Sanskrit, the "Tripitaka" in Pali, but he had acquired Hebrew to master the Old Testament, and Greek to read the New. At the weekly meetings, held in the new church, or temple, monotheistic hymns from Vedic literature were chanted, and moral maxims from the same source explained. A new religion was being evolved to fill up the void produced by the destruction of old beliefs, under the

[1] Adjective form from *Brāhmā*.

disintegrating influence of European teaching, and before some new system was developed to take its place.

In the same year, 1830, the Directors, in a further Despatch expressed their satisfaction that it was evidently becoming clear, both from the reports they received, and from the success of the Anglo-Indian College at Calcutta, that the higher ranks of the natives were prepared to welcome a further extension of the means of cultivating the English language and literature, and of acquiring a knowledge of European ideas and science. It was, in their opinion, of primary importance that English should be taught, both because of the higher tone and better spirit of European literature, and further, because it was "calculated to raise up a class of persons qualified, by their intelligence and morality, for high employment in the Civil Administration of India."

In the Report of the following year, 1831, the Committee of Public Education stated that, although measures for the diffusion of English were only in their infancy, the results obtained at the Vidyālaya, or College of Calcutta, surpassed all their expectations: "A command of the English language, and a familiarity with its literature and science has been acquired to an extent rarely equalled by any schools in Europe." They pointed out, in conclusion, that, "the moral effect has been equally remarkable, and an impatience of the restrictions of Hinduism, and a disregard of its ceremonies are equally avowed by many young men of respectable birth and talents, and entertained by many more who outwardly conform to the practices of their countrymen."

When the Company's Charter was renewed by Parliament in 1833, it was definitely laid down, in a resolution proposed by Mr Charles Grant, that the government of British India was entrusted to the Company for "the purpose of extending the commerce of the country, and of securing the good government, and promoting the religious and moral improvement of the people of India."

Lord Macaulay, who was appointed President of the Committee of Education on his arrival in India as Member of the Supreme Council, produced his celebrated "Minute" in 1835, which forever decided the question so momentous for the whole future intellectual history of the land. According to his view, the action of the Committee of Public Education, in confining their attention to the study of the classical languages of India, to the neglect of English, could only be paralleled by supposing that our own ancestors, in the fifteenth, or beginning of the sixteenth centuries, had been infatuated enough to neglect all classical literature, and continue the study of Anglo-Saxon chronicles and Norman-French romances. To the people of India, the language of England was to be their classic language. It was to do for them what the study of Greek and Latin had done for the West. To him the demand for the teaching of English was imperative.[1] Not only did it give access to the vast intellectual treasures of the past, not only was it likely to become the language of commerce in the Eastern seas, as it was in South Africa and Australasia, but further, "a single shelf of a good European library was worth the whole native literature of India and Arabia."[2]

The result was inevitable, Lord William Bentinck and

[1] "Lord Macaulay's celebrated 'Minute,' which, in 1835, determined the Anglicising of all the higher education, is not quite so triumphantly unanswerable as it is usually assumed to be; for we have to reckon, on the other side, the disappearance of the indigenous systems, and the decay of the study of the Oriental Classics in their own language."—Sir A. Lyall, "India Under Queen Victoria," *Nineteenth Century* (June 1897), p. 881.

[2] At this time, be it remembered, although H. H. Wilson had published his translation of the "Megha Dûta" in 1813, his "Sanskrit Dictionary" in 1819, his "History of Kashmîr, from the Râjâ Tarangini," and his four dramas in the "Theatre of the Hindus" in 1834, the essay of H. J. Colebrooke on the "Vedas" in the "Asiatic Researches" did not appear until 1837, and even then was the only information possessed on the subject of the ancient language and religion of the Hindus.

his Council finally decided, in 1835, that the educational policy of the Government should be confined to the promotion of European literature and science, and that for the future all funds set apart for education should be devoted to that purpose, and no portion of them be expended on the printing of Oriental works.

One other view of the situation has been ably given by Sir John Malcolm, Governor of Bombay, in a Minute of 1828, where he advocated, as the wisest policy, the education of a certain proportion of natives in the English language and science, for the object of enabling them to diffuse their knowledge through their own vernacular dialect to their own countrymen.

Although it was finally decided that the higher education of the native population should be through the medium of the English language, it was always acknowledged and understood that it was but a small class of the most advanced and educated natives who could be so instructed.[1] The hope and expectation was that those natives who had received a liberal education, from a Western standpoint, would by degrees communicate their knowledge to the mass of the people through the local vernaculars. It does not appear to have been foreseen at the time that natives educated on English lines might compose original works in the vernaculars, through which ideals and forms of thought, assimilated under Western influences, would disseminate themselves among the mass of the population. Whether the immediate object of the encouragement of the study of English was to raise a class of natives fitted for carrying on the duties of the public service, so that in time the language of public business might be English, is not of immediate importance. Be the motives what they may, from the point of view of the Directors, to obtain a class of

[1] "Printed Parliamentary Papers: Second Report of Select Committee of House of Lords" (Appendix I., p. 481, 1852-53); Syed Mahmoud, p. 57.

servants to carry on economically the duties of public servants, and to have ready means of obtaining accurate information of details of revenue affairs, or from the point of view of the missionaries, the hope that a liberal education would further the advance of Christianity, and prove the most effectual weapon for attack against what was palpably vicious, false, and erroneous in the popular beliefs, the result was that the study of English was almost exclusively encouraged. Lord Auckland, in 1839, somewhat modified Lord William Bentinck's resolution by upholding the Sanskrit and native colleges, and by setting aside funds for their encouragement. Further, by the Despatch of 1854, known as that of Sir Charles Wood, it was fully acknowledged that vernacular schools for elementary education should be encouraged, and that funds should be raised for the purpose by a special levy imposed on the land.

The object expressly desired by the Court of Directors was declared to be "the diffusion of the Improvements, Science, Philosophy, and Literature of Europe—in short, of European knowledge," and this was to be accomplished by the establishment, throughout India, of a graduated series of schools and colleges, with a central university for each of the Presidencies.

Universities, on the model of the University of London, were founded at Calcutta, Madras, and Bombay during the dark days of the Mutiny in 1857, and were followed by one for the Panjāb at Lahore in 1882, and one for the North-West Provinces at Allahabad in 1887.

As a result of an exhaustive investigation into the subject of education made by a Commission in 1882, the Government finally decided to retire, in all cases where it was possible, from competition with the private management and control of secondary education. The Government steadily pursued this policy, with a result that, although there was a vast increase during the succeeding ten years in secondary education, the cost to Government decreased, the expense being met from the fees charged. The ten years' result can be judged from the following table giving the number of colleges, schools, and pupils under education :—

Grade.	1881–82.		1891–92.	
	No.	Pupils.	No.	Pupils.
University { Arts	8	8,127	104	12,985
University { Professional	24	2,411	37	3,292
Secondary	4,432	418,412	4,872	473,294
Primary	90,700	2,537,502	97,109	2,837,607
Normal	135	4,949	152	5,146
Technical	189	8,503	402	16,586
TOTAL	95,566	2,979,904	102,676	3,348,910

So far as the higher education is concerned, the following statement, by Sir Raymond West, in the course of an address on "Higher Education in India" to the Oriental Congress of 1892, speaks for itself:—

"The youths receiving secondary education amount, after all, to only some five per cent. of the whole number recorded as under instruction in India. The students in colleges amount to no more than one per cent. In England the proportion is twice as great; in a German State four or five times as great, of youths under secondary instruction. In a German town, indeed, from a third to a half of the children are in the higher schools; but in Germany it is everywhere recognised, in direct opposition to the principle announced by the Government of India, that the State is more especially interested in the higher education, the town or locality in the lower. The contributions of Government are regulated accordingly.

According to the last Census Returns, prepared by Mr Baines, the annual average of candidates, during the previous five years, presenting themselves for matriculation at the Presidency colleges was 18,150, of whom 5,875 pass. The intermediate examination is reached by 2,213 students, the Bachelor of Arts degree is attained by 761 members, and the Master of Arts by only 54.

At the lower end of the scale there are only 109 males and 6 females in every 1000 of the population able to read and write, the corresponding numbers for the coloured population of the United States being 254 males and 217 females, and for Ireland 554 males and 501 females.

The formation of the Brāhma Samāj was the first uneasy movement made in slumbering Brāhmanism, as the clear-cut thought of the earliest recipients of English education pierced through the whole of Indian religious and philosophic speculations, and saw their strength and weakness when brought face to face with new ideals and new modes of reasoning.

Ram Mohun Roy, the first apostle of this new gospel, in which the old and new were strangely fused—the worship of Brahman of the "Vedānta," with much of Christianity—however lived and died a Brāhman, tended by his own Brāhman servant, and wearing his Brāhmanic thread. He was buried at Bristol in 1853 without any religious service.

He was succeeded by Debendra Nāth Tagore who, born in 1818, and educated at the Hindu College at Calcutta, joined the Brāhma Samāj in 1843.[1] By him a monthly periodical, the *Tattva-bodhinī-patrikā*, was started in 1843, and under the editorship of Akhay Kumar Datta, commenced the publication of Vedāntic literature. By 1847, upwards of seven hundred and sixty-seven Brāhmans had joined the society, and agreed to the essential Seven Articles of Faith, including the worship of a God, One without a

[1] Max Müller, "Biographical Essays," p. 37 (*note* 1):—"In 1838 or 1841." Monier-Williams, "Indian Theistic Reformers," J.R.A.S. (January 1881), gives 1841. In 1839 he had formed his own society, the "Tattva-bodhinī-Sabhā."

Second, the Cause of the Emanation (*srishti*), Stay, and Decay (*pralaya*) of the World, and the Cause of emancipation (*mukti karana*). The Seven Articles of Faith were as follows:—

First Vow.—"By loving God and by performing the works which He loves, I will worship God, the Creator, the Preserver, and the Destroyer, the Giver of Salvation, the Omniscient, the Omnipresent, the Blissful, the Good, the Formless, the One only without a Second."

Second Vow.—"I will worship no created object as the Creator."

Third Vow.—"Except the day of sickness or tribulation, every day, the mind being undisturbed, I will engage in love and veneration of God."

Fourth Vow.—"I will exert myself to perform righteous deeds."

Fifth Vow.—"I will be careful to keep myself from vicious deeds."

Sixth Vow.—"If, through the influence of passion, I have committed any vice, I will, wishing redemption from it, be careful not to do it again."

Seventh Vow.—"Every year, and as the occasion of every happy domestic event, I will bestow gifts upon the Brāhma Samāj. Grant me, O God, power to observe the duties of this great faith."

The essential point to note is, that the god worshipped, as clearly shown in the four essential principles set forth by Debendra Nāth, is the neuter essence, Brăhmă (nom. of *Brăhmăn*). The faith begins with the declaration that "before this universe existed, Brahma (the Supreme Being) was, nothing else whatever was," and then goes on to declare that "He created the Universe" (*tad idam sarvam asrijat*). The movement could not rest; it had yet left within it a respect for caste, the use of the sacred thread, a leaning towards the old, and ancestral rites. All these had to be swept away, as were already the belief in transmigration and the Vedāntic doctrine of Absorption of the Soul.[1]

[1] The first change came in 1845, when Debendra Nāth Tagore, and the Brāhma Samāj, decided that the "Vedas" could no longer be held as of Divine origin.

The leaven of English education had yet to sink deeper. In 1838 Keshab Chandar Sen was born, a Vaidya by caste, of orthodox Hindu family. He was educated at the Presidency College, Calcutta, and joined the Brāhma Samāj in the days of the Mutiny.

It may be safely prognosticated that the future great reformer of Hinduism, the reformer who will spread his influence and disturbing power all over India, and arouse the enthusiasm of Bengali, Sikh, Marātha, and Tamil, will not be a Bengali. The reformer—and it seems probable that one will appear—will arise without known parentage or nationality, and it may also safely be believed that he will be considered to be infused with the same spirit which Keshab Chandar Sen is said to have been infused with, when it is recorded that on his marriage, in 1856, he declared: "I entered the world with ascetic ideas, and my honeymoon was spent amid austerities in the house of the Lord."[1]

Under the guidance of Keshab Chandar Sen the Brāhma Samāj gradually cut itself adrift from Hindu rites and customs. In 1861, Debendra Nāth Tagore allowed his own daughter to be married by a simple Brāhmic ceremony, without the orthodox Hindu festivities, expenses, and rites. In 1864, a marriage was performed between members of different castes by Keshab Chandar Sen, who further insisted on the leaving-off of the sacred thread, the ancient birthright of all twice-born Aryans. These reforms were opposed to the conservative instincts of Debendra Nāth Tagore and those of the more orthodox Hindus who soon repudiated their new leader. Keshab Chandar Sen, with his cousin, Protab Chandar Mozoondar, accordingly, in 1866, founded a new and advanced Brāhma Samāj, with the *Indian Mirror* as its organ, leaving the old society the name of

[1] "Biographical Essays," p. 53.

the "Adi Brāhma Samāj," which had as its leader, Debendra Nāth Tagore, and as its secretary, Rāj Nārain Bose.

Between the two societies there were but few doctrinal differences. The old leaven of Vaishnava bhakti, or faith, still permeated Keshab Chandar Sen, and brought him close to Christianity—a faith which his pride in his own heritage from the past forbade him to accept. Brāhmanism might be outwardly discarded, nevertheless, the new progressive Samāj held that

> "God Himself never becomes man by putting on a human body. His divinity dwells in every man, and is displayed more vividly in some; as in Moses, Jesus Christ, Muhammad, Nānak, Chaitanya, and other great Teachers who appeared at special times, and conferred vast benefits on the world. They are entitled to universal gratitude and love. . . . Every sinner must suffer the consequences of his own sins sooner or later, in this world or the next. Man must labour after holiness by the worship of God, by subjugation of the passions, by repentance, by the study of Nature and of good books, by good company, and by solitary contemplation. These will lead, through the action of God's grace, to salvation."[1]

In England he set forth his own views as to the Christ the West had offered to the East:—

> "Methinks I have come into a vast market. Every sect is like a small shop where a peculiar kind of Christianity is offered for sale. As I go from door to door, from shop to shop, each sect steps forward and offers, for my acceptance, its own interpretations of the Bible, and its own peculiar Christian beliefs. I cannot but feel perplexed, and even amused, amidst countless and quarrelling sects. It appears to me, and has always appeared to me, that no Christian nation on earth represents fully and thoroughly Christ's idea of the kingdom of God. I do believe, and I must candidly say, that no Christian sect puts forth the genuine and full Christ as He was and as He is, but, in some cases, a mutilated, disfigured Christ, and what is more shameful, in many cases, a counterfeit Christ.

[1] Monier-Williams, "Indian Theistic Reformers," J.R.A.S. (January 1881), p. 25.

> Now, I wish to say that I have not come to England as one who has yet to find Christ. When the Roman Catholic, the Protestant, the Unitarian, the Trinitarian, the Broad Church, the Low Church, the High Church all come round me, and offer me their respective Christs, I desire to say to one and all: 'Think you that I have no Christ within me? Though an Indian, I can still humbly say, Thank God that I have my Christ.'"

The first important reform inaugurated by the new society was the passing of the Native Marriage Act of 1872, introducing, for the first time, a form of civil marriage for persons who did not profess the Christian, Jewish, Hindu, Muhammadan, Parsi, Buddhist, Sikh, or Jaina religions.

Into the religious struggles of Keshab Chandar Sen's life it would be unprofitable to enter, as they show no solid advance, drifting, as they did, between Christianity, Yogīism, Bhakti, and Asceticism, mingled with a practical propaganda for social reformation.

The times were not ripe for the missionary work of reformation he had set before him, although he possessed much to sway the mass: "A fine countenance, a majestic presence, and that soft look which of itself exerts an almost irresistible fascination over impressionable minds, lent wonderful force to a swift, kindling, and practical oratory, which married itself to his highly spiritual teaching as perfect music unto noble minds."[1]

In spite of all the efforts made by Keshab Chandar Sen for the abolition of early marriages, he lost ground in 1878 by permitting his own daughter, aged fourteen, to be married to the young Mahārāja of Kuch Behar, the result being that, in 1878, a new society called the "Sādhārana" (or general) "Brāhma Samāj" was formed. With all the brilliant eloquence of his fervid imagination, though with a waning of his undoubted intellectual powers, Keshab Chandar Sen

[1] *Indian Daily News*. Quoted in Max Müller's "Biographical Essays," p. 72.

continued his preaching, declaring himself to be the apostle of what he called the "New Dispensation Church," in which there was to be an amalgamation of all creeds in a belief in the Unity of the Godhead, the acceptance of Christ as an ideal Yogī, Oriental in His character and mission, Hindū in faith, whose Godhead he still denied. In his "Manifesto" of 1883, he poured forth, in the spirit of Walt Whitman, his rhapsody:—

"Keshab Chandar Sen, a servant of God, called to be an apostle of the Church of the New Dispensation, which is in the holy city of Calcutta, the metropolis of Āryāvarta.

"To all the great nations of the world, and to the chief religious sects in the East and the West; to the followers of Moses, of Jesus, of Buddha, of Confucius, of Zoroaster, of Mahomet, of Nānak, and the various branches of the Hindu Church, grace be to you and peace everlasting. Gather ye the wisdom of the East and the West, and assimilate the examples of the saints of all ages.

"Above all, love one another, and merge all differences in universal brotherhood.

"Let Asia, Europe, Africa, and America, with diverse instruments, praise the New Dispensation, and sing the Fatherhood of God and the Brotherhood of Man."[1]

More extraordinary was his "Proclamation," issued, in 1879, in the columns of the *Indian Mirror*, which has been abridged by Sir Monier Monier-Williams in his article on "Indian Theistic Reformers":—

"To all my soldiers in India my affectionate greeting. Believe that this Proclamation goeth forth from Heaven in the name and with the love of your Mother. Carry out its behests like loyal soldiers. The British Government is my Government. The Brāhma Samāj is my Church. My daughter Queen Victoria have I ordained. Come direct to me, without a mediator as your Mother. The influence of the earthly Mother at home, of the Queen-Mother at the head of the Government will raise the head of my Indian children to their Supreme Mother. I will give them peace and salvation. Soldiers, fight bravely and establish my dominion."

[1] Monier-Williams, "Hinduism," p. 573.

To all who understand the Eastern mode of thought, the following words spoken by Keshab Chandar Sen in a sermon, a masterpiece of eloquence, delivered in 1879 before the Bishop of Calcutta, other Europeans, and a thousand listeners, only represent what might have been expected as the furthest the new reformer would proceed in his fusing of Hinduism and Christianity:—

> "It is Christ who rules British India, and not the British Government. England has sent out a tremendous moral force in the life and character of that mighty prophet to conquer and hold this vast empire. None but Jesus, none but Jesus, none but Jesus ever deserved this bright, this precious diadem, India, and Jesus shall have it. Christ comes to us as an Asiatic in race, as a Hindu in faith, as a kinsman, and as a brother. . . . Christ is a true Yogī, and will surely help us to realise our national ideal of a Yogī. . . . In accepting Him, therefore, you accept the fulfilment of your national Scriptures and prophets."

Though the work of Keshab Chandar Sen was carried on by his brother, Krishna Behari Sen, Gaur Govind Roy, and others, and received the enthusiastic support of the Mahārāja and Mahārāni of Kuch Behar, its importance waned before the Sādhārāna Samāj, which numbered amongst its leaders the Hon. Ānanda Mohan Bose, the only native Cambridge wrangler, its able secretary, Rajani Nāth Roy, and its minister, Pandit Sivanāth Sāstri.

The full conservative Hindu reaction was marked by an effort to fall back on Vedic authority for a pure Theism, where there was to be but one formless abstract God worshipped by prayer and devotion, with the four "Vedas" as primary, and later Vedic writings as secondary, authorities in all matters of moral conduct.

During the last Census of 1891 there were 3,051 who returned themselves as followers of the faith of Brāhmanism, of whom 2,596 were in Bengal, while the followers of Dayānanda Saraswati, who, in 1877, founded a Theism based purely on Vedic authority, numbered 40,000, mostly writers or traders.

The recoil of orthodox Hindu thought back to the old was led by Dayānanda Saraswati, a Brāhman of Katthiāwār, who formed a new society called the "Ārya Samāj." He himself was from his youth brought up in the strictest school of Hindu orthodoxy. As he wrote, in the strange records of his life:[1]—

> "I was but eight when I was invested with the sacred Brāhmanic thread and taught the Gāyātri hymn, the Sandhyā (morning and evening) ceremony, and the 'Yajur Veda.' As my father belonged to the Śiva sect, I was early taught to worship the uncouth piece of clay representing Śiva, known as the 'Pārthiva Linga.'"

Dayānanda Saraswati early abandoned idol-worship, but he remained firm in his belief in Vedic revelation, the doctrine of metempsychosis, and the worship of One God, held to be the deity addressed by Vedic Aryans as Agni, Indra, and Sūrya.

Whatever form these strange minglings of "Veda," "Upanishad," "Kuran," "Tripitakas," "Zend Avesta," and Christian Bible, may assume in the future, they all denote an upheaval of thought among the educated classes of India, the result of the meeting of the new and old. To claim that movement as indicating a future triumph for Christianity would first necessitate a survey of the whole course of Christianity in India, the marking out of its success and the causes for its undoubted failures. It is hoped that time and opportunity may be found for undertaking such a task, for no work yet published has viewed the subject from an Indian standpoint; at present it must suffice to take refuge under the words of the learned

[1] Max Müller, "Biographical Essays," p. 172.

Sir Monier Monier-Williams, who has given deep thought to the subject :—

> "We may be quite sure that men like Debendra Nāth Tagore, Keshab Chandar Sen, and Ānanda Mohan Bose, are doing good work in a Christian self-sacrificing spirit, though they may fall into many errors, and may not have adopted every single dogma of the Athanasian Creed.
>
> "Let us hold out the right hand of fellowship to these noble-minded patriots—men who, notwithstanding their undoubted courage, need every encouragement in their almost hopeless struggle with their country's worst enemies—Ignorance, Prejudice, and Superstition. Intense darkness still broods over the land—in some places a veritable Egyptian darkness thick enough to be felt. Let Christianity thankfully welcome, and wisely make use of, every gleam and glimmer of true light, from whatever quarter it may shine."

All these movements, denoting as they do the disintegrating force of Western education, had their own influence in moulding the whole literature of the people to new forms and uses.

The strength of the barriers that the sacerdotal class had ranged round the sacred literature, so as to keep its secrets from vulgar gaze or scrutiny, can be judged from the fact that Romesh Chandra Dutt's translation of the "Rig Veda" into Bengalī was looked upon as a sacrilege, and vehemently opposed by his own countrymen. Amongst the few[1] who dared to support the undertaking were the wise and enlightened Isvara Chandra Vidyasagar and Akhay Kumar Datta, the two great writers who must be placed in the first rank of those who ably seconded the work of the Brāhma Samāj in perfecting Bengalī as a prose medium for a new school of writers who, trained in Western modes of thought, handed on their impressions and ideas to the mass of the people in the local vernaculars.

Akhay Kumar Datta, at the age of sixteen, commenced his education in English at the Oriental Seminary at

[1] R. C. Dutt, "The Literature of Bengal," p. 178.

Calcutta. He afterwards acquired a knowledge of Sanskrit, a language he ably used, for the purpose of enriching Bengali as a prose literature, in his work in the *Tattva-bodhinī-patrikā*, a monthly journal started in 1873 by Debendra Nāth Tagore. Isvara Chandra Vidyasagar, on the other hand, applied himself to the study of Sanskrit in the Sanskrit College at Calcutta, which he entered at the age of nine for the orthodox course of study. For three years he studied grammar, and by the age of twelve had read the greater portion of the best works of the classic period of Sanskrit verse. Sanskrit he afterwards read and wrote as well as his own vernacular. Being appointed, in 1841, head pandit of the Fort William College, he commenced his study of English and Hindi. By 1847 he published, in Bengalī, the "Betal Panchavimsati," translated from the Hindi, a work instinct with poetic feeling. This work raised him, in spite of much that was artificial and over-elaborated in it, to the position of an acknowledged master of a pure and classical prose style in the vernacular. In 1862, the publication of his "Exile of Sītā,"[1] based on Bhavabhūti's "Uttararāma Charitra," showed how Bengalī had become a classic prose language, with all the flexibility, dignity, and grace requisite for the purpose of interpreting to the mass of the people the old life-history of the nation, and the new phase of thought introduced from the West. Isvara Chandra Vidyasagar brought down on his head the bitter curses and ribald abuse, sung throughout the streets of Calcutta, of his more bigoted Brāhman brethren by his writings, in 1855, against the system of enforced widowhood, which his deep learning in Sanskrit lore enabled him to prove beyond question was no part of the decrees of the Vedic Scriptures. By his subsequent writings and efforts, he aided towards the first step in the course he had marked

[1] Sricharan Chakravarti, "Life of Pandit Isvara Chandra Vidyasagar" (Calcutta, 1896).

out, the passing of the Act of 1856, which enacted that the sons of re-married Hindu widows should be held as legitimate heirs.

The dangers feared were neither imaginary nor trifling. The ancient traditions of Brāhmanism were being scattered to the winds, and the system itself called upon to justify the inherent strength of its position before the newly-arisen scepticism. Ancient customs, habits, and beliefs, all finding their authority and sanction in the will of the Creator of the world, as revealed in the sacred literature of India, were being questioned. The hereditary custodians of the sacred lore, claiming as they did to be the specially created partakers of the confidence of the deity, were being forced to come forth and defend their birthright.

Ram Mohun Roy had shaken to its foundations the whole established fabric of Brāhmanic power by his fierce denunciations of, and irrefutable arguments against, idolatry and widow-burning. One task Vidyasagar had set his hand to he had to leave unaccomplished. He endeavoured in vain to put an end to the system whereby the class known as the Kulin Brāhmans of Bengal entered into marriages, sometimes formal, sometimes real, with daughters of those of their own class who, unable to obtain husbands, were glad to pay a Kulin Brāhman large sums of money for forming a matrimonial alliance which left them free to abandon the numerous women they had thus married. In 1871, his famous work, "Whether Polygamy Should be Done Away With," not only gave a list of these Kulin Brāhmans, showing the number of wives each of them had, but also proved that the custom could not possibly find any support from ancient law or history.

Akhay Kumar Datta at the same time continued to pour forth, in earnest and forcible prose, a series of articles scientific, biographical, and moral, printed in the *Tattva-bodhinī-patrikā*, uncompromising in their sincerity and love for truth until he at last saw, as the crowning reward of his labours, the Brāhma Samāj reject the belief in the infallibility and revealed authority of the "Vedānta."[1]

The work begun by Akhay Kumar Datta and Isvara Chandra Vidyasagar was followed by the efforts of a series of able writers who carried every widening current of reform further into the social life of the people by publishing works on history and biography, and by writing tales satirising social habits and customs.[2]

The spirit of the times may be judged from the fact that the first Bengalī play, the "Kulina Kula Sarvasa," composed in 1854 by Ram Narāyan Tarkaratna, and acted in 1856 at the Oriental Seminary, was a satire on the Kulin custom of polygamy. The play was followed by the "Nala Natak," in which the same author satirised the custom of child-marriage. Happily, the early efforts of the rising school to express their thoughts in English proved unsuccessful and unprofitable. Madhu Sudan Datta was the first to recognise the difficulty. He was educated in the Hindu College, founded in 1817, and at the age of nineteen forsook his own caste and religion and was baptised a Christian, adopting the name Michael. At seventeen he had already published some indifferent verse, in imitation of those of Byron. The influence of Western ideas had so permeated him that, after becoming a Christian, he married an English wife, daughter of an indigo planter in Madras, from whom, however, he soon separated, when he married a second English wife, the daughter of the Principal of the Madras Presidency College. His "Captive Ladie," published in 1849, telling, in English verse, the story of Prithivi Rāj, the famous Hindu King of Delhi and his

[1] Dutt, R. C., "The Literature of Bengal," p. 169.

[2] Such as the "Alaler-gharer Dulal," of Pyari Chand Mitra, which has been translated into English, and the "Hutam Pechar Naksha," of Kali Prasanna Sinha, who also translated the "Mahābhārata" into Bengali, a work also accomplished (1885) for the "Rāmāyana" by Hem Chandra Vidyaratna. *See* Dutt, R. C., "The Literature of Bengal," pp. 182-183.

wife, Sanjuta, clearly showed the impossibility even of a poetic genius, such as he undoubtedly was, ever finding an outlet for his imagination in the uncongenial trammels of an English garb.

The task has been essayed by nearly all the recent native writers who may be safely held to have been endowed with that unceasing striving, and indomitable perseverance that denotes genius, but never yet have they reached a result worthy of their efforts. Michael wisely turned away from English, and in 1858 produced an original play, the "Sarmishta," a second Padmāvati, and then, in 1859, set to work on two great works in blank verse. In these he abandoned the Bengalī rhyme, and in 1860 published the "Tillottama," and in 1861, the "Meghanad badh Kavya."

The work of the drama, abandoned by Madhu Sudan Datta for epic poetry, was resumed by others, the most striking being Dinabandu Mitra, who in 1860 produced his "Nil Darpan," a fierce satire on the indigo planters of Jessore and Nadiyā. The Rev. James Long published the play, as translated into English by a native, for which he was fined and imprisoned. An exhaustive enquiry into the subject by an Indigo Commission ultimately led to the failure of much of the indigo growing in Nadiyā, and a refusal of the cultivators to sow indigo. As the play has now only an historical and literary importance, and as a copy of it is now difficult, if not impossible, to procure, no fault can be found if it is used for the purpose of throwing some light on the thought of the time, when the drama had travelled from its ancient classic repose to an active power for social reform.

The introduction to the "Nil Darpan," or "Indigo Planting Mirror," states that, as the Bengali drama had exposed "the evils of Kulin Brāhmanism, widow-marriage prohibition, quackery, fanaticism," the "Nil Darpan" pleads the cause of those who are the feeble. It purports, according to the Introduction, to describe "a respectable *ryot*, a peasant proprietor, happy with his family in the enjoyment of his land till the indigo system compelled him to take advances" for the cultivation of indigo, to the neglect of his own land and crops, so that he became beggared, and reduced "to the condition of a serf and vagabond." The effect of all this system on his home, children, and relatives is "pointed out in language plain but true; it shows how arbitrary power debases the lord as well as the peasant. Reference is also made to the partiality of various magistrates in favour of planters, and to the act of last year penally enforcing indigo contracts."[1]

In the play itself the English planter is depicted as upbraiding his native manager for want of zeal, and is answered by the retorts: "Saheb, what signs of fear hast thou seen in me? When I have entered on this indigo profession I have thrown off all fear, shame, and honour; and the destroying of cows, Brāhmans, of women, and the burning-down of houses are become my ornaments."[2] The cultivators who refuse to accept advances are dragged before the planter, who twists their ears, beats them with a leather strap, calls them scoundrels, "bloody niggers," and then, with many "God damns!" and other words of chastisement, orders them to be imprisoned unless they accept advances binding them to grow indigo instead of rice. The ryots assemble together and declare there is no hope for them, for they had seen "the late Governor Saheb go about all the indigo factories, being feasted like a bridegroom just before the celebration of the marriage. Did you not see that the planter Sahebs brought him to this factory well-adorned like a bridegroom?" The whole despairing lot of the village is summed up in a favourite verse:—

> "The missionaries have destroyed the caste;
> The factory monkeys have destroyed the rice."[3]

[1] Long. Rev. J., "Nil Darpan," iii. [2] *Ibid.*, p. 13. [3] *Ibid.*, p. 29.

The "Indigo Planter" declares the fate in store for the cultivators: "We indigo planters are become the companions of death; can our factories remain if we have pity? By nature we are not bad; our evil disposition has increased by indigo cultivation. Before, we felt sorrow in beating one man; now we can beat ten persons with the leather strap, making them senseless, and immediately after, we can, with great laughter, take our dinner or supper."[1]

As a result, tragedy is piled on tragedy, to show that "the sorrows which the ryots endure in the preparation of the indigo is known only to themselves and the great God, the preserver of the poor." With less of exaggeration, and less of melodrama, the play would have served its purpose better, and had an independent artistic value.

The great interest of the play is now purely literary. The use of it, for a social purpose, shows how the new weapon, placed in the hands of the people, could serve a double purpose. Its realistic movement and over-wrought tragedy have been adapted from the West, probably, so far as can be judged, from the vague idea a translation necessarily gives of the original, from an imperfect reading of the spirit of "Macbeth," "Hamlet," and the "Merchant of Venice."

Traces are here and there to be seen of truly Eastern poetic charm and idealism. An extraordinary mixture of Eastern conventional symbolism, with ideas and touches borrowed from Elizabethan tragedy, occurs in the final scene, where the last surviving member of a family of cultivators pours forth his lamentation over his wife, Sarala, and all his relations, who have been brought to a tragic death through the wickedness of the indigo planter. In his deep sorrow the cultivator cries out:—

> "In this world of short existence, human life is as a bank of a river, which has a most violent course and the greatest depth. How

[1] "Nil Darpan," p. 53.

very beautiful are the banks, the fields covered over with new grass most pleasant to the view, the trees full of branches newly coming out; in some places the cottages of fishermen, in others the kine feeding with their young ones. To walk about in such a place, enjoying the sweet songs of the beautiful birds, and the charming gale full of the sweet smell of flowers, only wraps the mind in contemplation of that Being who is full of pleasure. . . . The cobra de capello, like the indigo planters, with mouths full of poison, threw all happiness into the flame of fire. The father, through injustice, died in the prison; the elder brother in the indigo field; and the mother, being insane through grief for her husband and son, murdered, with her own hands, a most honest woman. . . . The cry of mama, mama, mama, mama, do I make in the battle-field and the wilderness whenever fear arises in the mind. . . . Ah! ah! it bursts my heart not to know where my heart's Sarala is gone to. The most beautiful, wise, and entirely devoted to me; she walked as the swan, and her eyes were handsome as those of the deer. . . . The mind was charmed by thy sweet reading, which was as the singing of the bird in the forest. Thou, Sarala, hadst a most beauteous face, and didst brighten the lake of my heart. Who did take away my lotus with a cruel heart? The beautiful lake became dark. The world I look upon is as a desert full of corpses; while I have lost my father, my mother, my brother, and my wife!"[1]

The play, however weak and artificial, marks the grave dangers that must be faced when England gives India, in consideration of her political servitude, the fullest possible freedom of thought, of conscience, and of expression of her needs and aspirations. If not true to fact, the very exaggeration of such writings as the "Nil Darpan" train the people who know the truth to more sober views of the situation, and to gradual mistrust of similar effusions. To establish a new industry, and especially to expect an agricultural population to accept more profitable modes of cultivation than those followed by their forefathers, is a task difficult of success, and one that must invariably lead to the strongest opposition against those who strive to move habits which have become almost instincts. Perhaps, for many reasons, it was well for India that the cultivation

[1] "Nil Darpan," p. 101.

of indigo had a check, even as had the efforts to introduce the English plough, in preference to the surface-scratching native one, for speedy results, in a land like India, often mean speedy exhaustion, and permanent decay. The "Nil Darpan" was the instinctive reaction of a poetic mind, ever ready, through the stress of its imagination, to exaggerate the meaning of passing changes, and revolt against a system it could not fit into its conception of the times.

The whole course of England's mission is calmly to note the power of the old, mark its failing strength, and graft any of its lasting principles of vitality on to new ideals.

Nowhere better than in the novels of Bankim Chandra Chatterji can the full force of this strife between old and new be traced. The novels themselves owe their form to Western influences, but the subject-matter and spirit are essentially native. Bankim Chandra Chatterji himself was the first B.A. of the Calcutta University. Born in 1838, his earliest novel, "Durges Nandini,"[1] appeared in 1864, professedly inspired as a historical novel under the influence of the works of Sir Walter Scott. This work was followed by "Kopala Kundala,"[2] a tale of life in Bengal some two hundred and fifty years ago, and was succeeded by the "Mrinalini." In 1872 the novelist commenced, in his newly-started magazine, the *Banga Darsan*, the monthly publication of his novel of social life, the "Bisha Brikka," translated into English as "The Poison Tree" in 1884.[3] The "Debi Chaudhurani," "Ananda Mathar," and "Krishna Kanta's Will"[4] followed, the last being translated into English in 1895. The "Krishna Charitra," published in 1886, is, however, the work through which the name of Bankim Chandra Chatterji will probably remain famed in the memory of his own country-people.

[1] Translated by Charu Candra Mookerji (Calcutta, 1880).
[2] Translated by H. A. D. Phillips (Trübner & Co., 1885).
[3] Translated by Marian Knight, with Preface by Sir Edwin Arnold.
[4] Translated by Marian Knight, with Introduction by Prof. J. F. Blumhardt.

It is the crowning work of all his labours. It inculcates, with all the purity of style of which the novelist was so perfect a master, a pure and devout revival of Hinduism, founded on monotheistic principles. The object was to show that the character of Krishna was, in the ancient writings, an ideal perfect man, and that the commonly-received legends of his immorality and amours were the accretions of later and more depraved times. Bankim Chandra Chatterji is the first great creative genius modern India has produced. For the Western reader his novels are a revelation of the inward spirit of Indian life and thought.

As a creative artist he soars to heights unattained by Tulsi Dās, the first true dramatic genius India saw. To claim him solely as a product of Western influence would be to neglect the heritage he held ready to his hand from the poetry of his own country. He is, nevertheless, the first clear type of what a fusion between East and West may yet produce, and the type is one reproduced in his successor, Romesh Chandra Dutt, and in a varied manner by others, such as Kasinath Trimbak Telang, in Bombay. It is names such as Ram Mohun Roy, Keshab Chandar Sen, Bankim Chandra Chatterji, Toru Dutt, and Telang that would live in the future as the memorial of England's fostering care, if all the material evidences of Western civilisation were swept from off the land.

To those who would know something of the life, thoughts, feelings, and religions of the Indian people, no better instructor can be found than Bankim Chandra Chatterji. The English reader must not be surprised if, in the novels of the greatest novelist India has seen, there is much of Eastern form, much of poetic fancy and spiritual mysticism alien to a Western craving for objective realism. Bankim Chandra Chatterji, with all the insight of Eastern poetic genius, with all the artistic delicacy of touch so easily attained by the subtle deftness of a high-caste native of India, or a Pierre Loti, weaves a fine-spun drama of life, fashioning his characters and painting their surroundings with the same gentle touch, as though his fingers worked amid the frail petals of some flower, or moved along the lines of fine silk, to frame therewith a texture as unsubstantial as the dreamy fancies with which all life is woven, as warp and woof. So the "Kopala Kundala" opens with a band of pilgrims travelling by boat to the sacred place of pilgrimage, where the holy River Ganges pours its sin-destroying waters into the boundless ocean. The frail boat, with its weight of sin, is being swept by the rushing flood out towards the sea. The boatmen are powerless; they cry for help to the Muhammadan saints, the pilgrims wail to Durgā, the dreaded wife of Śiva, the Destroyer. One woman alone weeps not; she has cast her child into the flowing stream, for such was her vow of pilgrimage. In its unguided course the boat, by chance, touches land, and the hero, Nobo Kumar, volunteers to wander along the sandy shore in search of firewood. The tide rises, the boat is swept away, and Nobo Kumar is left to gaze after it in despair. The sandy waste is the abode of an ascetic worshipper of Kāli, who is waited on by the heroine, "Kopala Kundala," destined as a sacrifice to the fierce goddess. The ascetic sage is clothed in tiger skins; he is seated on a corpse, and wears a necklace of rudra seeds and human bones; his hair is matted and unshorn. The wild scene is depicted with all the dreamy, poetic repose which saturates the whole life of the East. The ocean is spread in front; across it speeds an English trading ship, with its sails spread out like the wings of some large bird; the blue waters gleam like gold beneath the setting sun; far out, in the endless expanse, the waves break in foam; along the glittering sands there runs a white streak of surf like to a garland of white flowers. The two scenes—one the lonely pilgrim and the near-seated, hideous, human-sacrificing ascetic, the other of the vastness and stillness of the sea—seem to picture forth the emptiness of man's imaginings and efforts amid the impassive immensity of the universe. Over all, the murmuring roll of the ocean, echoed as it is in the poet's words, seems as though it bore to the senses the wailing moan of a soul lost in time and space. In the midst of the mystic scene a woman, the heroine, appears. She is a maiden, with hair as black as jet trailing to her ankles in snake-like curls. Her face, encircled by her black hair, shines like the rays of the moon through the riven clouds. As Nobo Kumar gazes on her form, she tells him to fly from the ascetic Yogī, who has already prepared the sacrificial fire and awaits a human victim. Spellbound, Nobo Kumar has no power to fly from the devotee to Kāli; he follows to the place of sacrifice, and is there bound. Kopala Kundala, in the absence of the priest, appears, severs the bonds, and releases Nobo Kumar. The priest returns, seeks the sacrificial sword, then notes how his victim has been released. In his rage he rushes to and fro along the sandy dunes, from the summit of one of which he stumbles in the darkness, falls, "like a buffalo hurled from some mountain peak," and breaks his arms. The hero and heroine, before they fly from the waste of sands, are married. Kopala Kundala, however, longs to know the will of the goddess. A leaf placed at the foot of the dread deity falls to the ground, fatal omen that the goddess is displeased.

So the fate of man is, for the poet's purpose, as uncertain as the face of a trembling raindrop on a lotus leaf. The new-made wife departs, weeping, from the shrine. The novelist has now to follow her destiny to its relentless course. The shadow of her future soon throws its dark gloom across the soul of Kopala Kundala. Amid the intrigues of the Mughal court of the time of Jahangīr the course is prepared for the tragedy to close round Kopala

Kundala, whose husband grows to doubt her love, and then to witness what has been cunningly devised to seem her faithlessness. The ascetic sage, with broken arms, now appears before Nobo Kumar, and declares that the angered goddess still claims a sacrifice. In his rage, Nobo Kumar offers to sacrifice his wife, and so at once to appease Kāli and his own blind jealousy. Kopala Kundala has herself resolved to fulfil her fate. The relentless decrees, that hold the destiny of man at their beck and nod, have now almost worked out their purposes. The voice of the priest wails with pity as he calls on the victim; her husband seizes the sword, but his passion bursts forth in moaning cries to his beloved to assure him, at the last moment, that she has not been faithless. He hears the truth, that all his suspicions were roused by cunning design. Fate, typified by the will of the goddess, must be worked out. Nobo Kumar extends his arms to clasp his love, but Kopala Kundala steps back, and the waters of the Ganges rise to sweep her away in its sin-destroying flood, where Nobo Kumar also finds his death.

The novel throughout moves steadily to its purpose. There is no over-elaboration, no undue working after effect; everywhere there are signs of the work of an artist whose hand falters not as he chisels out his lines with classic grace. The force that moves the whole with emotion, and gives to it its subtle spell, is the mystic form of Eastern thought that clearly shows the new forms that lie ready for inspiring a new school of fiction with fresh life. Outside the "Mariage de Loti" there is nothing comparable to the "Kopala Kundala" in the history of Western fiction, although the novelist himself, and many of his native admirers, see grounds for comparing the works of Bankim Bābu with those of Sir Walter Scott, probably because they are outwardly historical.

A novel far surpassing "Kopala Kundala" in realistic

interest is the same novelist's "Poison Tree." This novel has its own artistic merits, but its chief value, for English readers, lies in the life-like pictures it presents of modern Indian life and thought. With subdued satire the interested efforts of would-be social reformers are shown to be founded often on motives of self-interest, dishonesty, or immorality. The evil results which too often follow the breaking-away from the strict seclusion and moral restraints of Hindu family life under the influence of Western education are indicated plainly. These modern movements are depicted as often leading the native more towards agnosticism and impatience of control than towards the implanting of a vigorous individuality, founded on a heightening of religious feelings, and wider views of the necessity of self-control and altruistic motives of action. It is a danger which grows graver daily; it is a movement which must be expected in the history of a nation's advance from bondage to freedom, and one to be resolutely met with a firm faith in the eternal elements underlying all enlightenment and social progress, and not with a hopelessness of a pessimistic despair. The novel itself is very simple. It deals with the same few human elements which always form the leading motive for any great creative work of universal and abiding interest. The hero, Nagendra Nāth, is a wealthy landlord, aged thirty, a model amongst men, wealthy and handsome, surrounded by friends, retainers, and relations, all of whom live an ideal life of happiness through his bounty. He rejoices in the possession of a beloved and loving wife, Surja Mukhi, aged twenty-six, who moves amid the household with a calm dignity and graceful gentleness, an ideal picture of a faithful Hindu spouse and well-educated, sensible woman. Nagendra, during a journey to Calcutta, befriends an orphan girl, Kunda, aged but thirteen—an age described as that in which all the charm of simplicity is combined with the radiance of the moonbeams and scent of sweet flowers. Nagendra brings the girl to his married sister at Calcutta, but, as he seems in no hurry to depart, his wife writes playfully upbraiding him, and suggesting in jest that he should bring his new-found treasure home and marry her himself, or give her to the village schoolmaster, who has not yet found a willing bride. The child is accordingly brought to the village and married to the schoolmaster. This schoolmaster, snub-nosed, conceited, and copper-coloured, is represented as an up-to-date product of an undigested surfeit of Western emancipation. He has received an English education at a free mission school, and planted himself amid the village community as a very mine of learned lore; it was whispered abroad that he had read the "Citizen of the World," and passed in three books of "Euclid." He extracted essays against idolatry, against the seclusion of women and child-marriage from the *Tattva-bodhinī*, and published them under his own name. He joined the local Brāhma Samāj, established by the spendthrift of the neighbourhood, who had imbibed all the Western vices and abandoned all the native virtues, who drank wine from decanters with cut-glass stoppers, carried a brandy flask, and ate roast mutton and cutlets, and who, when not drunk, occupied his time in encouraging the marriage of low-caste widows, so that he might pose as a local reformer. The satire is perfect, the characters satirised true to life. The new product of Western influences encouraged the infatuated schoolmaster to read papers and deliver eloquent addresses on the subject of the emancipation of women, and the moralising influence of bringing women out into public life, but finds that although the schoolmaster can be jeered into allowing him to visit Kunda, the outraged pride of the timid beauty bursts forth in a flood of indignant tears.

Luckily for Kunda, the schoolmaster dies. The widow

returns to the home of her former protector, the all-loving Nagendra. The gentle beauty of Kunda sinks deep into the heart of Nagendra, whose want of self-control sows the seeds of the poison tree, whose baneful fruit must be eaten. Nagendra's wife looks on in sorrow until her husband, unable to stifle his thoughts or bear her silent reproaches, seeks to drown his feelings in drink. At length he can bear the restraint no longer. Isvara Chandra Vidyasagar has proved, from the ancient law books, that widow-marriage is allowable, although no Hindu custom. His wife hides her wounded feelings, wondering if Isvara Chandra Vidyasagar be a pandit, who then is wanting in wisdom? She sacrifices all her feelings to her great love for her husband and prepares the marriage ceremonies, but once the marriage takes place, she steals away from the happy home where she was once sole mistress. She had made her resolve to wander as a mendicant from place to place, unable to remain at home and bear the pain of seeing Kunda claim her husband.

The suffering of Surja Mukhi, the despair of Nagendra when he finds his once loved wife has left, and that, as a consequence, his overwhelming passion for Kunda has turned to indifference, almost to loathing, are set forth with a fulness of sympathy and emotional feeling which a native can so deeply feel and express. To its bitterest depths the novelist traces the stern course of the unrelenting destiny which decrees that the seeds of sin once sown must grow, and the fruit be reaped.

A welcome relief comes when the story breaks into somewhat laboured humour. The eager servants of Nagendra go forth with coaches and palanquins in search of their mistress, whose face they have never seen. Every good-looking and high-caste woman along the road, by the bathing tanks, or river-side, is forcibly seized and brought, with cries of joy, to the unfortunate husband, to see if he can recognise among them his lost wife, so that, finally, no woman dare venture from home for fear of being brought to Nagendra. Surja Mukhi returns not. Her husband leaves his new wife, Kunda, to mourn alone over her destiny in the now deserted home, once so full of joy and happiness.

Nagendra returns after weary wanderings to end his life in pious deeds and holy living. Kunda he is resolved never more to speak to nor to see. For her, therefore, there is only death; the poisoned fruit must be eaten that grew from the seed of sin. Before she dies the long-lost wife reappears, and Kunda, in her dying moments, is received as a younger sister, and sinks to rest, her hands clasping her rival's feet, her head supported by her husband, whose love she had once won, and whom she now knows cannot abide by her.

In Nagendra's love for Kunda the novelist declares that he wished to depict the fleeting love of passion, as sung by Kālidāsa, Byron, and Jaya Deva, and in his love for Surja Mukhi, the deep love which sacrifices one's own happiness for the love of another, as sung by Shakespeare, Vālmīki, and Madame de Stäel.

The Bengali novelist could not so readily shake himself free from his Eastern form of thought, and view all things from an objective point of view. The love for Kunda is still the fettering of the soul by the objects of sense; the love of the husband for his first wife is still the mystic love of the soul for God.

The wealth of material which lies to the hand of the future great novelist of India has been virtually untouched. Bankim Chandra Chatterji, has but led the way and indicated the material which awaits the next great artist.

He leaves us in doubt whether he is depicting life as it throbbed around him, or whether he has hemmed in his characters with a surrounding of Eastern mysticism and romantic reserve born of Western conventionality.

If Bankim Chandra Chatterji has struck a chord which vibrates through the hearts of the many women of zenanas in India, whose eyes must have wept bitter tears over the agony of Surja Mukhi, deplorable indeed, and worthy of all his deep feeling as an artist, must be the condition of a vast multitude of suffering women in the East, who have been nurtured to see their life blasted by a rival love placed by their side to rejoice their lord's heart, or that a son may be born to save their husband's soul. We are, however, left in doubt as to whether Nagendra sinned in having a second wife—he defends polygamy in the course of the story—or whether his fault lay in marrying a widow against social custom. The motive for fatality of act should have been as clear and unmistakable as it was in the "Mud Cart," where the jealousies of the two rival wives who became reconciled do not influence the action.

The same idea is further worked out in "Krishna Kanta's Will." Here the true workings of the novelist's mind are apparent; a deeper vein is touched. The love of the erring husband for his wife, and the rival love by which he is infatuated, typifies a struggle between a Divine love and the ever-recurring phantasmal attraction of the soul to the objects of sense, from which freedom can only be reached by centring the mind on ideal perfections.

The praise of Krishna, as a perfected man, is sung by the poet in his greatest work, the "Krishna Charitra," published in 1862, as a contribution to a Hindu revival in the ancient national religion, which Romesh Chandra Dutt describes as "the nourishing and life-giving faith of the 'Upanishads,' and the 'Vedānta,' and the 'Bhagavad Gīta,' which has been, and ever will be, the true faith of the Hindus."[1]

A worthy follower of India's first great novelist appeared in Romesh Chandra Dutt, the ablest native member of the Indian Civil Service. His novels have now passed

[1] Dutt, R. C., "The Literature of Bengal," p. 235.

through five or six editions in the Bengalī. He has resisted all entreaties to translate them into English, although he is as able with his pen in English, as he is in Sanskrit and Bengalī. The advice given him by Bankim Chandra Chatterji now no longer applies; the Eastern form has fused sufficiently with the English motive force to make a prose translation by himself of his works not only widely acceptable by the Western public, but necessary for all students of history and literature.

Bankim Chandra's advice was given in 1872, and then mainly referred to poetry, not to prose: "You will never live by your writings in English," he said; "look at others. Your uncles, Govind Chandra and Shashi Chandra's English poems will never live. Madhu Sudan's Bengalī poetry will live as long as the Bengalī language will live."

In his own time the elder novelist clearly recognised the younger as a worthy rival, and on the appearance, in 1874 of Romesh Chandra Dutt's first novel, "Banga Bijeta," a tale of the times of Akbar, he wrote: "I am crowding my canvas with characters; it won't do for a veteran like me to be beaten by a youngster."

The other five novels of Romesh Chandra Dutt followed in quick succession. "Rājput Jiban Sandhya" (1878), a tale of the times of Jahangīr; "Madhalei Kankan" (1876), a tale of the times of Shāh Jahān; "Maharashtra Jiban Prabhat" (1877), a tale of the times of Aurangzīb; "Sansar" (1885); "Samaj" (1894); two social novels continuing the same story. His translation of the "Rig Veda Sanhita" into Bengalī appeared in 1887; his valuable "History of Civilisation of Ancient India," in English, in three volumes from 1889; his second edition of "The Literature of Bengal," so often quoted in this work, in 1895; and his selection of translations from the "Rig Veda Purānas," and "Hindu Sāstras," from 1895 to 1897.

A whole library of "Sorrow and Song" was poured forth by this Dutt family of Rambagan. Govind Chandra Dutt and Shashi Chandra Dutt first published the "Dutt Family Album," in 1870, in England, hoping, as they said, that their poems would be regarded in England as curiosities, and the work of foreigners educated at the Hindu College at Calcutta who had become Christians.

Their work, like much similar work of the same class —the "Lotus Leaves" of H. C. Dutt, the "Cherry Blossom" of G. C. Dutt, the "Vision of Sumeru," and other poems, by S. Chandra Dutt and others—indicate the enormous difficulties which lie before even the most gifted who work in English verse.

A few verses from "A Vision of Sumeru, and other Poems,"[1] by the estimable Shashi Chundra Dutt, a Rai Bahādur and Justice of the Peace at Calcutta, strike a key-note that wails of itself:—

MY NATIVE LAND.

"My native land, I love thee still!
There's beauty yet upon thy lonely shore;
And not a tree, and not a rill,
But can my soul with rapture thrill,
Though glory dwells no more."

. . . .

"What though those temples now are lone
Where guardian angels long did dwell;
What though from brooks that sadly run,
The naiads are for ever gone—
Gone with their sounding shell!"

. . . .

"Those days of mythic tale and song,
When dusky warriors, in their martial pride,
Strode thy sea-beat shores along,
While with their fame the valleys rung,
And turn'd the foe aside.

[1] Thacker Spink (Calcutta, 1879).

"Then sparkled woman's brilliant eye,
And heaved her heart, and panted to enslave;
And beauteous veils and flow'rets shy,
In vain to hide those charms did try
That flash'd to woo the brave.

"My fallen country! where abide
Thy envied splendour, and thy glory now?
The Páthán's and the Mogul's pride,
Spread desolation far and wide,
And stain'd thy sinless brow."

. . . .

"And beauty's eye retains its fire,
What though its lightnings flash not for the brave;
And beauteous bosoms yet aspire,
With passion strong and warm desire,
To wake the crouching slave.

"My country! fallen as thou art,
My soul can never cease to heave for thee:
I feel the dagger's edge, the dart
That rankles in thy widow'd heart,
Thy woeful destiny!"

The full force of the clashing of new and old reached its climax in the short, sad life of the "Jeune et célébre Hindoue de Calcutta."[1]

Toru Dutt, the gifted daughter of a gifted family, was born in Calcutta in 1856, where, as she sings:—

"The light green graceful tamarinds abound
Amid the mango clumps of green profound.
And palms arise, like pillars grey, between,
And o'er the quiet pools the seemuls lean."[2]

She died at the early age of twenty-one, but in her short span of life she had crowded her imaginative mind with imagery gleaned from French, German, English, and Sanskrit literature, and with her retentive memory had

[1] "Le Journal de Mdlle. d'Arvers par Toru Dutt" (Paris, 1879).
[2] Toru Dutt, "Ballads and Legends of Hindustan" (1885).

stored up an unique knowledge which she afterwards showed in "A Sheaf gleaned in French Fields," published in 1876, containing unaided translations from the French, some by her sister Aru, and criticisms, amongst others, of Leconte de Lisle, Alfred de Musset, Victor Hugo, François Coppée, and Théophile Gautier. More remarkable was "Le Journal de Mdlle. d'Arvers," a romance in French, published with an account of Toru Dutt's life and work by Mdlle. Clarisse Bader in 1879. The work, however, by which she will be best known to English readers is her "Ancient Ballads and Legends of Hindustān," published in 1885, with an introduction by Edmund Gosse. The poems often faultless as they are in technical execution, sometimes the verse, as Mr Gosse truly says, being exquisite to a hypercritical ear, can never take an abiding-place in the history of English or Indian literature. The old ballads and legends have lost all their plaintive cadence, all the natural charm they bore when wrapped round with the full-sounding music of the Sanskrit, or in what lay ready to the hands of the poetess, her own classical Bengalī.

The imagery, the scenery has even lost its own Oriental colour and profusion of ornamentation. The warmth of expression and sentiment has of necessity been toned down by the very use of a language which, even had it been plastic in the hands of Toru Dutt, could never have afforded her the delicate touch and colour which she found in the French.

In her poem "Jogadhya Uma," her own creative powers have found their fullest play. In her own vernacular the poem would have been sung to music so weird and soothing, the words would have been attuned to feelings so deep and sincere, that, although she had parted from her ancient faith and become a Christian, it would have been a poem destined to live in the religious poetry of Hinduism, and take a place among the songs of the people. As it is, while it shows all her innate resources, it also shows the lack of power of her choice of a medium to express her ideals. The story is one she has learned for herself:—

"Absurd may be the tale I tell,
 Ill-suited to the marching times,
I loved the lips from which it fell,
 So let it stand among my rhymes."

In the poem a pedlar wanders to and fro crying his wares:—

"Shell bracelets, ho! Shell bracelets, ho!
Fair maids and matrons come and buy!"

As he cries,

"A fair young woman with large eyes,
 And dark hair falling to her zone,
She heard the pedlar's cry arise,
 And eager seemed his ware to own."

A shell bracelet is bought, and the woman tells the pedlar to go to her home, a manse near the village temple where her father is priest. The pedlar goes to the priest and demands the price, and from the story he tells, the priest discerns that it was the goddess Uma who had appeared to the pedlar.

The priest cries:—

"How strange! how strange! Oh blest art thou
 To have beheld her, touched her hand,
Before whom Vishnu's self must bow,
 And Brahma and his heavenly band.
Here have I worshipped her for years,
 And never seen the vision bright.
Vigil and fasts and secret tears
 Have almost quenched my outward sight;
And yet that dazzling form and face
 I have not seen, and thou, dear friend,
To thee, unsought-for, comes the grace.
 What may its purport be, and end?"

They hasten back to the water-side, where the goddess had been seen bathing, but there

> "The birds were silent in the wood,
> Over all the solitude.
> A heron as a sentinel,
> Stood by the bank. . . ."

The goddess had disappeared, but in answer to the priest's prayer for her reappearance

> "Sudden from out the water sprung
> A rounded arm on which they saw,
> As high the lotus buds among
> It rose, the bracelet white. . . ."
>
> . . . .
>
> "It sinks.
> They bowed before the mystic Power,
> And as they home returned, in thought
> Each took from thence a lotus flower,
> In memory of the day and spot.
> Years, centuries have passed away,
> And still before the temple shrine,
> Descendants of the pedlar pay
> Shell bracelets of the old design,
> As annual tribute. Much they own
> On land, and gold,—but they confess
> From that eventful day alone,
> Dawned on their industry,—success."

A novel of great interest, entitled "Induleka," has passed almost unnoticed in England, although it was translated by the able Malayālam scholar, Mr Dumergue of the Indian Civil Service. It appeared in 1889, and was written in the vernacular language of the Malabar coast, Travancore, and Cochin by Mr O. Chandu Menon. It was avowedly written for the purpose of introducing the Western form of fiction to the home of the novelist, so that when "stories composed of incidents true to national life, and attractively and gracefully written, are once introduced, then, by degrees, the old order of books, filled with the impossible and the supernatural, will change, giving place to the new."

In the course of the story, the newly-acquired thoughts and habits of natives educated on English lines, are contrasted with those of the old school of conservative and orthodox Hindus.

The inward life of a Nair family or Tarwad, ruled, according to the local custom, by the chief of the house, or "Karnavan," is laid bare, with the conflict waged by the younger members against their "unprogressive" elders.

The author, in his preface, describes the hero, Madhavan, as "a graduate both in Arts and Law. He is extremely handsome in appearance, and extraordinarily intelligent, and a good Sanskrit scholar. He excelled in sports and English games, such as cricket and lawn-tennis." As the novel is to be "a novel after the English fashion," the author confesses that "it is evident that no ordinary Malayalee lady could fill the rôle of the heroine of such a story. My Induleka is not, therefore, an ordinary Malayalee lady. She knows English, Sanskrit, music, etc., and is at once a very beautiful and a very accomplished young lady of about seventeen years of age when our story opens."

That the reader should not imagine that the character is altogether untrue to life, the novelist hastens to add: "I myself know two or three respectable Nair ladies now living, who, in intellectual culture (save and except in the knowledge of English), strength of character, and general knowledge, can well hold comparison with Induleka. As for beauty, personal charms, refined manners, simplicity of taste, conversational powers, wit and humour, I can show hundreds of young ladies, in respectable Nair Tarwads, who would undoubtedly come up to the standard of my Induleka."

The story of the trials of the hero and heroine and of

the final triumph of their love, is well worked out on the lines of English fiction, with the added interest and charm of Eastern life and Eastern scenery.

One chapter towards the end of the story gives, in the form of a conversation between Madhavan, the hero, his father, Govinda Panikkar, a "bigoted Hindu," and his cousin, Govinda Kutti Menon, the current native view on such subjects as religion, education, and the National Congress. Madhavan's father first upbraids his son with want of love, faith, and veneration :—

> "The cause of all this, I say, is English education. Faith in God and piety should rank foremost in the hearts of men, but you who learn English have neither. . . . Your new-fangled knowledge and notions have ruined everything. I see you continually forsaking the good old practices which we Hindus have observed from time immemorial. . . . All this hostility to our time-honoured rules of virtuous life, is due to nothing but the study of English. If the acquisition of human knowledge and human culture comes into conflict with faith in things Divine, then they are most utterly worthless. It behoves each and every man to cling to the faith of his forefathers, but you apparently think that the Hindu religion is altogether contemptible."

The usual arguments on the subjects of theism, atheism, and agnosticism follow. The father, Govinda Panikkar, at length retorts :—

> "If you say that God is omnipresent, can you therefore make up your mind not to go to the temples? Besides, do you really mean to say that there are no saints upon earth who have freed themselves from all worldly cares and passions?"
>
> "I certainly do," answered Madhavan. "I maintain emphatically that, except when all natural appetites and desires are quenched by sickness, there is no man devoid of the impulses and passions which are inherent in the flesh."
>
> "This is dreadful," exclaimed Govinda Panikkar. "Just think how many great devotees and ascetics have conquered all fleshly lusts."
>
> "I don't believe there are any who have," replied Madhavan.
>
> "Then are you an atheist altogether, my son?"
>
> "I am no atheist; on the contrary, I firmly believe there is a God."
>
> "Then what about the ascetics?"

"I do not believe there are any such men as you mentioned, whether they are devotees or not."

"But I saw an ascetic once who lived on nothing but seven pepper-corns and seven neem leaves a day. He never even drank water."

"He must have been an uncommonly clever impostor," said Govinda Kutti Menon, "and I have no doubt he humbugged you."

"He stayed for nine days in the lodge with me," returned Govinda Panikkar, "and ate nothing the whole time."

"You did not see him eat anything, brother," said Govinda Kutti Menon, "and believed that he ate nothing; that's all. A man cannot live without food. It is so ordained by nature, and what is the use of any one telling lies about it?"

"There, now," said Govinda Panikkar, "this perversity comes from your intercourse with English people. You never believe a word we say."

Long extracts from the writings of Bradlaugh are quoted to break down the faith of the orthodox Hindu in all his ancient religion. The story of creation and of Adam, as dealt with by Bradlaugh, are next discussed :—

"But there is no mention of any man named Adam in our 'Shāstras' and 'Purānas,' and I don't believe a word of what you have read," objected Govinda Panikkar.

"You need not believe in Adam," replied Govinda Kutti Menon. "But the account given by the Christian Scriptures of the curse which is said to have fallen on Adam, and the tribulation which is described as resulting from the wrath of God, is nothing compared with similar accounts in our 'Purānas.' According to them, it is not only God, but also saintly men and minor deities, and Brāhmans, and, more than this, women, that are paragons of virtue, who, in their wrath, take cruel and manifold vengeance on immortals and mortals, and the dumb brute creation from one birth to another. None of this rank, preposterous folly appears in the Christian Scriptures."

"Don't speak like that," said Govinda Panikkar. "What do you mean by saying such things of our 'Purānas,' Govinda Kutti? Do you imagine any one will believe you when you condemn as rank folly our 'Purānas,' which are as old as the world itself, simply because you have read an English book, a creation of yesterday? But, apart from that, if there is no God, then what you say must amount to this, that man called himself into existence."

"It amounts to more," replied Govinda Kutti, "because I say that not only man, but also the whole world, came into existence through various elements and forces, and is attaining complete development spontaneously."

"Then, in that case, when a man dies, what becomes of the spirit of life?" asked Govinda Panikkar.

"Nothing," replied Govinda Kutti Menon. "It simply becomes extinct. If you put out a lighted candle, what becomes of the flame? Surely nothing; it is simply extinguished, and so it is with the spirit of life."

"Then man has no future state! All is ended in death!" exclaimed Govinda Panikkar. "Verily, this is a creed fit only for devils!"

The unfortunate father has, however, to sit still and listen to a discussion over the relative merits of the writings of Darwin, Huxley, Herbert Spencer, and other English writers, and those of the Indian sages. The case for and against the National Congress is next considered, Madhavan's cousin vehemently opposing its purposes and methods:—

"Even for the English, with all their unity of caste and fusion of race, Parliamentary Government is a matter of difficulty, and how preposterous then is the idea entertained by some bawling Babus, Brāhmans, and Mudalis of forming, out of the inhabitants of India, who are divided by ten thousand differences of caste into sections as antagonistic to each other as a mongoose is to a snake, an assembly like Parliament for the administration of the country? The project is sheer folly, nothing else. It is simply their fear of being knocked over by bullets and their weakness that has made the nations between the Himālayas and Cape Comorin live at peace with one another since the advent of the English, but let the English leave India to-morrow, and then we shall see the greatness and valour of the Babus. Will these open-mouthed demagogues be able to protect the country for a single minute? Why, if they really possessed that fine feeling of self-esteem which they profess, they would long ago have obtained the privileges they so earnestly desire. But in truth they possess neither courage, nor strength, nor energy, nor patience. Clamour is almost everything with them. Their sole object, their one set ambition is to make a fine speech in English. If the English Government, working on its present lines, gradually introduces changes and reforms into India for the next generation, this is all that is required. There are thousands of customs and institutions in India which are wholly imperfect or disgraceful, and should be developed and improved. Why should the supporters of the Congress neglect them utterly and go beyond all bounds in grasping first of all at sovereignty? Why, for instance, do they make no attempt to remove the obstacles to improvement and progress which are interposed by so many unnecessary distinctions of caste? Why do they not, in order to relieve the poverty of the land, try to teach its nations trade with foreign countries, better modes of agriculture, manufacture, mechanical engineering? Why not endeavour to spread education among women? Why not seek to reform our obscure household customs and barbarous practices? It is now many years since the railway, and telegraph, and other wonderful inventions, were introduced into India, and why should no efforts be made to instruct Hindus and Muhammadans how to construct them and work them?"

The case for the Congress is argued out by Madhavan, who sets forth its objects shortly in the following words:—

"With the beginning of their administration began not only the diffusion of knowledge and education among the natives of India, but also a desire to participate in the privileges to which knowledge affords us a title. Inasmuch then as we have every reason to believe that the English Government will, in justice grant us the fulfilment of this desire if we ask for it, the Congress has been established in order to prefer our request by all lawful and reasonable means."

In Madras the two novels "Saguna," and "Kamala" were written by Mrs S. Satthianadhan, whose fragile life passed away in 1894. She was born in 1862, her parents, Haripunt and Radhabai, being the first Brāhman converts to Christianity in the Bombay Presidency.[1] Her novels are now well known in England. The two conspicuous features of her novels—both derived from her English education and surroundings—are seen in the following extract from "Saguna." The scene is one she witnessed with her brother in the Deccan. The objective mode of

[1] "Kamala: a Story of Hindu Life," by Mrs S. Satthianadhan, with Memoir by Mrs H. B. Grigg (Madras, 1894). "Saguna: a Story of Native Christian Life," with Preface by Mrs R. S. Benson (Madras, 1895).

viewing Nature is peculiarly the outcome of Western influence, to which influence must also be ascribed her sincerely Christian piety.

> "The mountain path with its loose stones, moss-grown and dark, the trees loaded with foliage, the twisted, gnarled trunks springing from the midst of granite rocks and stones, the huge serpentine creepers swinging overhead, and over it all the faint glimmering light of dawn—all this formed a picture too full of living beauty, light and shade, to be ever forgotten. We ascended a little rocky eminence, and were looking at the wonders round us, the mists and the shadows, and the play of the light over all, when suddenly the scene changed, and the sun emerged from behind a huge rock. In a moment the whole place was bathed in light. Did the birds make a louder noise, or was the echo stronger, for I thought I heard, with the advent of light, quite an outburst of song and merriment? My brother, in his usual earnest way, remarked that it is just like this, shadowy, dark, mystic, weird, with superstition and bigotry lurking in every corner, before the light of Christianity comes into a land. When the sun rises, he said, all the glory of the trees and the rocks comes into view, each thing assumes its proper proportions and is drawn out in greater beauty and perfection. So it is when the sunbeams of Christianity dispel the darkness of superstition in a land."

In later years the names crowd round of those who show that

> During the last two generations India has gone through a new and unique development, fraught with momentous consequences to itself and to the British Empire. Under Western influences the former traditional moorings are already being gradually left behind, and the educated classes are drifting towards another goal."[1]

It would be almost an endless task to even enumerate the names of those whose works and labours show evidences of this new influence, this awakening of the torpid Hindu intellect from the sleep into which it had been thrown by the fierce, foreign rule of the Muhammadans during seven centuries. Of all the names, that of Behramji Malabari is

[1] Karkaria, "India: Forty Years of Progress and Reform," p. 13.

most familiar to English readers, from his well-known work, "The Indian Eye on English Life," and his "Guzarat and the Guzaratis."

Malabari, a Parsi, was born in 1853 at Baroda, in the dominion of the Gaikwad, now one of surviving representatives of the great Marātha power. Failing to pass the matriculation examination at Bombay, he commenced a desultory course of reading described by himself:—

"I have ranged aimlessly over a very wide field of poetry, English as well as Indian; also Persian and Greek translated. As to English masters, Shakespeare was my daily companion during schooldays, and a long while after that. Much of my worldly knowledge I owe to this greatest of seers and practical thinkers. Milton filled me with awe. Somehow I used to feel unhappy when the turn came for 'Paradise Lost.' His torrents of words frightened me as much by their stateliness as by monotony. Nor could I sympathise with some of the personal teachings of this grand old singer. Wordsworth is my philosopher, Tennyson is my poet."[1]

The command Malibari obtained over Guzarati resulted in the production of his "Nīti Vinod," or "Pleasures of Morality," and his acquaintance with English emboldened him to risk his "Indian Muse in English Garb," to an English public. From the latter a few lines[2] will indicate the spirit in which the new reformer commenced his work, and the style of his verse:—

"O mourn thou not in vain regrets
  That fancied wrong thy peace alloys;
When thy ungrateful heart forgets
  What bliss thy conquered race enjoys.
What if thy English brother lords
  It o'er thee, with contempt implied?
Recall the day when Moslem swords
  Cut thee and thine in wanton pride!
Think how a generous nation strives
  To win thee back thy prestige lost;
Of what dear joys herself deprives
  To aid thee at a frightful cost!"

[1] Karkaria, "Indiaec," p. 40.   [2] *Ibid.*, p. 67.

During his active life Malabari cast the whole of the power his command over Guzarati and English gave him into the tasks of endeavouring to soften race antipathies, and to introduce some of the more obviously required reforms into Indian society. As editor of the *Spectator* he exercised an influence far-spread and deep, being, in the words of Mr Martin Wood, the editor of the *Times of India*, "peculiarly fitted for being a trustworthy interpreter between rulers and ruled, between the indigenous and immigrant branches of the great Aryan race. It is easy to see that he thoroughly understands the mental and moral characteristics of these two great divisions of the Indian community, not only as presented in Bombay, but in other provinces in India." In his notes on "Infant Marriage and Enforced Widowhood," Malabari pointed out forcibly the two gravest social blots in Indian life. As a result of his labours, both in the Press and on the platform, in England as well as in India, he had the satisfaction of seeing the "Age of Consent Bill of 1891" passed, during the administration of Lord Lansdowne, by which the age of consummation of marriage was raised from ten to twelve.

In his "Sketch of the Life and Times of Behramji M. Malabari," R. P. Karkaria points out, from an Indian point of view, the tendencies, so apparent to all, in one direction of the continued contact with a new and Western civilisation:—

> "The work of destruction is being done effectively; belief in the old religion is giving way among the men who receive an English training. This may not be perhaps quite desirable, as it is better to be, in the phrase of Wordsworth, 'a Pagan suckled in a creed outworn,' than to have no creed at all. The old creeds are found to be outworn by them, but they have taken definitely to no new creed. The ground for such a one, however, is being cleared. What that creed is to be is a matter for speculation. That it will be Christianity in any dogmatic form, one cannot hope. The present agnostic tendency of European thought seems to have a fascination for the Indian intellect, and there are signs here and there to show that atheism is spreading and

taking the place of the old superstitions. The writings of agnostics and atheists are growing in favour with our academic youths, who seem to consider all religion as superstition, and every creed to be an anachronism."[1]

In the same work the opinion of Malabari is quoted on this problem of the future, the most momentous, not only for India, but for the whole civilised world :—

"I know not if India will become Christian, and when. But this much I know, that the life and work of Christ must tell in the end. After all, He is no stranger to us Easterns. How much of our own He brings back to us, refined and modernised? His European followers seek Him most for His Divine attributes, to me, Jesus is most Divine in His human element. He is so human, so like ourselves, that it will not be difficult to understand Him, though it is doubtful if the dogmas preached in His name will acquire a firm hold on the East."[2]

What may be expected in the near future, as a result of a contact between the intensely earnest and brooding thought of the East with the best of what may be called Western civilisation, can, in some measure, be dimly shadowed forth, as some hope of encouragement to England in the work she has undertaken, if the lines are read and re-read of a brilliant article that has appeared on the situation by Sir Raymond West, in his review of the life and work of Kasinath Trimbak Telang, a Judge of the High Court of Bombay, who died in 1894.

Kasinath Trimbak Telang was born, in 1850, of a respectable family in Bombay. He early perfected himself in Marathī and Sanskrit, and by 1869 had taken the degree of M.A. and LL.B. in the Bombay University. In 1872 he became an advocate, and soon, "in all matters of Hindu law, Telang was, by general acknowledgment, *facile princeps* of the Bombay Bar."

To a native alone can be known the true force of the various schools of Hindu law among the varied classes

[1] Karkaria, "Sketch of the Life and Times of B. M. Malabari," p. 67.

[2] *Ibid.*, p. 81.

of the community, and in how far local circumstances, habits, or customs have the binding force of law outside all the formulated codes of the Brāhmanical legislators. The English judge naturally accepts these Brāhmanical codes as of universal authority, and as being generally known or accepted as such. That the Brāhmanical codes were made by a special class, and for a special class, of the community is evident to all acquainted with the literary history of India. To the overworked and practical administrator, or advocate, a law is accepted as law, and applied without those restrictions which only an intimate acquaintance with the past history or present life of the people would suggest. The peculiar province of a native advocate or judge, such as Telang, is to impress these facts on their English legislators and jurists. In the words of Sir Raymond West,[1] Telang "felt very strongly that in Hindu Law, as elsewhere, life implies growth and adaptation. He hailed with warm welcome the principle that custom may ameliorate, as well as fix, even the Hindu law, and it was refreshing sometimes to hear him arguing for modernization, while, on the other side, an English advocate, to whom the whole Hindu system must have seemed more or less grotesque, contended for the most rigorous construction of some antique rule."

Telang received, as a fitting recognition of his position as "the most capable of Hindus of our generation," a Judgeship of the High Court of Bombay, in 1889, and afterwards the Vice-Chancellorship of the University. As a Legislative Member of the Council at Bombay he threw the whole weight of his scholarship and power as an advocate against such of his orthodox countrymen as opposed the raising of the age of consummation of marriage for child-wives. He showed that by neither Vedic authority, nor by the wording of the Queen's

[1] West Sir Raymond, J R.A.S. (1894).

Proclamation was the English Government anything but free to legislate on the subject. "It is the bounden duty of the Legislative," he said, "to do what it is now doing in the interests of humanity, and of the worldly interests of the communities committed to its charge, and for such a purpose as the present to disregard, if need be, the 'Hindu Shāstras.'"[1]

As a profound Sanskrit scholar, he is known as author of many valued works. As a debater whose "language of a limpid purity would have done credit to an English-born orator," he is remembered for his stirring addresses on such subjects as the Ilbert Bill, Licence and Salt Taxes, his advocacy for the extended admission of natives to the Indian Civil Service, and on many other important measures and topics. In these addresses "his style was framed on the classic writers, and expressed his meaning with admirable force and clearness. It may, indeed, be doubted if any native orator has equalled him in lucidity and that restraint which is so much more effective than exaggeration and over-embellishment."[2]

As a member of the Education Commissioners of 1882 his report is, "in some respects, the most valuable of a crushingly voluminous collection," and, as Vice-Chancellor of the University, he warmly supported all the great efforts of Lord Reay[3] for the establishment and encouragement of technical education, and convinced as he was that "success in the modern world was to be obtained only by adaptation to the needs of modern life, he wished his fellow-Hindus to unite an inner light of Divine philosophy, drawn from the traditional sources, and generously interpreted, to a mastery of the physical sciences, and the means of natural improvement." Jurist, statesman, scholar, orator, poet, lover of Nature, and meditative sage, he remains to the West the

[1] West, Sir Raymond, J.R.A.S. (1894), p. 119. [2] *Ibid.*, 113.
[3] *See* Hunter, Bombay, "A Study in Indian Administration," p. 157.

convincing proof that "it is by the word and the example of him and his like that India must be regenerated, and the moral endowments of her children made noble, serviceable for the general welfare of mankind."

To his fellow-countrymen, he is the example of how "the present generation of cultivated Hindus want only physical robustness and public experience, or a modest sense of inexperience and reasonable limitation of practical aims, to be outwardly distinguished from the mass of pushing, intelligent Europeans with whom they mingle."

There are other well-known names whose places and fame future times will have to record and note, as affording clear evidences that East and West have met, and sent new forces out into the world for the solving of its plan and mysteries. There are names, such as Rajendra lāl Mitra, Bhagvan lāl Indraji,[1] Ram Krishna Gopal Bhandarkar, which tell how India, with a newly-awakened respect for historical accuracy, and perspective combined with labour, can produce works fully able to rank with those of the best of Western scholarship.

The West has plainly recognised how the subtle, nervous temperament, the quick co-relation between thought and action joined to untiring perseverance, can produce a cricketer, probably the keenest the world has seen; and yet there are doubts that the same qualities cannot produce, and have not produced, their due effect in the realms more congenial to them, those of thought, where for the present their true working must remain more or less hidden from our gaze.

Men such as Ram Mohun Roy, Keshab Chandar Sen, Michael Sudan Datta, Bankim Chandra Chatterji, Kasinath Trimbak Telang are no bastard bantlings of a Western civilisation; they were creative geniuses worthy to be reckoned in the history of India with such men of old as Kālidāsa, Chaitanya, Jaya Deva, Tulsi Dās, and Śānkara

[1] *See* "Memoir" in J.B.R.A.S., vol. xvii. p. 18.

Āchārya, and destined in the future to shine clear as the first glowing sparks sent out in the fiery furnace where new and old were fusing.

Year by year the leaders of Indian thought in India spread their influence over ever-widening circles, though what the final result may be when these leaders, infused with all the best of the spirit of the East and West, rise up to proclaim that East and West have met, and from the union new forms of thought, new modes of artistic expression, new ways of viewing life, new solutions of religious, social, and moral problems have been produced, as produced they must be, is one that the whole past history of the world teaches us is to be watched with hope, not fear or doubt. Slowly the movement will take place, and in each step there will be unrest and dangers both to State and people, and in a land like India fierce commotion, taking all the steadying hand of the English rule to direct and guide it towards a safe haven. The words of one of the many of the great thinkers of India, who has received, in his own sphere of thought, a recognition that might be extended more liberally to all those who strive to find expression for what the West has inplanted in them, may be quoted as some hope for the future, though not, perhaps, in the sense intended by Professor Bose :[1]—

> "How blind we are! How circumscribed is our knowledge! The little we can see is nothing compared to what actually is! But things which are dark now will one day be made clear. Knowledge grows little by little, slowly but surely. Patient and long-continued work will one day unravel many of the mysteries with which we are surrounded. Many wonderful things have recently been discovered, much more wonderful things still remain to be discovered. We have already caught broken glimpses of invisible lights. Some day, perhaps not far distant, we shall be able to see light-gleams, visible or invisible, merging one into the other, in unbroken sequence."

[1] *Indian Magazine and Review* (May 1897), p. 237; S. J. L. Bose, on "Electric Waves."

A SHORT LIST OF USEFUL WORKS RECOMMENDED FOR FURTHER STUDY

A SHORT LIST OF USEFUL WORKS RECOMMENDED FOR FURTHER STUDY.

BADEN-POWELL, B. H. The Indian Village Community. 1896.

BARTH, A. The Religions of India. Authorised Translation. By Rev. J. Wood. *London*, 1882.

BERGAIGNE, ABEL. La Religion Védique. 3 vols. *Paris*, 1878-83.

BIGANDET, Bishop. The Life or Legend of Gaudama. *Rangoon*, 1858. *London*, 1880.

CAMPBELL, F. Index Catalogue of Bibliographical Works relating to India. *London*, 1897.

CHATTERJEE, B. C. Poison Tree. Translated. *London*, 1884.

——— Kopala Kundala. Translated. *London*, 1885.

——— Krishna Kanta's Will. Translated. *London*, 1895.

COLEBROOKE, H. T. Essays on the Religion and Philosophy of the Hindus. *London*, 1882.

COWELL, E. B., and A. E. Gough. Sarva Darsana Sangraha.

COWELL, Professor E. B., and Mr THOMAS of Trinity College, Cambridge. Bâna's Harsa Carita. Oriental Translation Series. 1897.

CROOKE, W. The Tribes and Castes of the North-West Provinces and Oudh. *Calcutta*, 1896.

CROOKE, W. Popular Religion and Folk-Lore of Northern India. 2 vols. *London*, 1896.

DAHLMANN, JOSEPH. Das Mahâbhârata als Epos und Rechtsbuch. *Berlin*, 1895.

DARMESTETER, J. English Studies. 1896.

DAVIDS, T. W. RHYS. Buddhist Birth-Stories. *London*, 1880.
—— Buddhism. 2nd edit. *London*, 1894.
—— Buddhism: Its History and Literature (American Lectures). 1896.
DAVIES, J. Bhagavad-gita. *London*, 1882.
DAVIES, Rev. J. Hindu Philosophy. 1881.
DEUSSEN, P. Das System des Vedānta. 1883.
DUFF, J. G. A History of the Mahrattas. 3 vols. *London*, 1826. Later Editions.
DUTT, J. C. Kings of Kashmīr. *Calcutta*. 1879.
DUTT, R. C. A History of Civilisation in Ancient India. 2 vols. *London*, 1893.
—— Literature of Bengal. *London*, 1895.
DUTT, TORU. Journal de Mdlle. d'Arvers.
—— Lays and Ballads of Hindustān. *London*, 1882.

EDUCATION in India, Progress of. *Second Quinquennial Review. Calcutta*, 1893.

FERGUSSON, Dr J. Tree and Serpent Worship. *London*, 1868.
—— History of Indian and Eastern Architecture. *London*, 1876.
FICK, R. Die Sociale Gliederung in N. Östlichen Indien zu Bhudda's Zeit. *Kiel*, 1897.

GARBE, R. Śankhya Philosophie.
GOUGH, A. E. The Philosophy of the Upanishads. Oriental Series. 1882.
GRIFFITH, R. Sama Veda. *Benares*, 1893.
—— Atharva Veda. 2 vols. *Benares*, 1896.
GROWSE, F. S. Ramayana of Tulsi Das. Translated from the Hindi.

HAUG, MARTIN. Aitareya Brāhmana. Text, Translation, and Notes. 2 vols. *Bombay*, 1863.
HIBBERT LECTURES:—
—— LECTURES on the Growth of Religion, as Illustrated by some Points in the History of Indian Buddhism. By T. W. Rhys Davids. *London*, 1881.
—— LECTURES on the Origin and Growth of Religion, as Illustrated by the Religions of India. By F. Max Müller. 2nd edit. *London*, 1878.
HOLTZMANN, A. Das Mahābhārata, 1892-1895.

HOPKINS, E. W. Religions of India. *Boston*, 1895.
—— The Social and Military Position of the Ruling Caste in Ancient India. Reprint. *Newhaven*, 1889.
HUNTER, Sir WILLIAM WILSON. The Indian Empire: Its History, People, and Products. *London*, 1893. 3rd edit.
—— Annals of Rural Bengal. 5th edit.
—— Orissa: Its History and People. 2 vols. *London*, 1872.
—— Our Indian Musalmans. 3rd edit.
—— Rulers of India Series. Edited by Oxford.

Indian Magazine and Review. A Monthly Publication. *London.*

JEVONS, F. B. Introduction to the History of Religions. *London*, 1896.

KAEGI, Professor A. The Rig Veda. Translated by Arrowsmith, R. 1886.
KARKARIA, R. P. India: Forty Years of Progress and Reform. *London*, 1896.

LASSEN, C. Indische Alterthumskunde. *Bonn*, 1847-61. 2nd edit. *Leipzig*, 1867-74.
LEVI, S. Théatre Indien. *Paris*, 1890.
LUDWIG, ALFRED. Der Rigveda, oder die heiligen Hymnen der Brâhmana. A Translation in German. 6 vols. *Prague*, 1876-88.
LYALL, Sir ALFRED. Asiatic Studies. *London*, 1882.

MACCRINDLE, J. W. The Invasion of India by Alexander the Great, as described by Q. Curtius, Diodorus, Plutarch, and Justin. With an Introduction containing a Life of Alexander. 1893.
MACDONELL, A. A. Vedic Mythology (Grundriss der Indo-Arischen Philologie und Altertumskunde, herausgegeben von Georg Bühler). 1897.
MAHÂBHÂRATA, The, of Krishna Dwaipayana Vyasa. Translated into English Prose by Pratapa Chandra Ray. *Calcutta*, 1893-96.
MANNING, Mrs. Ancient and Mediæval India. *London*, 1869.
MITCHELL, J. MURRAY. Hinduism, Past and Present. *London*, 1885.
MONIER-WILLIAMS, Sir MONIER. Non-Christian Religious Systems: Hinduism. *London*, 1877.
—— Indian Wisdom. 1876.

MONIER-WILLIAMS, Sir MONIER. Brāhmanism and Hinduism. 1891.

—— Religious Life and Thought in India. 1893.

—— Sakuntala of Kalidasa. 1887.

MUIR, J. Metrical Translations from Sanskrit Writers. 1879.

—— Original Sanskrit Texts. Translated into English. 5 vols. 1858-61. 2nd edit. 1868-73.

MÜLLER, MAX. A History of Ancient Sanskrit Literature. *London*, 1859.

—— Chips from a German Workshop. 2nd edit. *London*, 1868.

—— India: What Can It Teach us. *London*, 1892.

—— Biographical Essays. 1884.

—— Biographies of Words. *London*, 1888.

—— Sacred Books of the East. Translated by various Scholars, and edited by Prof. Max. Müller.

OLDENBERG, H. Buddha, sein Leben, etc. *Berlin*, 1881. Translation. *London*, 1882.

—— Die Religion Des Veda. *Berlin*, 1894.

OMAN, J. C. Indian Life, Religious and Social. 1889.

PADFIELD, Rev. J. E. The Hindu at Home. 1896.

POPE, Rev. G. U. Nalādiyar. *Oxford*, 1893.

RAE, G. MILNE. The Syrian Church in India. *London*, 1892.

RAGOZIN, Z. A. Vedic India: Story of the Nations. 1896.

RĀMĀYANA of Valmiki. Translated into English Verse, by R. T. H. Griffith. 1 vol. *Benares*, 1895.

RENDALL, G. H. Cradle of the Aryans. 1889.

SAMUELSON, JAMES. India, Past and Present. *London*, 1890.

SCHRADER, Dr O. Prehistoric Antiquities of the Aryan People. Translated by Jevons, F. Byron. 1890.

SENART, E. Les Castes dans l'Inde. 1896.

—— Essai sur la Légende du Buddha, son Caractère et ses Origines. *Paris*, 1882.

STEVENSON, Rev. J. Translation of the Sama Veda. 1841.

TASSY, GARCIN DE. Les Auteurs Hindoustanis et leurs Ouvrages. 2nd edit. *Paris*, 1868.

TASSY, GARCIN DE. Histoire de la Littérature Hindouie et Hindoustanie. 3 vols. 2nd edit. *Paris*, 1870-71.

TAYLOR, ISAAC. Origin of the Aryans. 1890.

THIBAUT, G. Vedānta Sūtras, S.B.E. Vols. XXXIV. and XXXVIII. 1890-96.

TOD, Lieut.-Col. J. Annals and Antiquities of Rajasthan. *London*, 1829-32.

TRUMPP, E. The Ādi Granth. Translated from the Gurmukhi. *London*, 1877.

TUKĀ RĀMA, The Poems of. Edited by Vishnu Parashurām Shāstrī Pandit, with a Life of the Poet in English. *Bombay*, 1869.

WALLIS, H. W. The Cosmology of the Rig-Veda. *London*, 1887.

WARREN, H. C. Buddhism in Translations. 1896.

WEBER, ALBRECHT. The History of Indian Literature. *London*, 1878.

WEST, Sir RAYMOND. Higher Education in India : Its Position and Claims. Transactions of the Ninth Oriental Congress. *London*, 1892.

WILSON, H. H. Translation of Hymns of the Rig Veda, continued by Professor E. B. Cowell and W. F. Webster. 1850-88.

——— Select Specimens of the Theatre of the Hindus. 2 vols. 1835.

——— The Vishnu Purana. *London*, 1840.

——— Sketch of the Religious Sects of the Hindus. *Calcutta*, 1846.

——— Complete Works of. 12 vols. *London*, 1862-77.

WINDISCH, E. Der griechische Einfluss im indischen Drama. *Berlin*, 1882.

ZEITSCHRIFT der deutschen Morgenländischen Gesellschaft. Quoted throughout as Z.D.M.G.

INDEX

Published by

Facsimile Publisher
Ashok Vihar, Delhi-110052 (India)
Website: www.facsimilepublisher.com

Distributed by

Gyan Books Pvt. Ltd.
5, Ansari Road, Daryaganj, New Delhi-110002 (India)
E-mail: books@gyanbooks.com, Website: www.gyanbooks.com

2 222000 012281